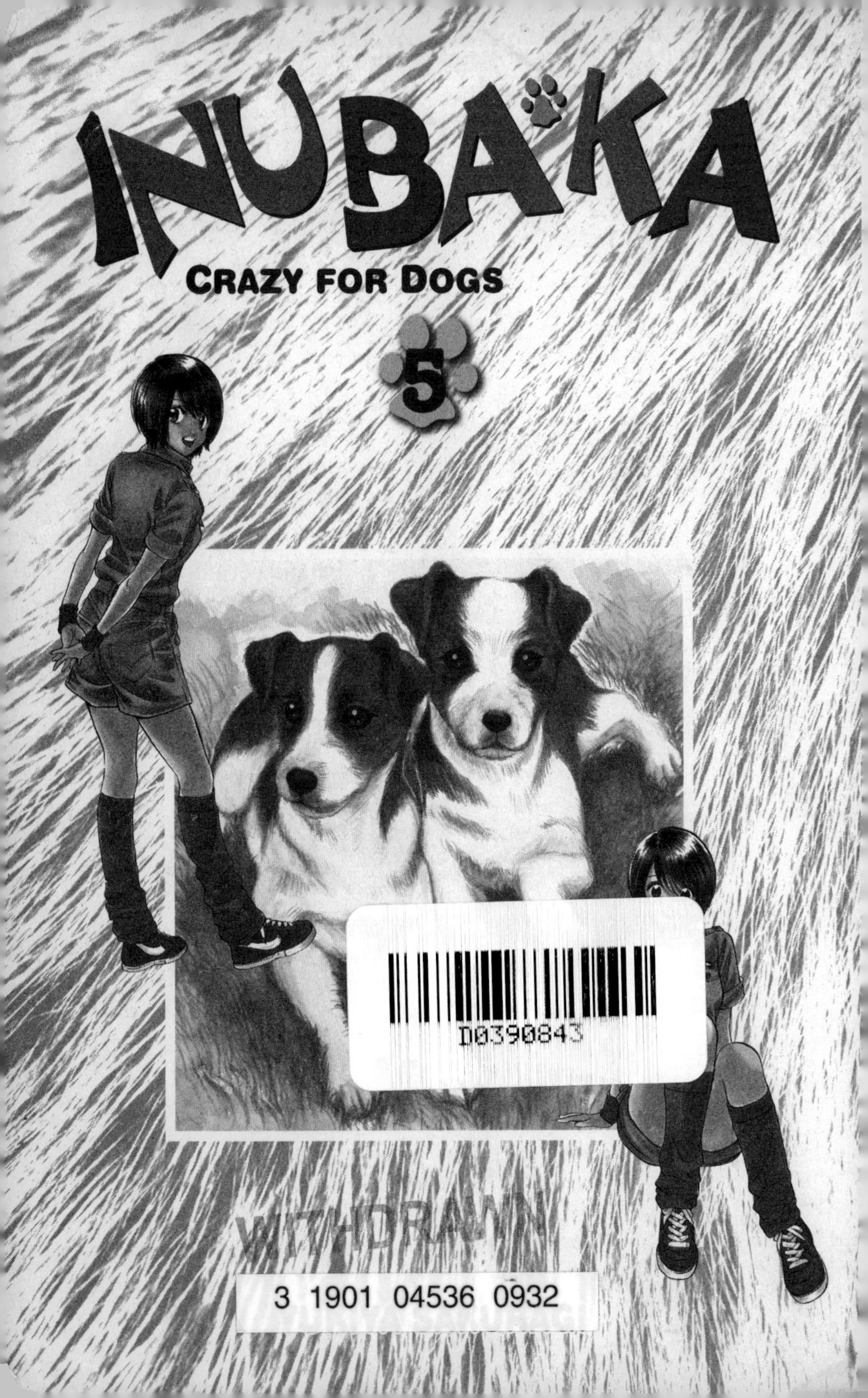
INUBAKA
CRAZY FOR DOGS
5

Contents

Story thus far

Teppei is the manager of the recently opened pet shop Woofles. He intended to breed his black Labrador Noa with a champion dog, but instead Noa was "taken advantage of" by an unknown and unfixed male dog!

The unknown dog's owner was Suguri Miyauchi and her dog was a mutt named Lupin. Suguri is now working at Woofles to make up for her dog's actions.

Suguri's enthusiasm is more than a little unique. She has eaten dog food (and said it was tasty), caught dog poop with her bare hands, and caused dogs to have "happy pee" in her presence. Teppei is starting to realize that Suguri is indeed a very special girl.

Kentaro and Suguri live at Teppei's house. Kentaro wants to be a musician and live a carefree life. His sister Mika, a junior high school student, has taken to visiting the shop after school to play with the puppies. Suguri suggests she play with Lupin instead. Mika follows Suguri's suggestion and goes to a rooftop to play with Lupin, but what's she doing with that box cutter in her hand...?

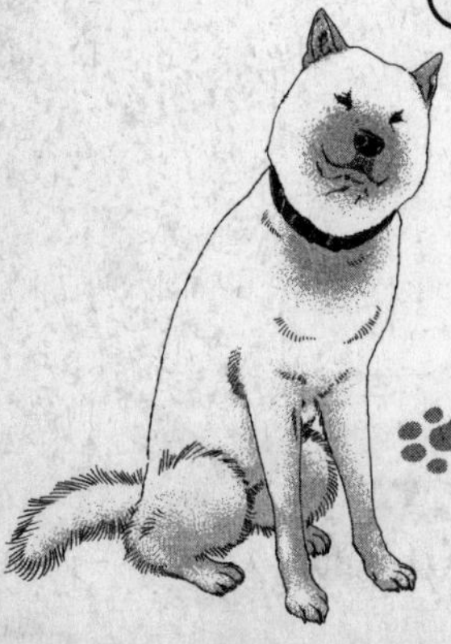

CHARACTERS

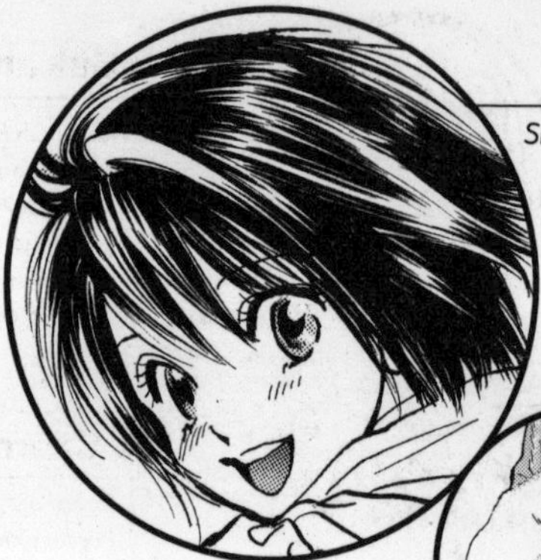

Suguri Miyauchi

She seems to possess an almost supernatural connection with dogs. When she approaches them they often urinate with great excitement! She is crazy for dogs and can catch their droppings with her bare hands. She is currently a trainee at the Woofles Pet Shop.

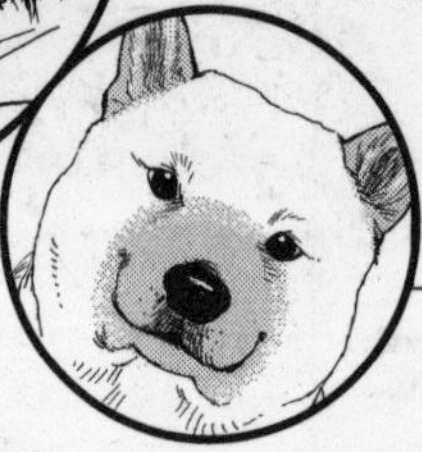

Lupin

♂ *Suguri's mutt (mongrel)*

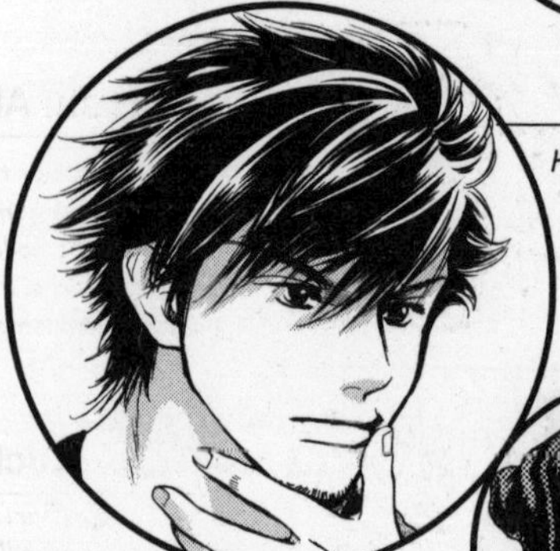

Teppei Iida

He is the manager of the recently opened pet shop Woofles. He is aware of Suguri's special ability and has hired her to work in his shop. He also lets Suguri and Kentaro crash with him.

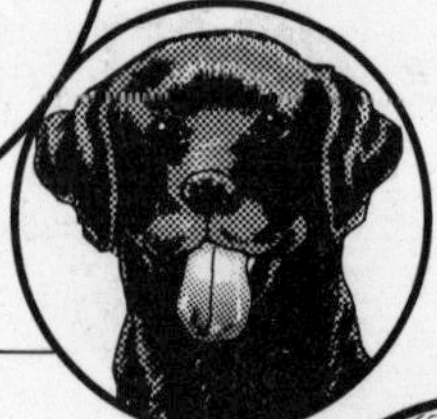

Noa

♀ *Teppei's Labrador retriever*

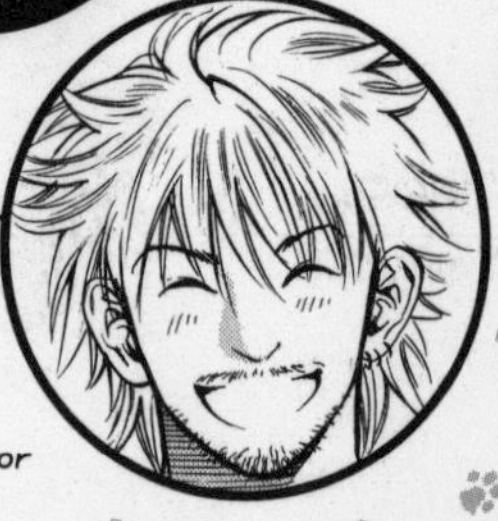

Kentaro Osada

A wanna-be musician and buddy of Teppei's from high school. Teppei saved Kentaro when he was a down-and-out beggar. He has a crush on the piano instructor Kanako, but not her dog...

Melon

♂ Chizuru's Chihuahua

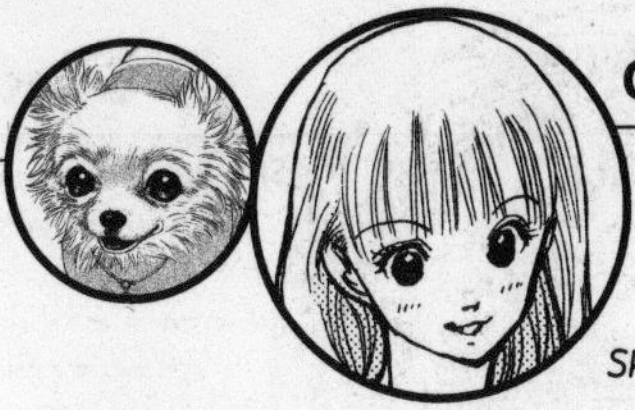

Chizuru Sawamura

She adopted a Chihuahua, Melon, after her long-time pet Golden Retriever Ricky alerted her that he was ill. She works at a hostess bar to repay Melon's medical fees.

Kanako Mori

She teaches piano on the second floor of the same building as Woofles. Her love for her dog, Czerny, is so great that it surprises even Suguri!

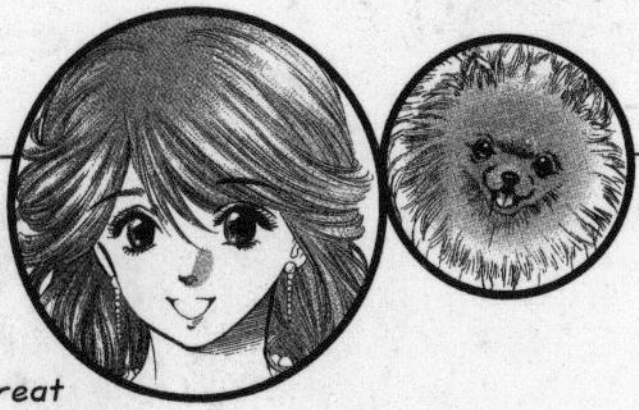

Czerny

♀ Kanako's Pomeranian

Zidane

♂ Hiroshi's French bulldog

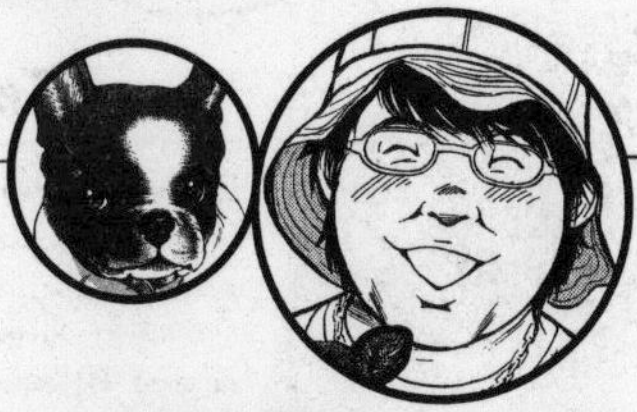

Hiroshi Akiba

Pop-idol otaku turned dog otaku. His dream is to publish a photo collection of his dog, Zidane. He is a government employee.

Mari Yamashita

She is a model whose nickname is Yamarin. She decided to keep an unsold Papillon, Lucky, who was her co-star in a bread commercial.

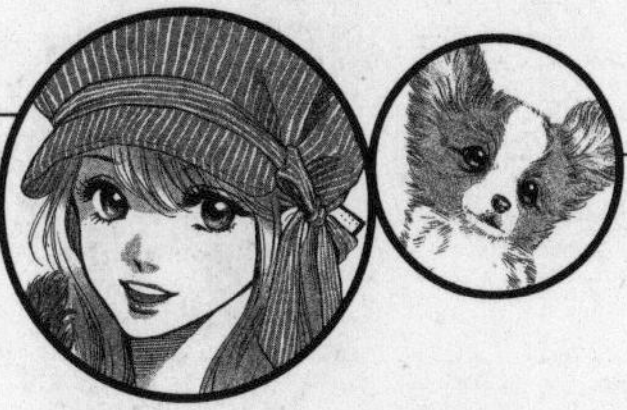

Lucky

♂ Mari's Papillon

Chanta

♀ Kim's Shiba

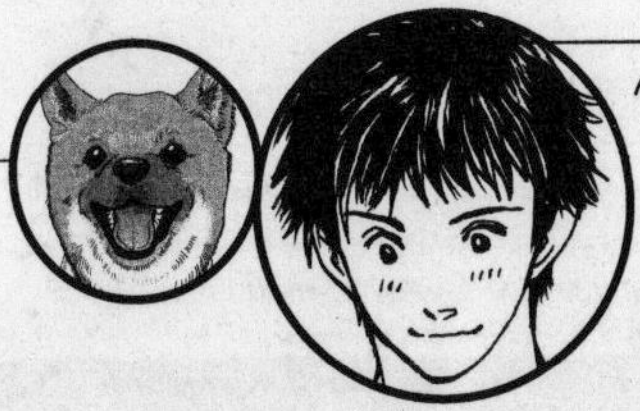

Kim

A Korean friend of Kentaro. He had a phobia of dogs, but he has been working hard to get over it in order to get close to Suguri, whom he has a crush on. He bought a Shiba dog!

INUBAKA

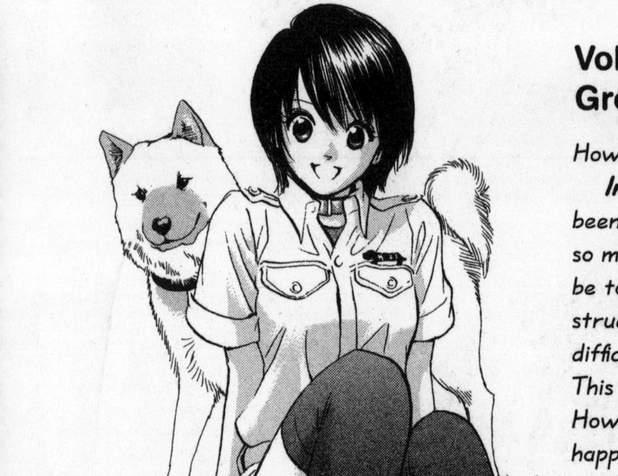

Volume 5 Greeting

How are you all doing?

Inubaka volume 5 has been published! There are so many stories that can be told about dogs, but structuring them is more difficult than I thought. This is always on my mind. However, I'll be quite happy if you just enjoy reading the manga and realize that <u>dogs are cute</u>.

I'll do my best to write a lot of doggy stories.

February 2006
Yukiya Sakuragi

LET'S GO to the main story of *Inubaka*!

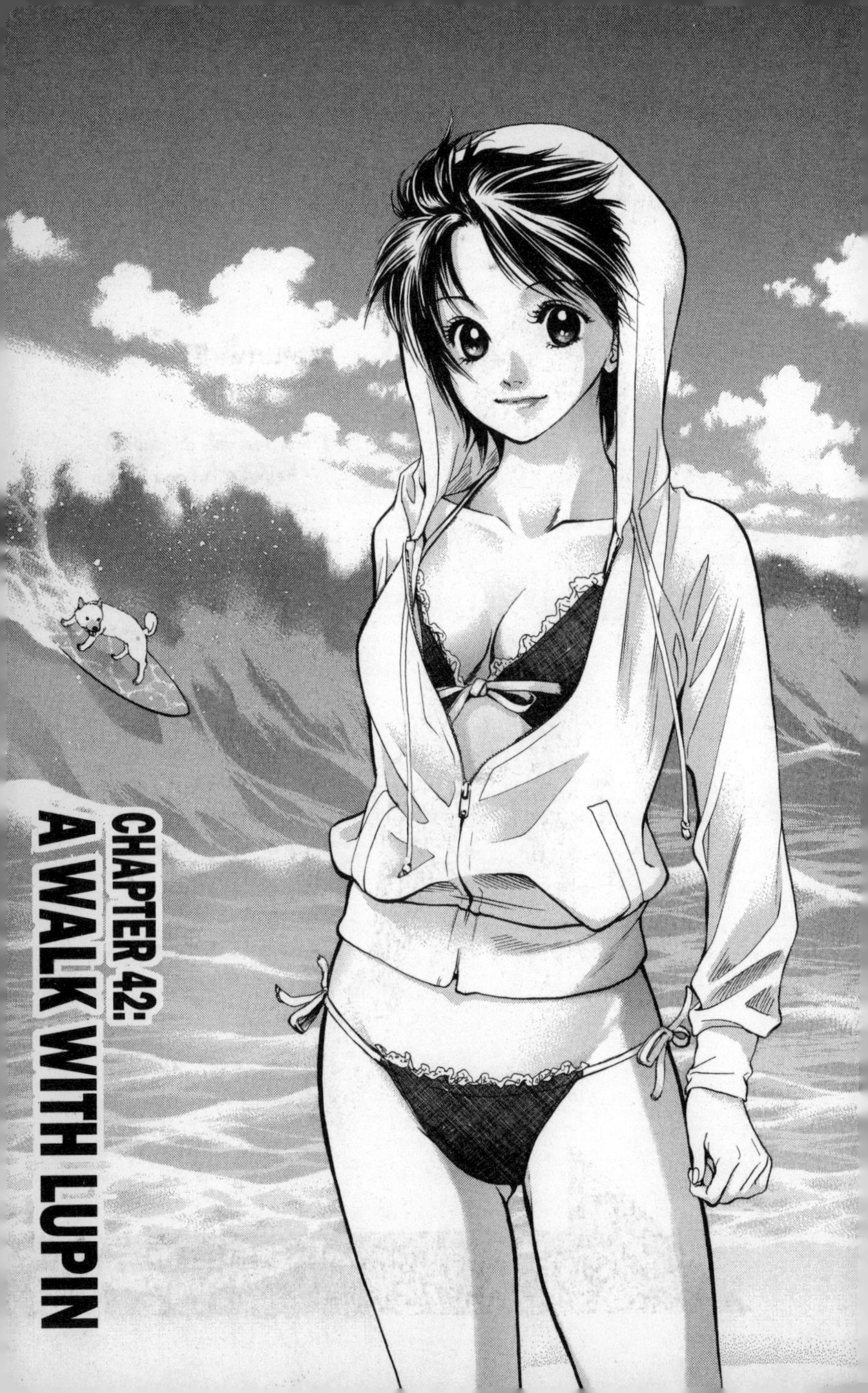
CHAPTER 42:
A WALK WITH LUPIN

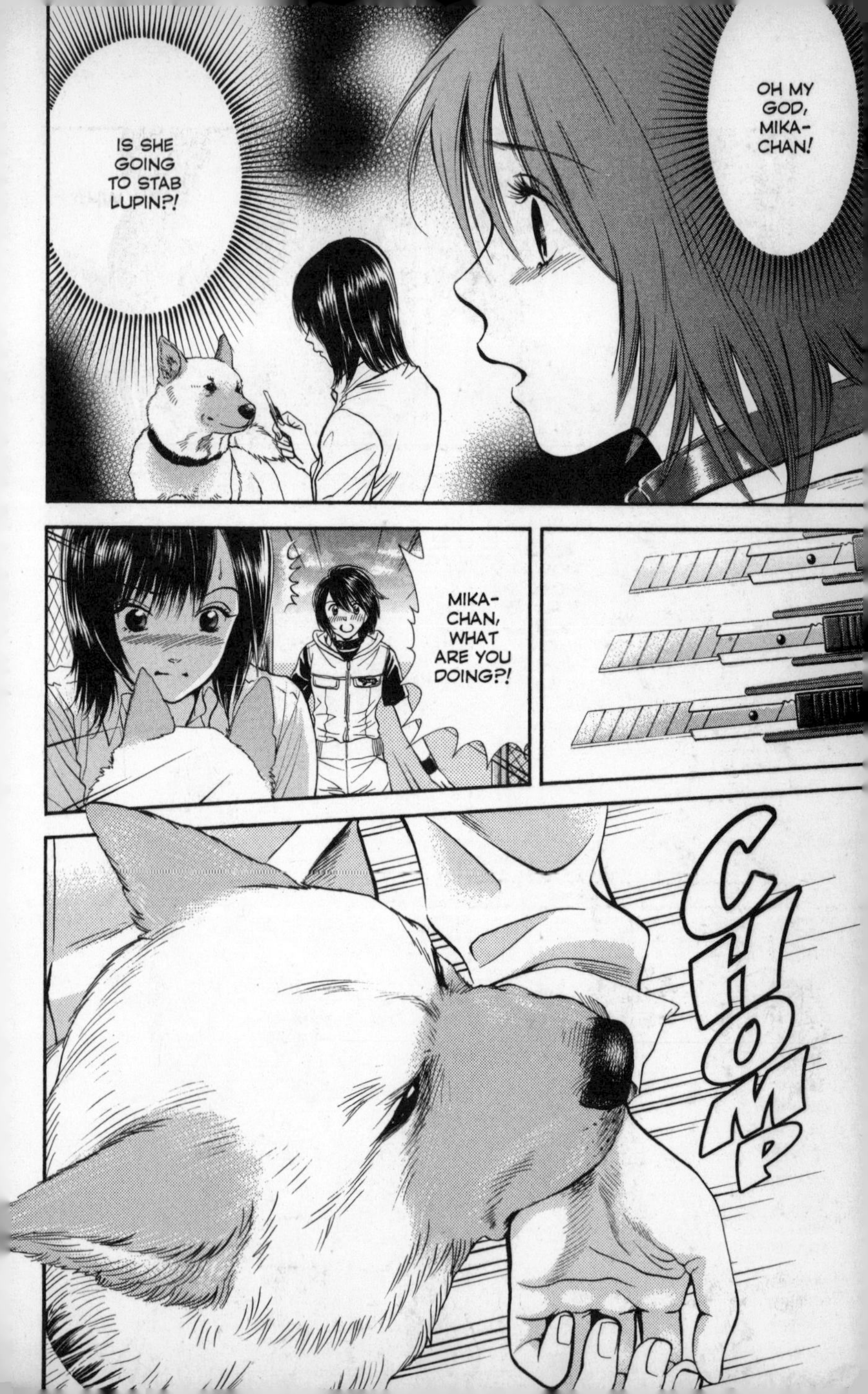
OH MY GOD, MIKA-CHAN!
IS SHE GOING TO STAB LUPIN?!
MIKA-CHAN, WHAT ARE YOU DOING?!
CHOMP

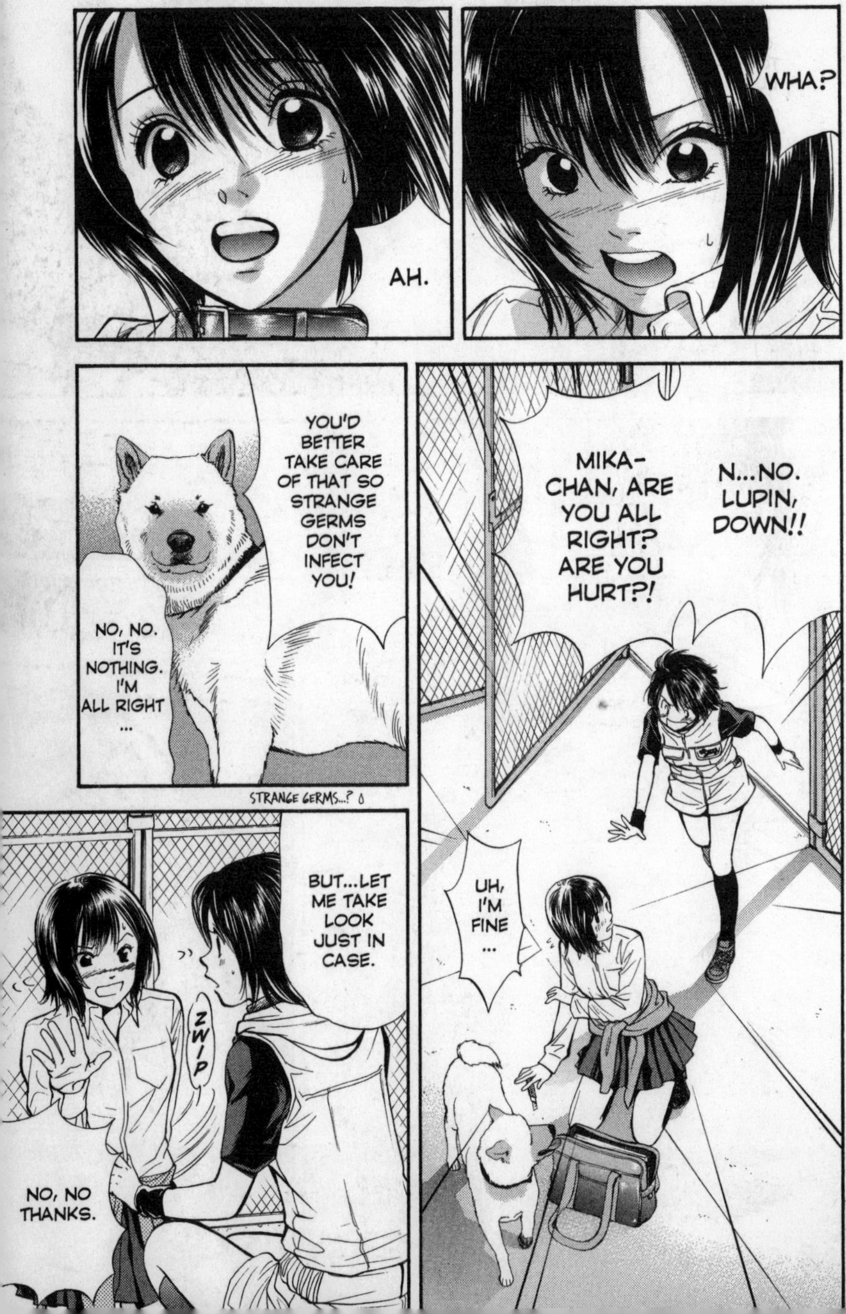
WHA?
AH.
N...NO. LUPIN, DOWN!!
MIKA-CHAN, ARE YOU ALL RIGHT? ARE YOU HURT?!
UH, I'M FINE ...
YOU'D BETTER TAKE CARE OF THAT SO STRANGE GERMS DON'T INFECT YOU!
NO, NO. IT'S NOTHING. I'M ALL RIGHT ...
STRANGE GERMS...?
BUT...LET ME TAKE LOOK JUST IN CASE.
ZWIP
NO, NO THANKS.

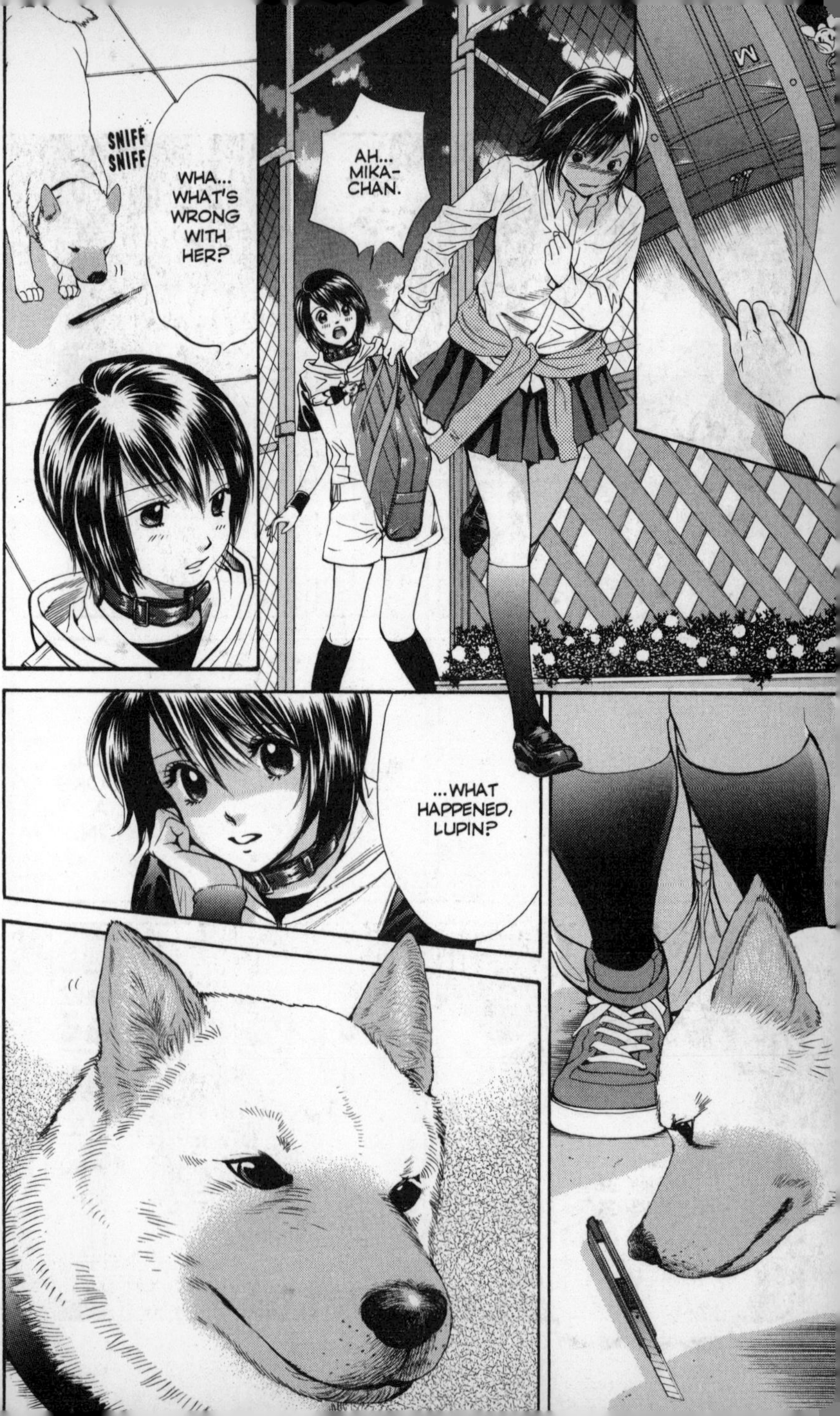
AH... MIKA-CHAN.
SNIFF SNIFF
WHA... WHAT'S WRONG WITH HER?
...WHAT HAPPENED, LUPIN?

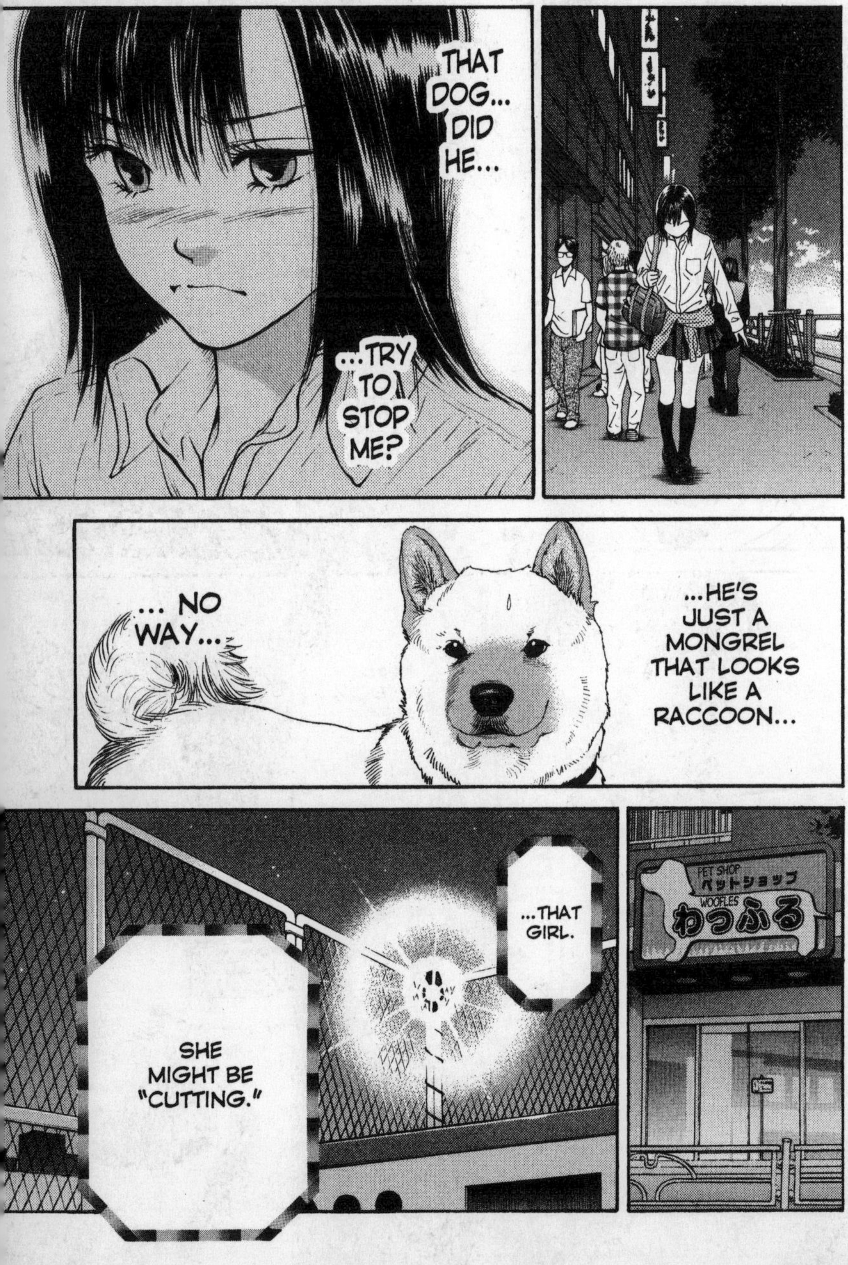
THAT DOG... DID HE...
...TRY TO STOP ME?
...HE'S JUST A MONGREL THAT LOOKS LIKE A RACCOON...
... NO WAY...
PET SHOP
ペットショップ
WOOFLES
わっふる
...THAT GIRL.
SHE MIGHT BE "CUTTING."

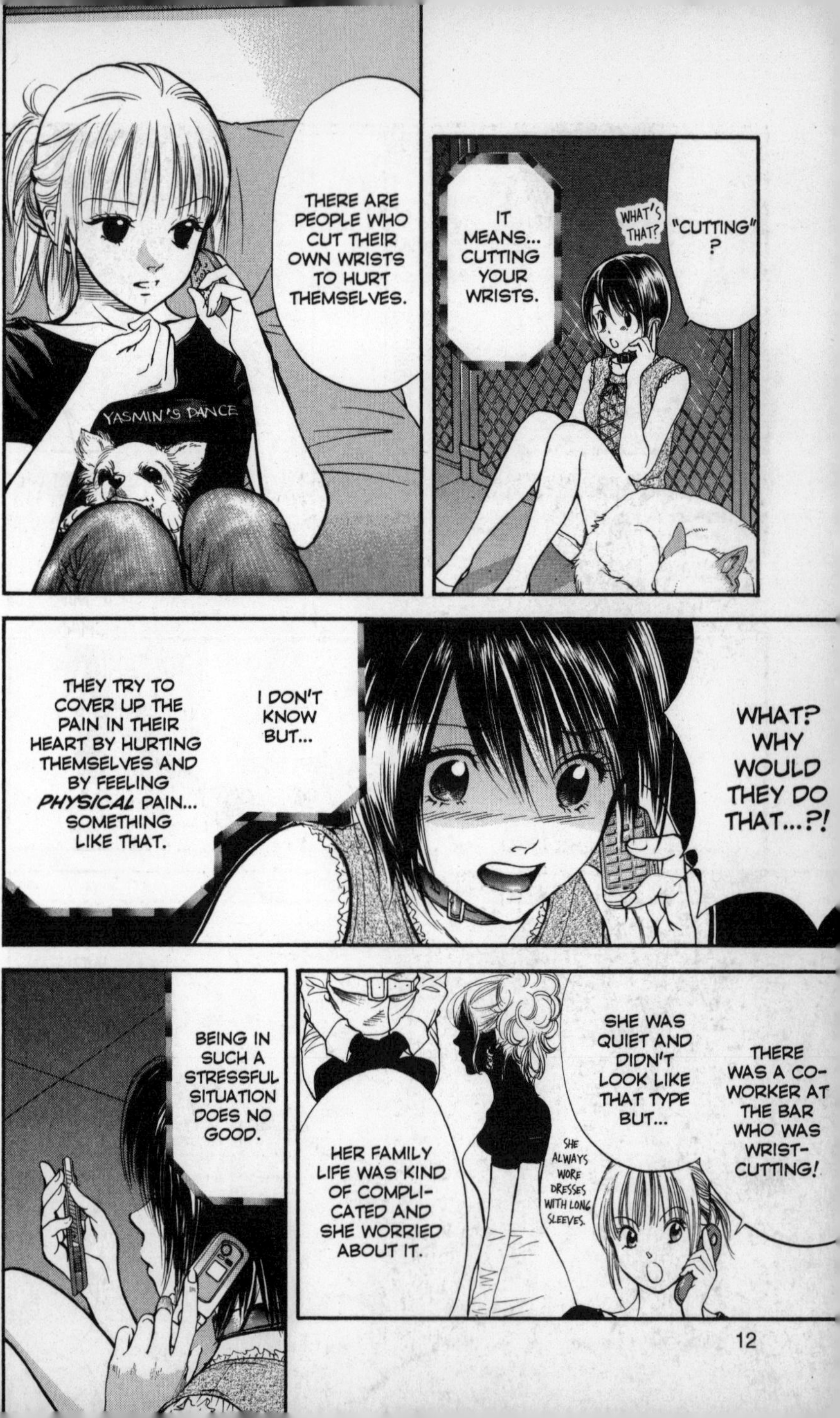
"CUTTING"?
WHAT'S THAT?
IT MEANS... CUTTING YOUR WRISTS.
THERE ARE PEOPLE WHO CUT THEIR OWN WRISTS TO HURT THEMSELVES.
YASMIN'S DANCE
WHAT? WHY WOULD THEY DO THAT...?!
I DON'T KNOW BUT...
THEY TRY TO COVER UP THE PAIN IN THEIR HEART BY HURTING THEMSELVES AND BY FEELING *PHYSICAL* PAIN... SOMETHING LIKE THAT.
THERE WAS A CO-WORKER AT THE BAR WHO WAS WRIST-CUTTING!
SHE WAS QUIET AND DIDN'T LOOK LIKE THAT TYPE BUT...
SHE ALWAYS WORE DRESSES WITH LONG SLEEVES.
HER FAMILY LIFE WAS KIND OF COMPLICATED AND SHE WORRIED ABOUT IT.
BEING IN SUCH A STRESSFUL SITUATION DOES NO GOOD.

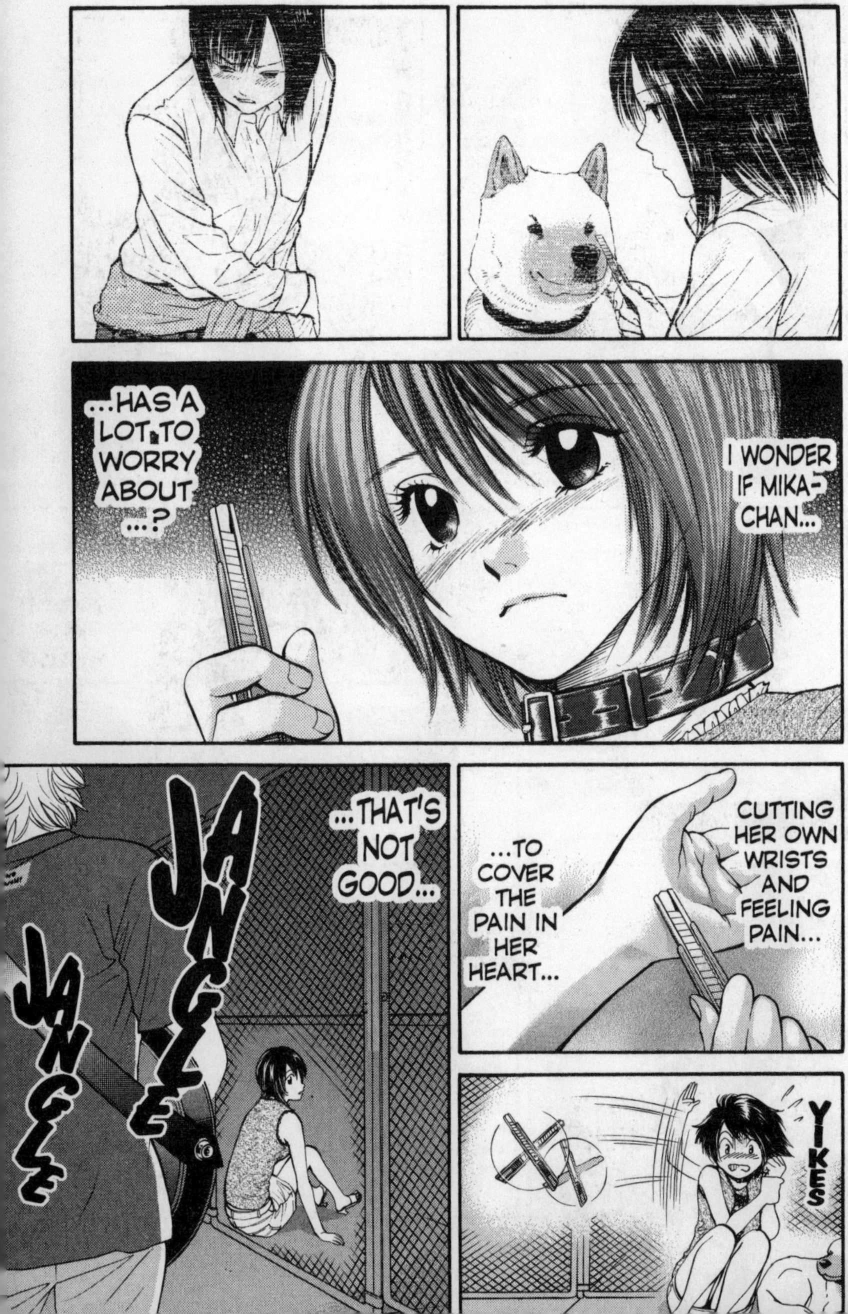
I WONDER IF MIKA-CHAN...
...HAS A LOT TO WORRY ABOUT...?
CUTTING HER OWN WRISTS AND FEELING PAIN...
...TO COVER THE PAIN IN HER HEART...
YIKES
...THAT'S NOT GOOD...
JANGLE
JANGLE

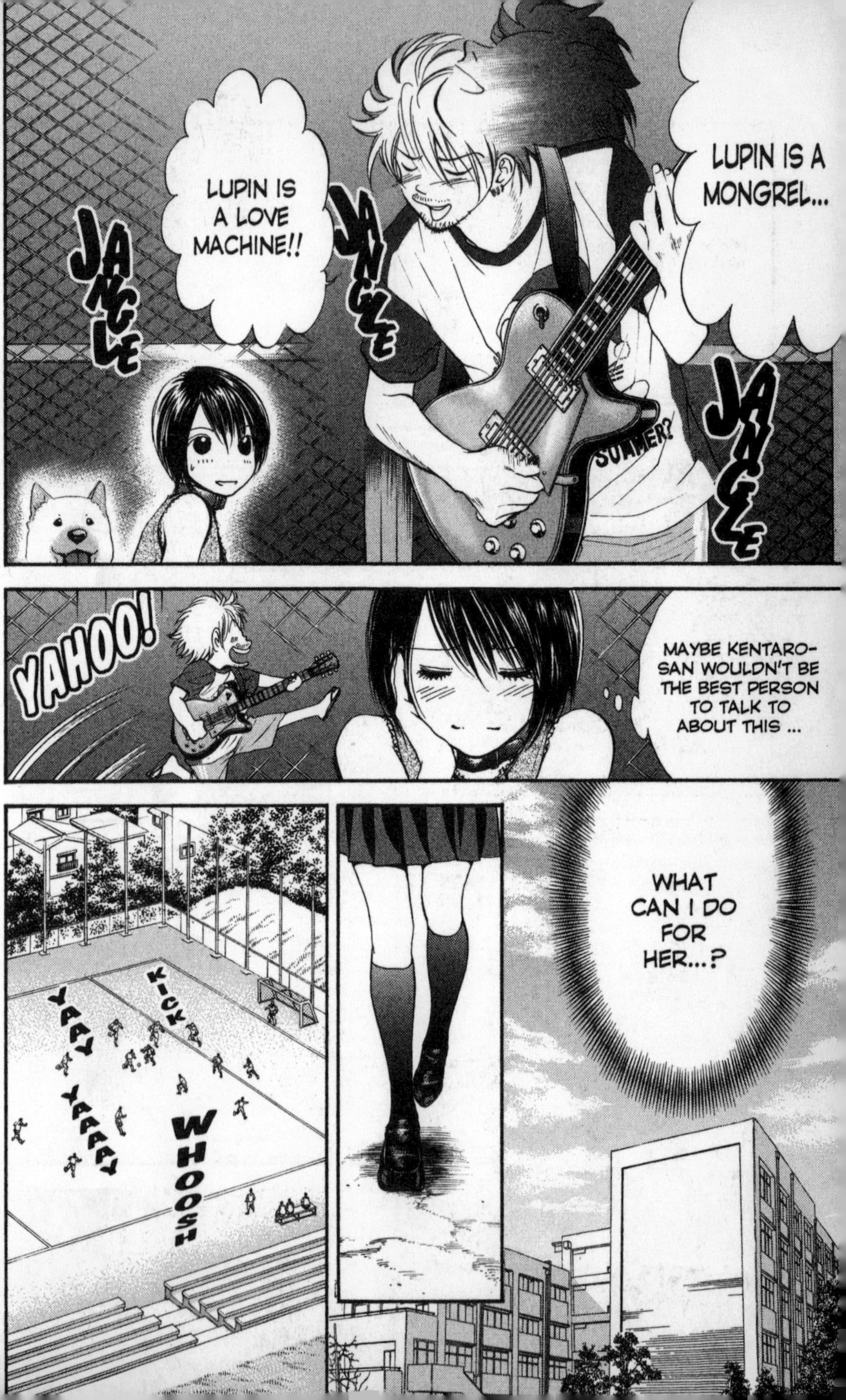
LUPIN IS A MONGREL...
JANGLE
SUMMER?
JANGLE
LUPIN IS A LOVE MACHINE!!
JANGLE
MAYBE KENTARO-SAN WOULDN'T BE THE BEST PERSON TO TALK TO ABOUT THIS ...
YAHOO!
WHAT CAN I DO FOR HER...?
KICK
WHOOSH
YAAY
YAAAAY

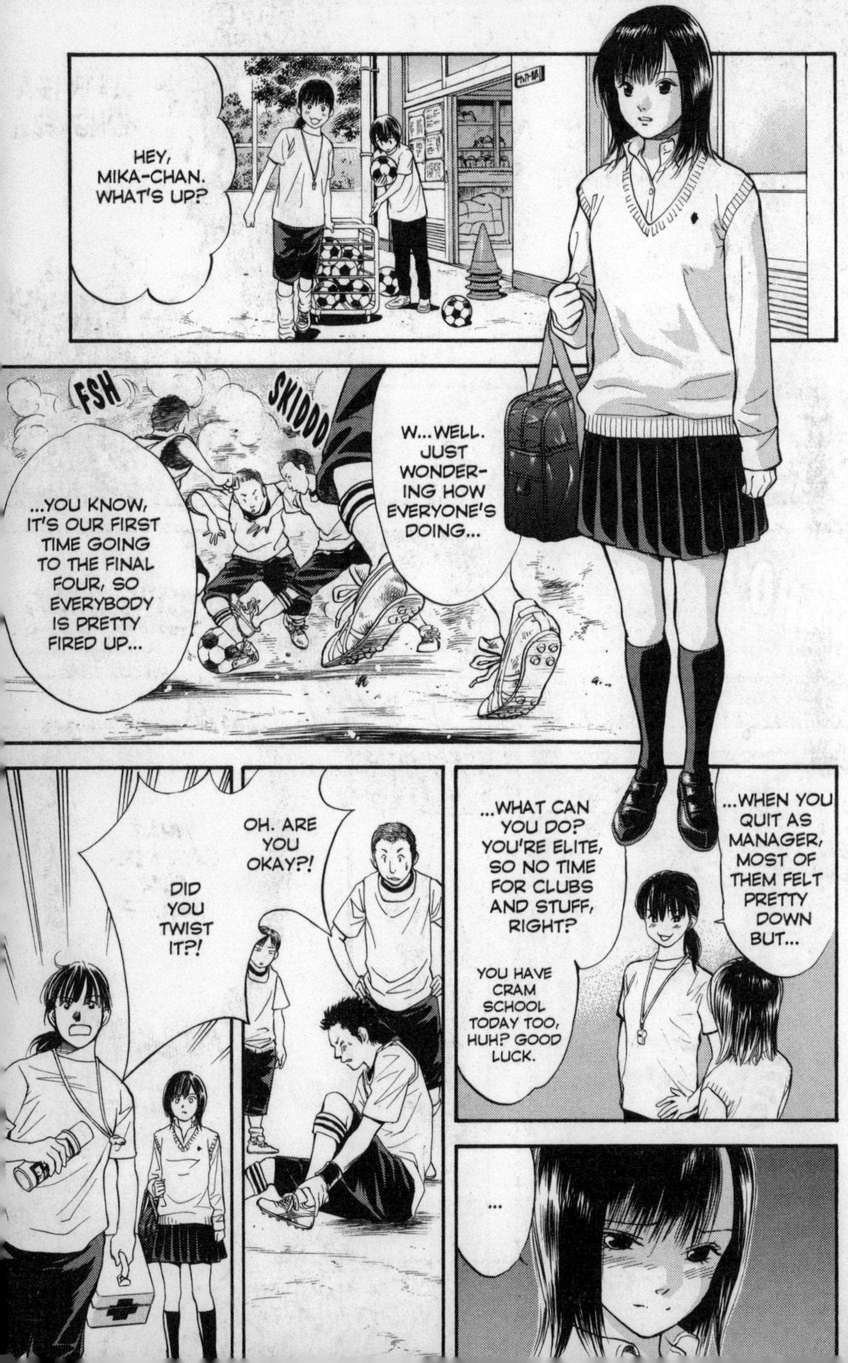
HEY, MIKA-CHAN. WHAT'S UP?
W...WELL. JUST WONDERING HOW EVERYONE'S DOING...
SKIDDD
FSH
...YOU KNOW, IT'S OUR FIRST TIME GOING TO THE FINAL FOUR, SO EVERYBODY IS PRETTY FIRED UP...
...WHEN YOU QUIT AS MANAGER, MOST OF THEM FELT PRETTY DOWN BUT...
...WHAT CAN YOU DO? YOU'RE ELITE, SO NO TIME FOR CLUBS AND STUFF, RIGHT?
YOU HAVE CRAM SCHOOL TODAY TOO, HUH? GOOD LUCK.
...
OH. ARE YOU OKAY?!
DID YOU TWIST IT?!

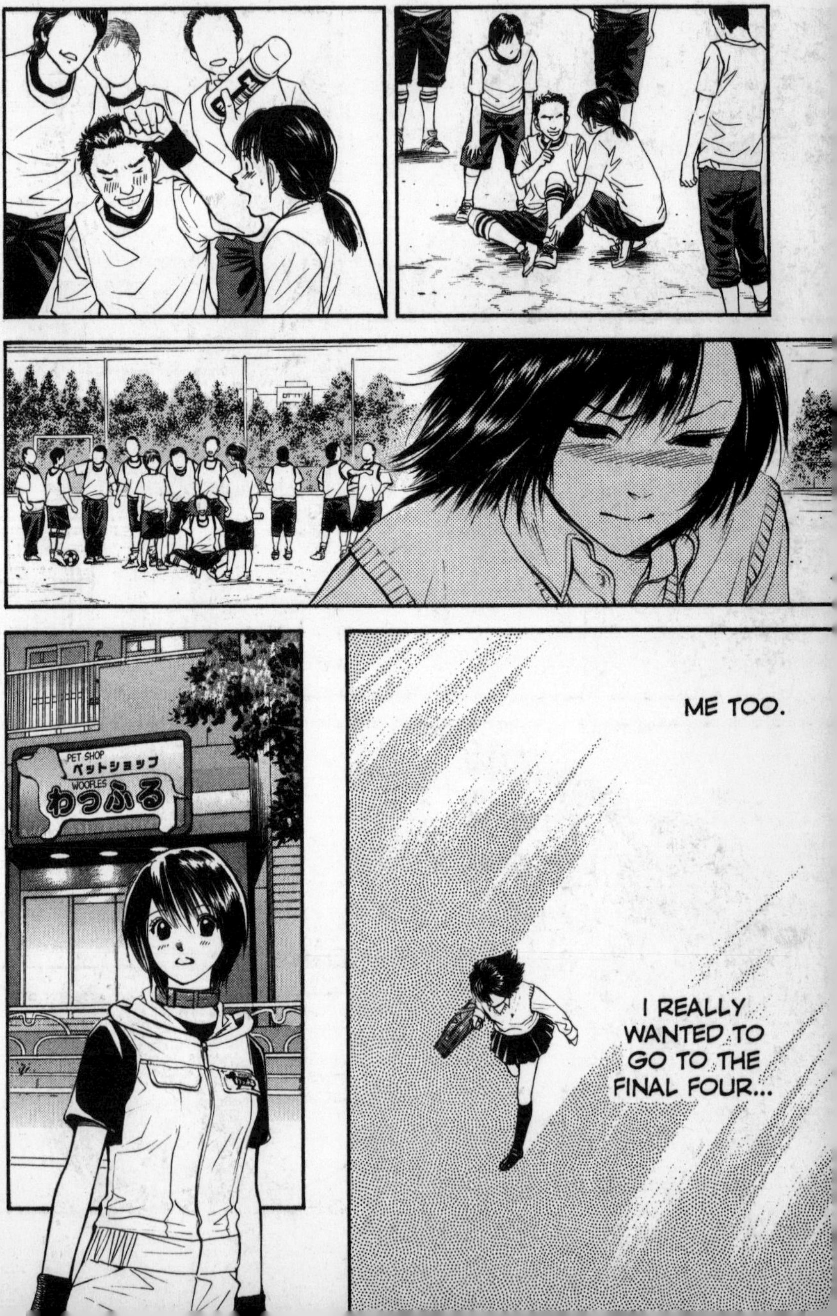
ME TOO.
I REALLY WANTED TO GO TO THE FINAL FOUR...
PET SHOP
ペットショップ
WOOFLES
わっふる

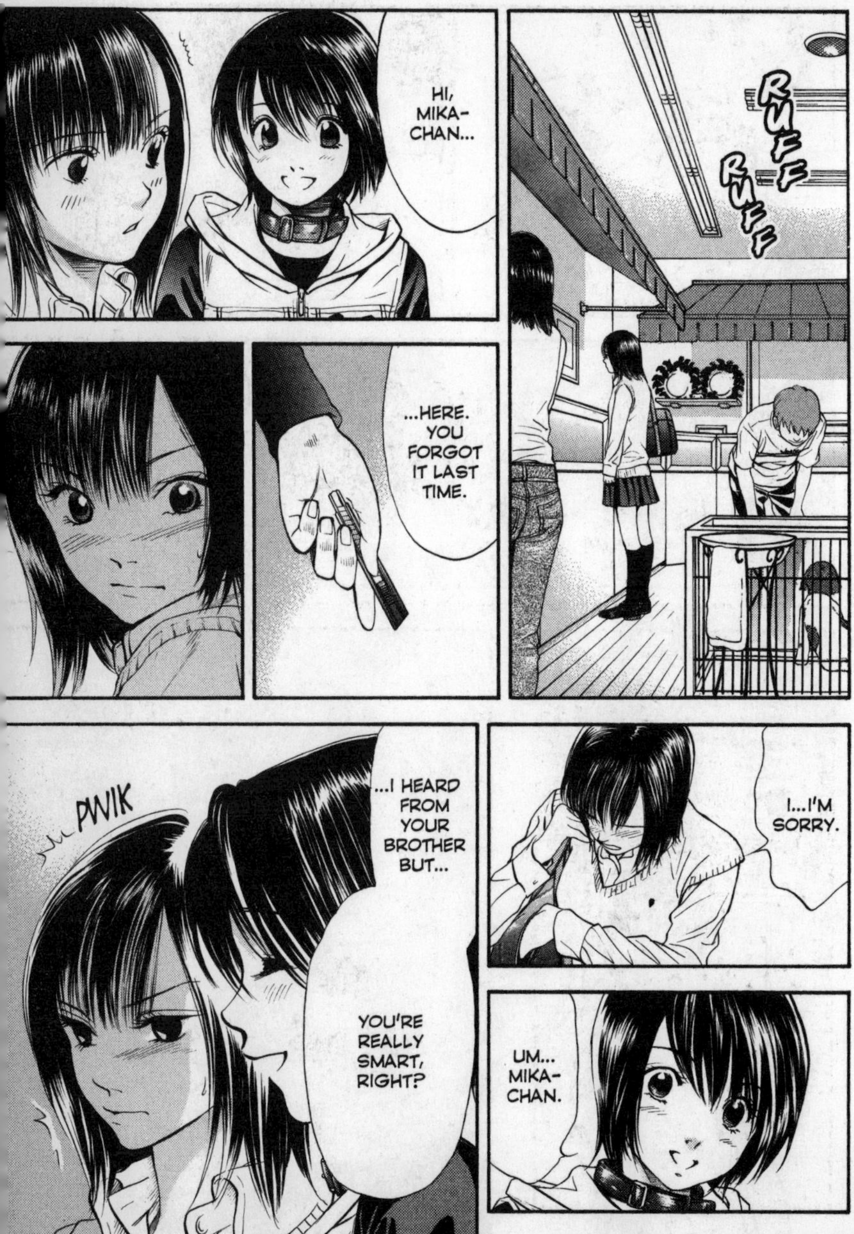
RUFF
RUFF
HI, MIKA-CHAN...
...HERE. YOU FORGOT IT LAST TIME.
I...I'M SORRY.
UM... MIKA-CHAN.
PWIK
...I HEARD FROM YOUR BROTHER BUT...
YOU'RE REALLY SMART, RIGHT?

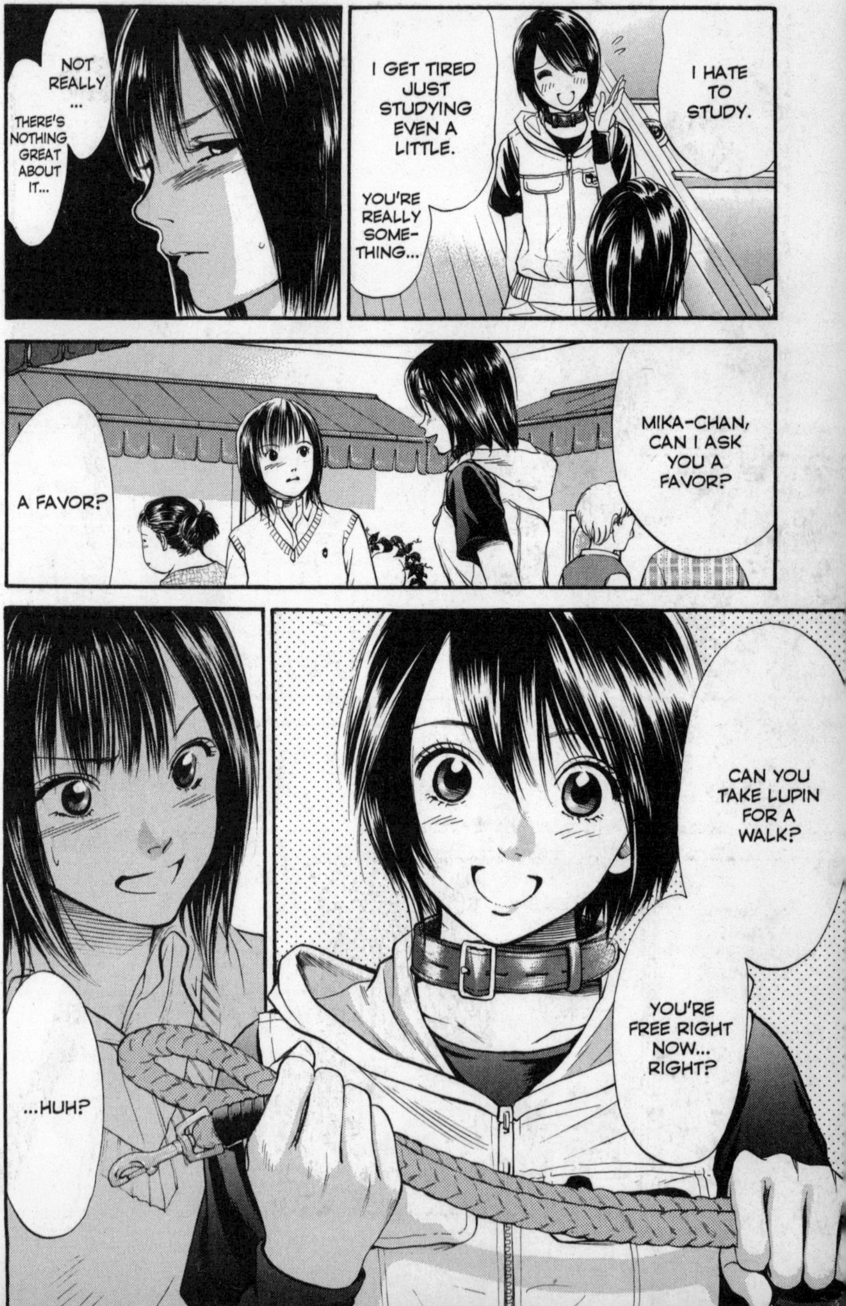
I HATE TO STUDY.
I GET TIRED JUST STUDYING EVEN A LITTLE.
YOU'RE REALLY SOME-THING...
NOT REALLY ...
THERE'S NOTHING GREAT ABOUT IT...
MIKA-CHAN, CAN I ASK YOU A FAVOR?
A FAVOR?
CAN YOU TAKE LUPIN FOR A WALK?
YOU'RE FREE RIGHT NOW... RIGHT?
...HUH?

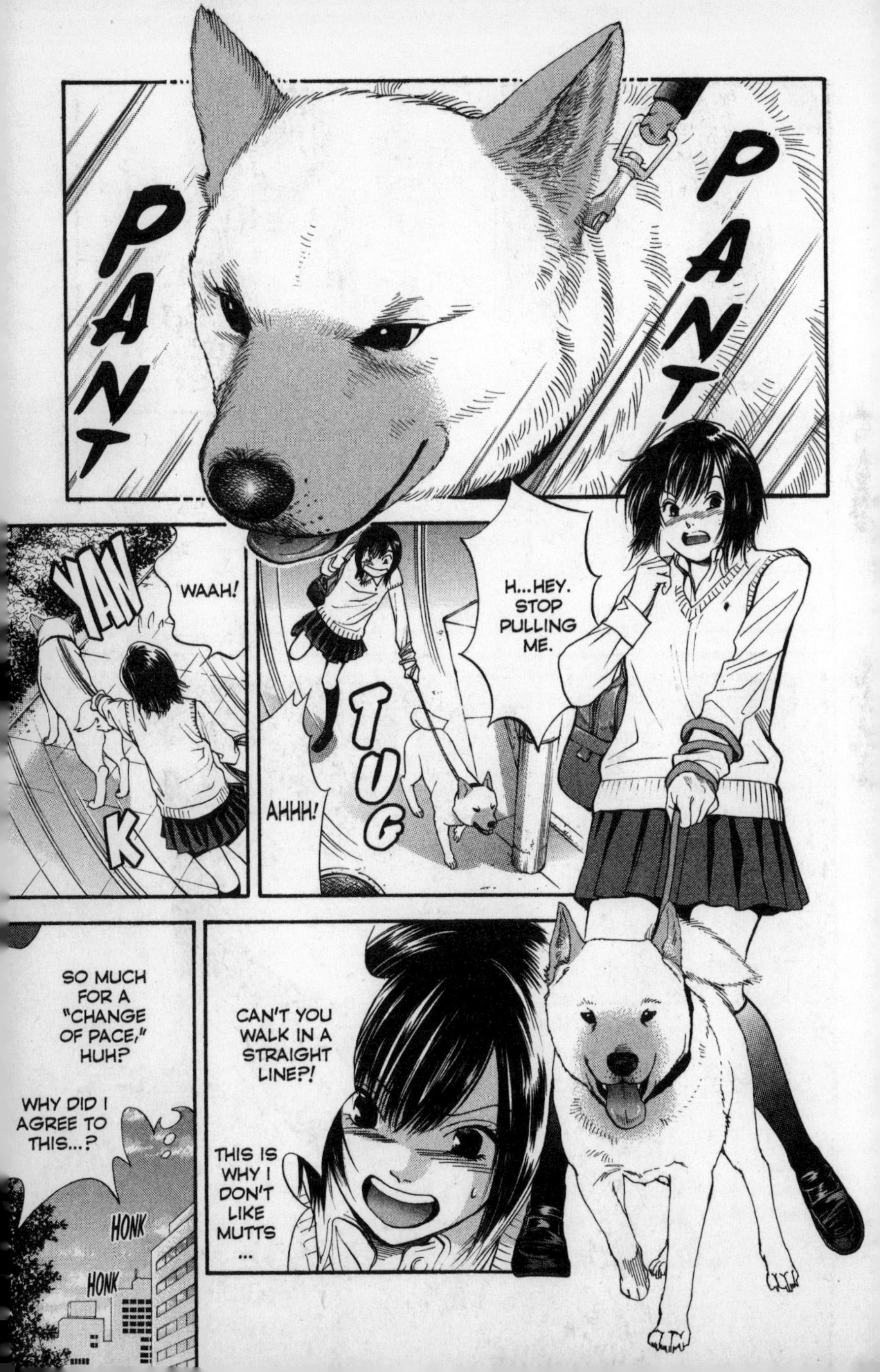
PANT
PANT
H...HEY. STOP PULLING ME.
TUG
AHHH!
YANK
WAAH!
CAN'T YOU WALK IN A STRAIGHT LINE?!
THIS IS WHY I DON'T LIKE MUTTS ...
SO MUCH FOR A "CHANGE OF PACE," HUH?
WHY DID I AGREE TO THIS...?
HONK
HONK

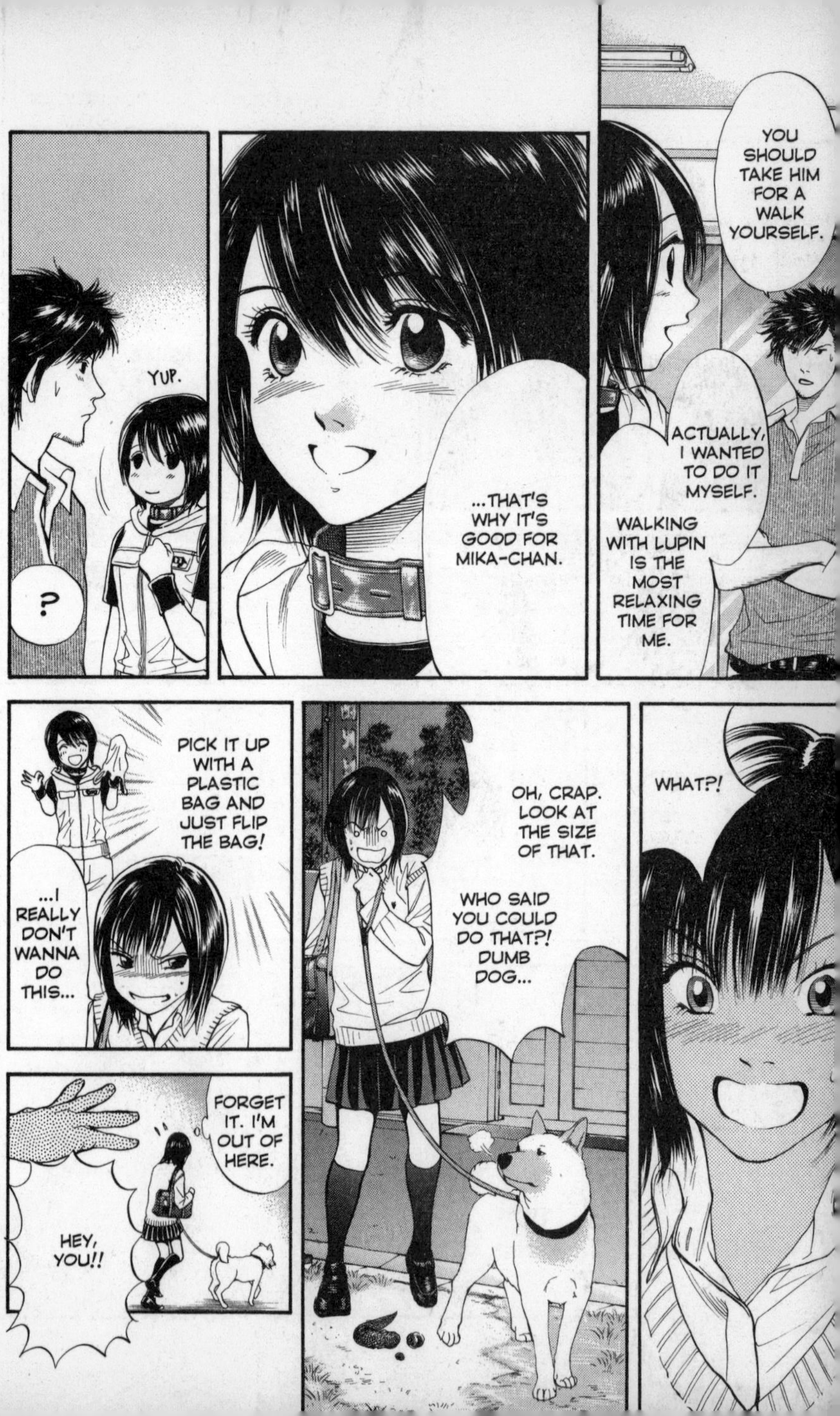
YOU SHOULD TAKE HIM FOR A WALK YOURSELF.
ACTUALLY, I WANTED TO DO IT MYSELF.
WALKING WITH LUPIN IS THE MOST RELAXING TIME FOR ME.
...THAT'S WHY IT'S GOOD FOR MIKA-CHAN.
YUP.
?
WHAT?!
OH, CRAP. LOOK AT THE SIZE OF THAT.
WHO SAID YOU COULD DO THAT?! DUMB DOG...
PICK IT UP WITH A PLASTIC BAG AND JUST FLIP THE BAG!
...I REALLY DON'T WANNA DO THIS...
FORGET IT. I'M OUT OF HERE.
HEY, YOU!!

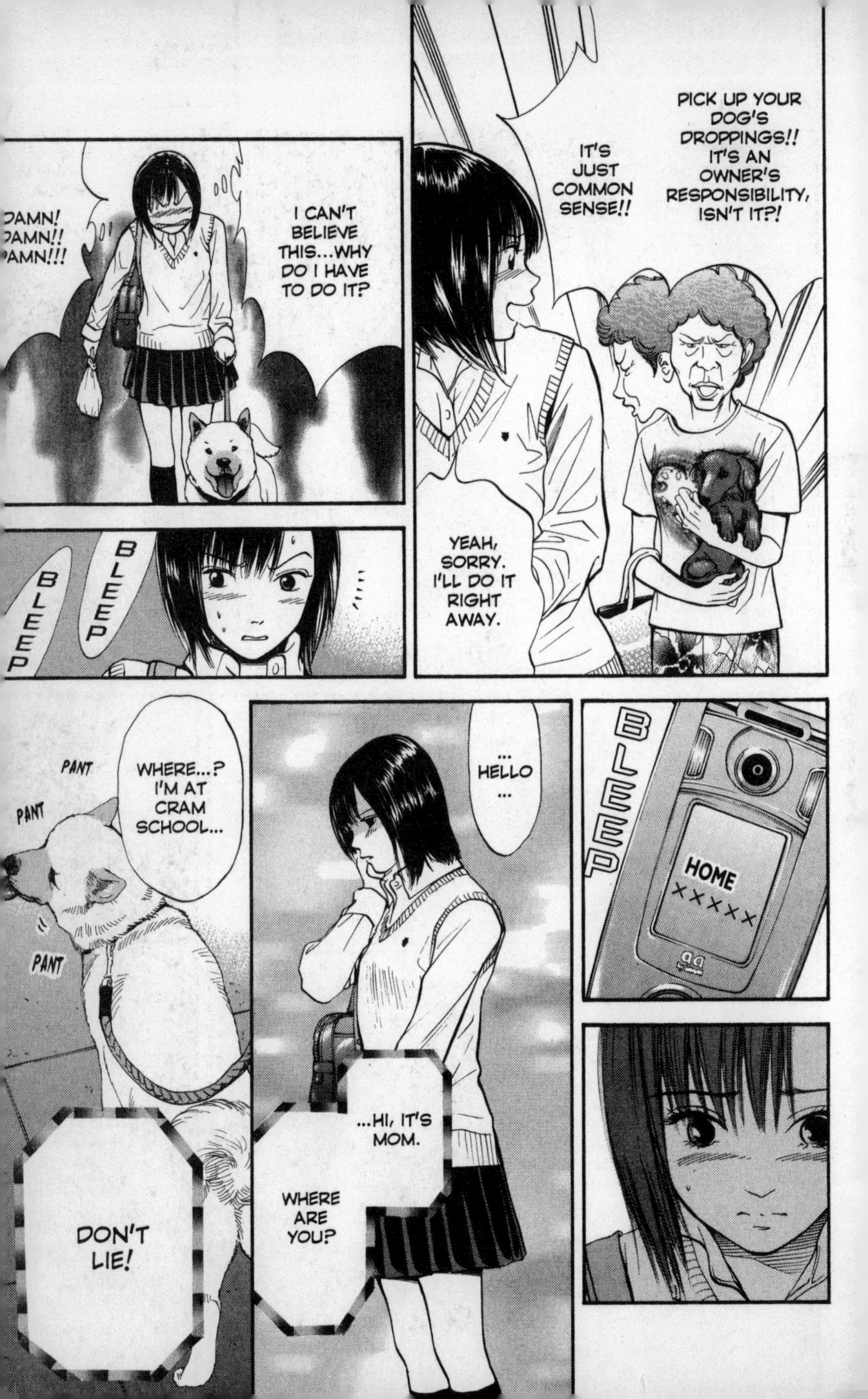
PICK UP YOUR DOG'S DROPPINGS!! IT'S AN OWNER'S RESPONSIBILITY, ISN'T IT?!
IT'S JUST COMMON SENSE!!
YEAH, SORRY. I'LL DO IT RIGHT AWAY.
I CAN'T BELIEVE THIS...WHY DO I HAVE TO DO IT?
DAMN! DAMN!! DAMN!!!
BLEEP
BLEEP
BLEEP
HOME
×××××
... HELLO ...
...HI, IT'S MOM.
WHERE ARE YOU?
WHERE...? I'M AT CRAM SCHOOL...
PANT
PANT
PANT
DON'T LIE!

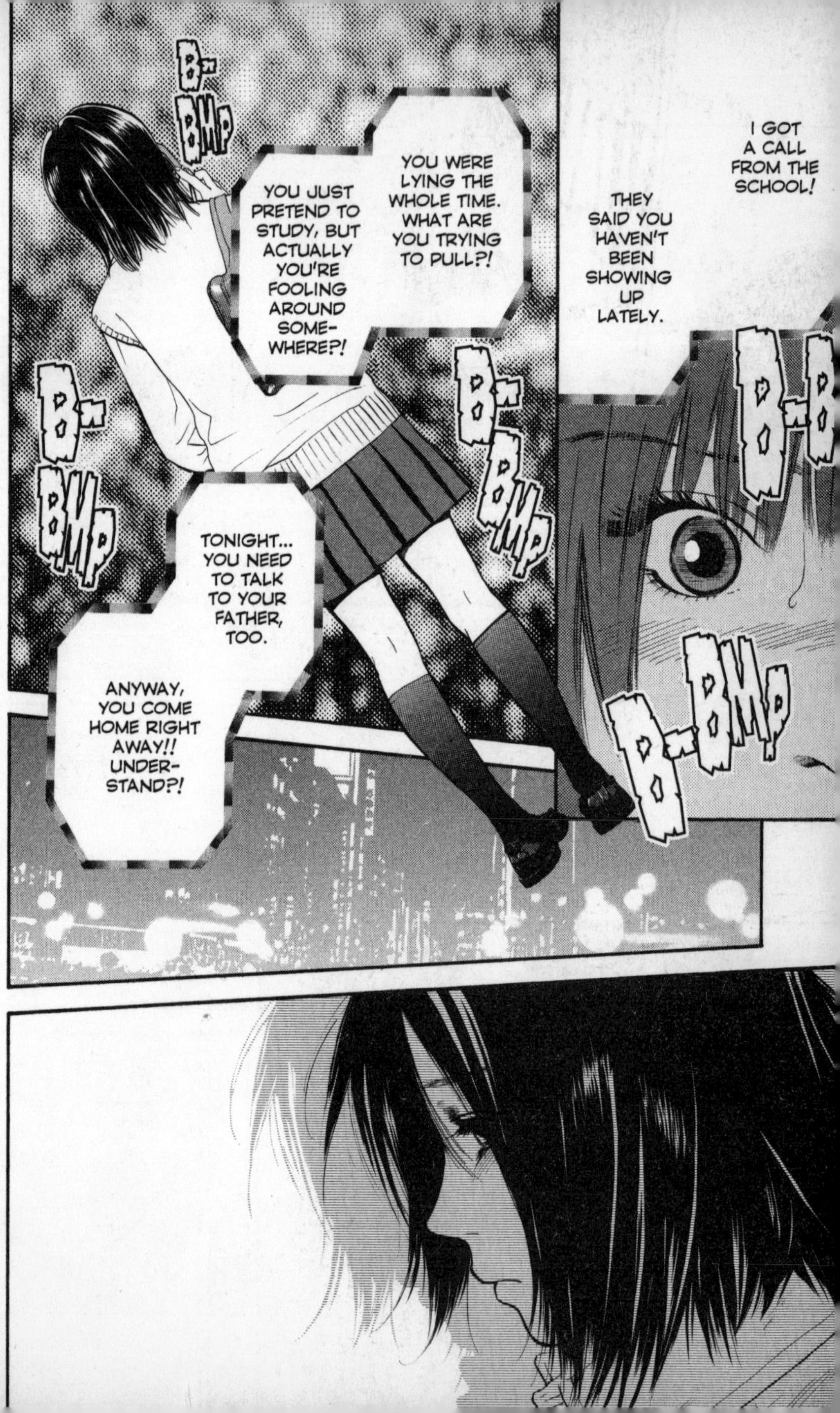
I GOT A CALL FROM THE SCHOOL!
THEY SAID YOU HAVEN'T BEEN SHOWING UP LATELY.
B-B
B-BMP
YOU WERE LYING THE WHOLE TIME. WHAT ARE YOU TRYING TO PULL?!
YOU JUST PRETEND TO STUDY, BUT ACTUALLY YOU'RE FOOLING AROUND SOME-WHERE?!
B-BMP
B-BMP
B-BMP
TONIGHT... YOU NEED TO TALK TO YOUR FATHER, TOO.
ANYWAY, YOU COME HOME RIGHT AWAY!! UNDER-STAND?!

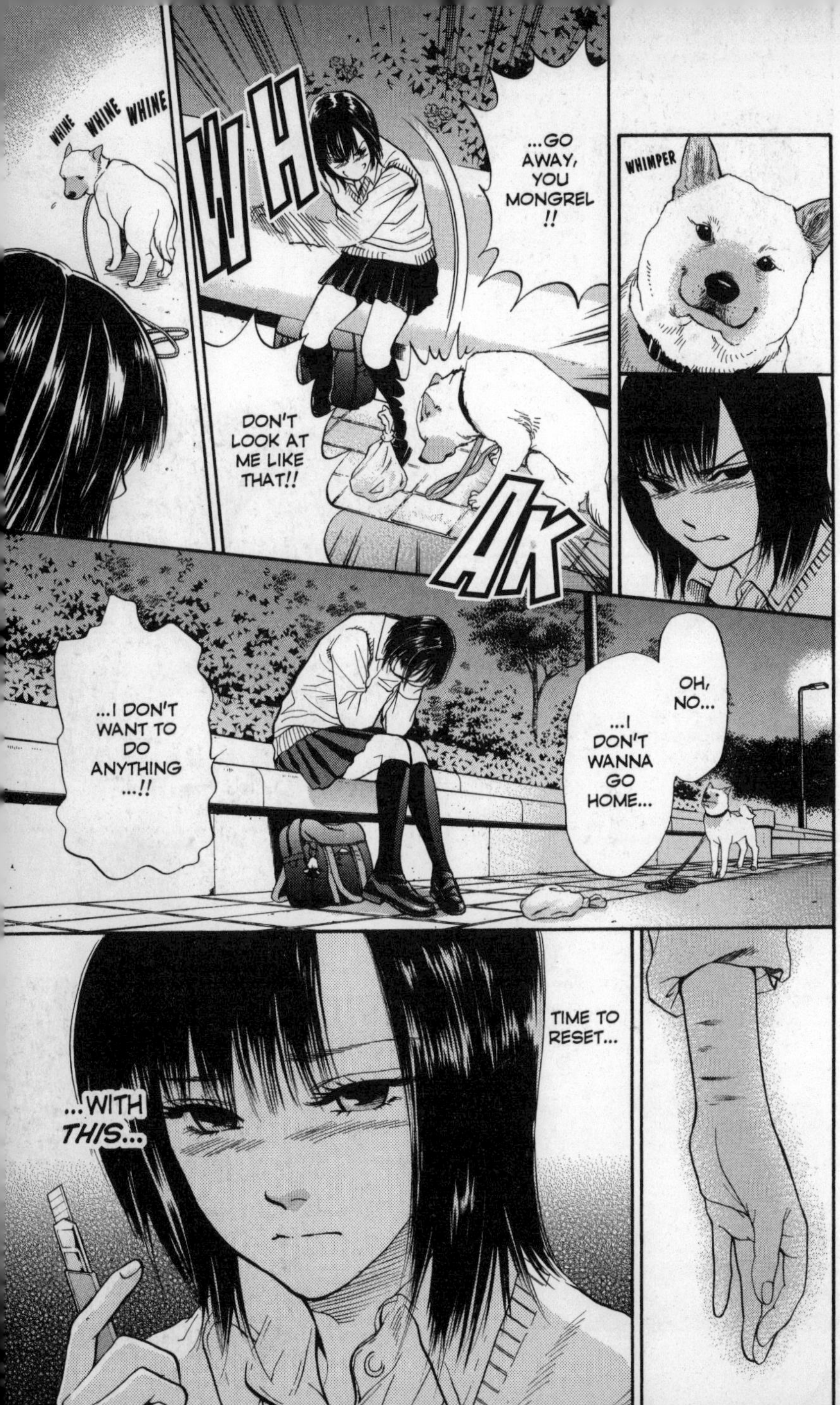
WHIMPER
...GO AWAY, YOU MONGREL!!
WH
AK
DON'T LOOK AT ME LIKE THAT!!
WHINE WHINE WHINE
OH, NO...
...I DON'T WANNA GO HOME...
...I DON'T WANT TO DO ANYTHING...!!
TIME TO RESET...
...WITH *THIS*...

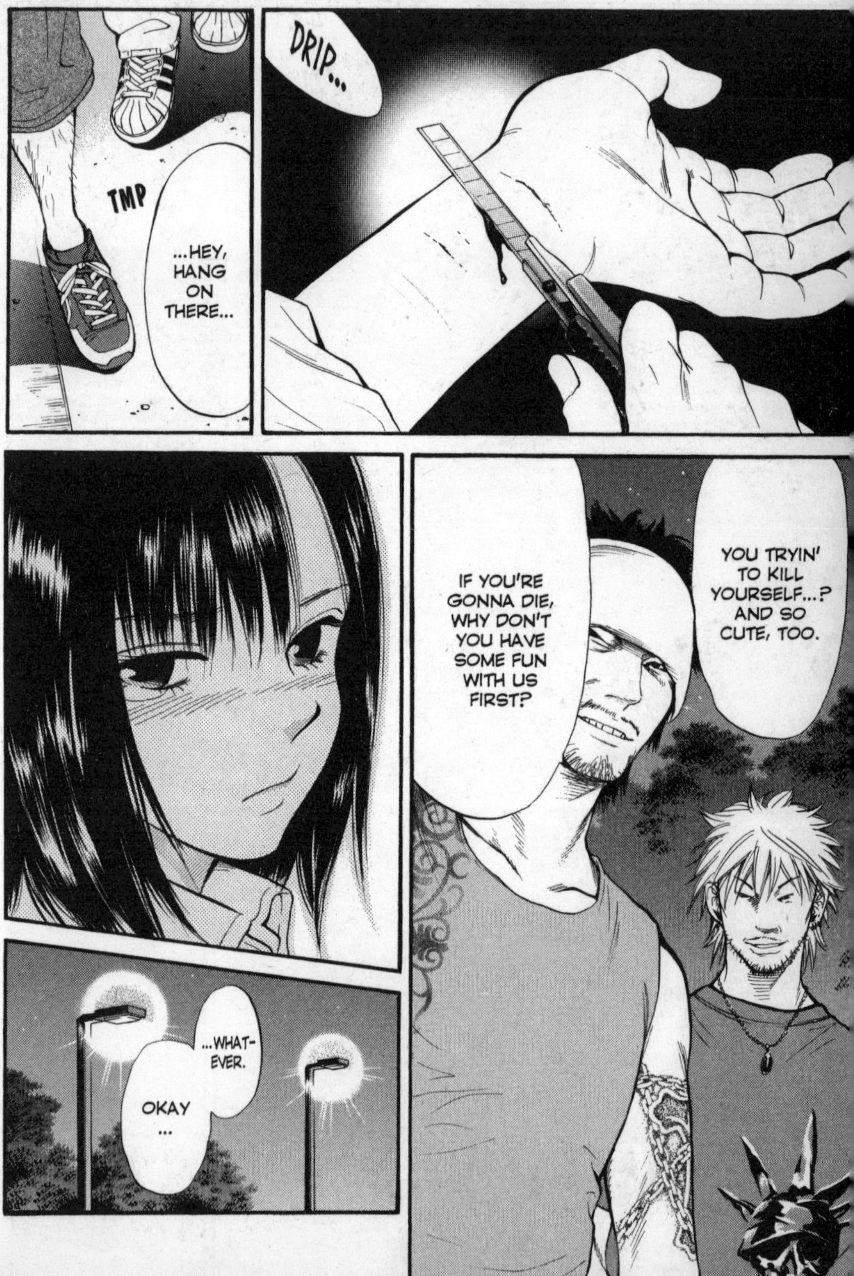
DRIP...
TMP
...HEY, HANG ON THERE...
YOU TRYIN' TO KILL YOURSELF...? AND SO CUTE, TOO.
IF YOU'RE GONNA DIE, WHY DON'T YOU HAVE SOME FUN WITH US FIRST?
...WHAT-EVER.
OKAY ...

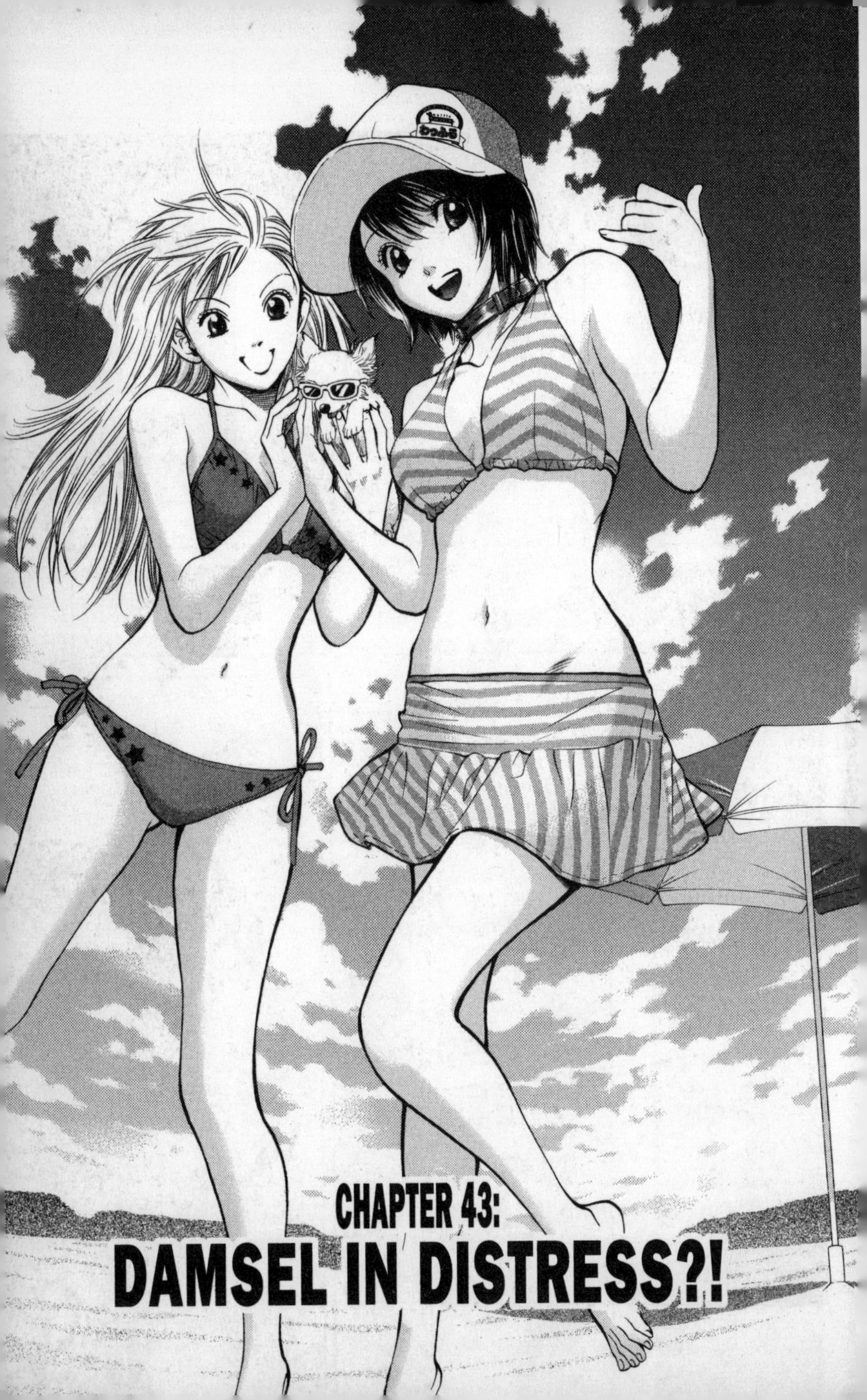

CHAPTER 43:
DAMSEL IN DISTRESS?!

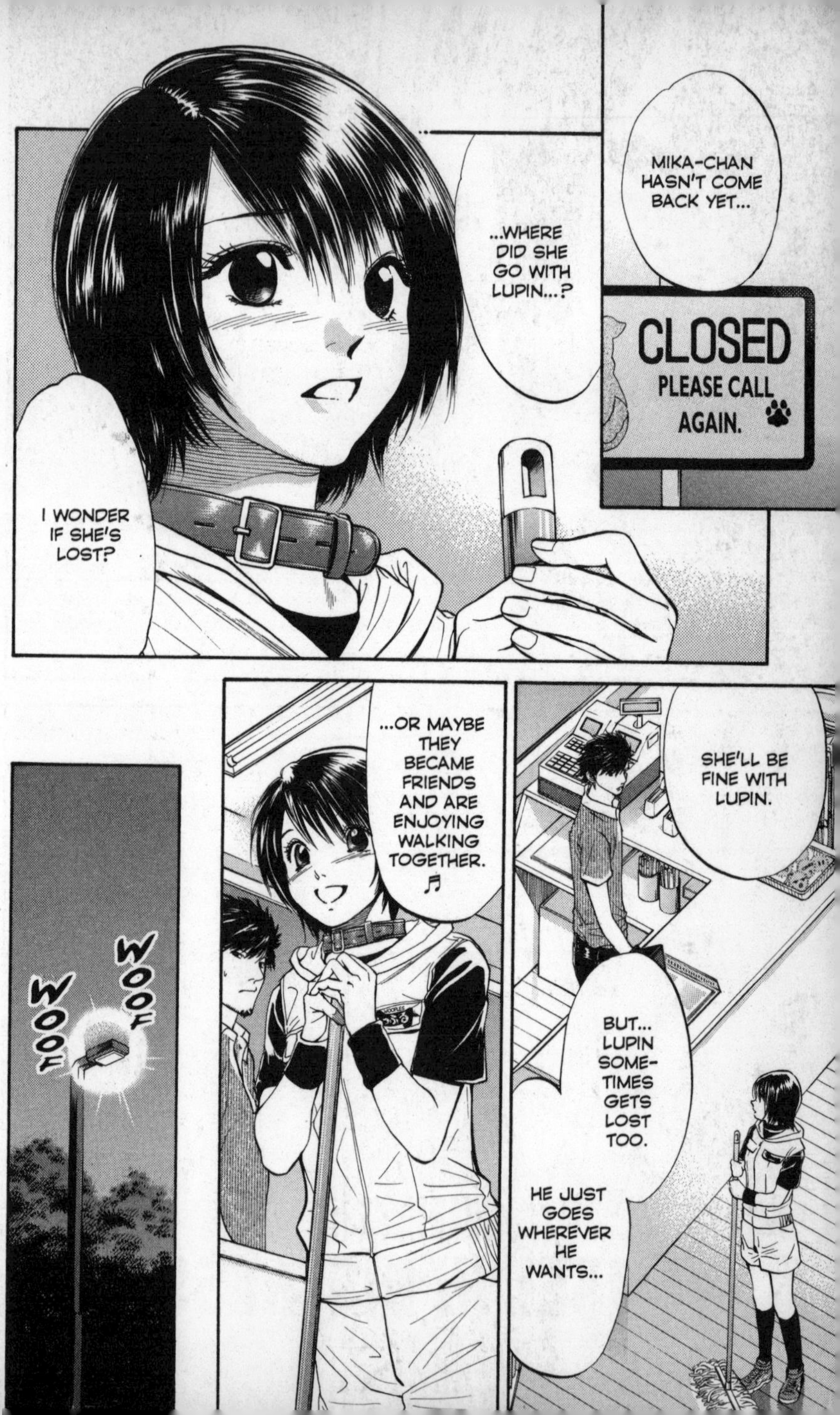
MIKA-CHAN HASN'T COME BACK YET...
CLOSED
PLEASE CALL AGAIN.
...WHERE DID SHE GO WITH LUPIN...?
I WONDER IF SHE'S LOST?
SHE'LL BE FINE WITH LUPIN.
BUT... LUPIN SOME-TIMES GETS LOST TOO.
HE JUST GOES WHEREVER HE WANTS...
...OR MAYBE THEY BECAME FRIENDS AND ARE ENJOYING WALKING TOGETHER. ♬
WOOF
WOOF

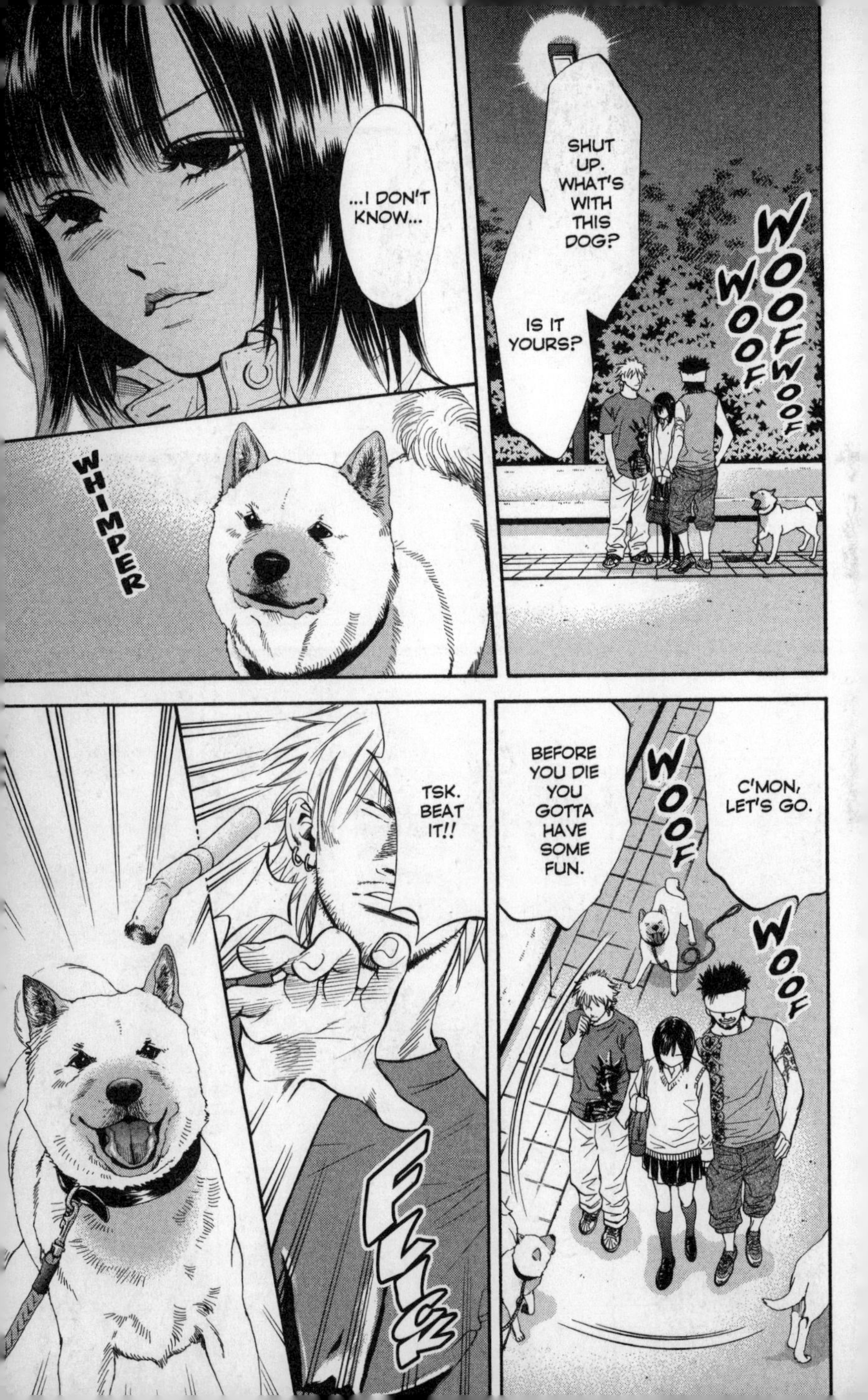
SHUT UP. WHAT'S WITH THIS DOG?
IS IT YOURS?
WOOF WOOF
WOOF WOOF
...I DON'T KNOW...
WHIMPER
C'MON, LET'S GO.
WOOF
WOOF
BEFORE YOU DIE YOU GOTTA HAVE SOME FUN.
TSK. BEAT IT!!

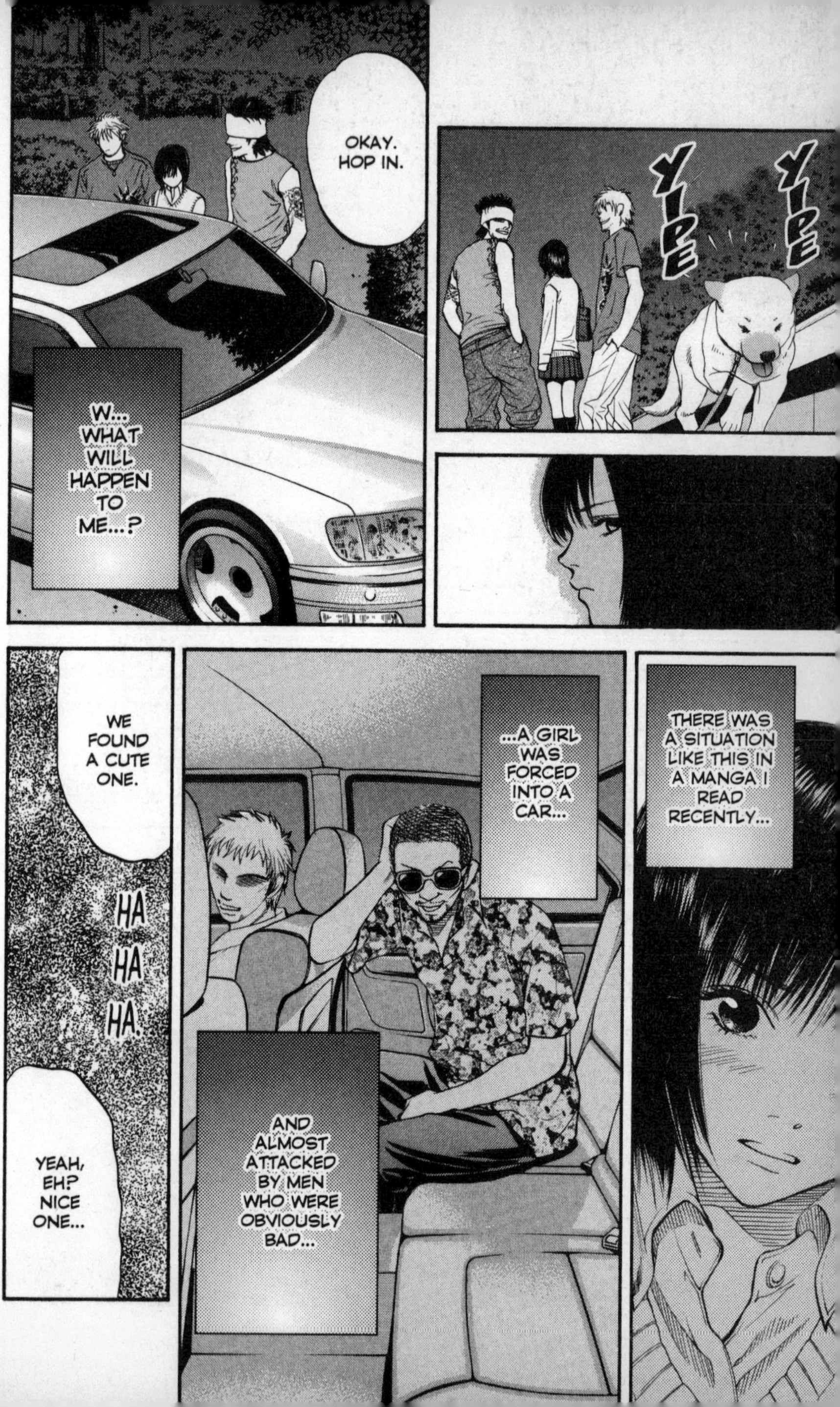
YIPE
YIPE
OKAY. HOP IN.
W... WHAT WILL HAPPEN TO ME...?
THERE WAS A SITUATION LIKE THIS IN A MANGA I READ RECENTLY...
...A GIRL WAS FORCED INTO A CAR...
AND ALMOST ATTACKED BY MEN WHO WERE OBVIOUSLY BAD...
WE FOUND A CUTE ONE.
HA HA HA.
YEAH, EH? NICE ONE...

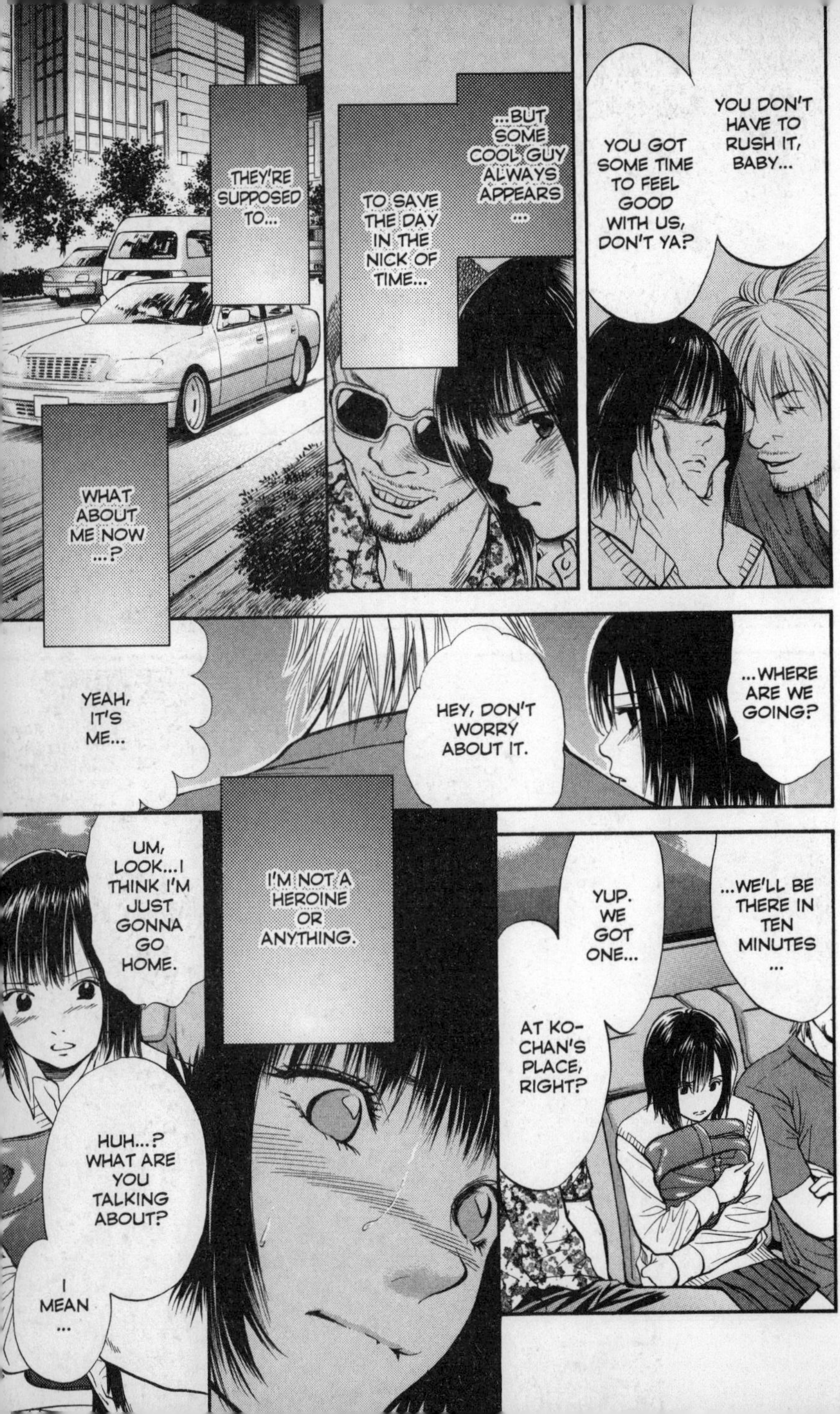
YOU DON'T HAVE TO RUSH IT, BABY...
YOU GOT SOME TIME TO FEEL GOOD WITH US, DON'T YA?
...BUT SOME COOL GUY ALWAYS APPEARS...
TO SAVE THE DAY IN THE NICK OF TIME...
THEY'RE SUPPOSED TO...
WHAT ABOUT ME NOW...?
...WHERE ARE WE GOING?
HEY, DON'T WORRY ABOUT IT.
YEAH, IT'S ME...
...WE'LL BE THERE IN TEN MINUTES...
YUP. WE GOT ONE...
AT KO-CHAN'S PLACE, RIGHT?
I'M NOT A HEROINE OR ANYTHING.
UM, LOOK...I THINK I'M JUST GONNA GO HOME.
HUH...? WHAT ARE YOU TALKING ABOUT?
I MEAN...

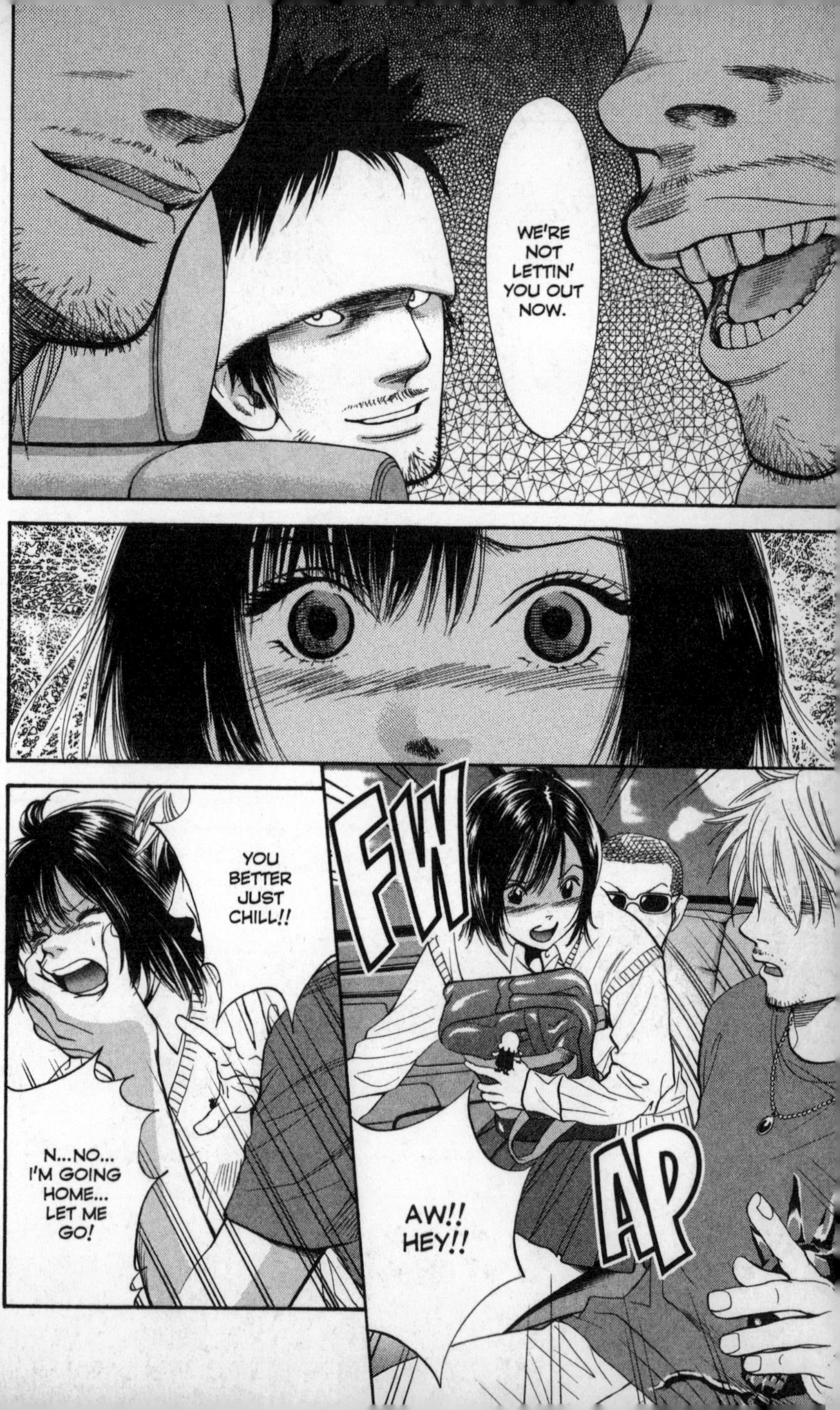
WE'RE NOT LETTIN' YOU OUT NOW.
FW
AP
AW!! HEY!!
YOU BETTER JUST CHILL!!
N...NO... I'M GOING HOME... LET ME GO!

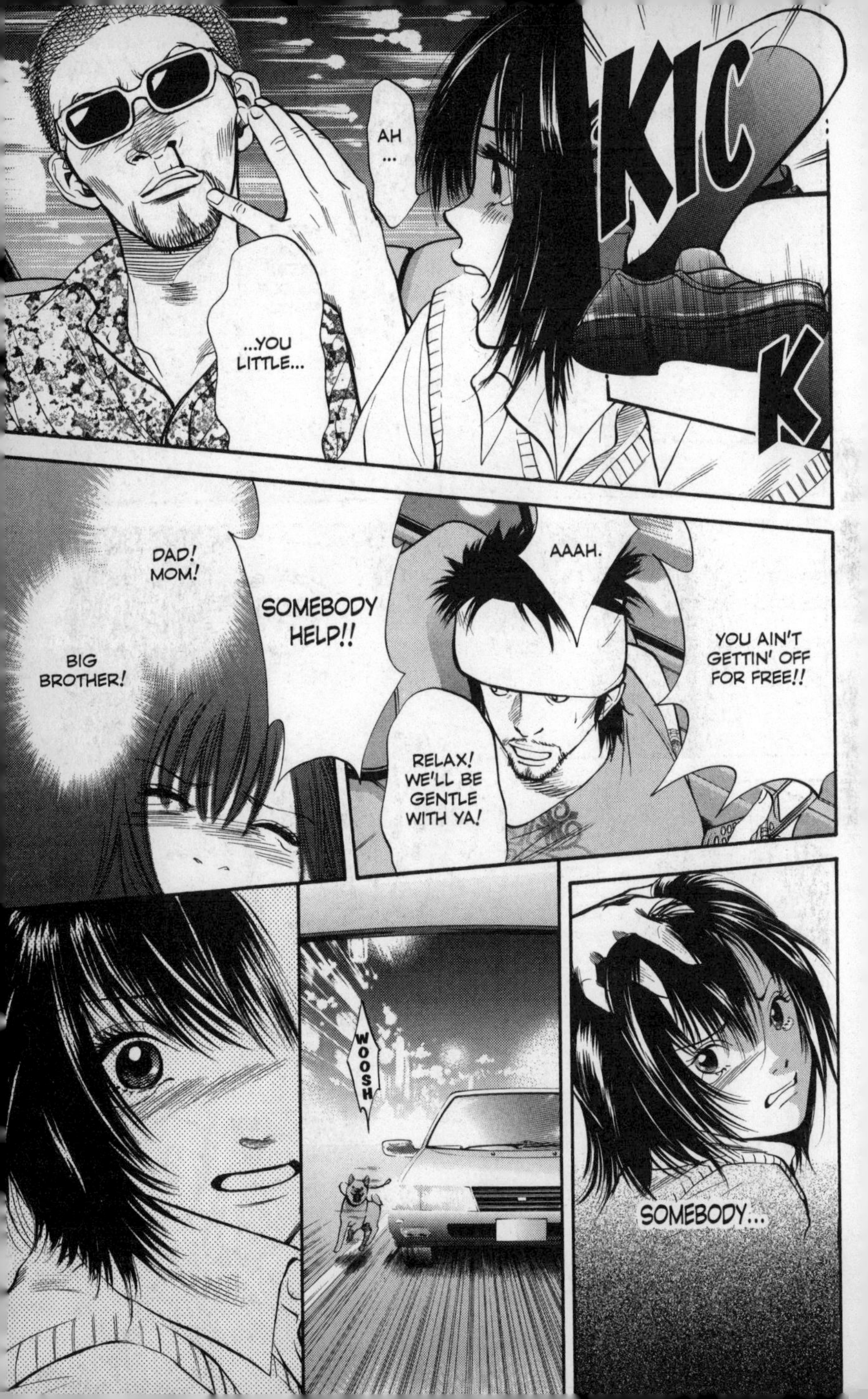

KIC
K
AH ...
...YOU LITTLE...
AAAH.
YOU AIN'T GETTIN' OFF FOR FREE!!
RELAX! WE'LL BE GENTLE WITH YA!
SOMEBODY HELP!!
DAD! MOM!
BIG BROTHER!
SOMEBODY...
WOOSH

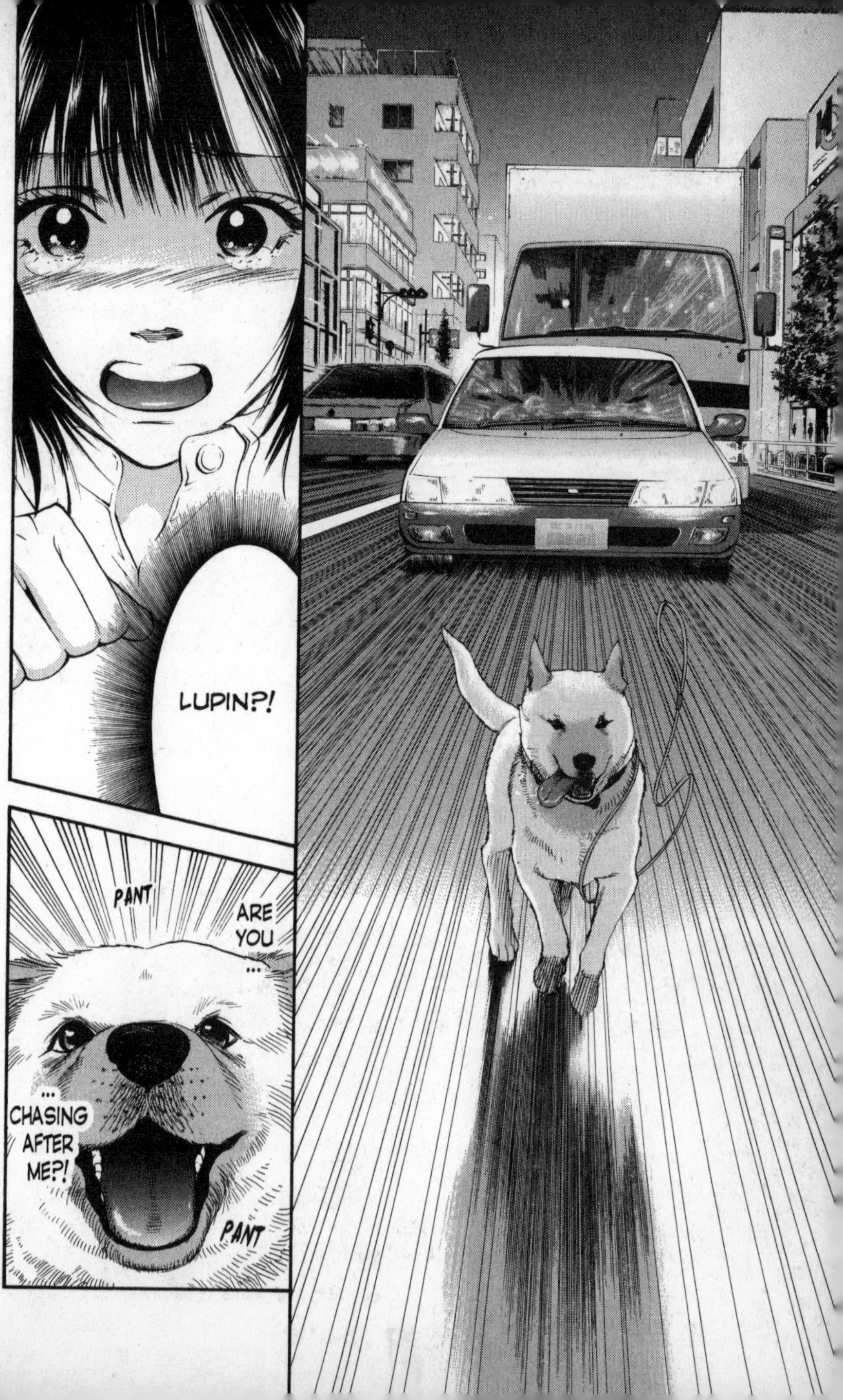
LUPIN?!
PANT
ARE YOU ...
... CHASING AFTER ME?!
PANT

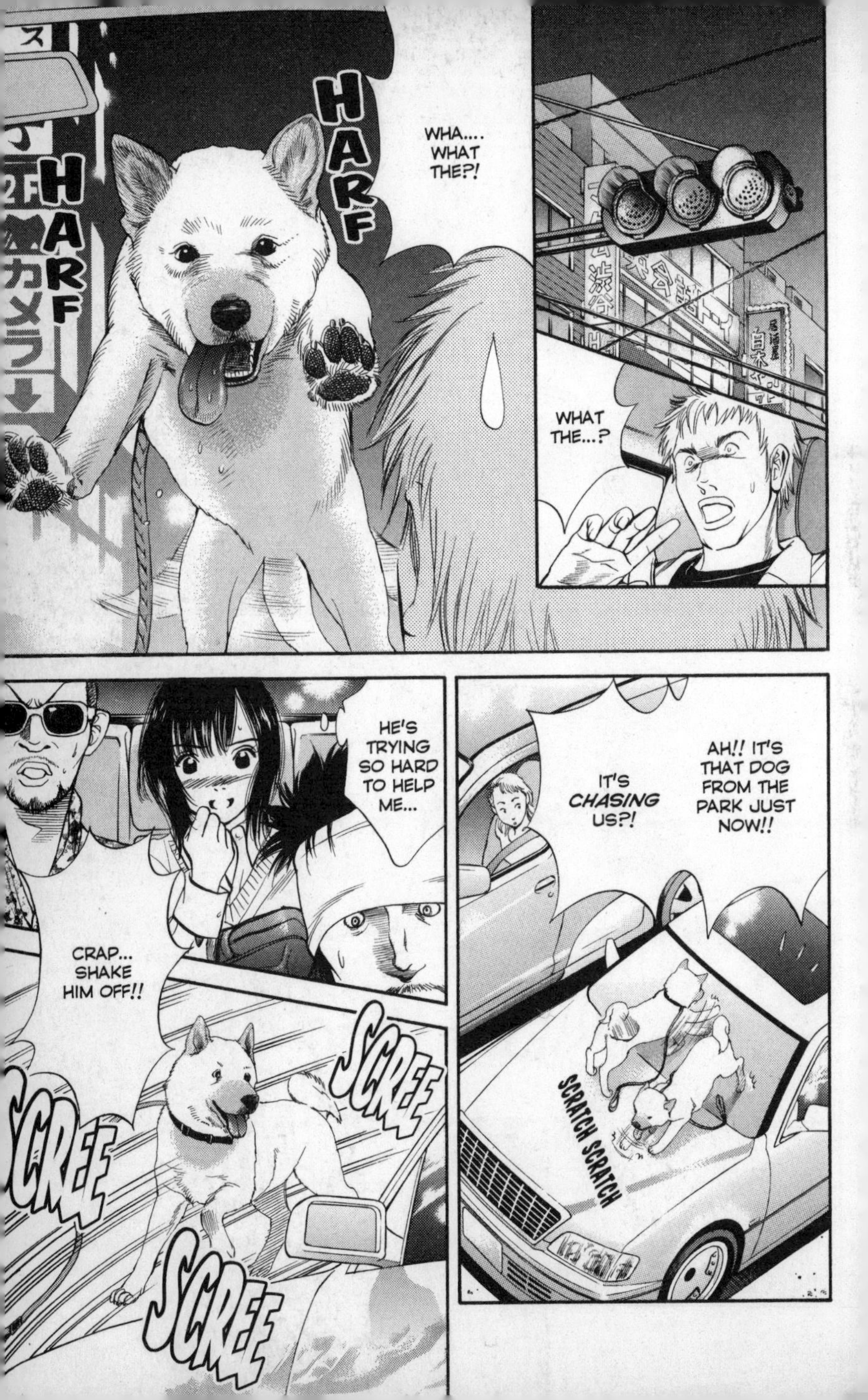
WHAT THE...?
HARF
HARF
WHA.... WHAT THE?!
AH!! IT'S THAT DOG FROM THE PARK JUST NOW!!
IT'S CHASING US?!
SCRATCH SCRATCH
HE'S TRYING SO HARD TO HELP ME...
CRAP... SHAKE HIM OFF!!
SCREE
SCREE
SCREE

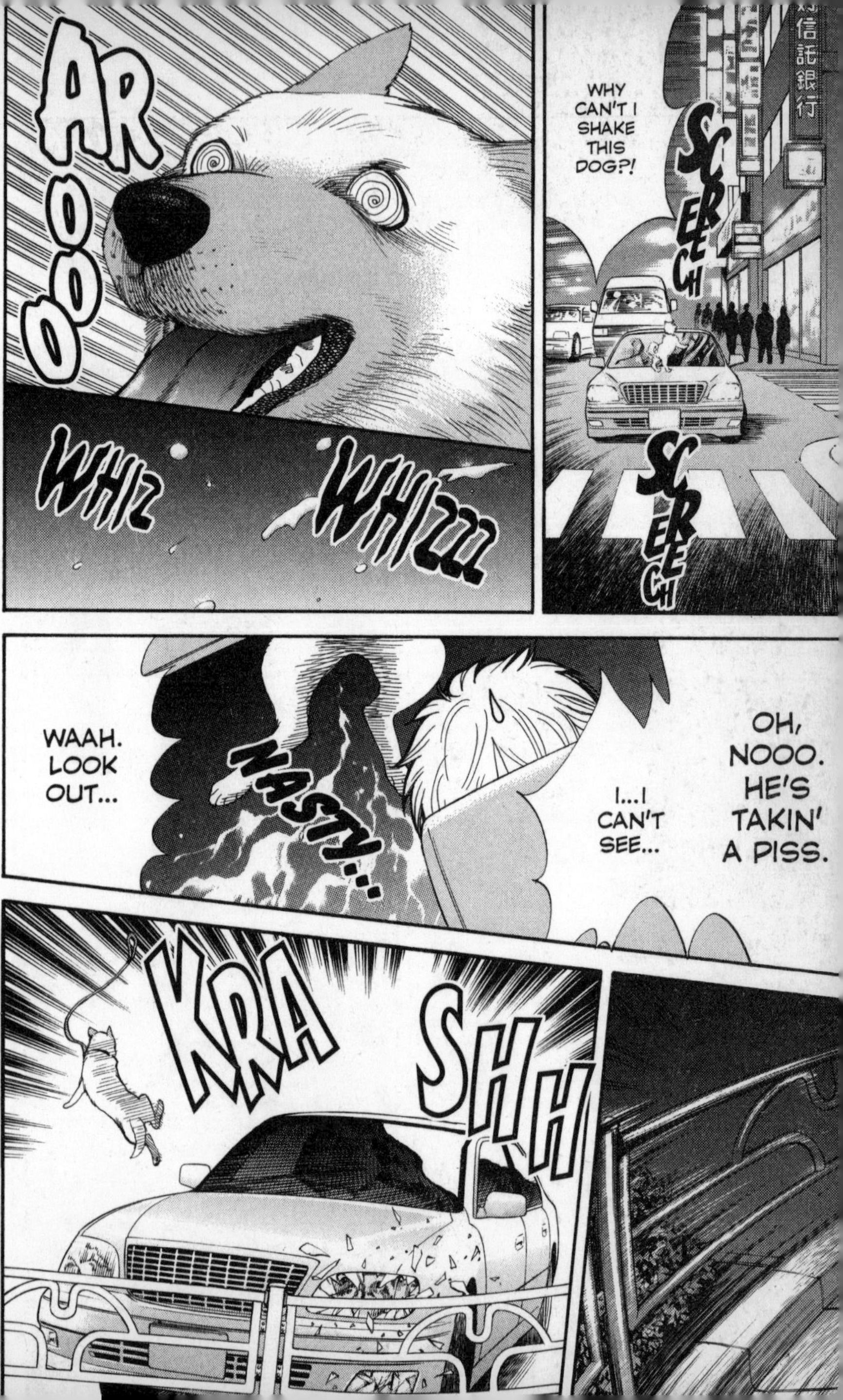

信託銀行
WHY CAN'T I SHAKE THIS DOG?!
SCREECH
SCREECH
AROOOOO
WHIZ
WHIZZZ
OH, NOOO. HE'S TAKIN' A PISS.
I...I CAN'T SEE...
NASTY...
WAAH. LOOK OUT...
KRASHH

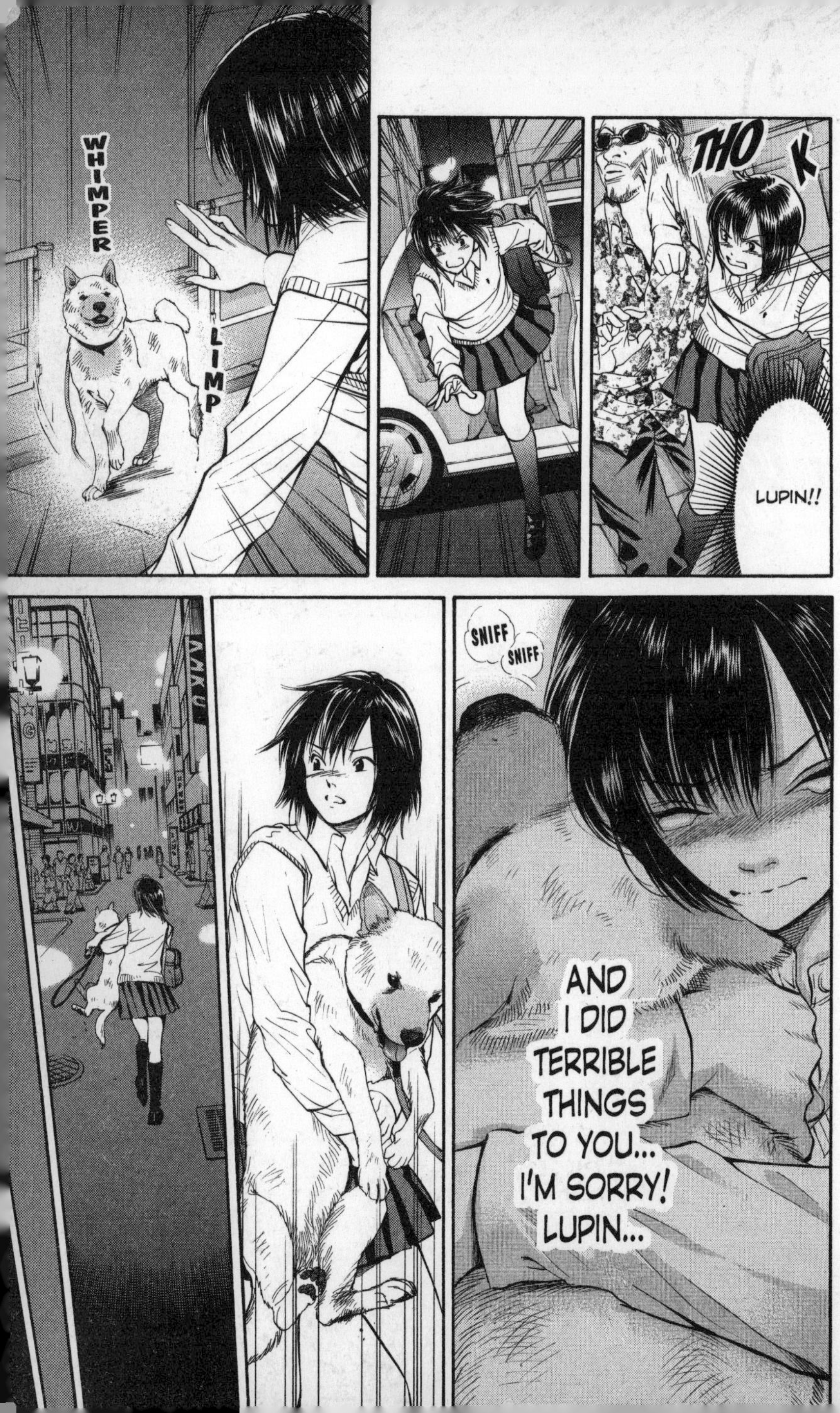
THO K
LUPIN!!
WHIMPER
LIMP
SNIFF
SNIFF
AND I DID TERRIBLE THINGS TO YOU... I'M SORRY! LUPIN...

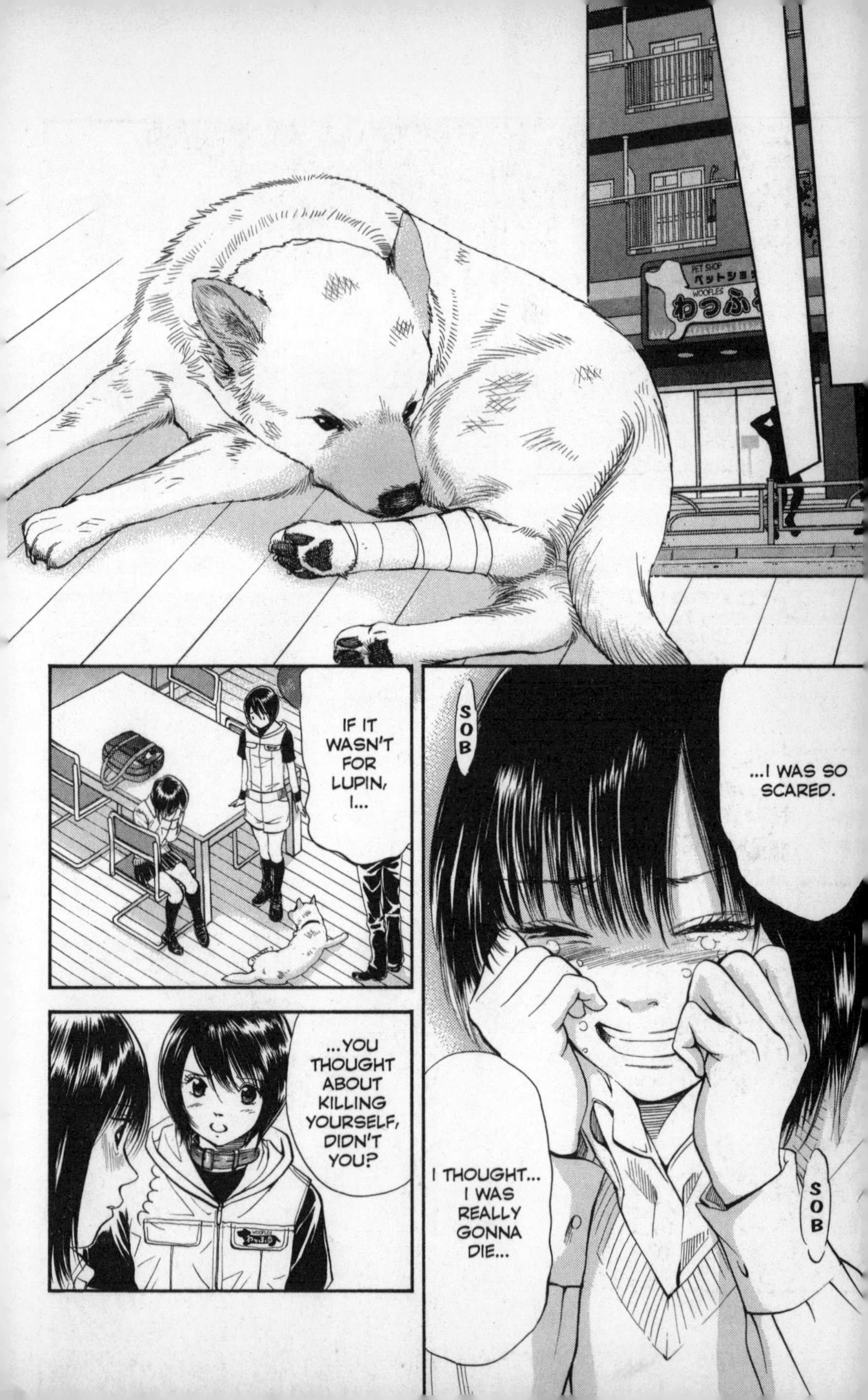
PET SHOP
WOOFLES
SOB
...I WAS SO SCARED.
I THOUGHT... I WAS REALLY GONNA DIE...
SOB
IF IT WASN'T FOR LUPIN, I...
...YOU THOUGHT ABOUT KILLING YOURSELF, DIDN'T YOU?

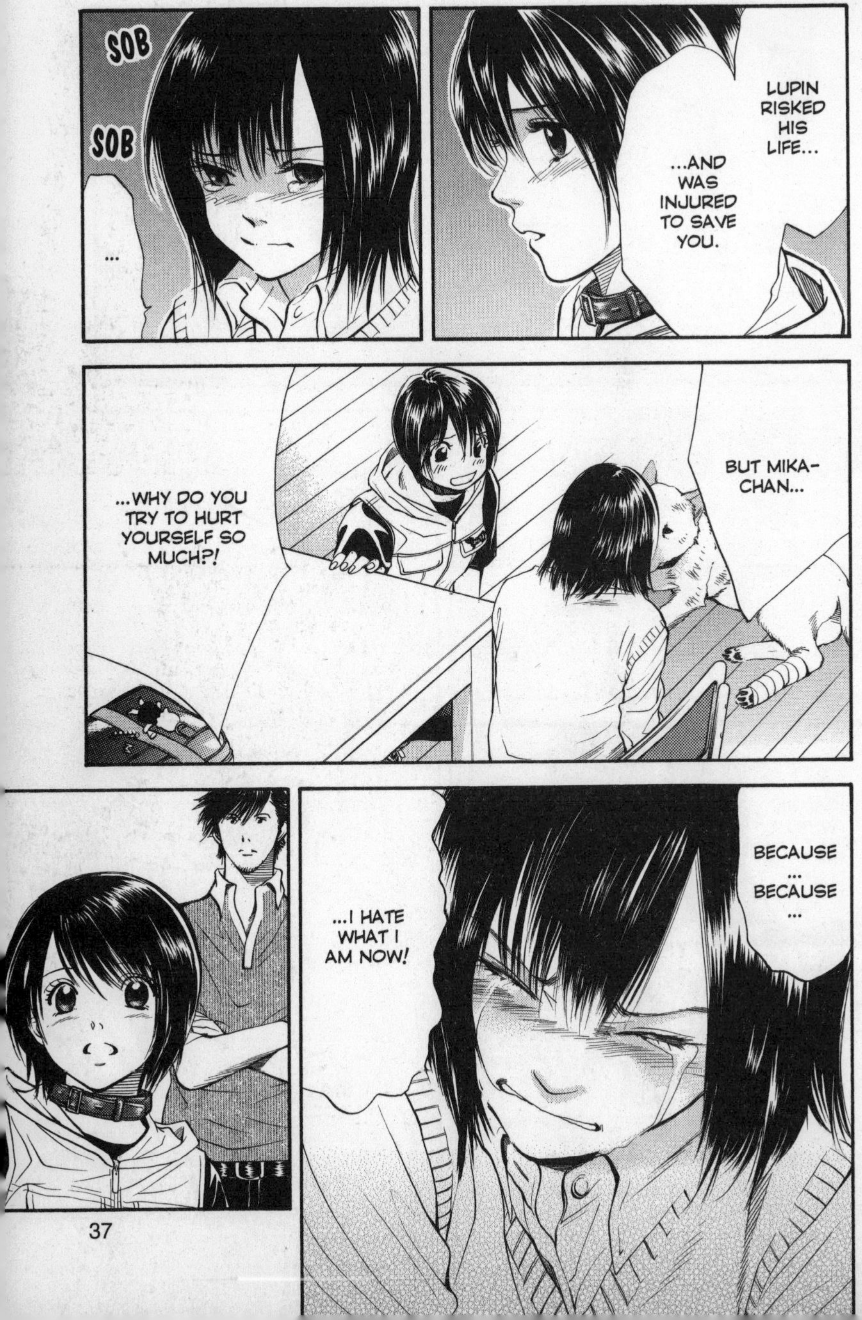
LUPIN RISKED HIS LIFE...
...AND WAS INJURED TO SAVE YOU.
SOB
SOB
...
BUT MIKA-CHAN...
...WHY DO YOU TRY TO HURT YOURSELF SO MUCH?!
BECAUSE ... BECAUSE ...
...I HATE WHAT I AM NOW!

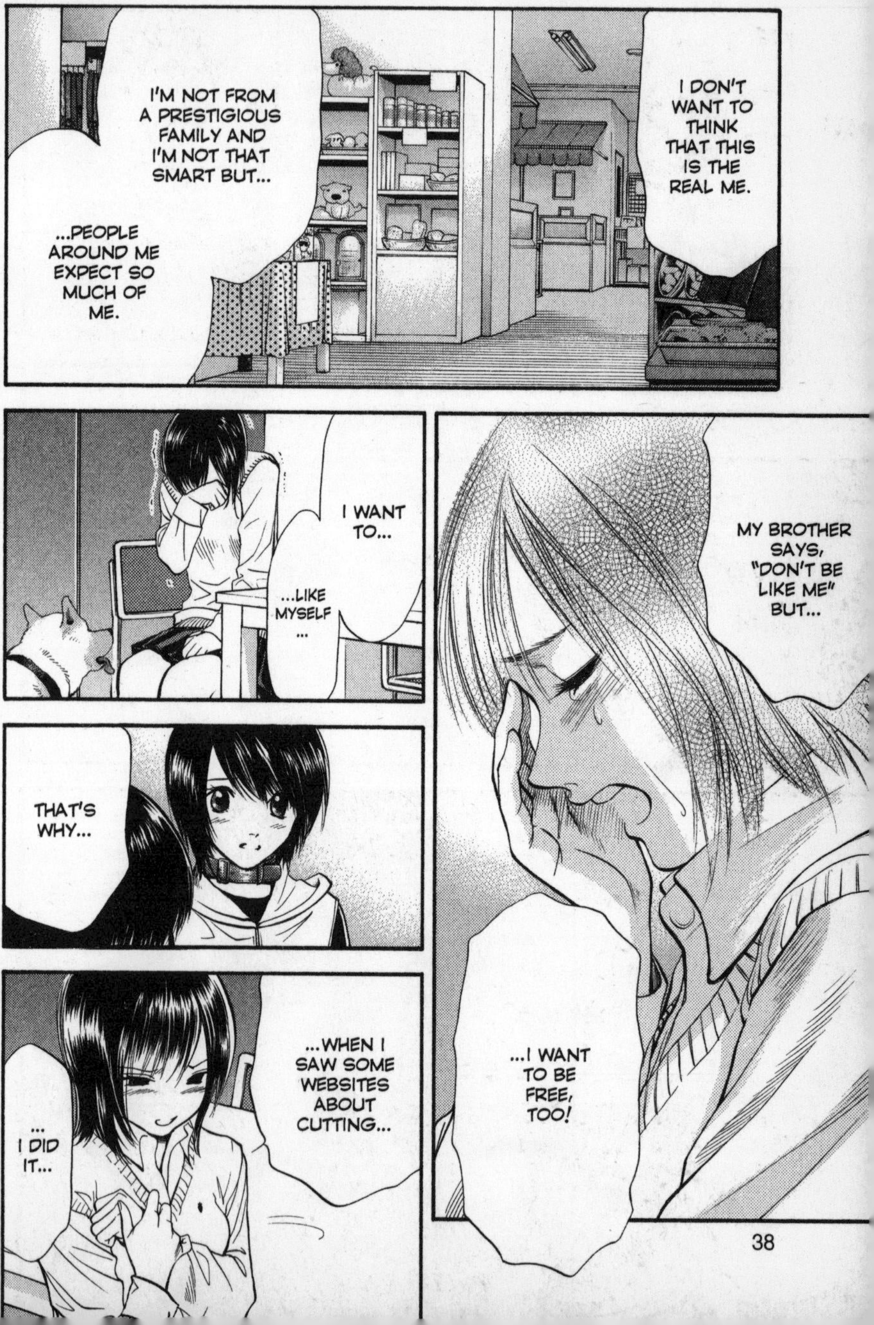
I DON'T WANT TO THINK THAT THIS IS THE REAL ME.
I'M NOT FROM A PRESTIGIOUS FAMILY AND I'M NOT THAT SMART BUT...
...PEOPLE AROUND ME EXPECT SO MUCH OF ME.
MY BROTHER SAYS, "DON'T BE LIKE ME" BUT...
...I WANT TO BE FREE, TOO!
I WANT TO...
...LIKE MYSELF ...
THAT'S WHY...
...WHEN I SAW SOME WEBSITES ABOUT CUTTING...
... I DID IT...

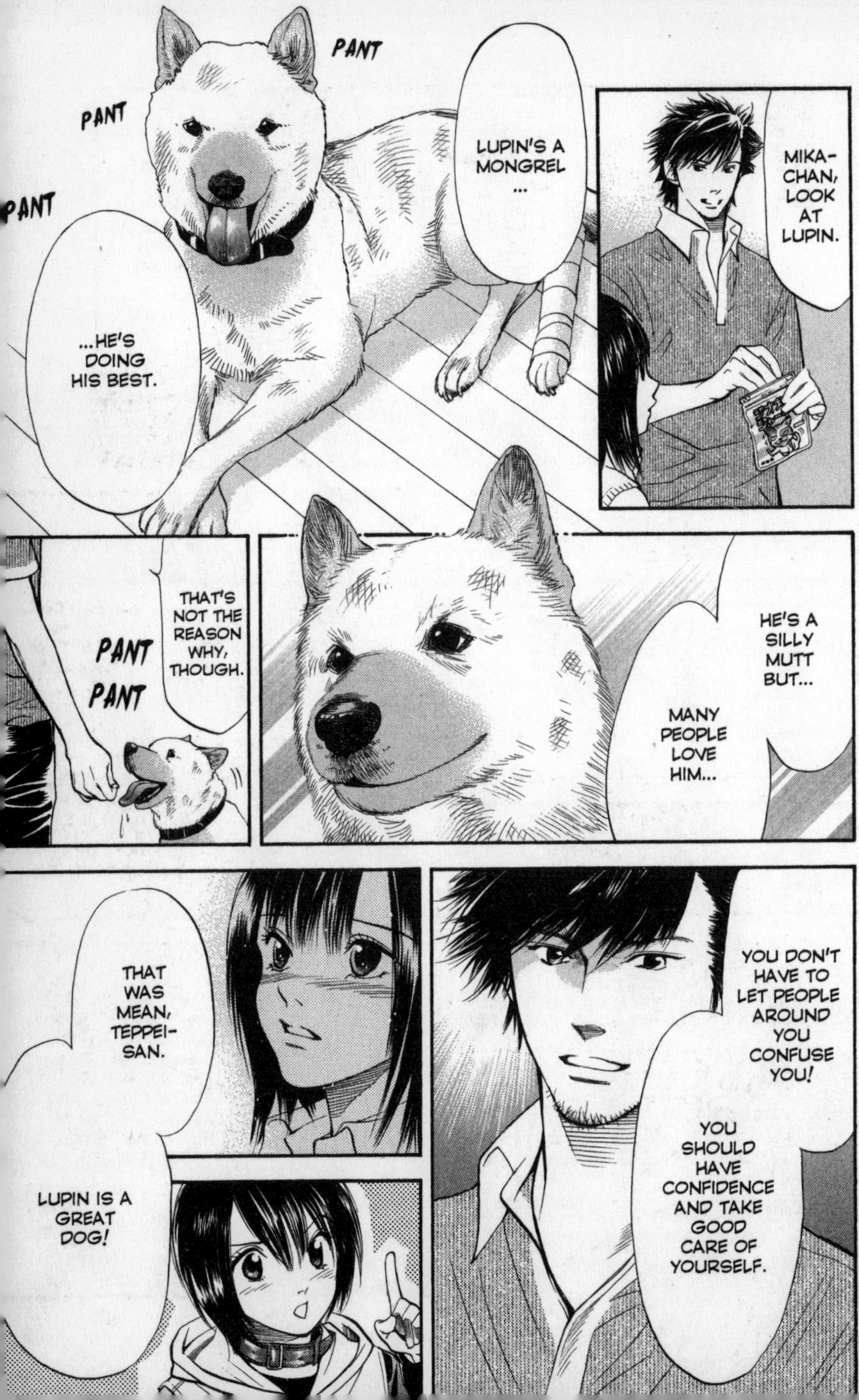
MIKA-CHAN, LOOK AT LUPIN.
PANT
LUPIN'S A MONGREL ...
PANT
PANT
...HE'S DOING HIS BEST.
HE'S A SILLY MUTT BUT...
MANY PEOPLE LOVE HIM...
THAT'S NOT THE REASON WHY, THOUGH.
PANT
PANT
YOU DON'T HAVE TO LET PEOPLE AROUND YOU CONFUSE YOU!
YOU SHOULD HAVE CONFIDENCE AND TAKE GOOD CARE OF YOURSELF.
THAT WAS MEAN, TEPPEI-SAN.
LUPIN IS A GREAT DOG!

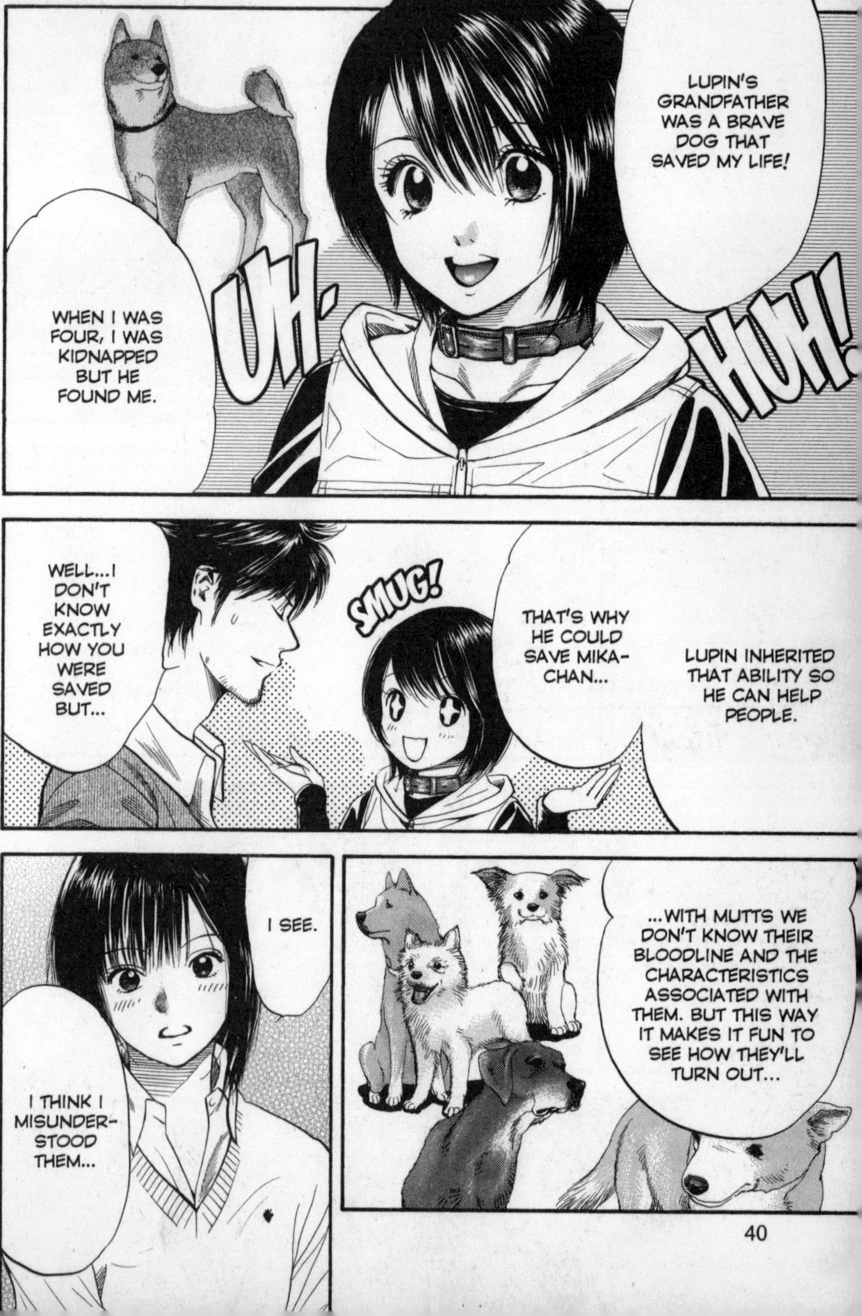
LUPIN'S GRANDFATHER WAS A BRAVE DOG THAT SAVED MY LIFE!
UH-HUH!
WHEN I WAS FOUR, I WAS KIDNAPPED BUT HE FOUND ME.
LUPIN INHERITED THAT ABILITY SO HE CAN HELP PEOPLE.
THAT'S WHY HE COULD SAVE MIKA-CHAN...
SMUG!
WELL...I DON'T KNOW EXACTLY HOW YOU WERE SAVED BUT...
...WITH MUTTS WE DON'T KNOW THEIR BLOODLINE AND THE CHARACTERISTICS ASSOCIATED WITH THEM. BUT THIS WAY IT MAKES IT FUN TO SEE HOW THEY'LL TURN OUT...
I SEE.
I THINK I MISUNDERSTOOD THEM...

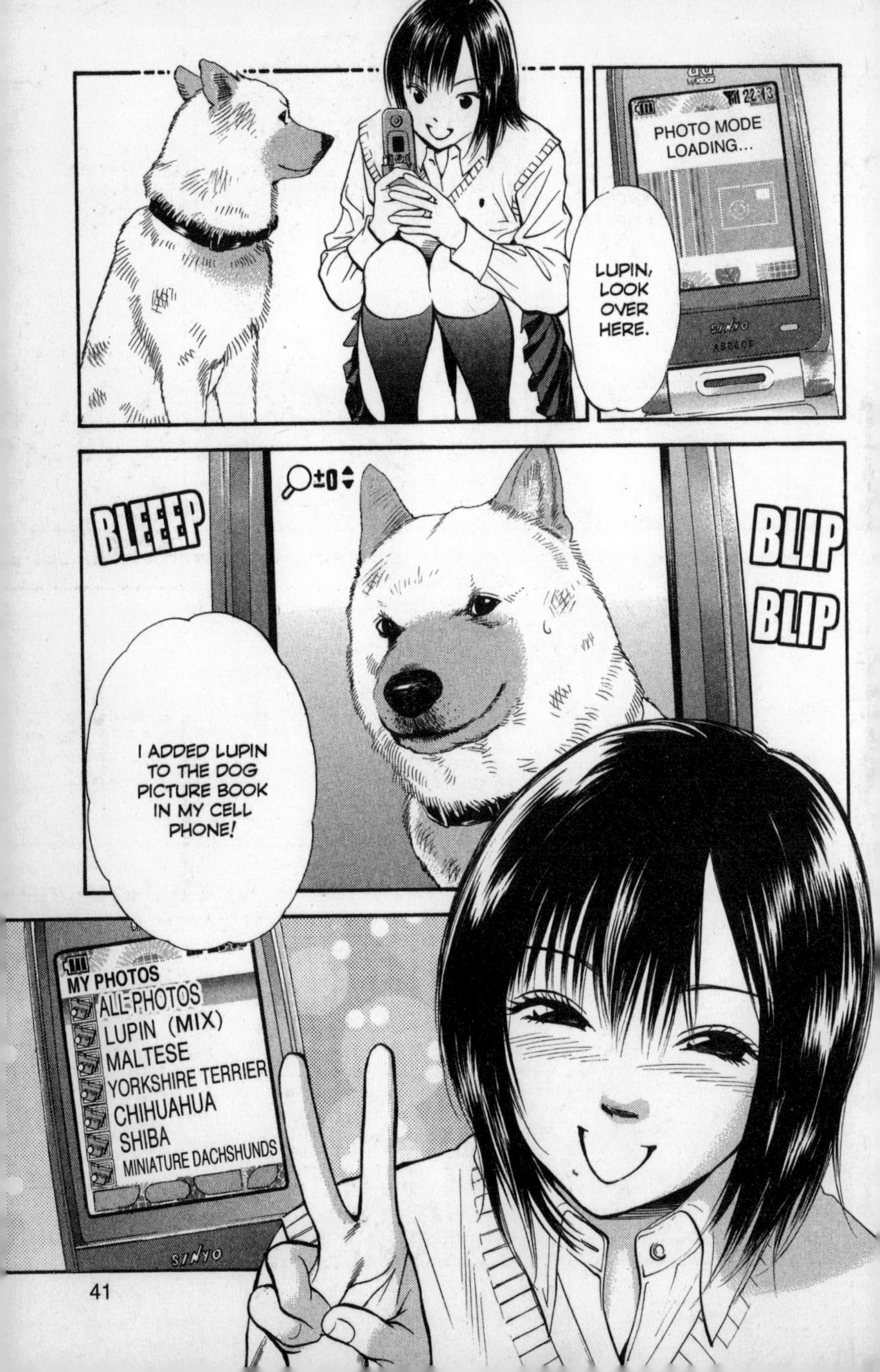
22:13
PHOTO MODE LOADING...
LUPIN, LOOK OVER HERE.
SINYO
BLIP BLIP
±0
BLEEEP
I ADDED LUPIN TO THE DOG PICTURE BOOK IN MY CELL PHONE!
MY PHOTOS
ALL PHOTOS
LUPIN (MIX)
MALTESE
YORKSHIRE TERRIER
CHIHUAHUA
SHIBA
MINIATURE DACHSHUNDS
SINYO

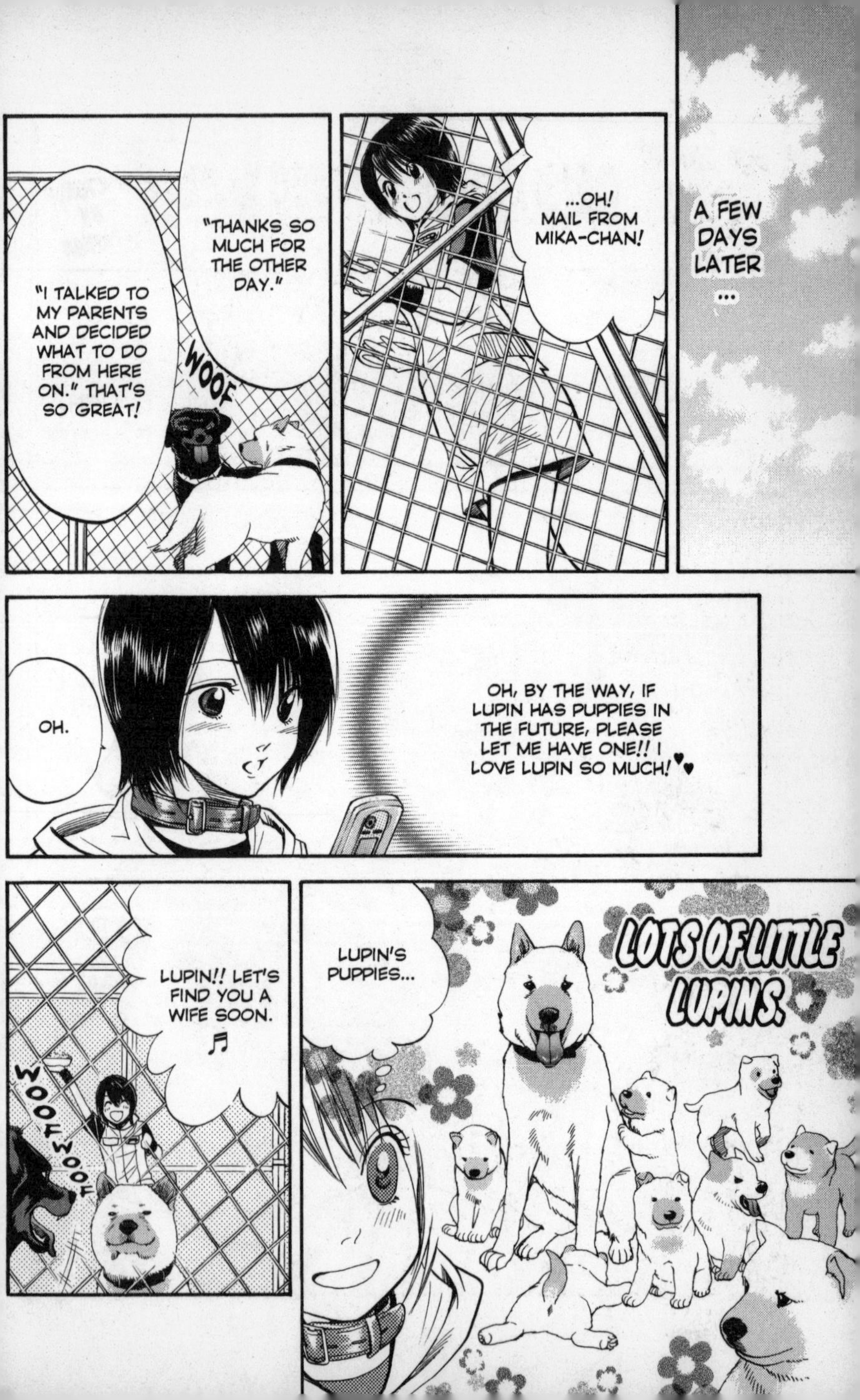

A FEW DAYS LATER ...
...OH! MAIL FROM MIKA-CHAN!
"THANKS SO MUCH FOR THE OTHER DAY."
"I TALKED TO MY PARENTS AND DECIDED WHAT TO DO FROM HERE ON." THAT'S SO GREAT!
WOOF
OH, BY THE WAY, IF LUPIN HAS PUPPIES IN THE FUTURE, PLEASE LET ME HAVE ONE!! I LOVE LUPIN SO MUCH! ♥♥
OH.
LOTS OF LITTLE LUPINS.
LUPIN'S PUPPIES...
LUPIN!! LET'S FIND YOU A WIFE SOON. ♫
WOOF WOOF

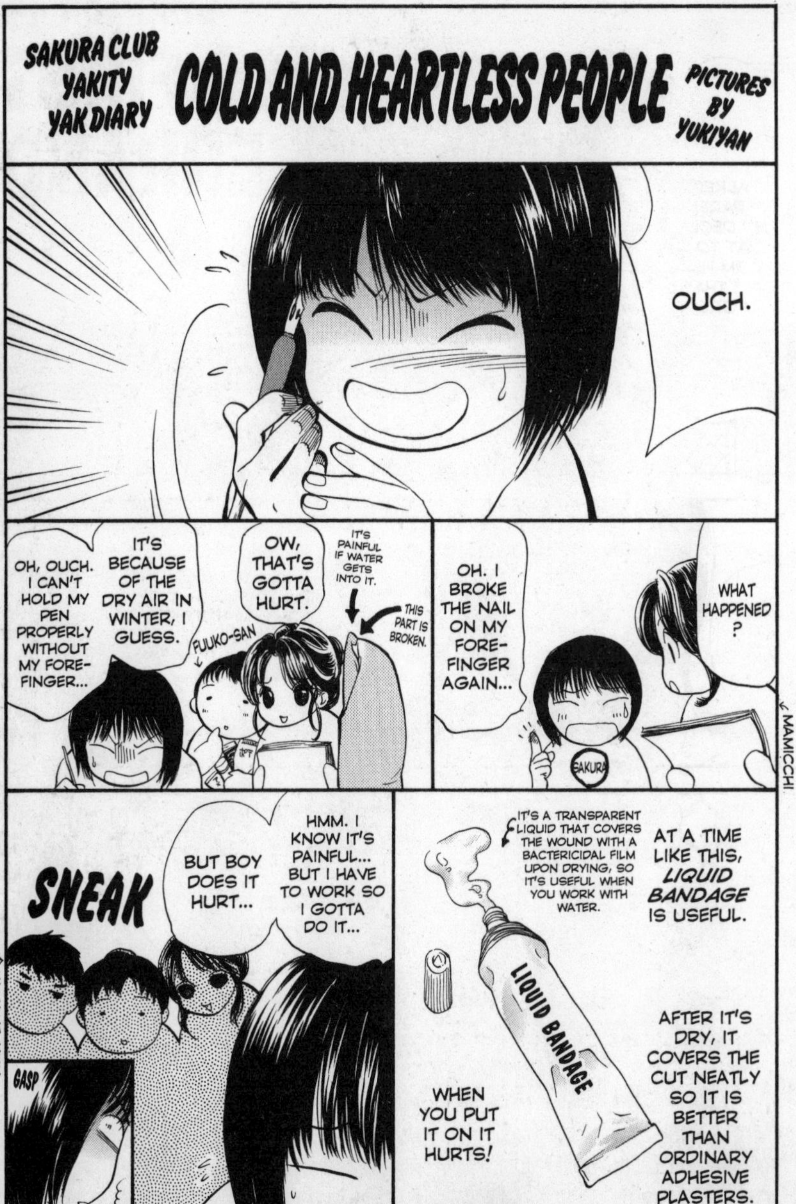
SAKURA CLUB YAKITY YAK DIARY
COLD AND HEARTLESS PEOPLE
PICTURES BY YUKIYAN
OUCH.
WHAT HAPPENED?
MAMICCHI.
OH. I BROKE THE NAIL ON MY FORE-FINGER AGAIN...
SAKURA
IT'S PAINFUL IF WATER GETS INTO IT.
THIS PART IS BROKEN.
OW, THAT'S GOTTA HURT.
FUUKO-SAN
IT'S BECAUSE OF THE DRY AIR IN WINTER, I GUESS.
OH, OUCH. I CAN'T HOLD MY PEN PROPERLY WITHOUT MY FORE-FINGER...
AT A TIME LIKE THIS, *LIQUID BANDAGE* IS USEFUL.
IT'S A TRANSPARENT LIQUID THAT COVERS THE WOUND WITH A BACTERICIDAL FILM UPON DRYING, SO IT'S USEFUL WHEN YOU WORK WITH WATER.
LIQUID BANDAGE
AFTER IT'S DRY, IT COVERS THE CUT NEATLY SO IT IS BETTER THAN ORDINARY ADHESIVE PLASTERS.
WHEN YOU PUT IT ON IT HURTS!
HMM. I KNOW IT'S PAINFUL... BUT I HAVE TO WORK SO I GOTTA DO IT...
BUT BOY DOES IT HURT...
SNEAK
YAMANE-KUN
GASP

CONTINUED ON PAGE 81.

CHAPTER 44: HER FIRST ERRAND

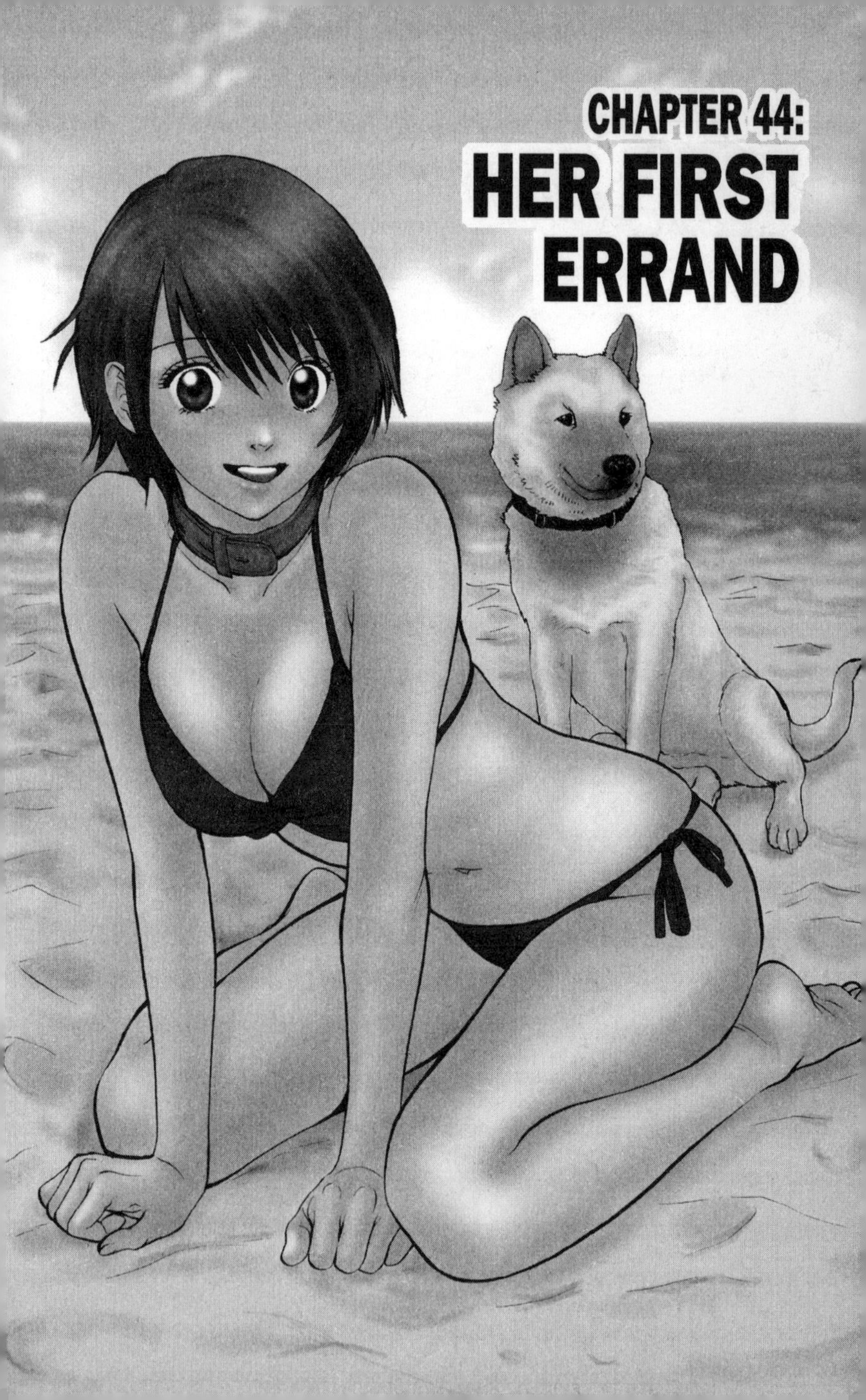

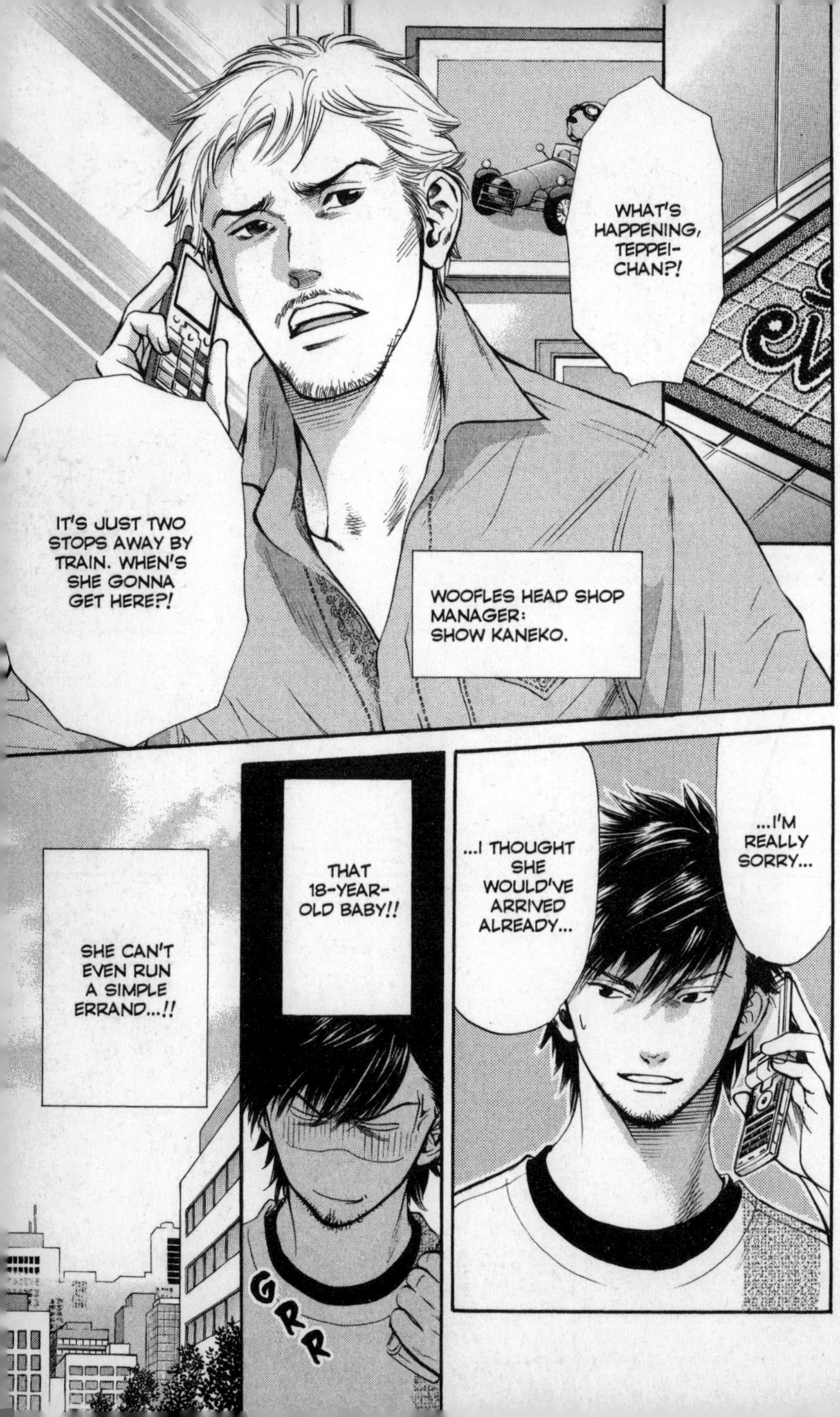
WHAT'S HAPPENING, TEPPEI-CHAN?!
WOOFLES HEAD SHOP MANAGER: SHOW KANEKO.
IT'S JUST TWO STOPS AWAY BY TRAIN. WHEN'S SHE GONNA GET HERE?!
...I'M REALLY SORRY...
...I THOUGHT SHE WOULD'VE ARRIVED ALREADY...
THAT 18-YEAR-OLD BABY!!
GRR
SHE CAN'T EVEN RUN A SIMPLE ERRAND...!!

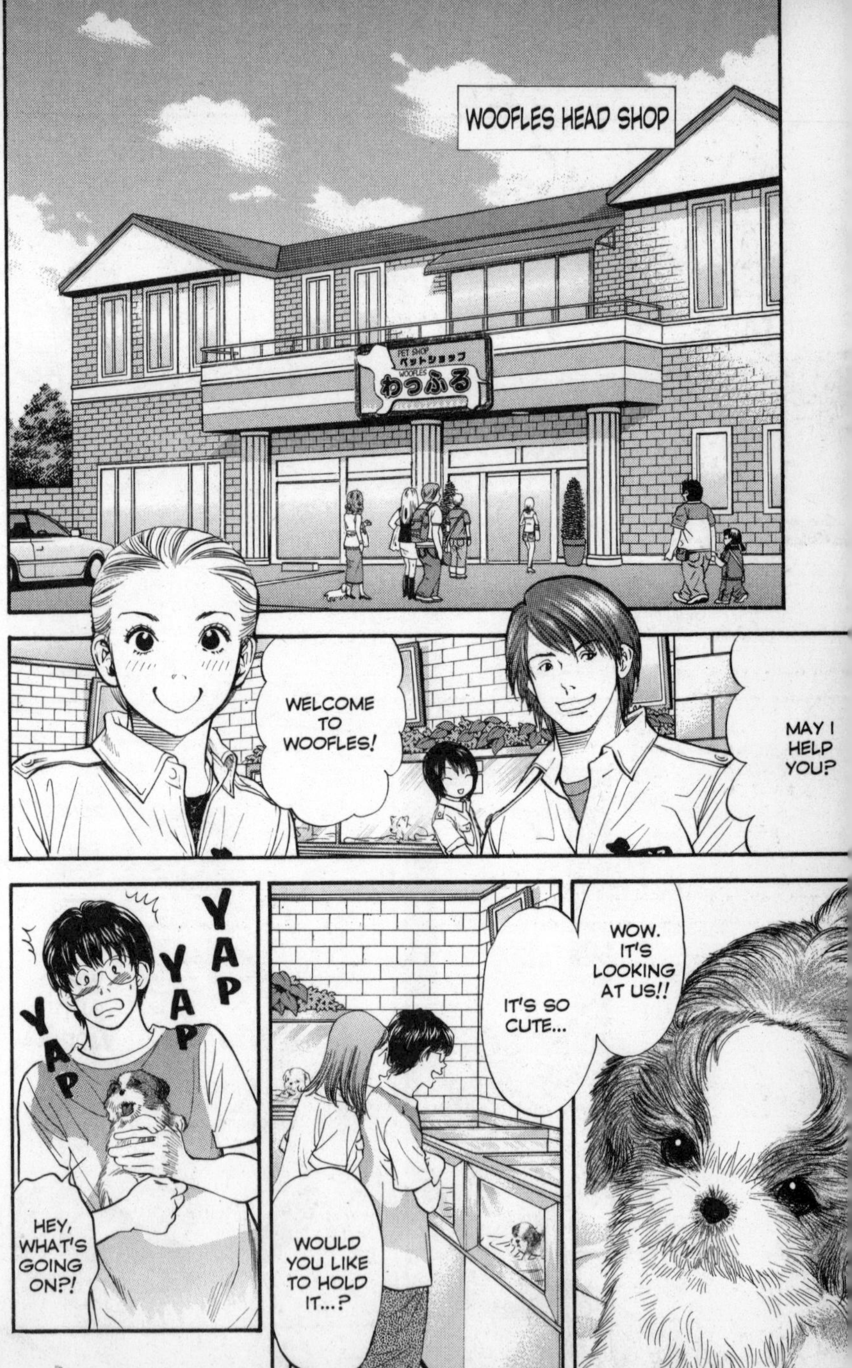
WOOFLES HEAD SHOP
PET SHOP
ペットショップ
WOOFLES
わっふる
MAY I HELP YOU?
WELCOME TO WOOFLES!
WOW. IT'S LOOKING AT US!!
IT'S SO CUTE...
WOULD YOU LIKE TO HOLD IT...?
YAP
YAP
YAP
YAP
HEY, WHAT'S GOING ON?!

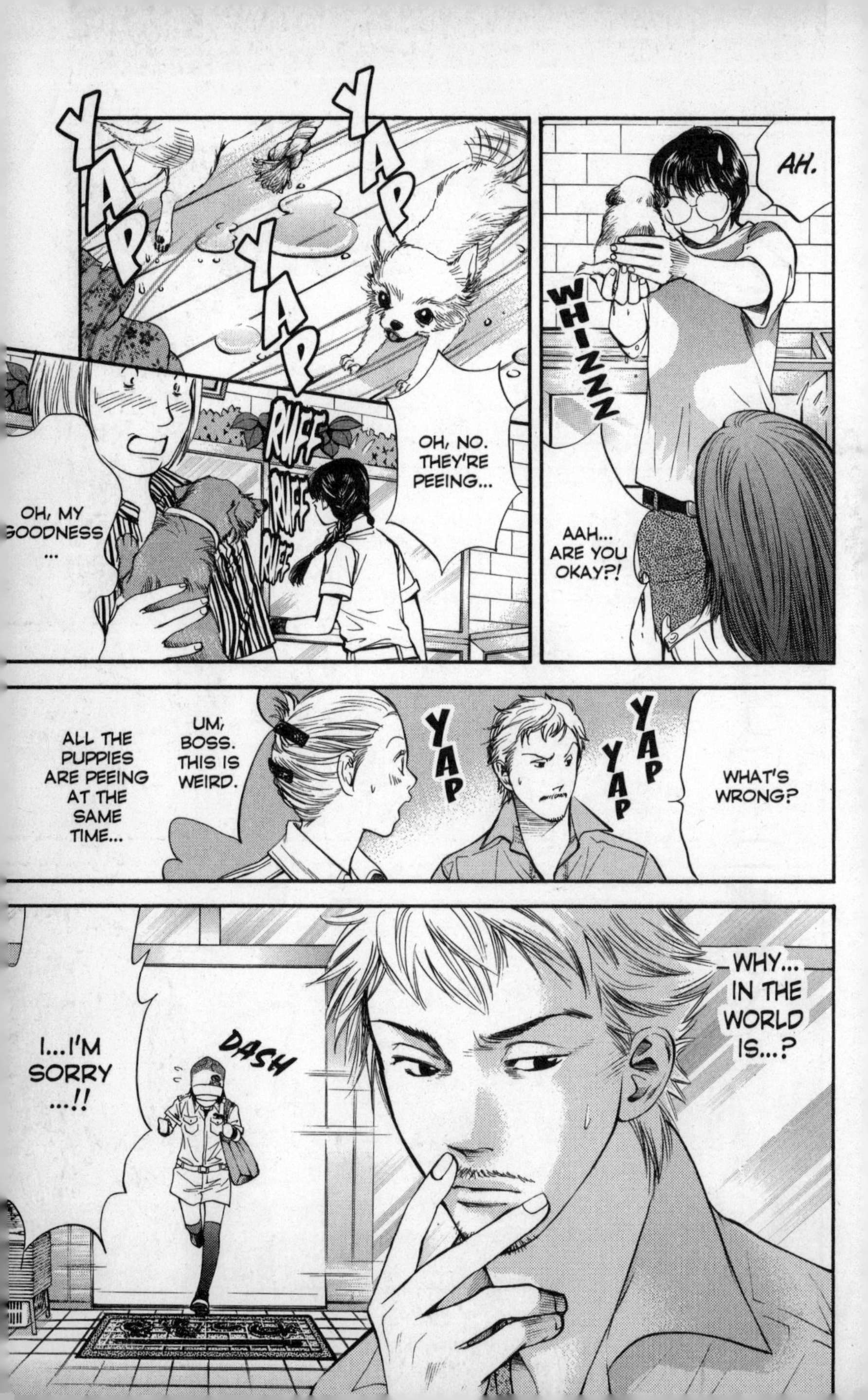
AH.
WHIZZZ
AAH... ARE YOU OKAY?!
YAP YAP
YAP YAP
YAP YAP
OH, NO. THEY'RE PEEING...
RUFF RUFF RUFF
OH, MY GOODNESS ...
WHAT'S WRONG?
YAP YAP
YAP
UM, BOSS. THIS IS WEIRD.
ALL THE PUPPIES ARE PEEING AT THE SAME TIME...
WHY... IN THE WORLD IS...?
DASH
I...I'M SORRY ...!!

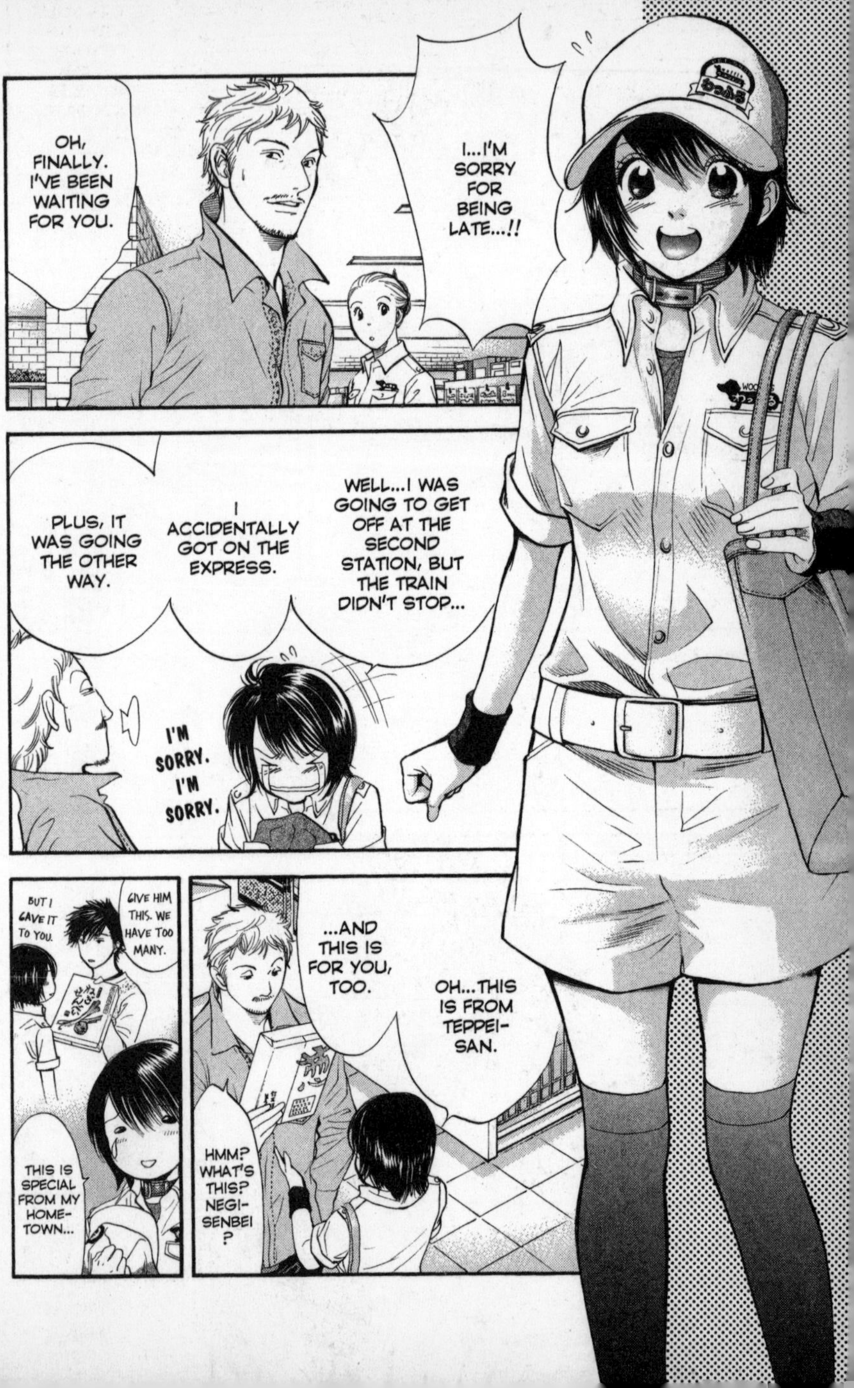
I...I'M SORRY FOR BEING LATE...!!
OH, FINALLY. I'VE BEEN WAITING FOR YOU.
WELL...I WAS GOING TO GET OFF AT THE SECOND STATION, BUT THE TRAIN DIDN'T STOP...
I ACCIDENTALLY GOT ON THE EXPRESS.
PLUS, IT WAS GOING THE OTHER WAY.
I'M SORRY. I'M SORRY.
OH...THIS IS FROM TEPPEI-SAN.
...AND THIS IS FOR YOU, TOO.
HMM? WHAT'S THIS? NEGI-SENBEI?
GIVE HIM THIS. WE HAVE TOO MANY.
BUT I GAVE IT TO YOU.
THIS IS SPECIAL FROM MY HOME-TOWN...

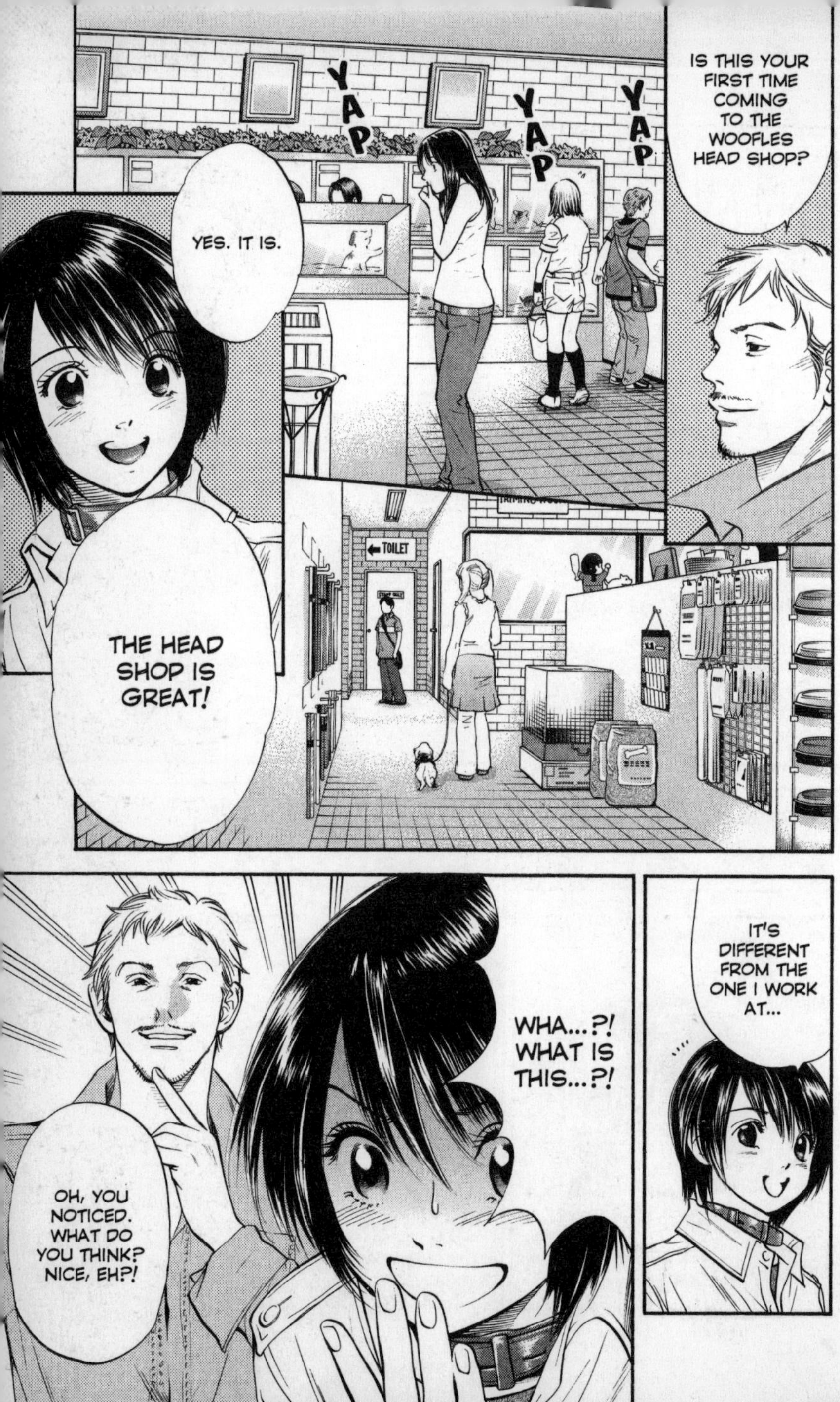
IS THIS YOUR FIRST TIME COMING TO THE WOOFLES HEAD SHOP?
YAP
YAP
YAP
TOILET
YES. IT IS.
THE HEAD SHOP IS GREAT!
IT'S DIFFERENT FROM THE ONE I WORK AT...
...
WHA...?! WHAT IS THIS...?!
OH, YOU NOTICED. WHAT DO YOU THINK? NICE, EH?!

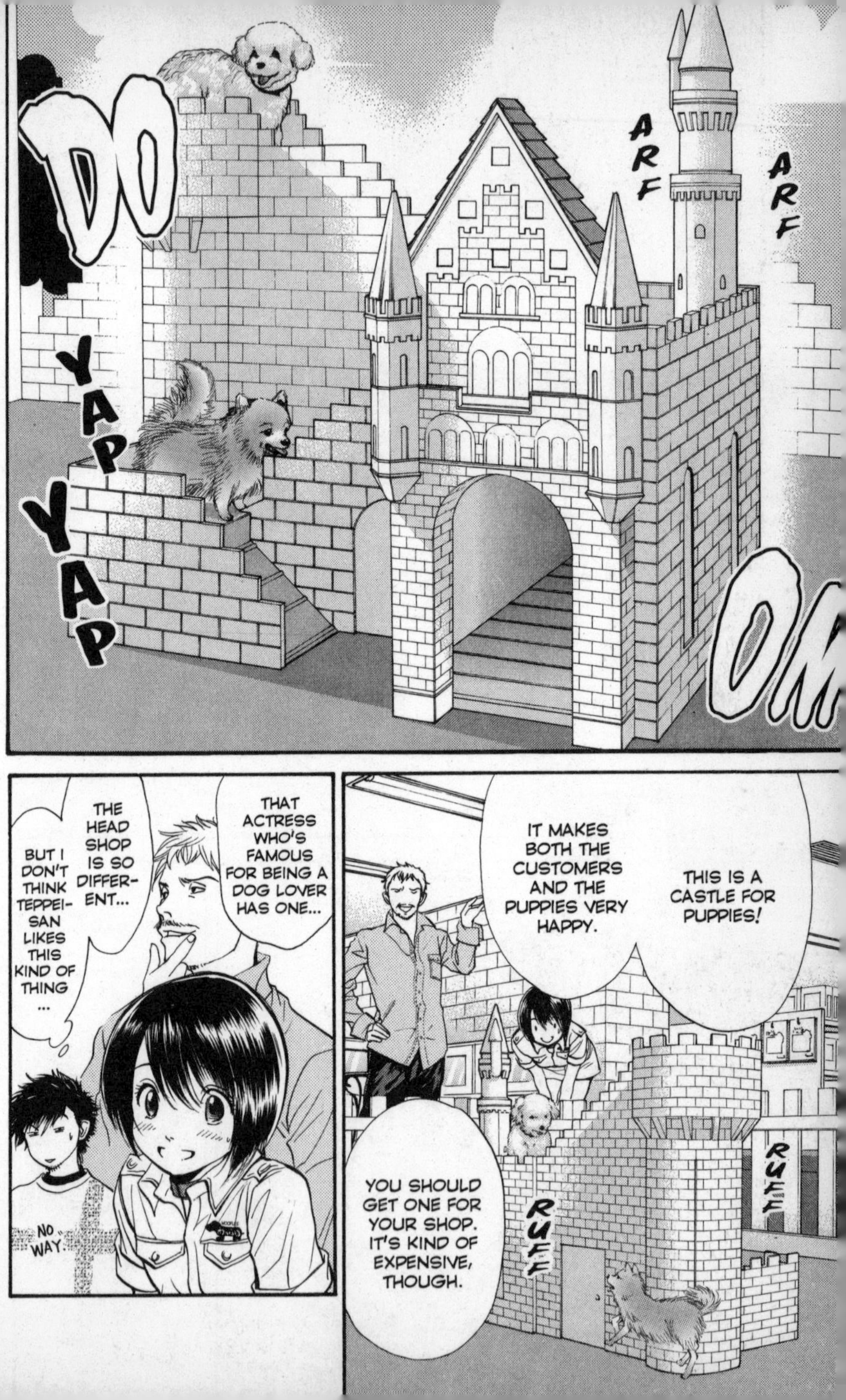
ARF
ARF
DO
OM
YAP YAP
YAP YAP
THIS IS A CASTLE FOR PUPPIES!
IT MAKES BOTH THE CUSTOMERS AND THE PUPPIES VERY HAPPY.
RUFF
RUFF
YOU SHOULD GET ONE FOR YOUR SHOP. IT'S KIND OF EXPENSIVE, THOUGH.
THAT ACTRESS WHO'S FAMOUS FOR BEING A DOG LOVER HAS ONE...
THE HEAD SHOP IS SO DIFFERENT...
BUT I DON'T THINK TEPPEI-SAN LIKES THIS KIND OF THING...
NO WAY.

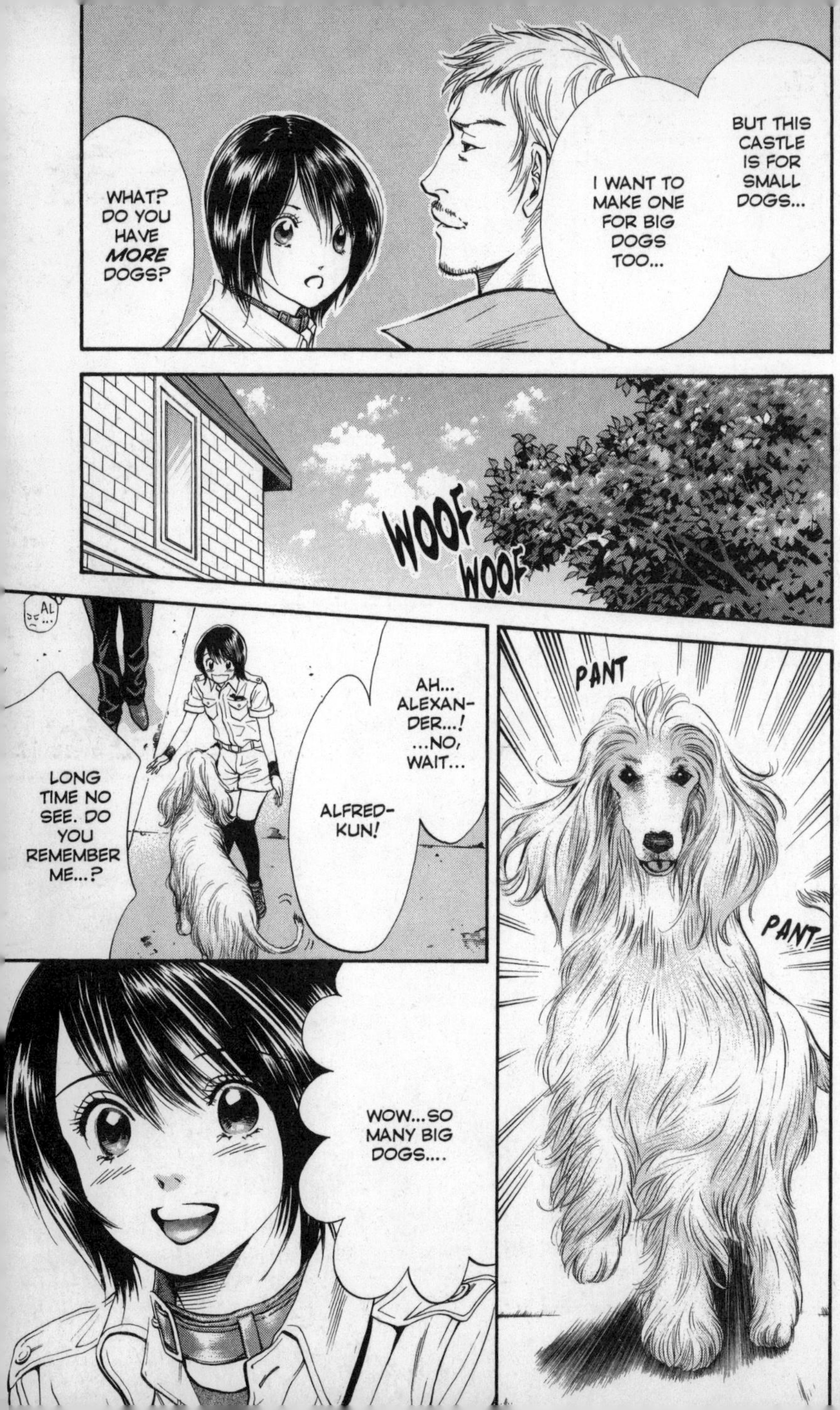
BUT THIS CASTLE IS FOR SMALL DOGS...
I WANT TO MAKE ONE FOR BIG DOGS TOO...
WHAT? DO YOU HAVE *MORE* DOGS?
WOOF
WOOF
PANT
PANT
AH... ALEXANDER...! ...NO, WAIT...
ALFRED-KUN!
LONG TIME NO SEE. DO YOU REMEMBER ME...?
AL...
WOW...SO MANY BIG DOGS....

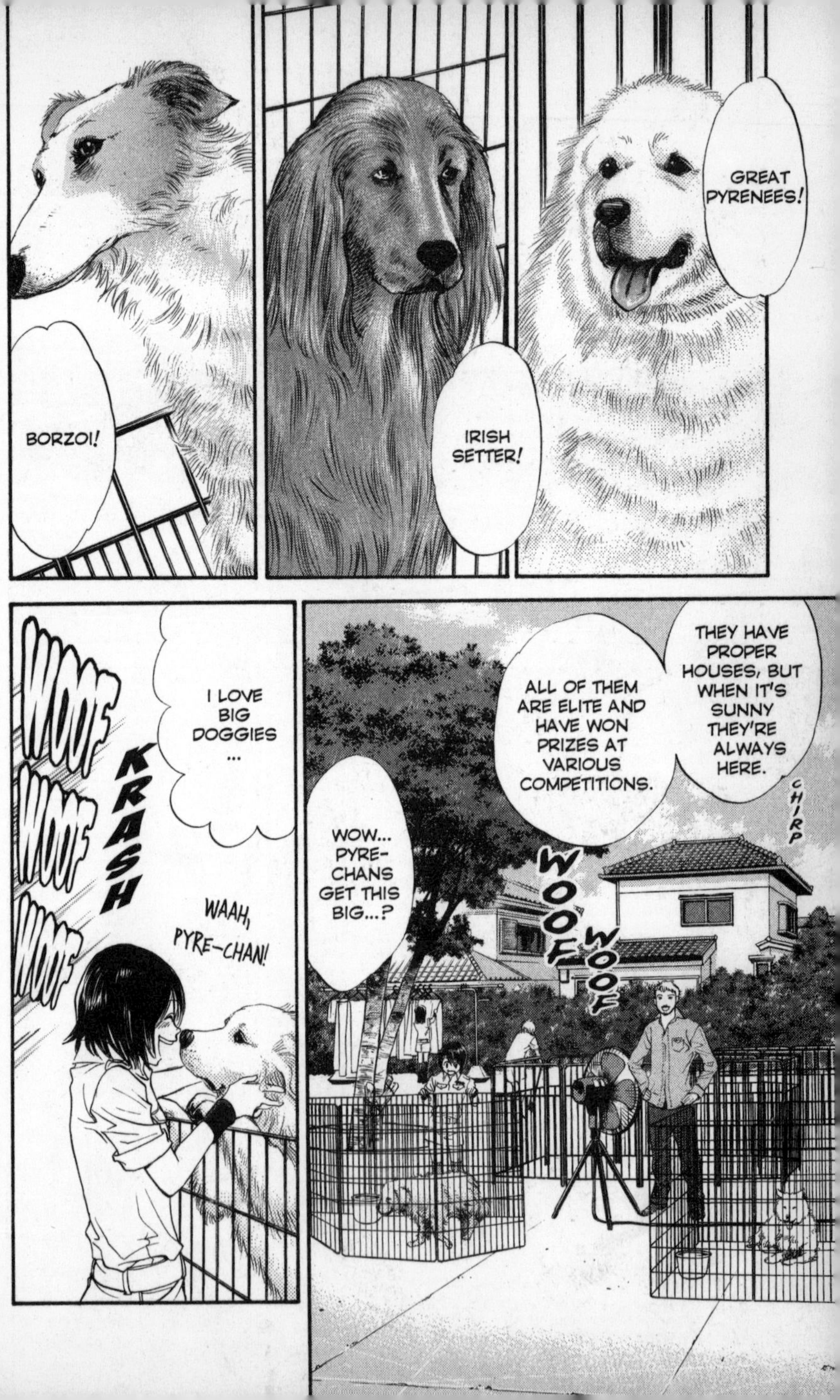
GREAT PYRENEES!
IRISH SETTER!
BORZOI!
THEY HAVE PROPER HOUSES, BUT WHEN IT'S SUNNY THEY'RE ALWAYS HERE.
CHIRP
ALL OF THEM ARE ELITE AND HAVE WON PRIZES AT VARIOUS COMPETITIONS.
WOOF WOOF
WOW... PYRE-CHANS GET THIS BIG...?
I LOVE BIG DOGGIES ...
KRASH
WOOF WOOF WOOF
WAAH, PYRE-CHAN!

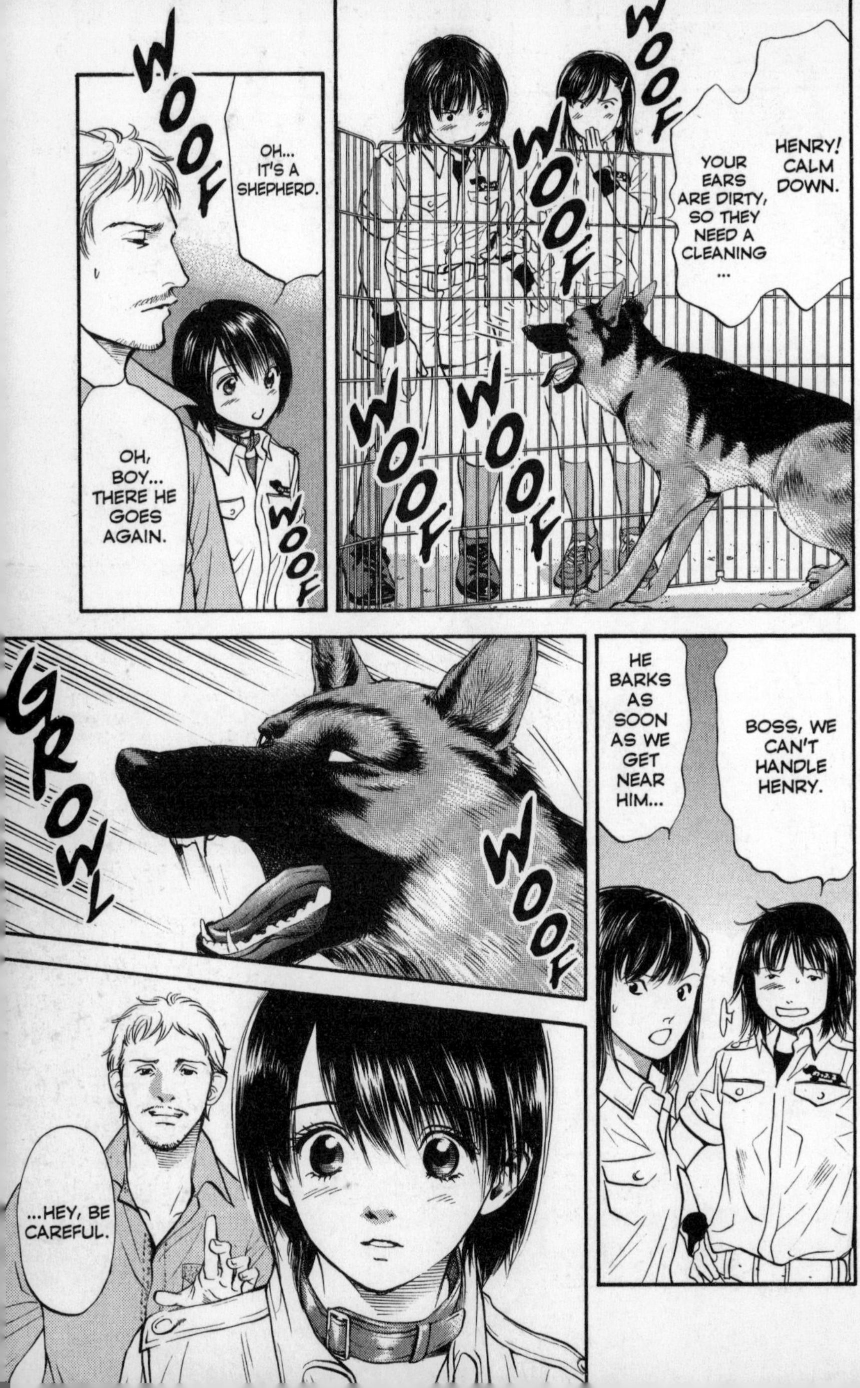
WOOF
HENRY! CALM DOWN.
YOUR EARS ARE DIRTY, SO THEY NEED A CLEANING ...
WOOF
WOOF
WOOF
WOOF
WOOF
OH... IT'S A SHEPHERD.
OH, BOY... THERE HE GOES AGAIN.
WOOF
BOSS, WE CAN'T HANDLE HENRY.
HE BARKS AS SOON AS WE GET NEAR HIM...
WOOF
GROWL
...HEY, BE CAREFUL.

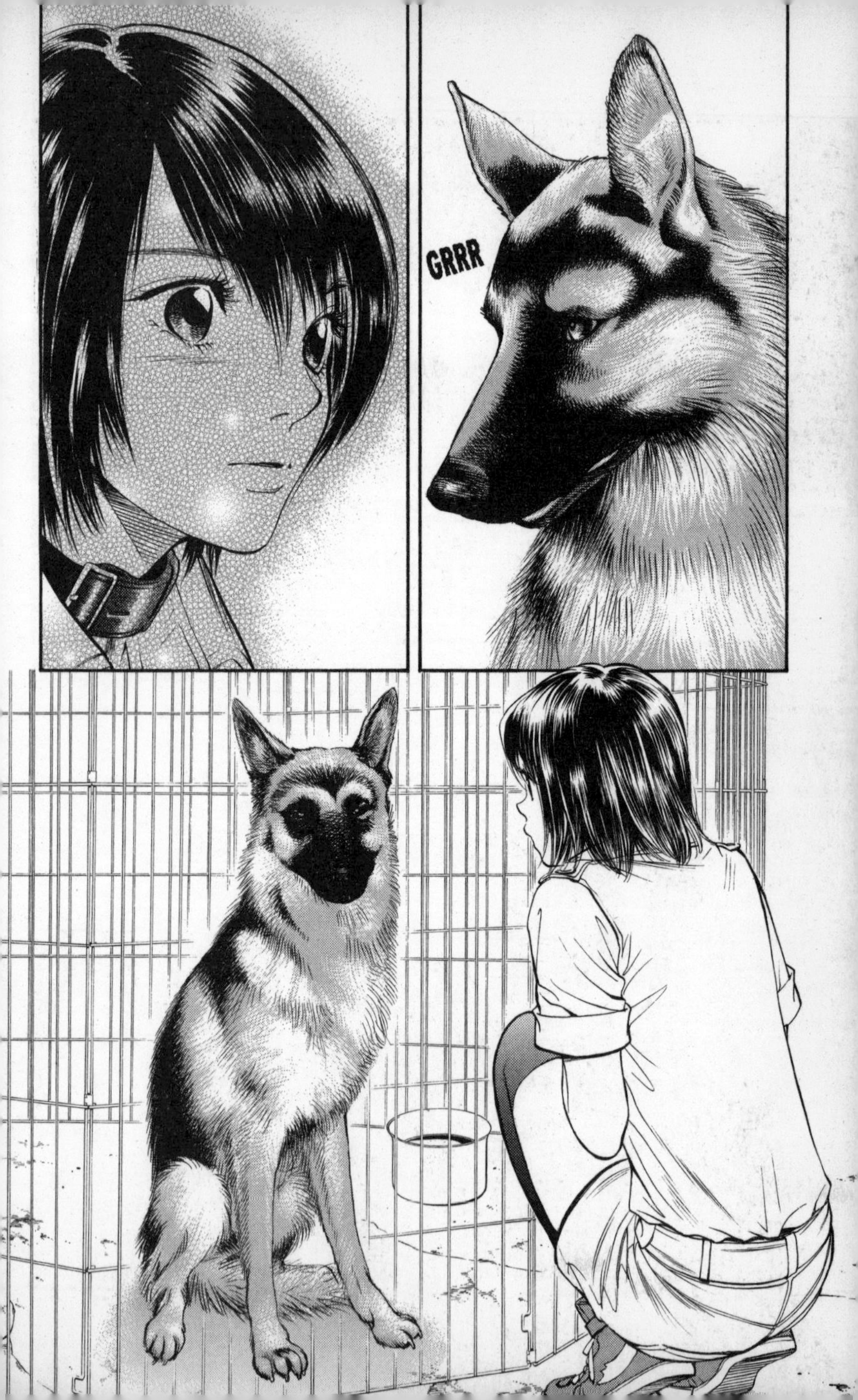
GRRR

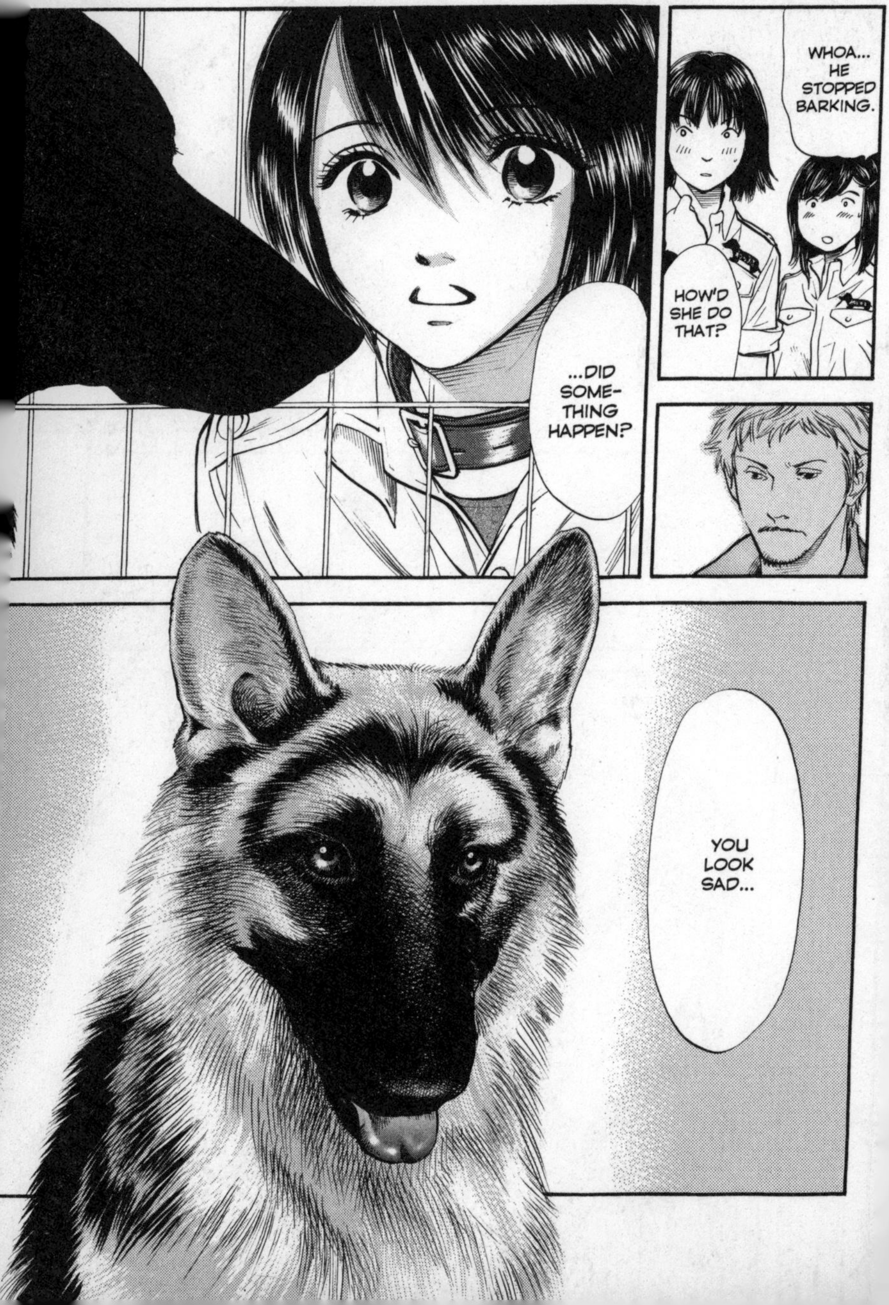
WHOA... HE STOPPED BARKING.
HOW'D SHE DO THAT?
...DID SOME-THING HAPPEN?
YOU LOOK SAD...

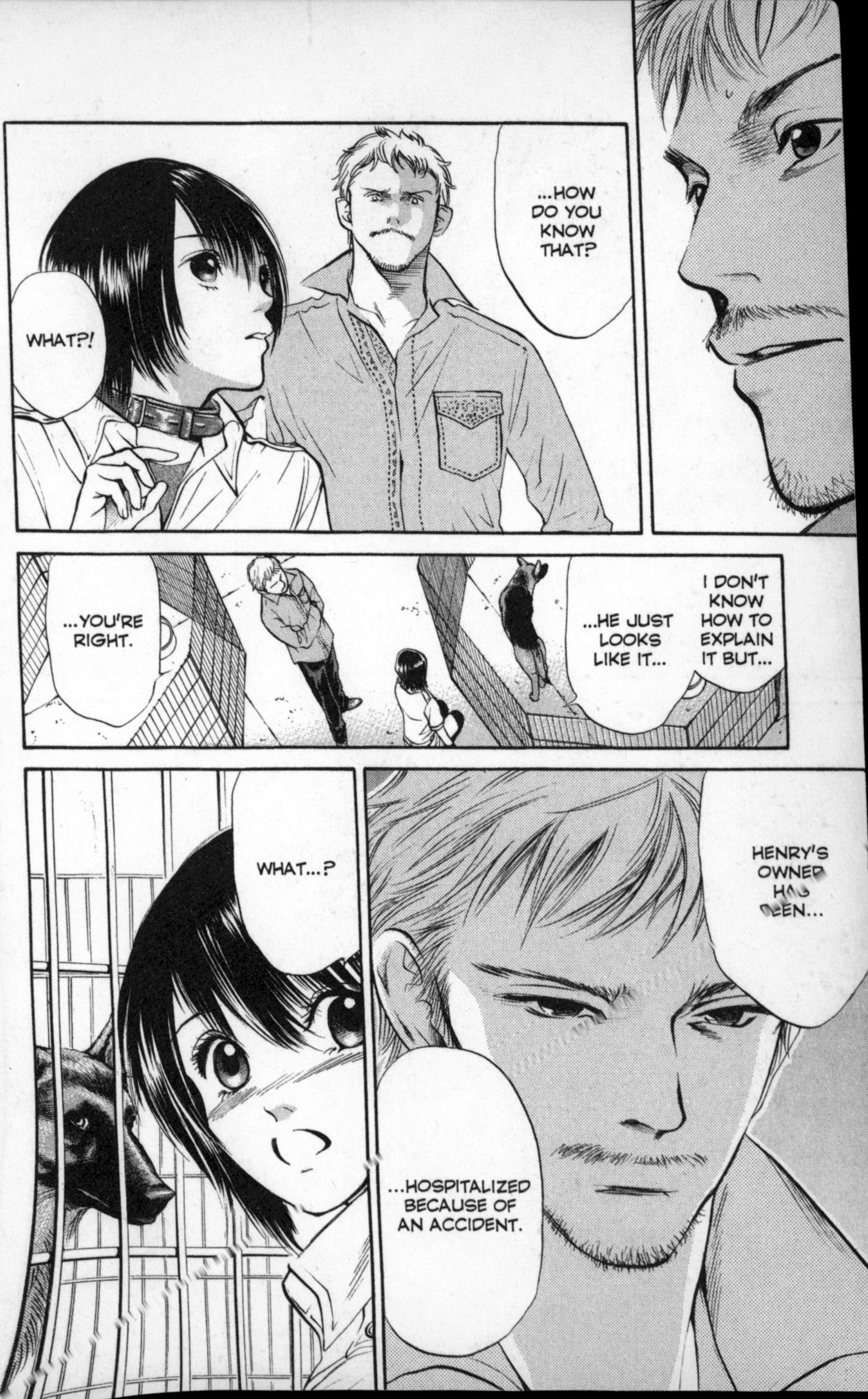
...HOW DO YOU KNOW THAT?
WHAT?!
I DON'T KNOW HOW TO EXPLAIN IT BUT...
...HE JUST LOOKS LIKE IT...
...YOU'RE RIGHT.
HENRY'S OWNER HAS BEEN...
...HOSPITALIZED BECAUSE OF AN ACCIDENT.
WHAT...?

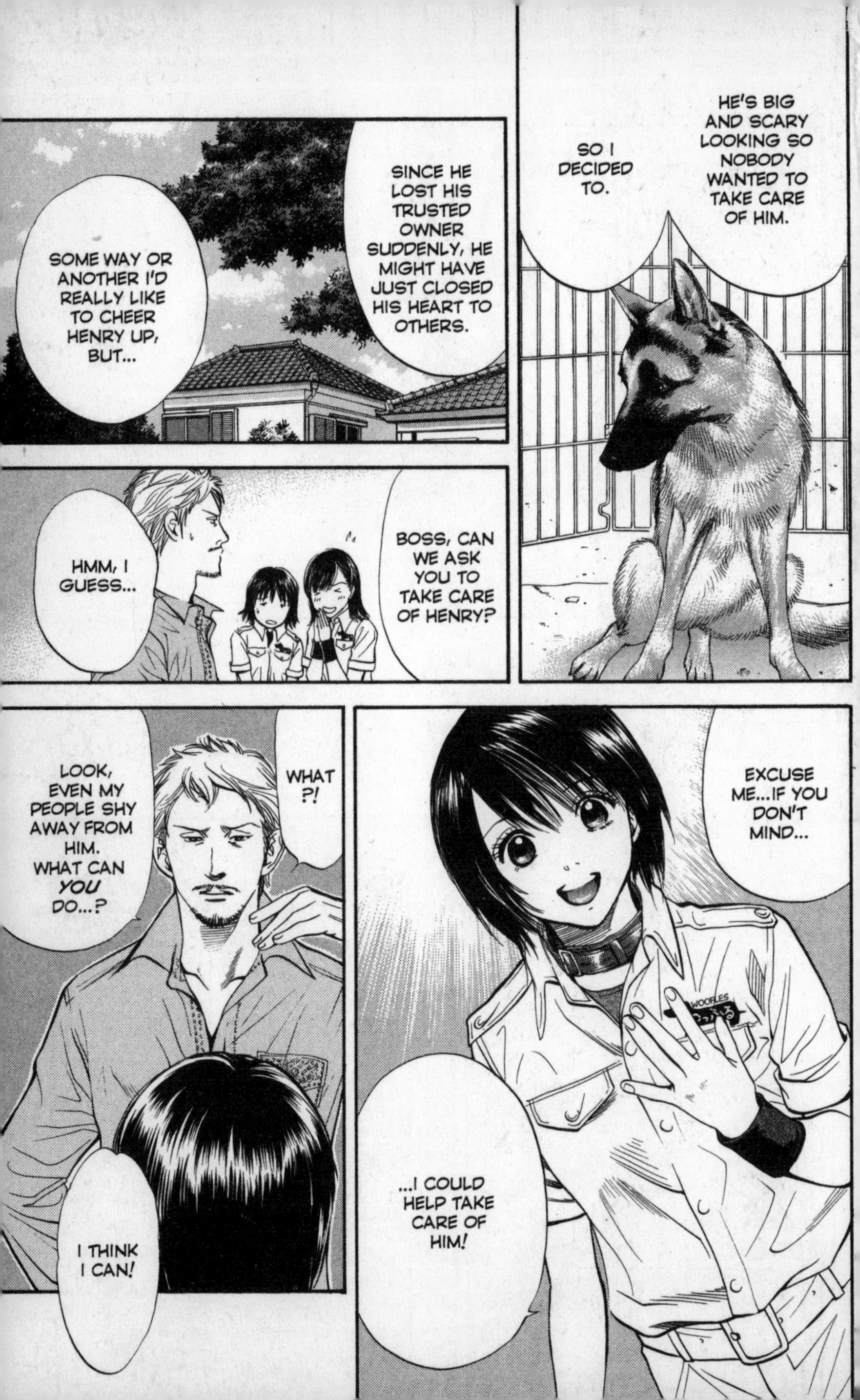
HE'S BIG AND SCARY LOOKING SO NOBODY WANTED TO TAKE CARE OF HIM.
SO I DECIDED TO.
SINCE HE LOST HIS TRUSTED OWNER SUDDENLY, HE MIGHT HAVE JUST CLOSED HIS HEART TO OTHERS.
SOME WAY OR ANOTHER I'D REALLY LIKE TO CHEER HENRY UP, BUT...
BOSS, CAN WE ASK YOU TO TAKE CARE OF HENRY?
HMM, I GUESS...
EXCUSE ME...IF YOU DON'T MIND...
WOOFLES
...I COULD HELP TAKE CARE OF HIM!
WHAT?!
LOOK, EVEN MY PEOPLE SHY AWAY FROM HIM. WHAT CAN *YOU* DO...?
I THINK I CAN!

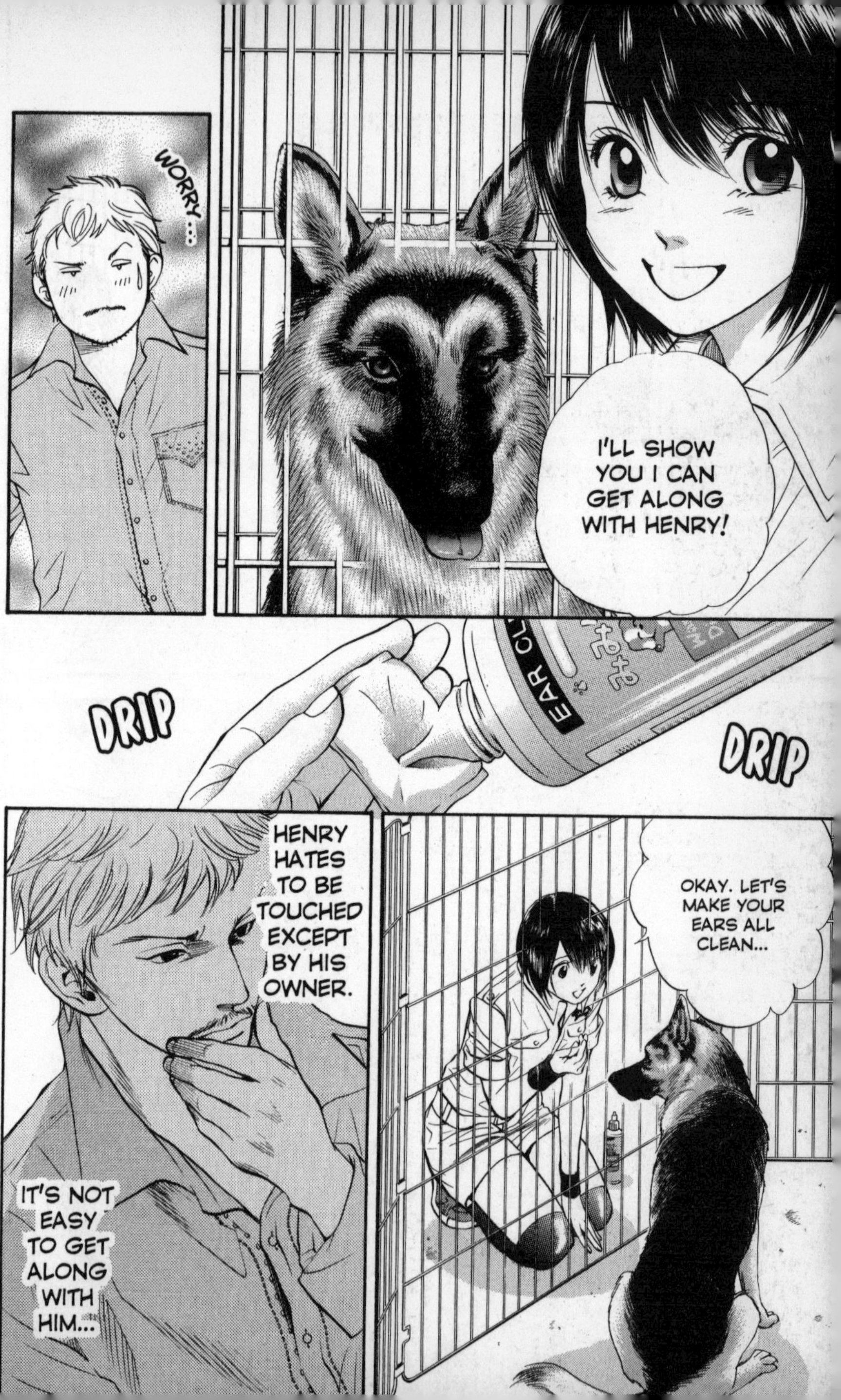
I'LL SHOW YOU I CAN GET ALONG WITH HENRY!
WORRY...
DRIP
DRIP
OKAY. LET'S MAKE YOUR EARS ALL CLEAN...
HENRY HATES TO BE TOUCHED EXCEPT BY HIS OWNER.
IT'S NOT EASY TO GET ALONG WITH HIM...

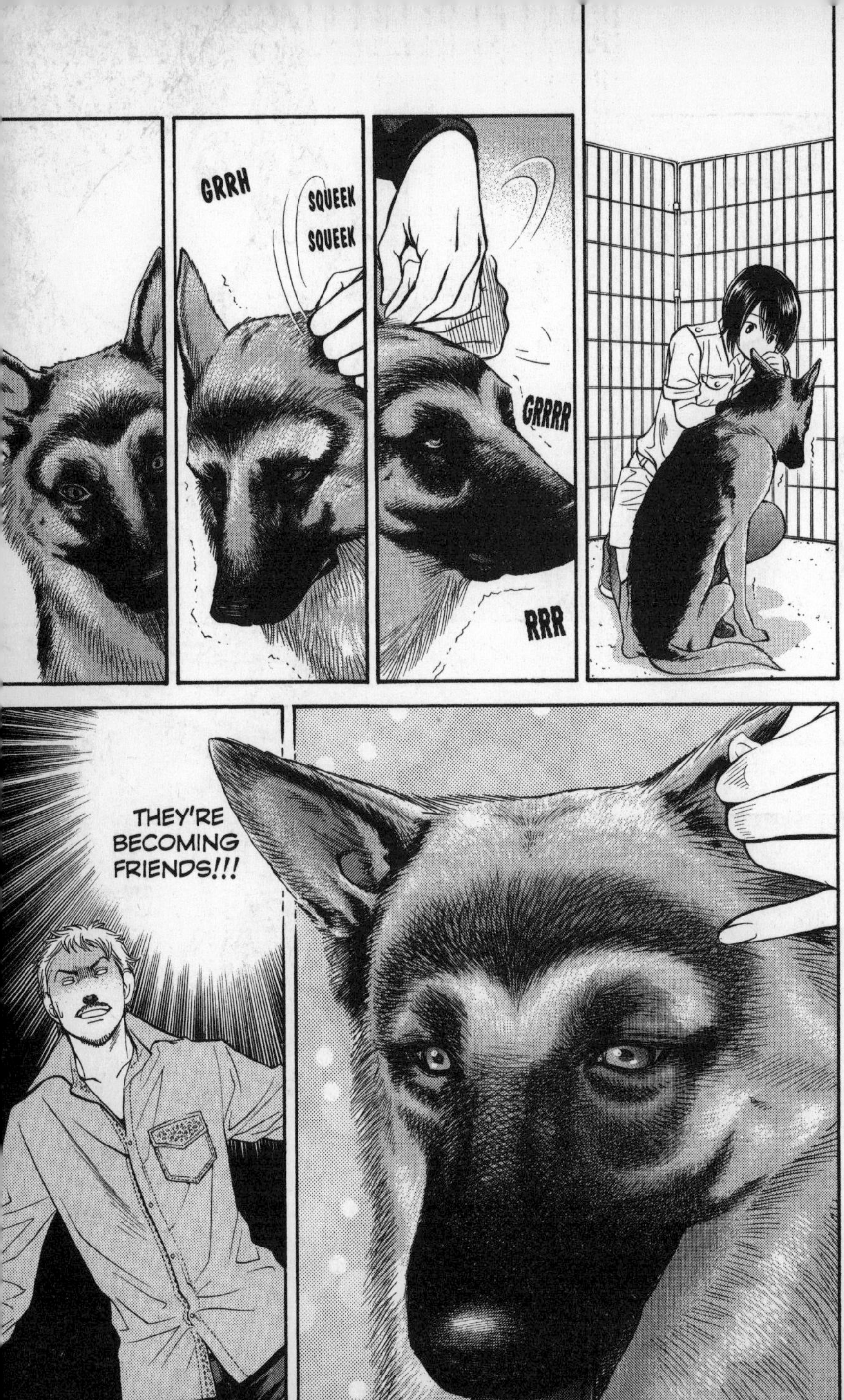
GRRRR
RRR
SQUEEK
SQUEEK
GRRH
THEY'RE BECOMING FRIENDS!!!

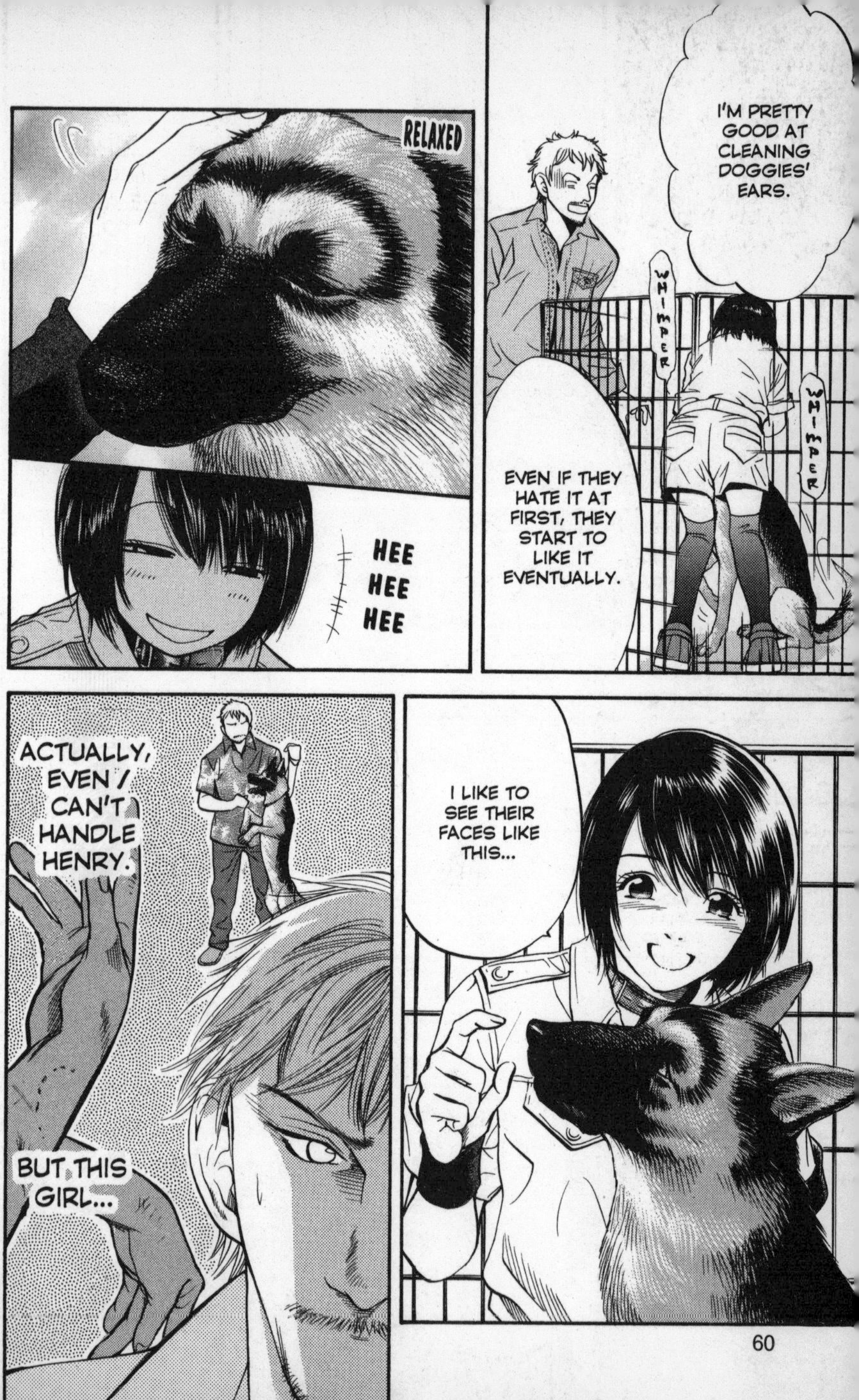
I'M PRETTY GOOD AT CLEANING DOGGIES' EARS.
WHIMPER
WHIMPER
EVEN IF THEY HATE IT AT FIRST, THEY START TO LIKE IT EVENTUALLY.
RELAXED
HEE HEE HEE
I LIKE TO SEE THEIR FACES LIKE THIS...
ACTUALLY, EVEN I CAN'T HANDLE HENRY.
BUT THIS GIRL...

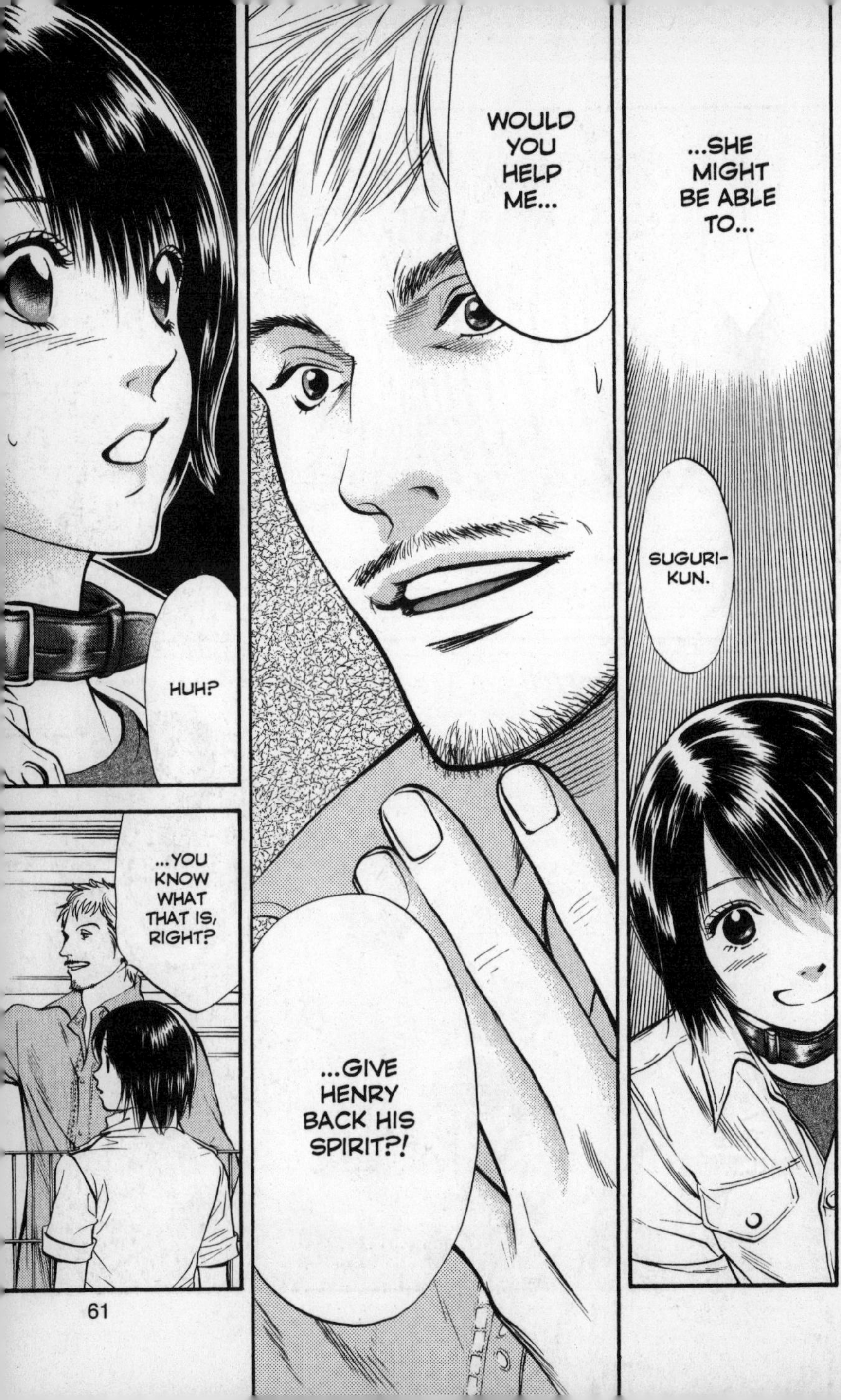

...SHE MIGHT BE ABLE TO...
SUGURI-KUN.
WOULD YOU HELP ME...
...GIVE HENRY BACK HIS SPIRIT?!
HUH?
...YOU KNOW WHAT THAT IS, RIGHT?

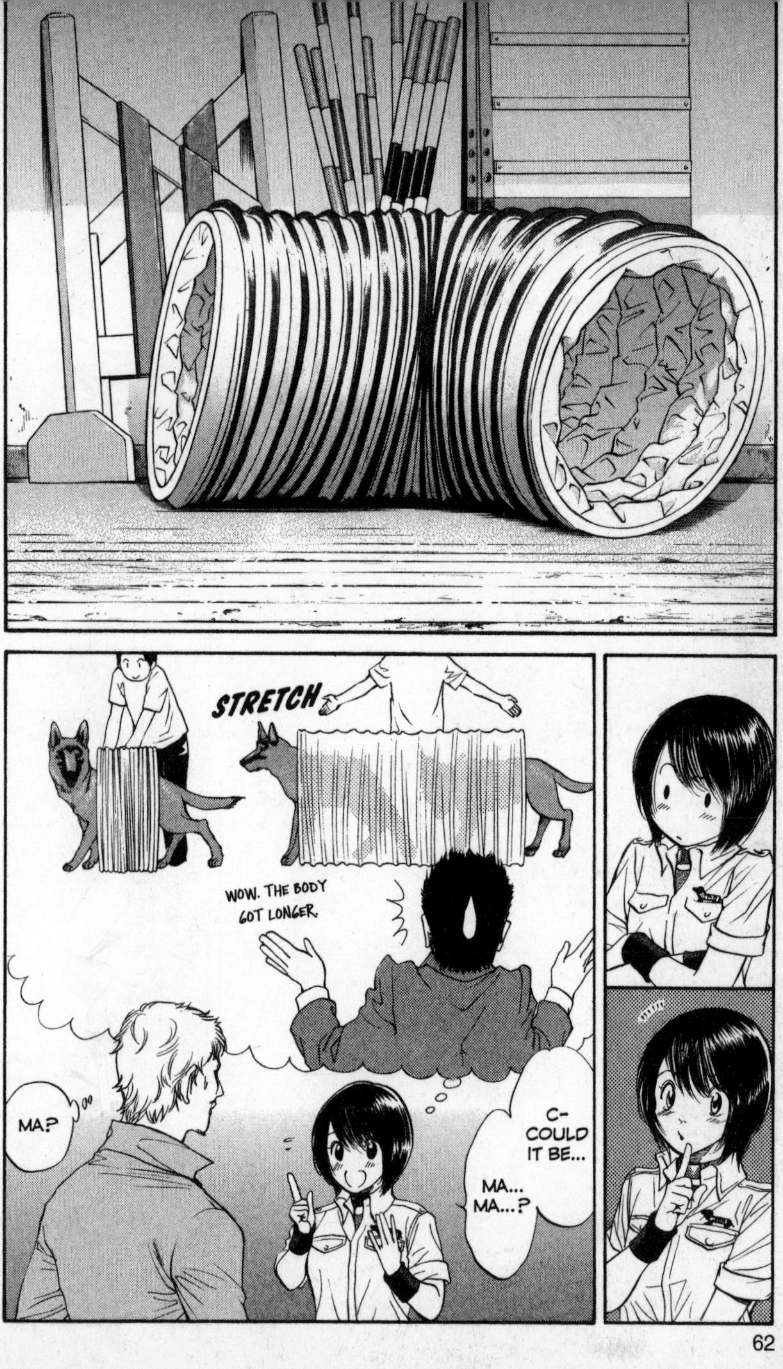
STRETCH
WOW. THE BODY GOT LONGER.
C-COULD IT BE...
MA... MA...?
MA?

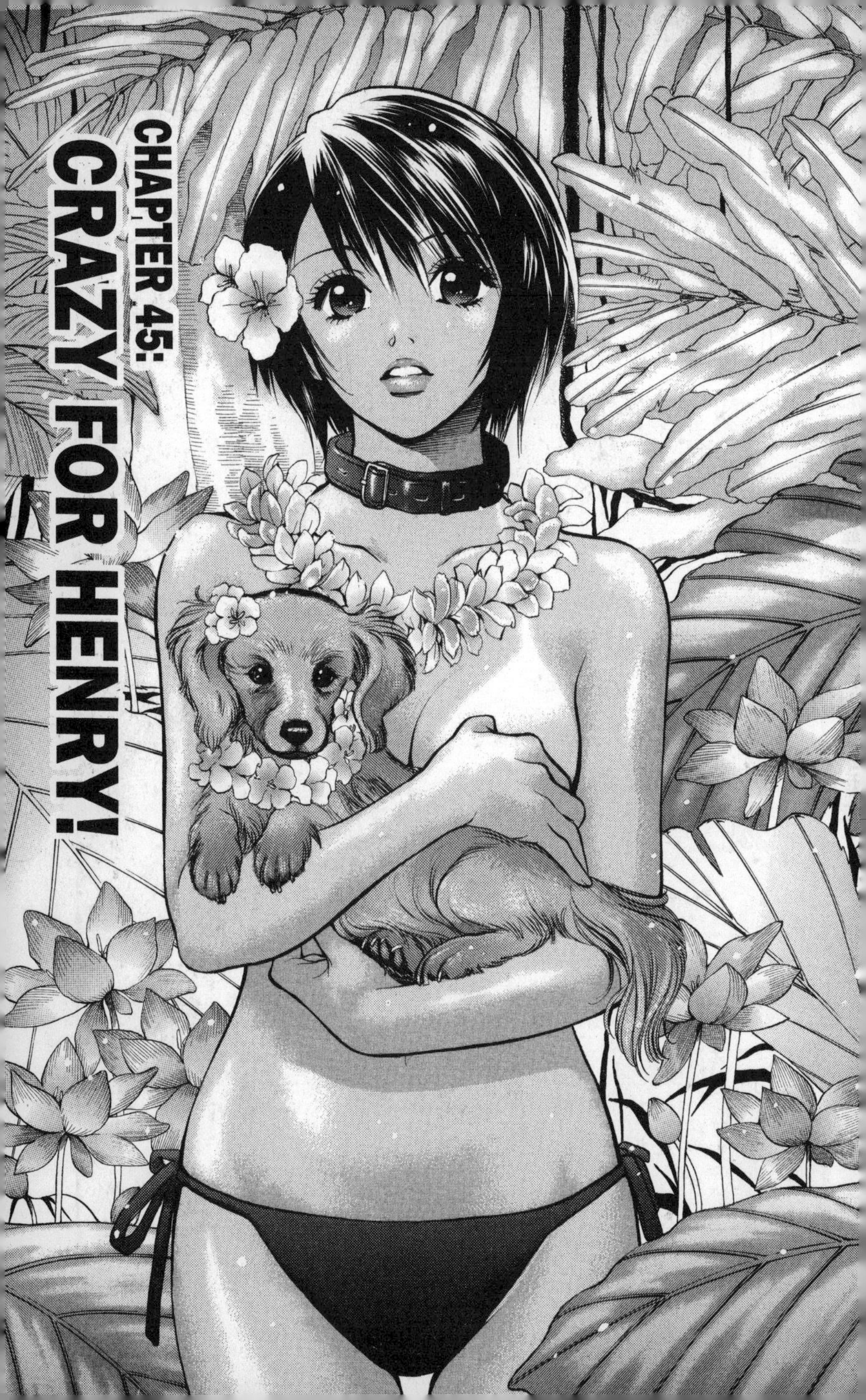
CHAPTER 45:
CRAZY FOR HENRY!

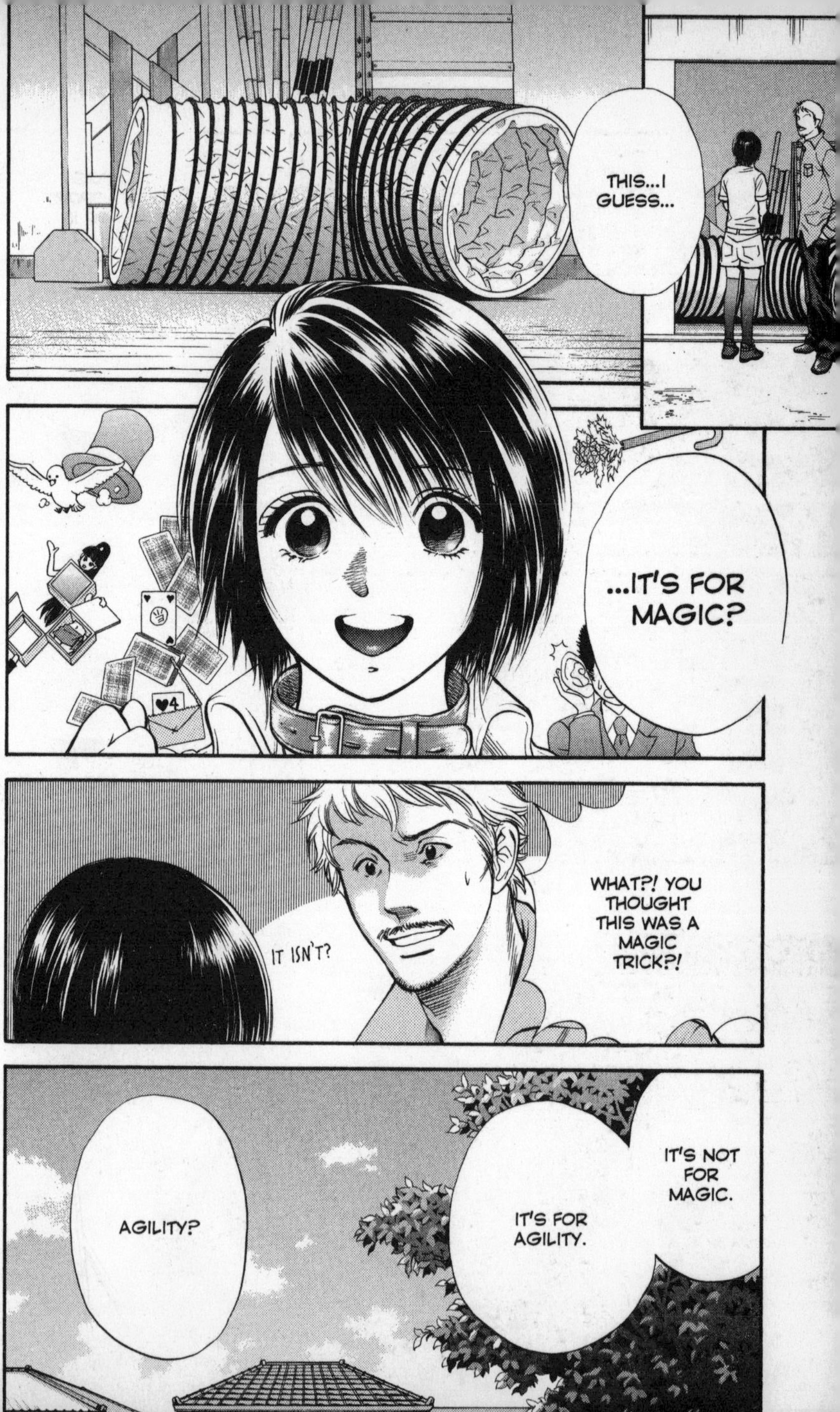
THIS...I GUESS...
...IT'S FOR MAGIC?
WHAT?! YOU THOUGHT THIS WAS A MAGIC TRICK?!
IT ISN'T?
IT'S NOT FOR MAGIC.
IT'S FOR AGILITY.
AGILITY?

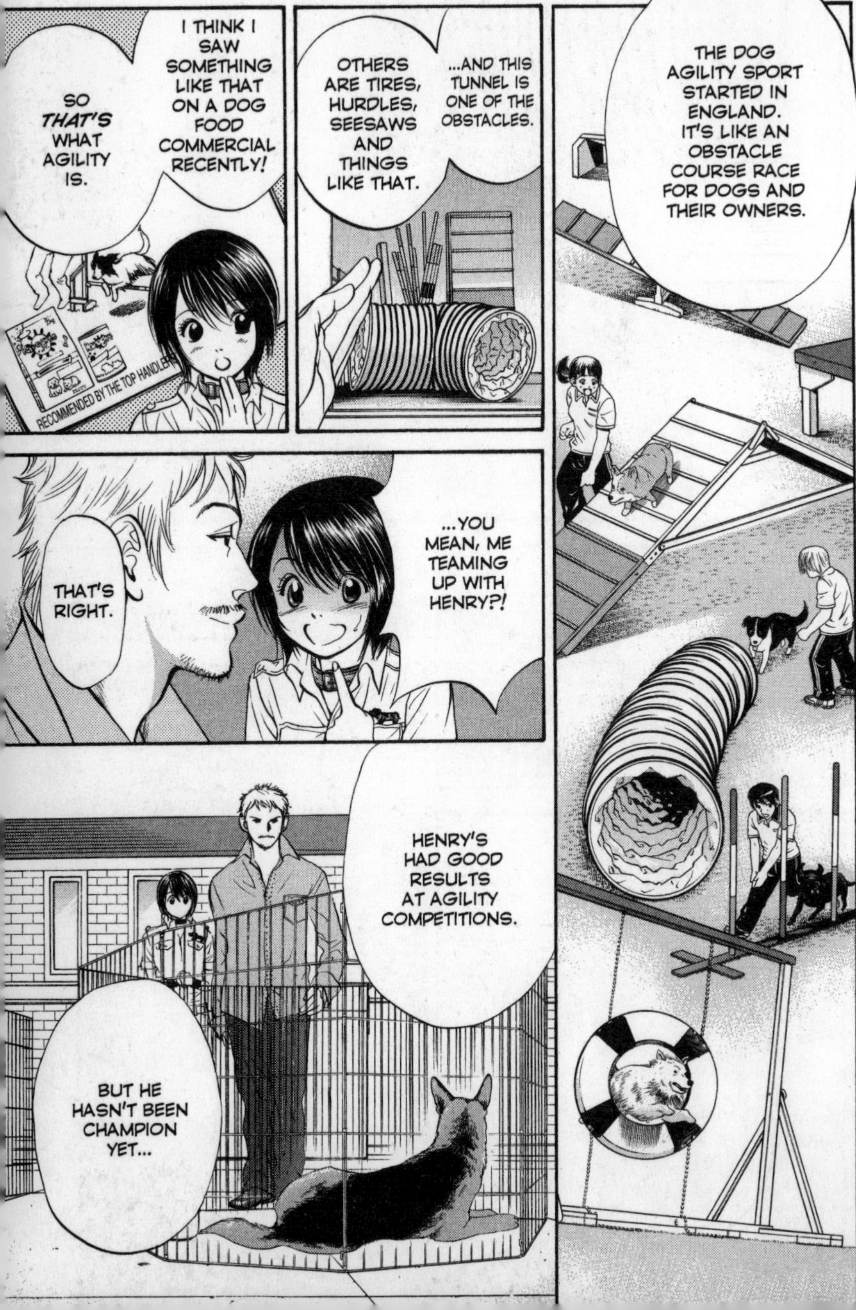
THE DOG AGILITY SPORT STARTED IN ENGLAND. IT'S LIKE AN OBSTACLE COURSE RACE FOR DOGS AND THEIR OWNERS.
...AND THIS TUNNEL IS ONE OF THE OBSTACLES.
OTHERS ARE TIRES, HURDLES, SEESAWS AND THINGS LIKE THAT.
I THINK I SAW SOMETHING LIKE THAT ON A DOG FOOD COMMERCIAL RECENTLY!
SO *THAT'S* WHAT AGILITY IS.
RECOMMENDED BY THE TOP HANDLER
...YOU MEAN, ME TEAMING UP WITH HENRY?!
THAT'S RIGHT.
HENRY'S HAD GOOD RESULTS AT AGILITY COMPETITIONS.
BUT HE HASN'T BEEN CHAMPION YET...

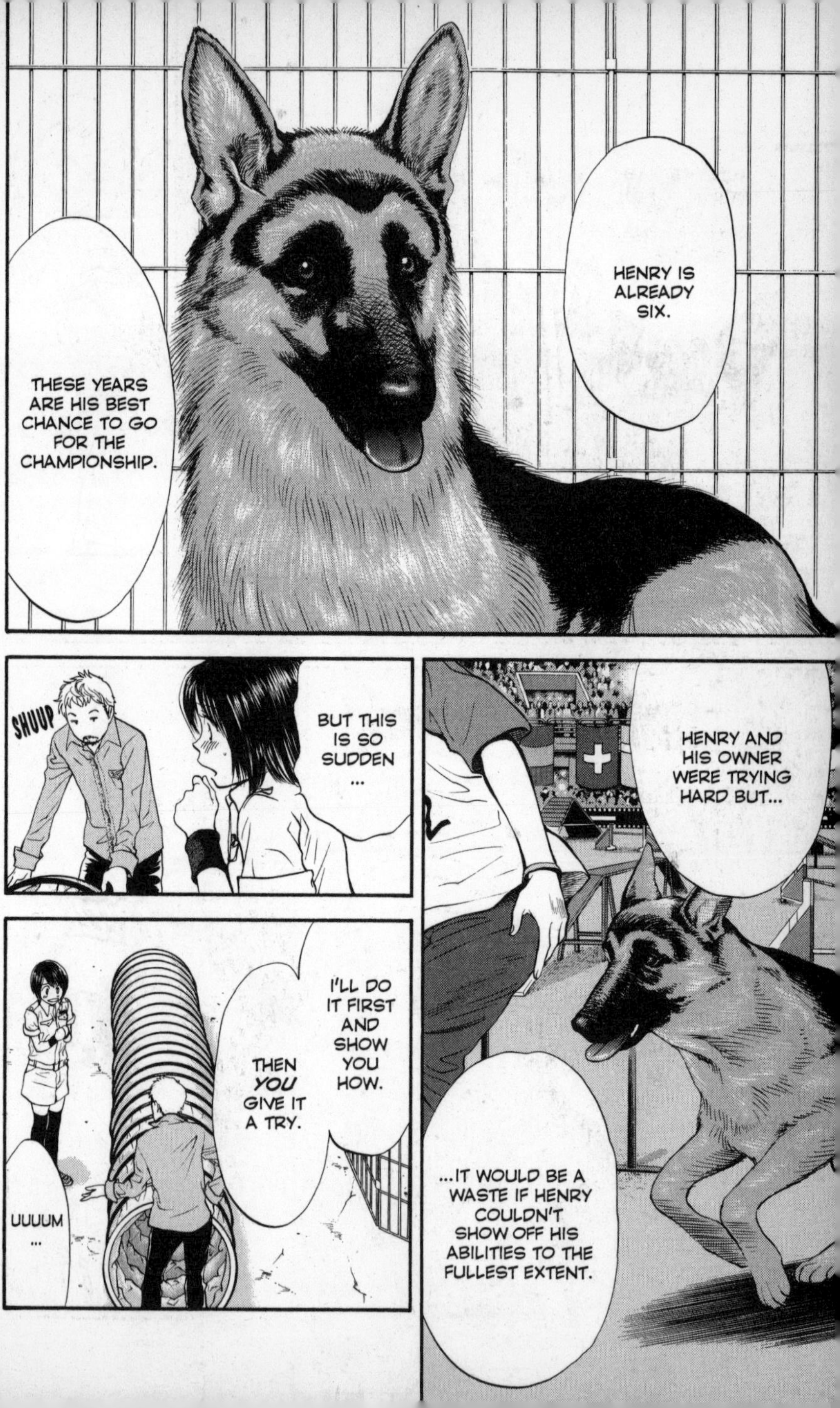
HENRY IS ALREADY SIX.
THESE YEARS ARE HIS BEST CHANCE TO GO FOR THE CHAMPIONSHIP.
HENRY AND HIS OWNER WERE TRYING HARD BUT...
...IT WOULD BE A WASTE IF HENRY COULDN'T SHOW OFF HIS ABILITIES TO THE FULLEST EXTENT.
BUT THIS IS SO SUDDEN ...
SHUUP
I'LL DO IT FIRST AND SHOW YOU HOW.
THEN *YOU* GIVE IT A TRY.
UUUUM ...

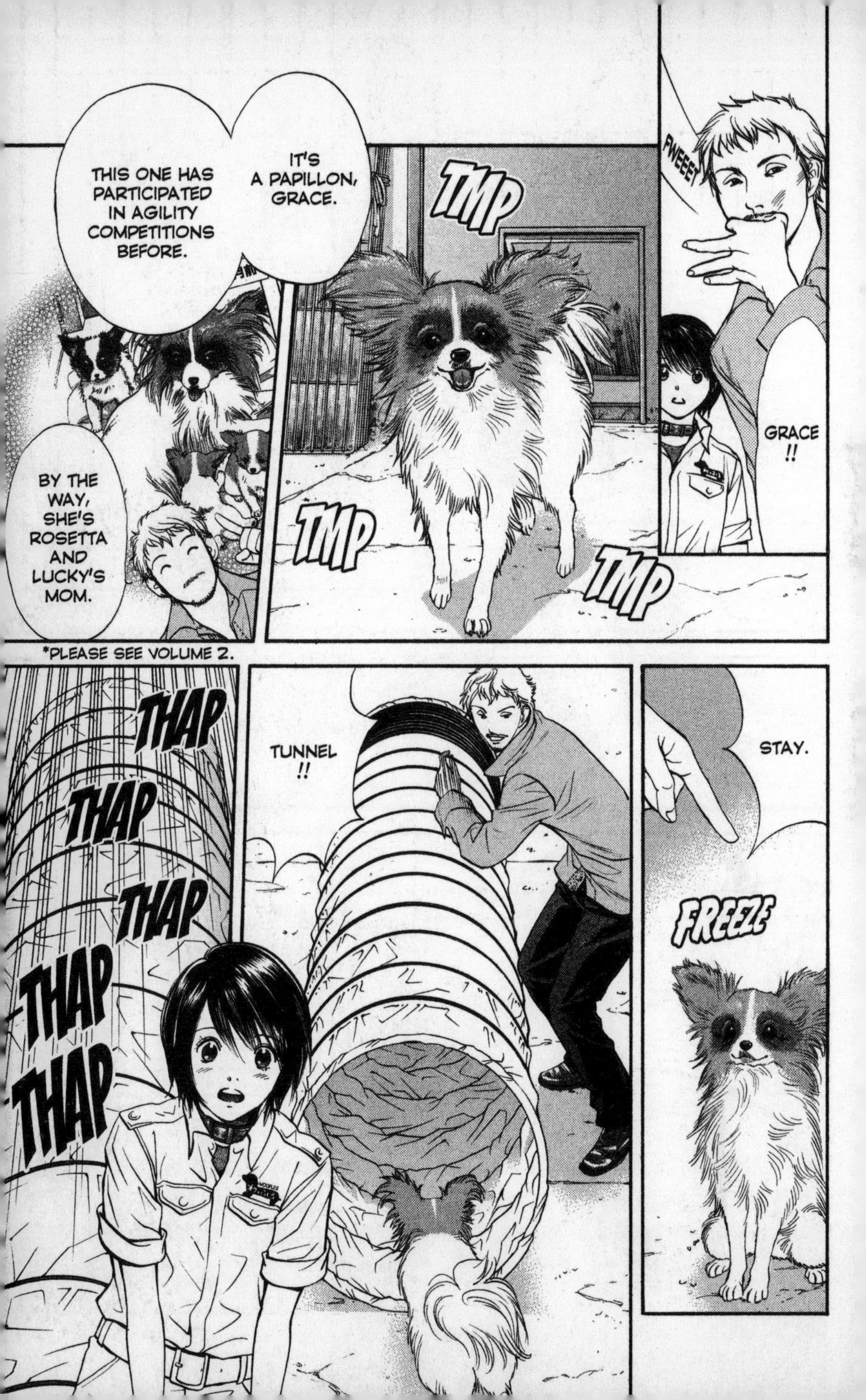
FWEEEE!
GRACE !!
TMP
TMP
TMP
IT'S A PAPILLON, GRACE.
THIS ONE HAS PARTICIPATED IN AGILITY COMPETITIONS BEFORE.
BY THE WAY, SHE'S ROSETTA AND LUCKY'S MOM.
*PLEASE SEE VOLUME 2.
STAY.
FREEZE
TUNNEL !!
THAP
THAP
THAP
THAP
THAP

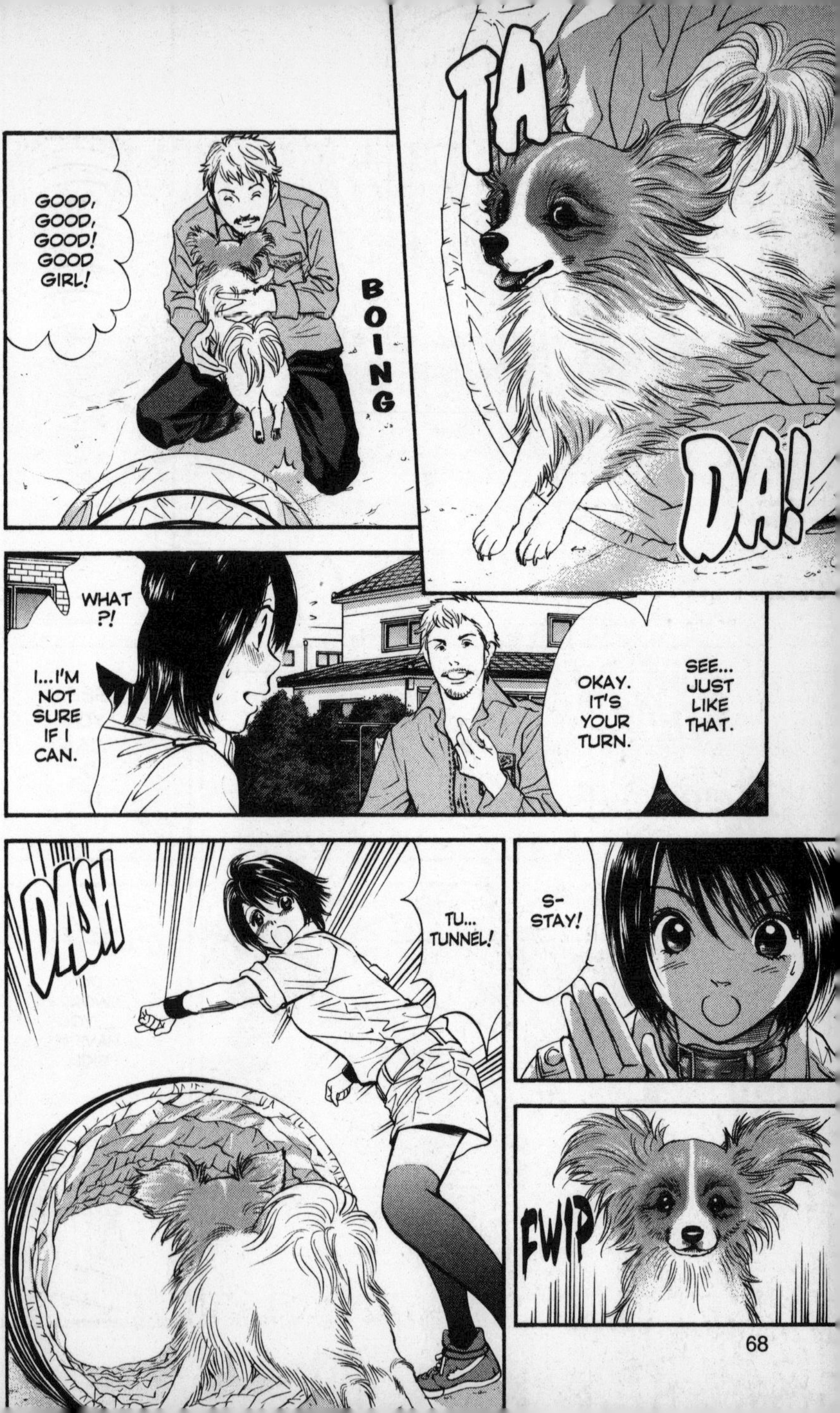
TA
DA!
GOOD, GOOD, GOOD! GOOD GIRL!
BOING
SEE... JUST LIKE THAT.
OKAY. IT'S YOUR TURN.
WHAT?!
I...I'M NOT SURE IF I CAN.
S-STAY!
FWIP
TU... TUNNEL!
DASH

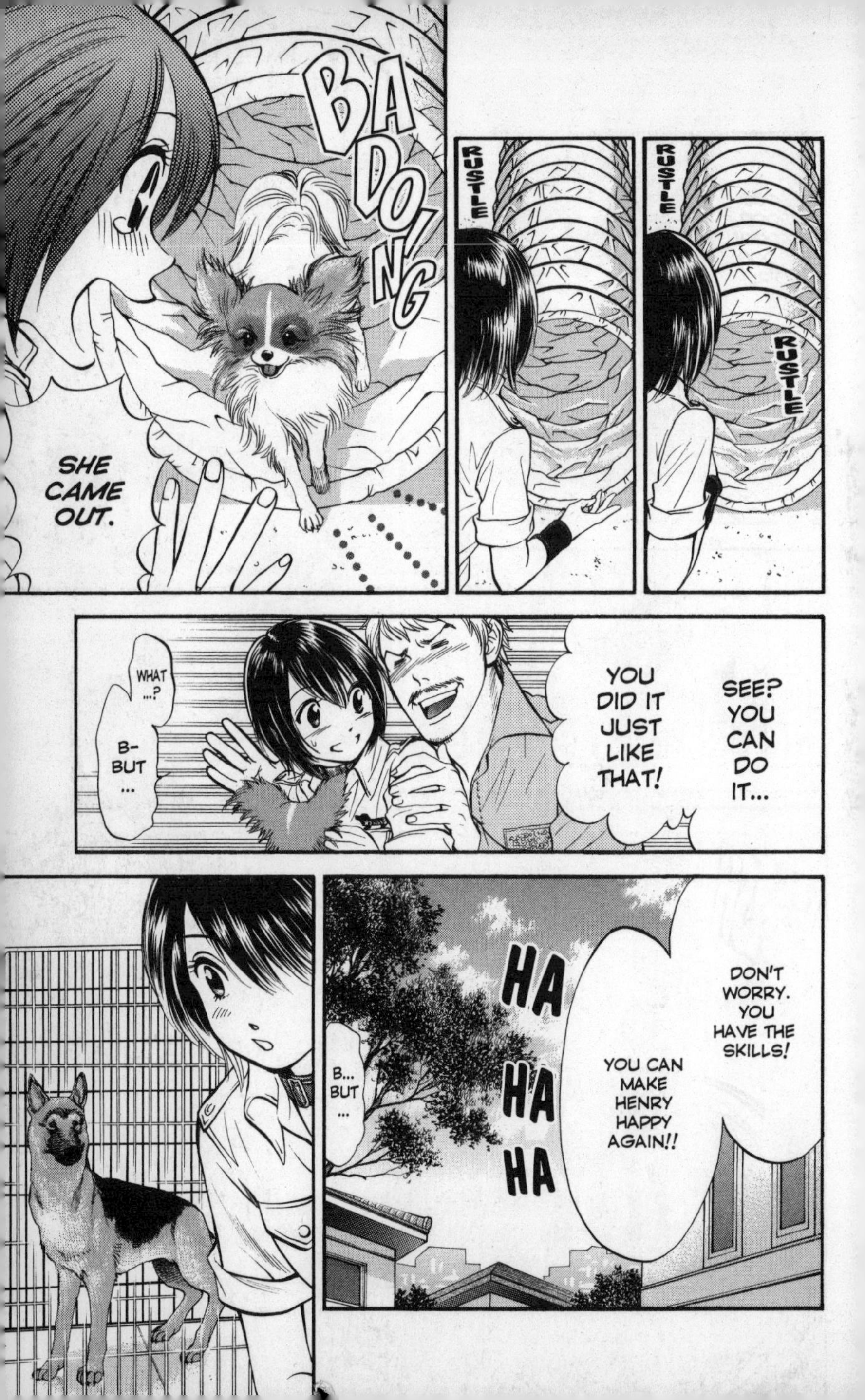

RUSTLE
RUSTLE
RUSTLE
BADOING
SHE CAME OUT.
SEE? YOU CAN DO IT...
YOU DID IT JUST LIKE THAT!
WHAT ...?
B- BUT ...
DON'T WORRY. YOU HAVE THE SKILLS!
YOU CAN MAKE HENRY HAPPY AGAIN!!
HA HA HA HA
B... BUT ...

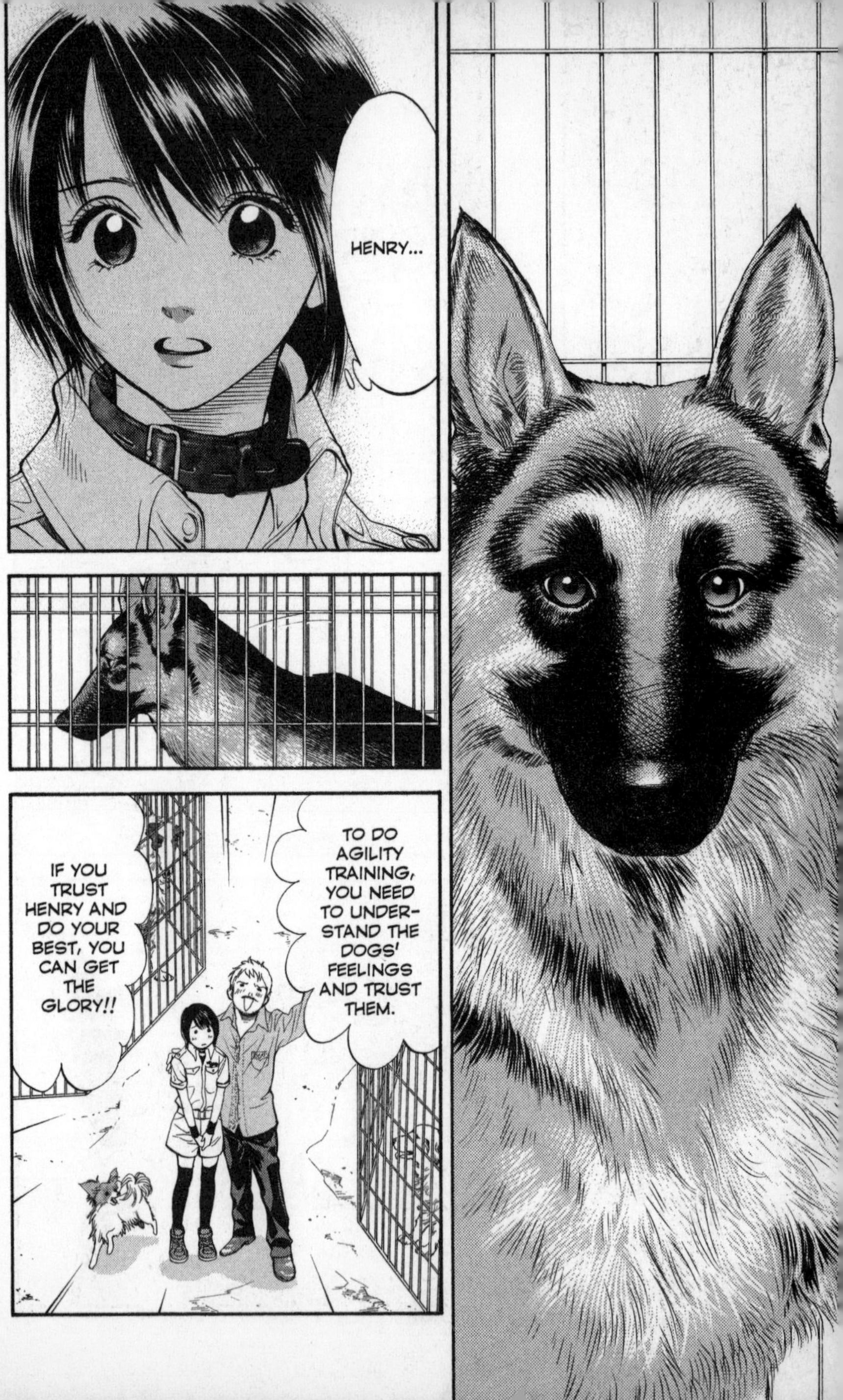
HENRY...
TO DO AGILITY TRAINING, YOU NEED TO UNDER-STAND THE DOGS' FEELINGS AND TRUST THEM.
IF YOU TRUST HENRY AND DO YOUR BEST, YOU CAN GET THE GLORY!!

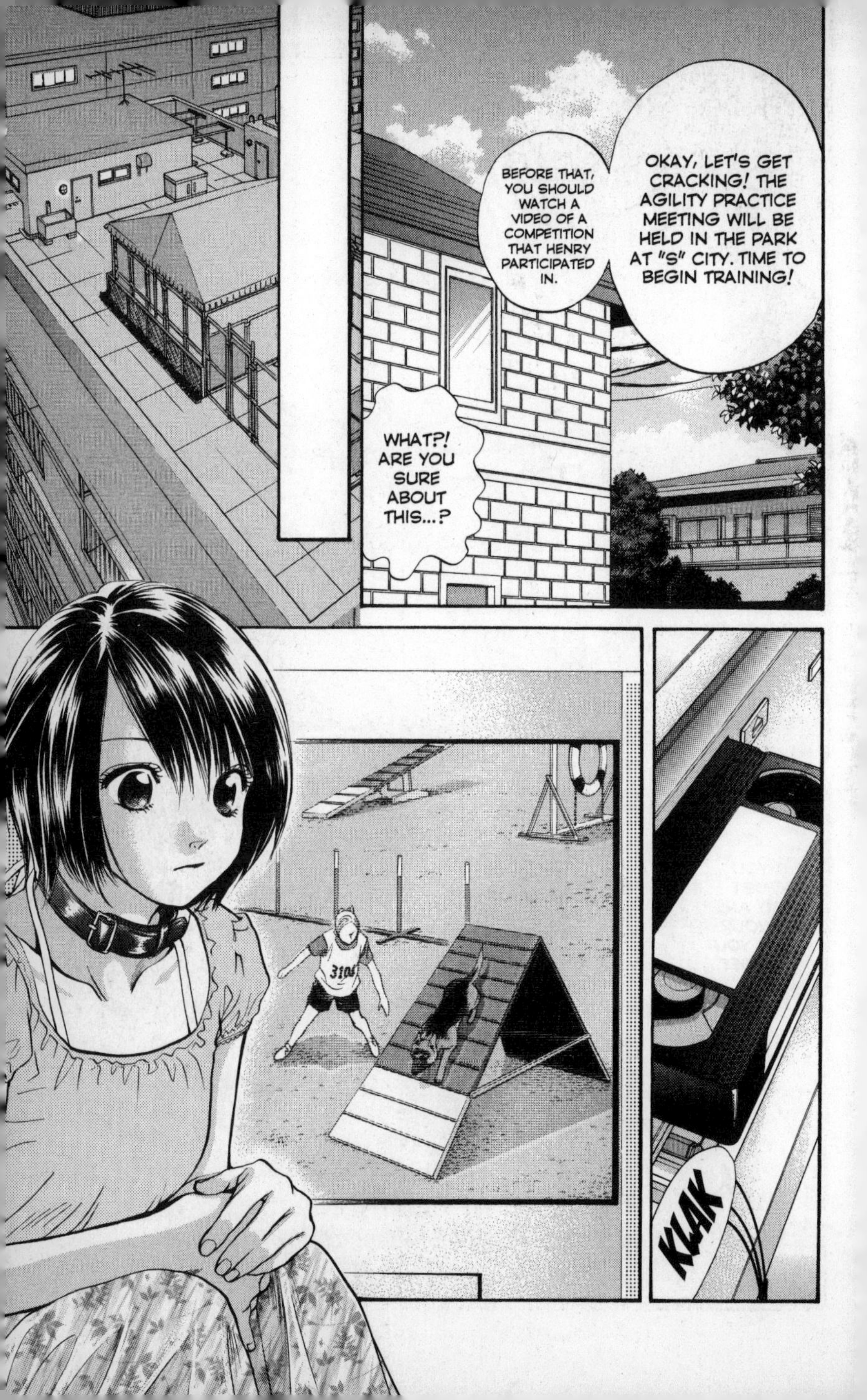
OKAY, LET'S GET CRACKING! THE AGILITY PRACTICE MEETING WILL BE HELD IN THE PARK AT "S" CITY. TIME TO BEGIN TRAINING!
BEFORE THAT, YOU SHOULD WATCH A VIDEO OF A COMPETITION THAT HENRY PARTICIPATED IN.
WHAT?! ARE YOU SURE ABOUT THIS...?
KLAK
3104

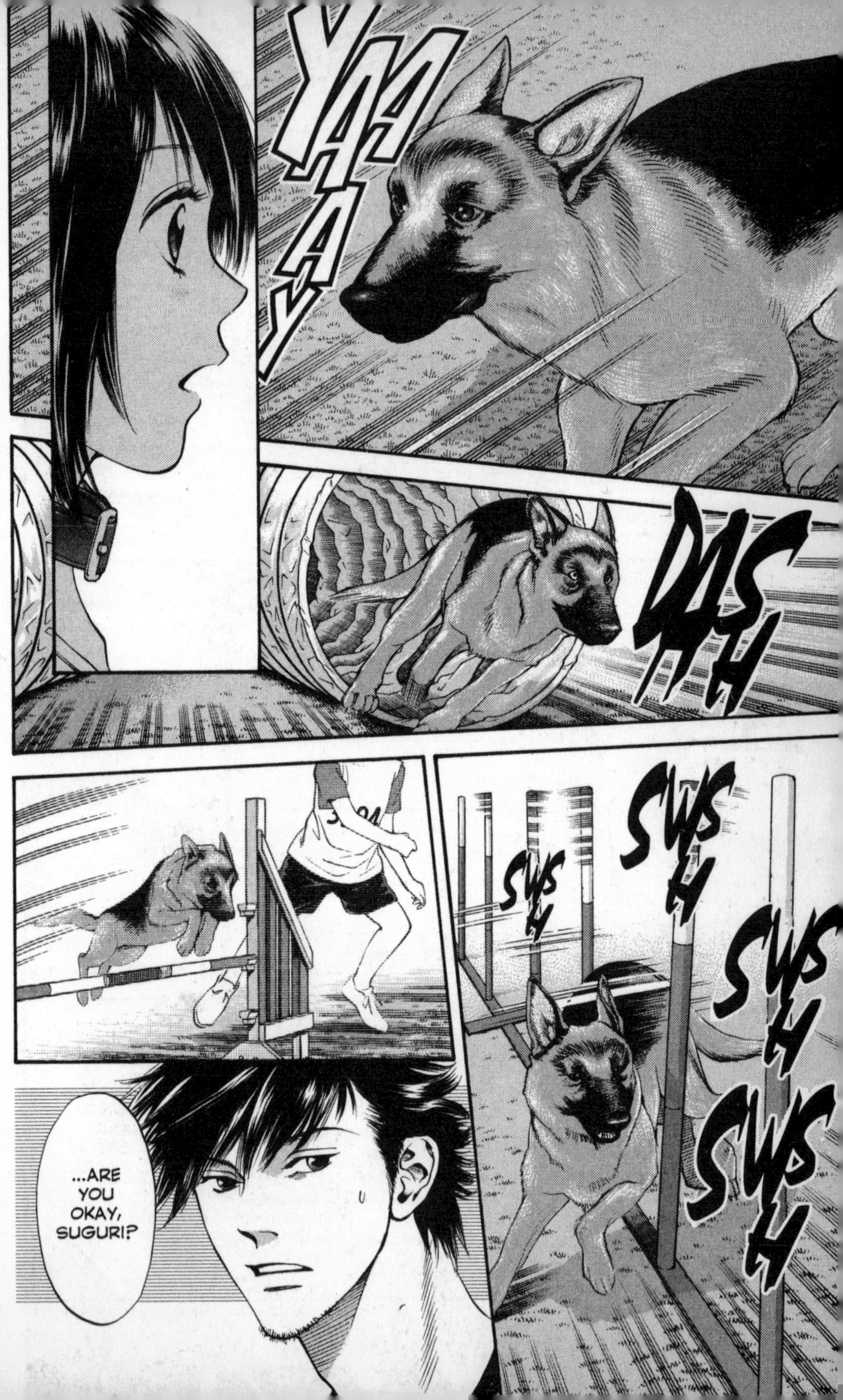
YAAAY
DASH
SWISH
SWISH
SWISH
SWISH
...ARE YOU OKAY, SUGURI?

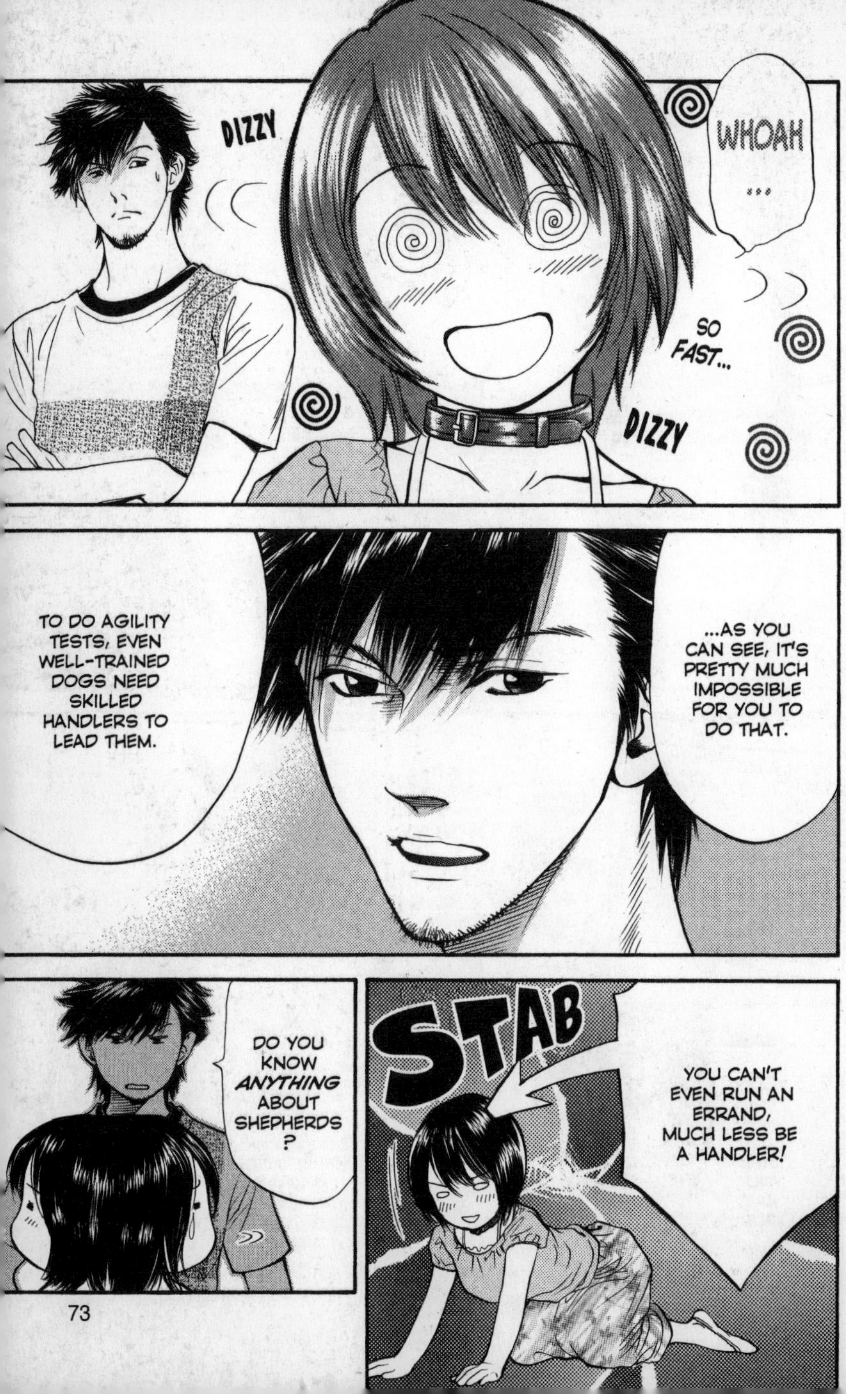
WHOAH ...
SO FAST...
DIZZY
DIZZY
...AS YOU CAN SEE, IT'S PRETTY MUCH IMPOSSIBLE FOR YOU TO DO THAT.
TO DO AGILITY TESTS, EVEN WELL-TRAINED DOGS NEED SKILLED HANDLERS TO LEAD THEM.
YOU CAN'T EVEN RUN AN ERRAND, MUCH LESS BE A HANDLER!
STAB
DO YOU KNOW *ANYTHING* ABOUT SHEPHERDS ?

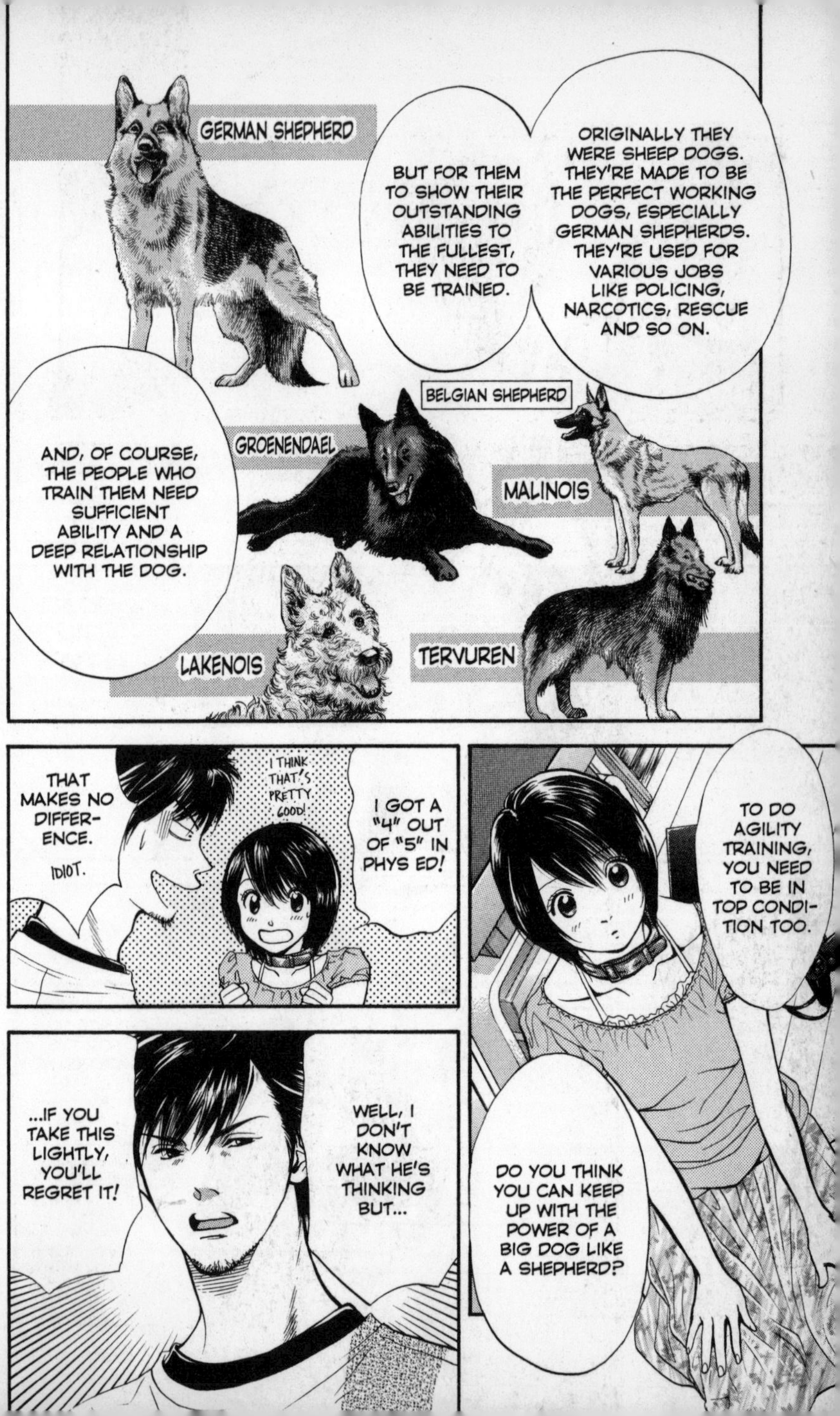
ORIGINALLY THEY WERE SHEEP DOGS. THEY'RE MADE TO BE THE PERFECT WORKING DOGS, ESPECIALLY GERMAN SHEPHERDS. THEY'RE USED FOR VARIOUS JOBS LIKE POLICING, NARCOTICS, RESCUE AND SO ON.
BUT FOR THEM TO SHOW THEIR OUTSTANDING ABILITIES TO THE FULLEST, THEY NEED TO BE TRAINED.
GERMAN SHEPHERD
BELGIAN SHEPHERD
MALINOIS
GROENENDAEL
AND, OF COURSE, THE PEOPLE WHO TRAIN THEM NEED SUFFICIENT ABILITY AND A DEEP RELATIONSHIP WITH THE DOG.
TERVUREN
LAKENOIS
TO DO AGILITY TRAINING, YOU NEED TO BE IN TOP CONDITION TOO.
DO YOU THINK YOU CAN KEEP UP WITH THE POWER OF A BIG DOG LIKE A SHEPHERD?
I GOT A "4" OUT OF "5" IN PHYS ED!
I THINK THAT'S PRETTY GOOD!
THAT MAKES NO DIFFERENCE.
IDIOT.
WELL, I DON'T KNOW WHAT HE'S THINKING BUT...
...IF YOU TAKE THIS LIGHTLY, YOU'LL REGRET IT!

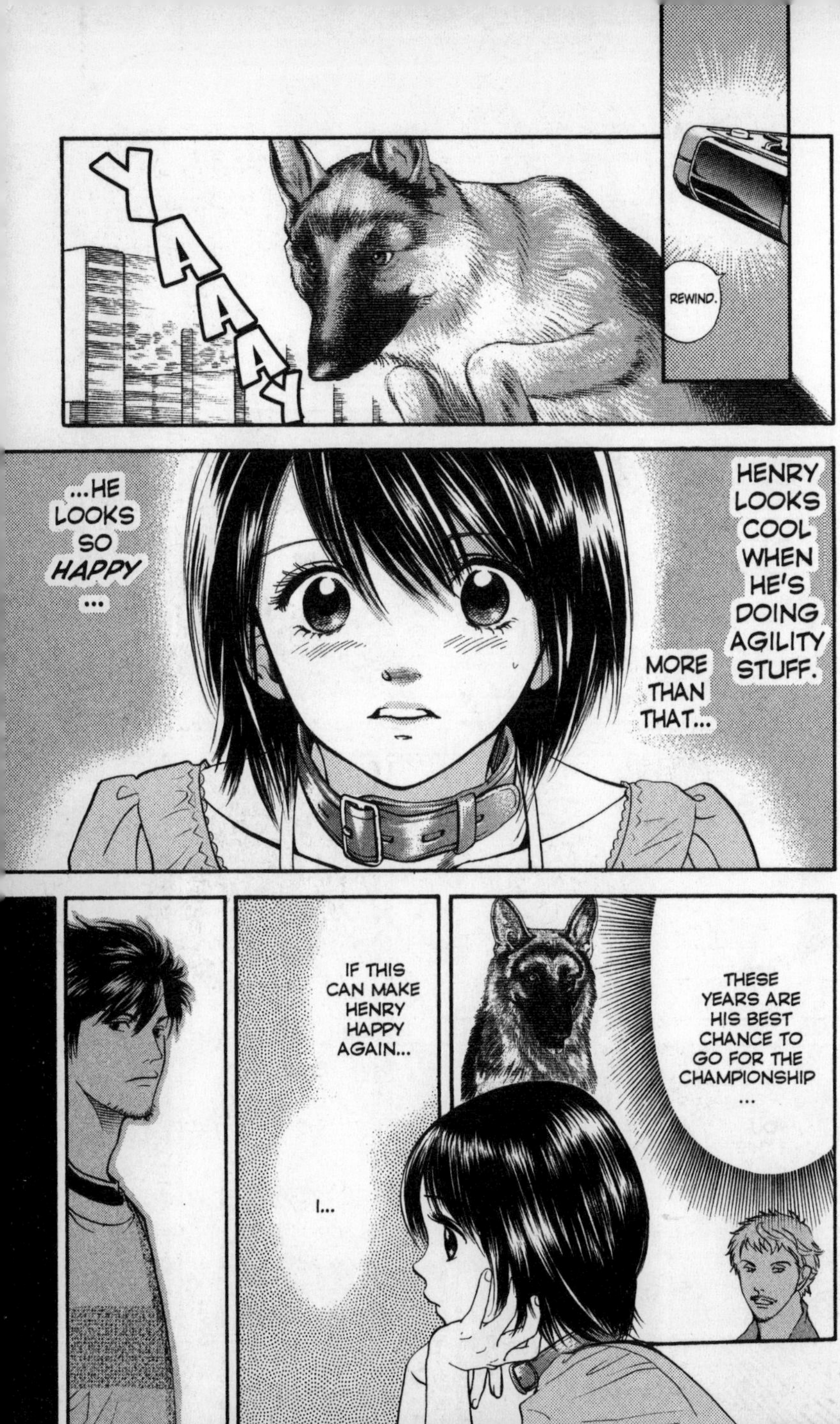
REWIND.
YAAAAY
HENRY LOOKS COOL WHEN HE'S DOING AGILITY STUFF.
MORE THAN THAT...
...HE LOOKS SO *HAPPY*...
THESE YEARS ARE HIS BEST CHANCE TO GO FOR THE CHAMPIONSHIP...
IF THIS CAN MAKE HENRY HAPPY AGAIN...
I...

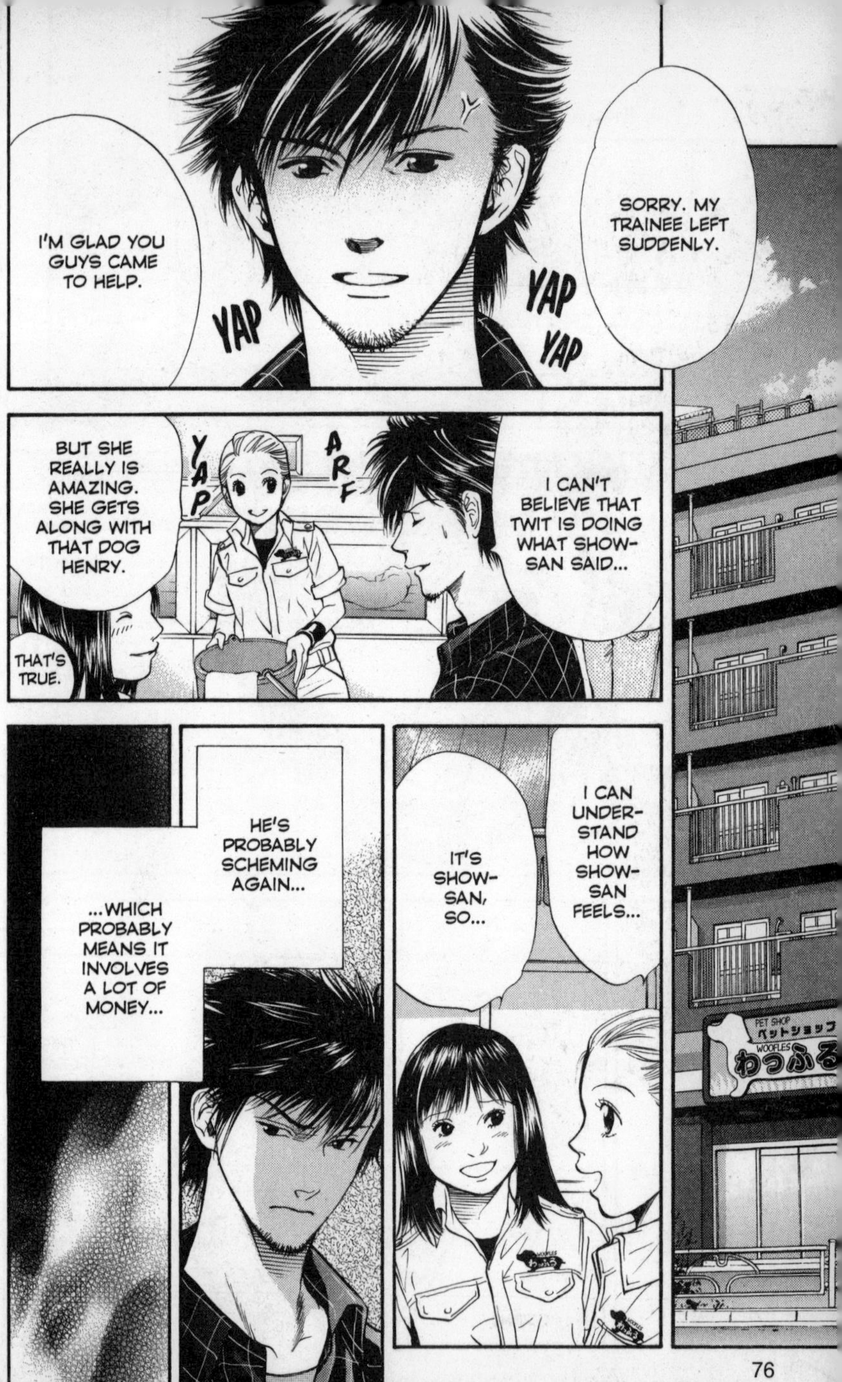
SORRY. MY TRAINEE LEFT SUDDENLY.
YAP
YAP
I'M GLAD YOU GUYS CAME TO HELP.
YAP
I CAN'T BELIEVE THAT TWIT IS DOING WHAT SHOW-SAN SAID...
ARF
YAP YAP
BUT SHE REALLY IS AMAZING. SHE GETS ALONG WITH THAT DOG HENRY.
THAT'S TRUE.
PET SHOP
WOOFLES
I CAN UNDERSTAND HOW SHOW-SAN FEELS...
IT'S SHOW-SAN, SO...
HE'S PROBABLY SCHEMING AGAIN...
...WHICH PROBABLY MEANS IT INVOLVES A LOT OF MONEY...

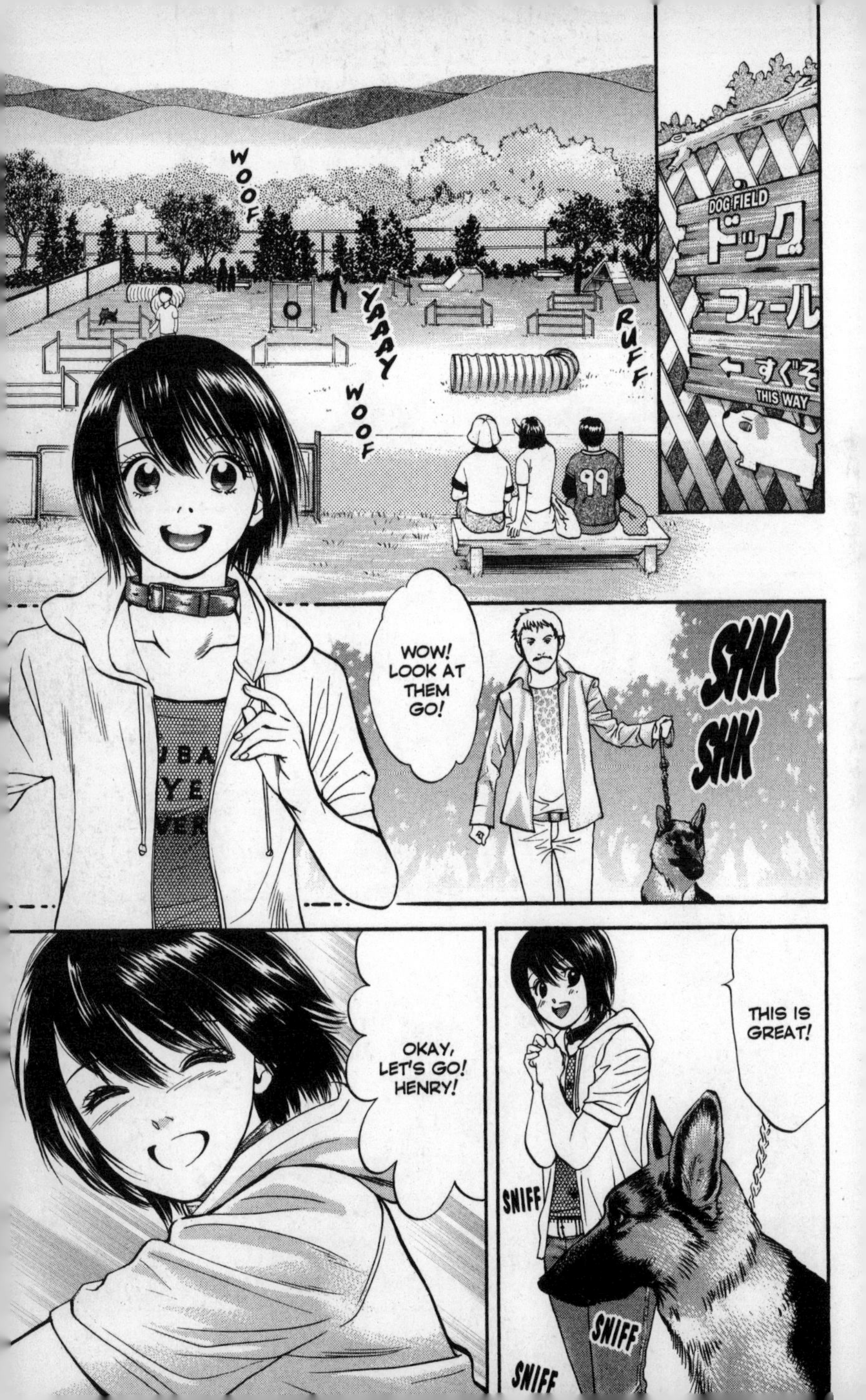
DOG FIELD
ドック
フィール
← すぐそ
THIS WAY
RUFF
YAAAY
WOOF
WOOF
SHK SHK
WOW! LOOK AT THEM GO!
THIS IS GREAT!
SNIFF
SNIFF
SNIFF
OKAY, LET'S GO! HENRY!

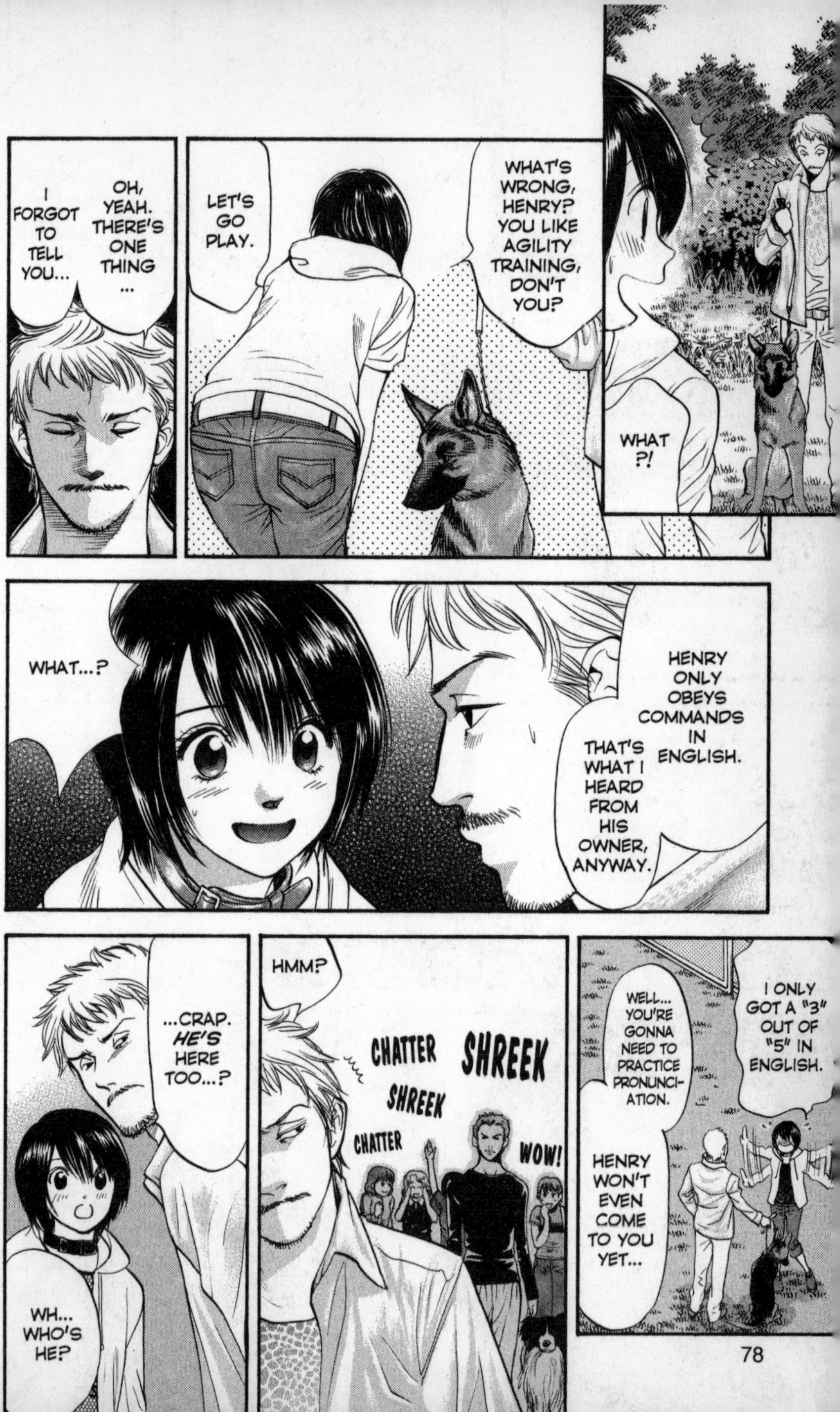
WHAT ?!
WHAT'S WRONG, HENRY? YOU LIKE AGILITY TRAINING, DON'T YOU?
LET'S GO PLAY.
OH, YEAH. THERE'S ONE THING ...
I FORGOT TO TELL YOU...
HENRY ONLY OBEYS COMMANDS IN ENGLISH.
THAT'S WHAT I HEARD FROM HIS OWNER, ANYWAY.
WHAT...?
I ONLY GOT A "3" OUT OF "5" IN ENGLISH.
WELL... YOU'RE GONNA NEED TO PRACTICE PRONUNCIATION.
HENRY WON'T EVEN COME TO YOU YET...
HMM?
SHREEK
CHATTER
SHREEK
CHATTER
WOW!
...CRAP. *HE'S* HERE TOO...?
WH... WHO'S HE?

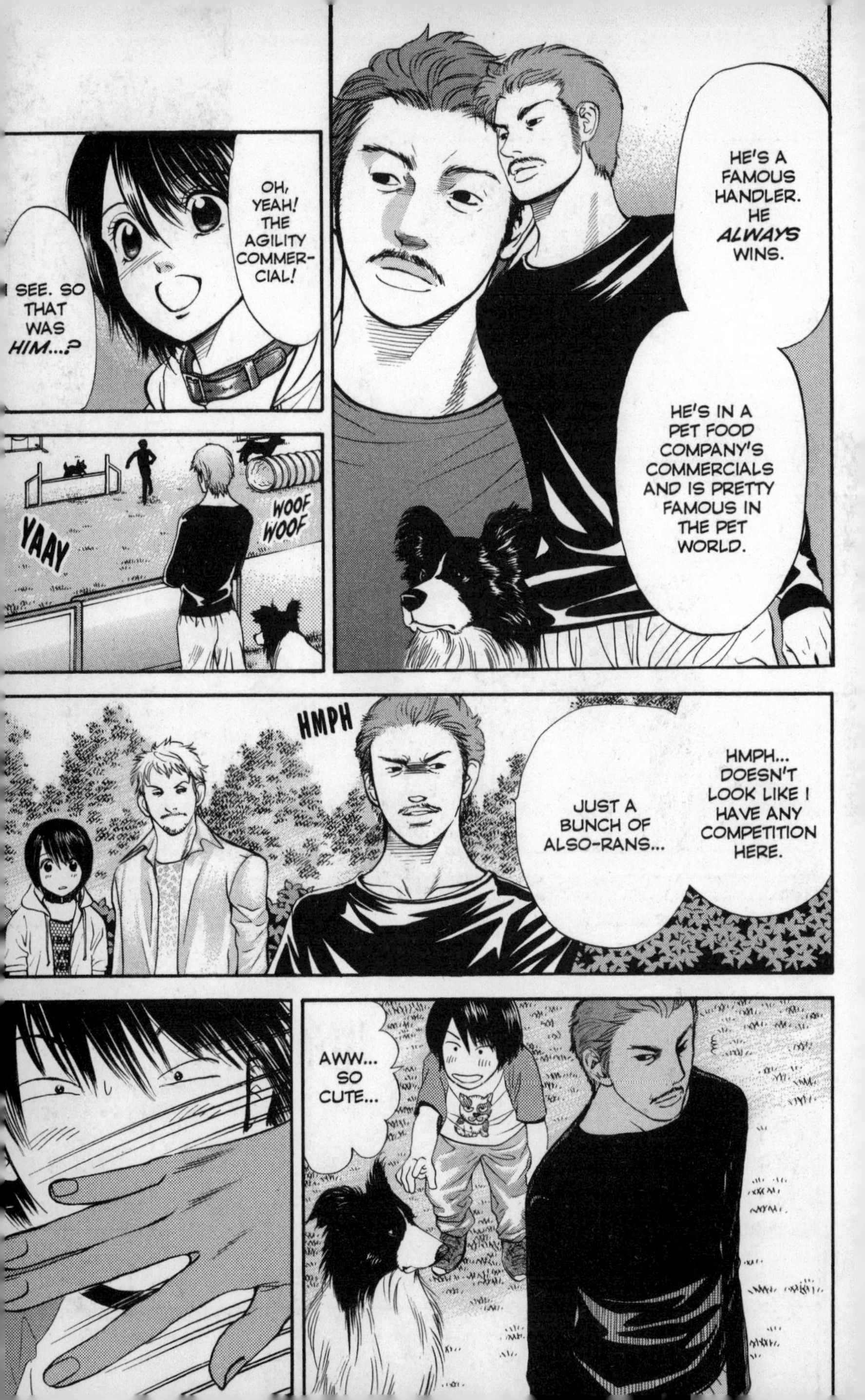
HE'S A FAMOUS HANDLER. HE *ALWAYS* WINS.
HE'S IN A PET FOOD COMPANY'S COMMERCIALS AND IS PRETTY FAMOUS IN THE PET WORLD.
OH, YEAH! THE AGILITY COMMERCIAL!
I SEE. SO THAT WAS *HIM*...?
WOOF WOOF
YAAY
HMPH
HMPH... DOESN'T LOOK LIKE I HAVE ANY COMPETITION HERE.
JUST A BUNCH OF ALSO-RANS...
AWW... SO CUTE...

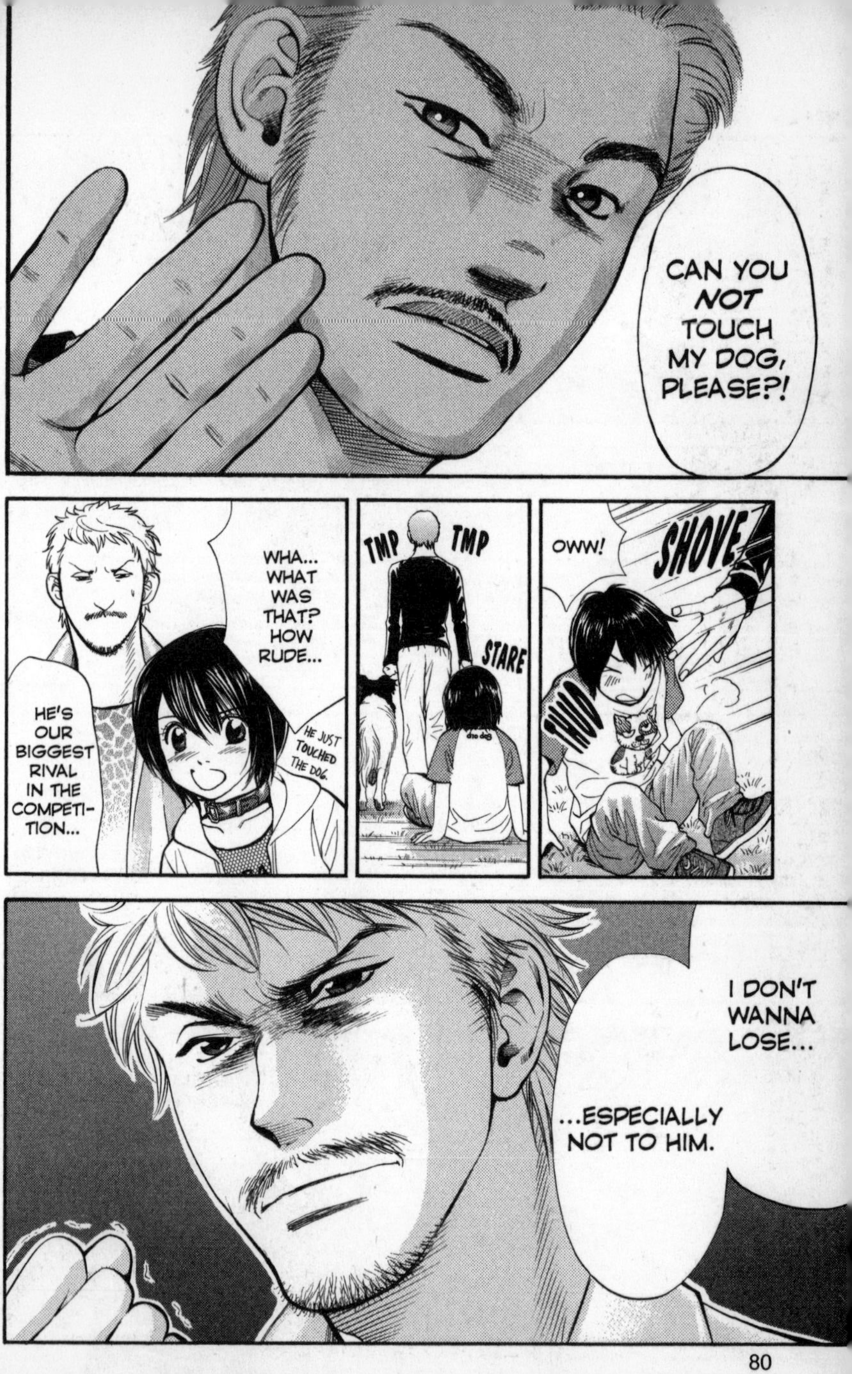

CAN YOU *NOT* TOUCH MY DOG, PLEASE?!
OWW!
SHOVE
THUD
TMP
TMP
STARE
WHA... WHAT WAS THAT? HOW RUDE...
HE JUST TOUCHED THE DOG.
HE'S OUR BIGGEST RIVAL IN THE COMPETITION...
I DON'T WANNA LOSE...
...ESPECIALLY NOT TO HIM.

BONUS MANGA CONTINUATION

THEIR EXCUSES.

MAMICCHI: SHE SHOULD GET IT TO HEAL FAST TO KEEP WORKING. I FORCED MYSELF TO DO IT...HOLDING BACK TEARS. IT WAS ALL FOR HER.

FUUKO: BUT I DID IT FOR HER. OH, WELL. I'LL GET MY REVENGE ON HER BY DOING ** TO **'S **...

YAMANE: DO I HAVE SUCH AN EVIL-LOOKING FACE? I CAN'T BELIEVE IT...I'LL BE LOOKING FORWARD TO THE NEXT TIME...

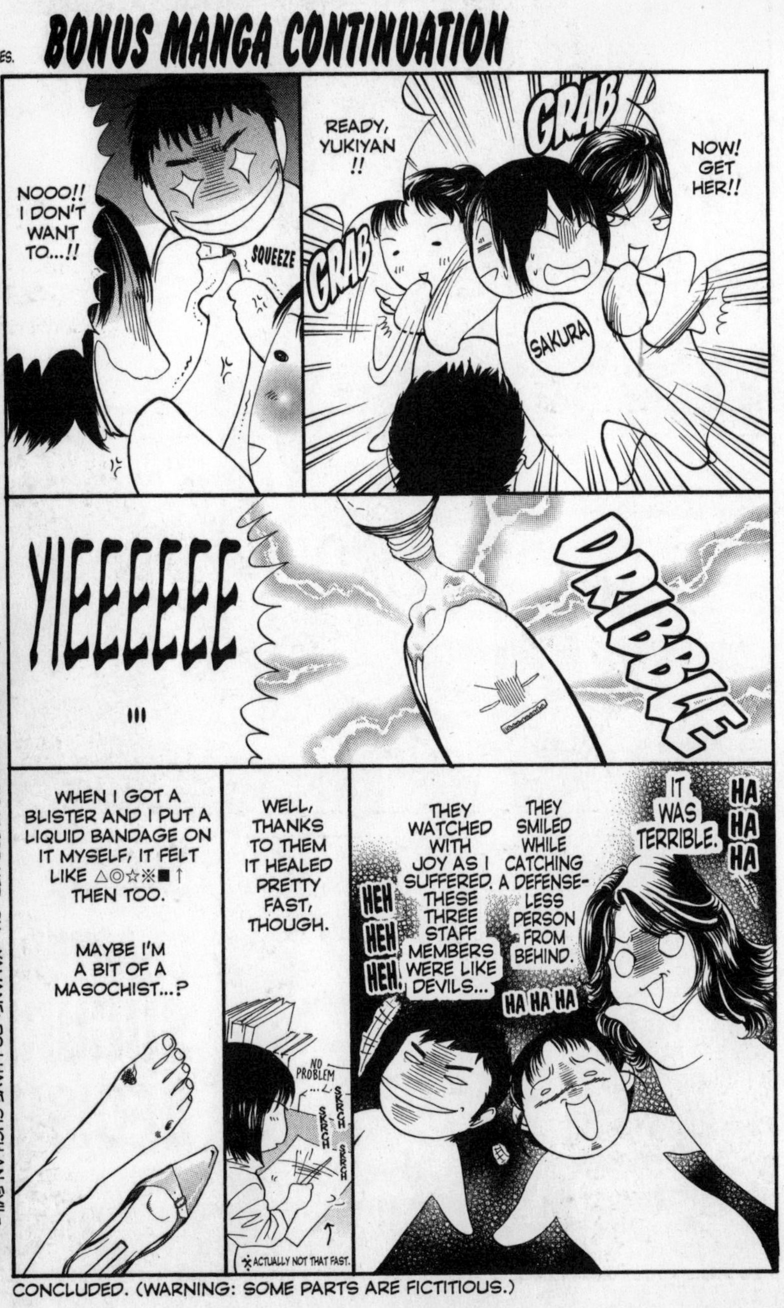
GRAB
NOW! GET HER!!
READY, YUKIYAN!!
GRAB
SAKURA
NOOO!! I DON'T WANT TO...!!
SQUEEZE
DRIBBLE
YIEEEEEE!!!
HA HA HA
IT WAS TERRIBLE.
THEY SMILED WHILE CATCHING A DEFENSELESS PERSON FROM BEHIND.
THEY WATCHED WITH JOY AS I SUFFERED. THESE THREE STAFF MEMBERS WERE LIKE DEVILS...
HEH HEH HEH.
HA HA HA
WELL, THANKS TO THEM IT HEALED PRETTY FAST, THOUGH.
NO PROBLEM ...
SKRCH SKRCH SKRCH SKRCH
*ACTUALLY NOT THAT FAST.
WHEN I GOT A BLISTER AND I PUT A LIQUID BANDAGE ON IT MYSELF, IT FELT LIKE △◎☆※■↑ THEN TOO.
MAYBE I'M A BIT OF A MASOCHIST...?

CONCLUDED. (WARNING: SOME PARTS ARE FICTITIOUS.)

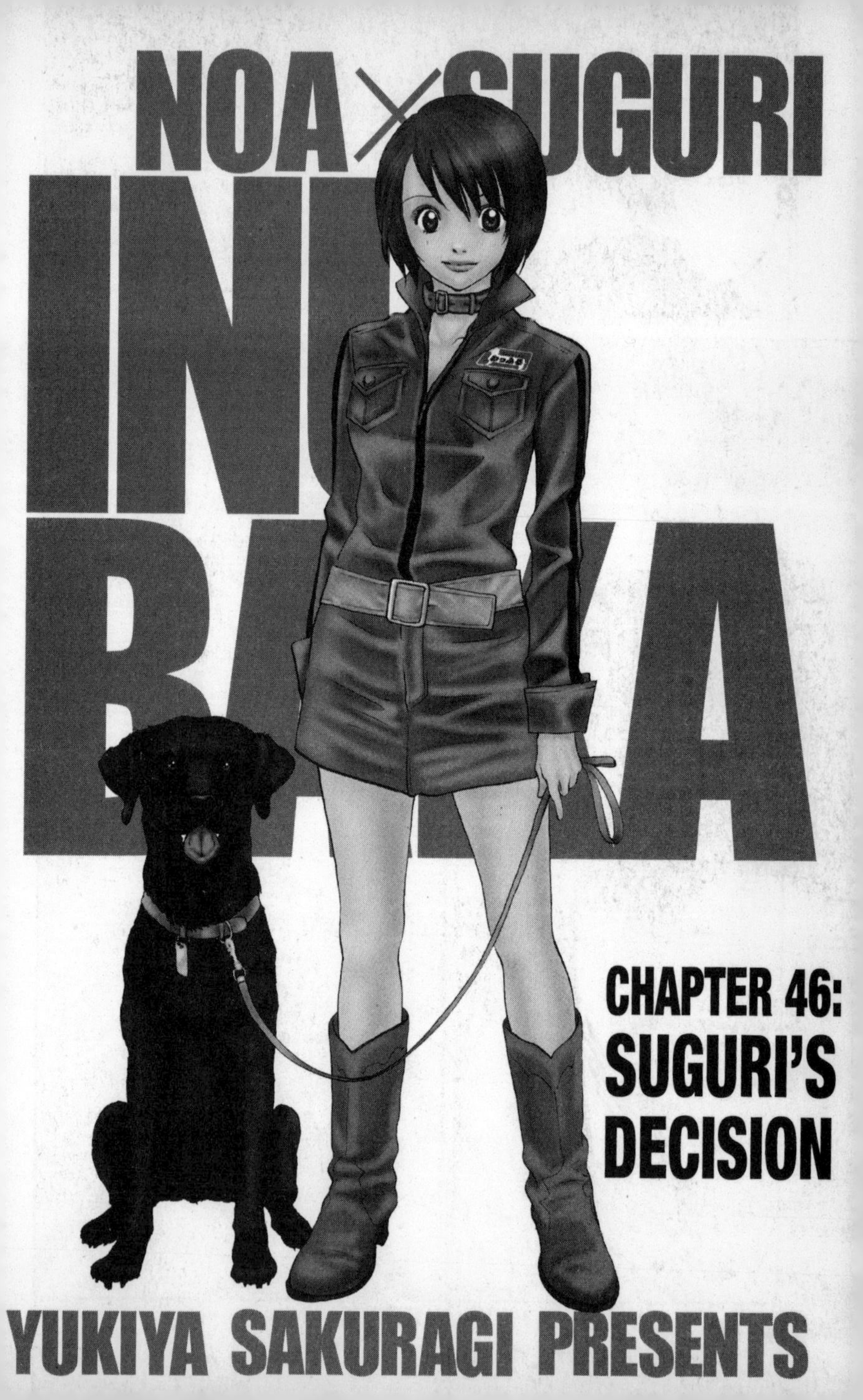
NOA×SUGURI
INU BAKA
CHAPTER 46:
SUGURI'S
DECISION
YUKIYA SAKURAGI PRESENTS

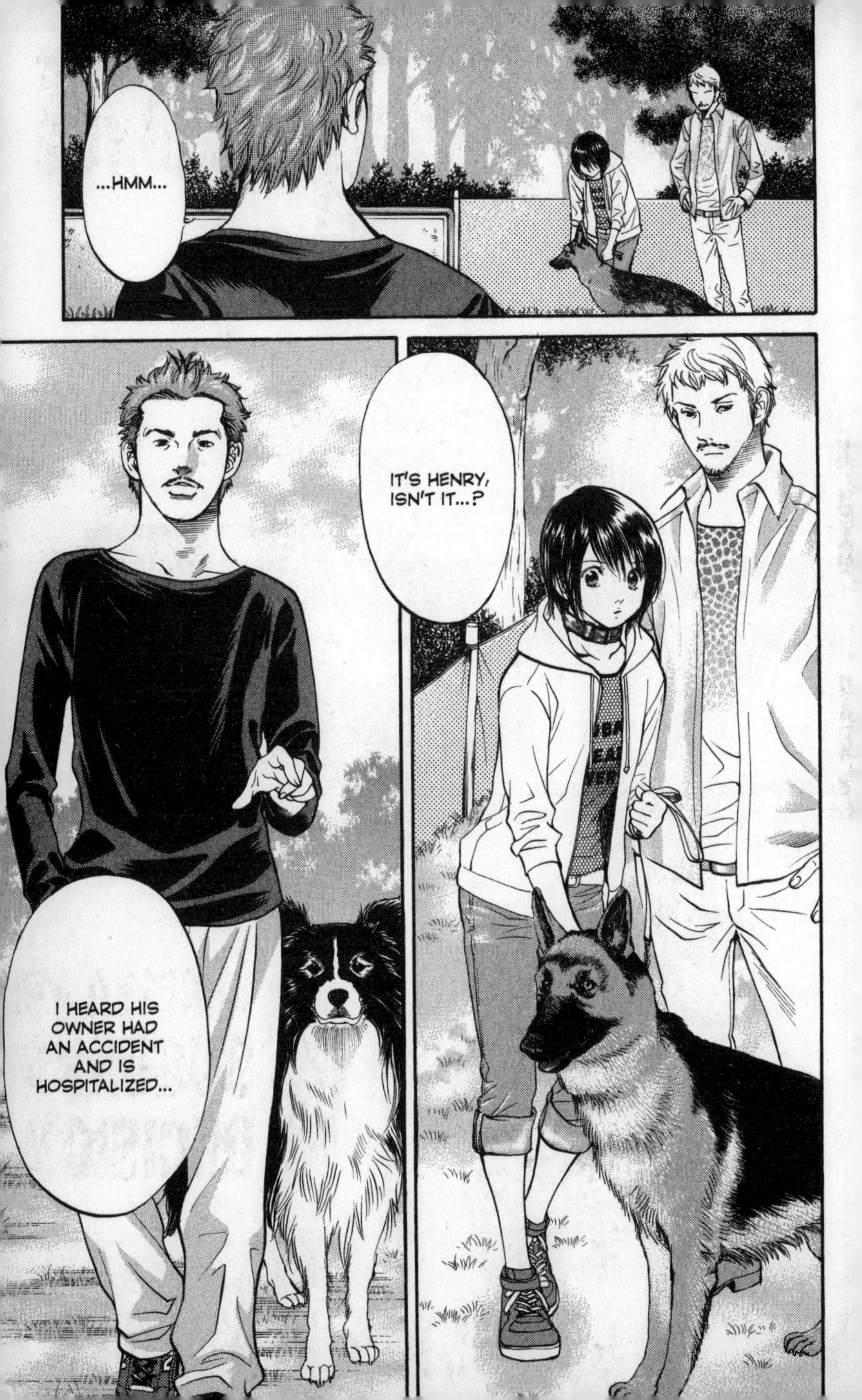
...HMM...
IT'S HENRY, ISN'T IT...?
I HEARD HIS OWNER HAD AN ACCIDENT AND IS HOSPITALIZED...

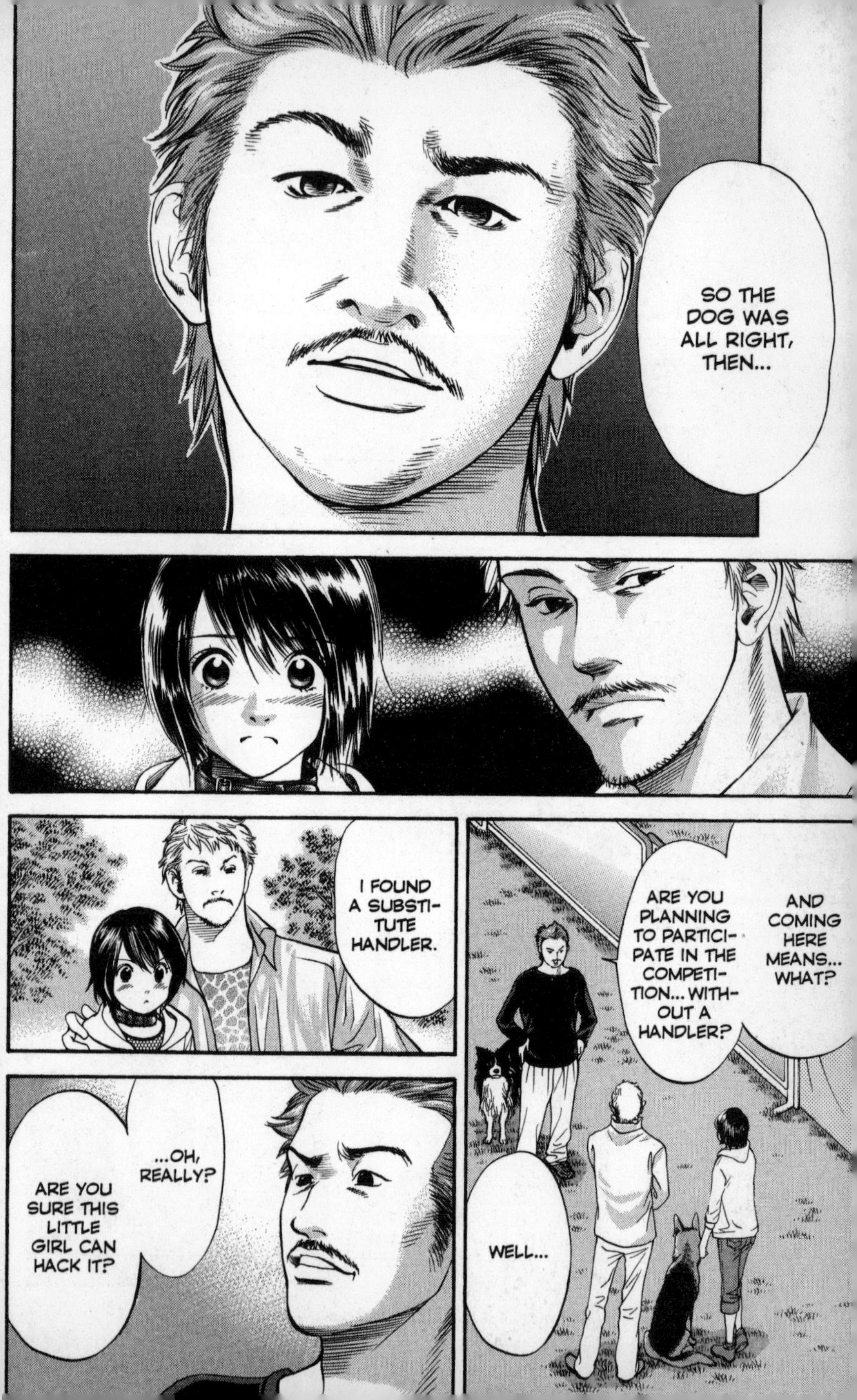
SO THE DOG WAS ALL RIGHT, THEN...
AND COMING HERE MEANS... WHAT?
ARE YOU PLANNING TO PARTICIPATE IN THE COMPETITION... WITHOUT A HANDLER?
WELL...
I FOUND A SUBSTITUTE HANDLER.
...OH, REALLY?
ARE YOU SURE THIS LITTLE GIRL CAN HACK IT?

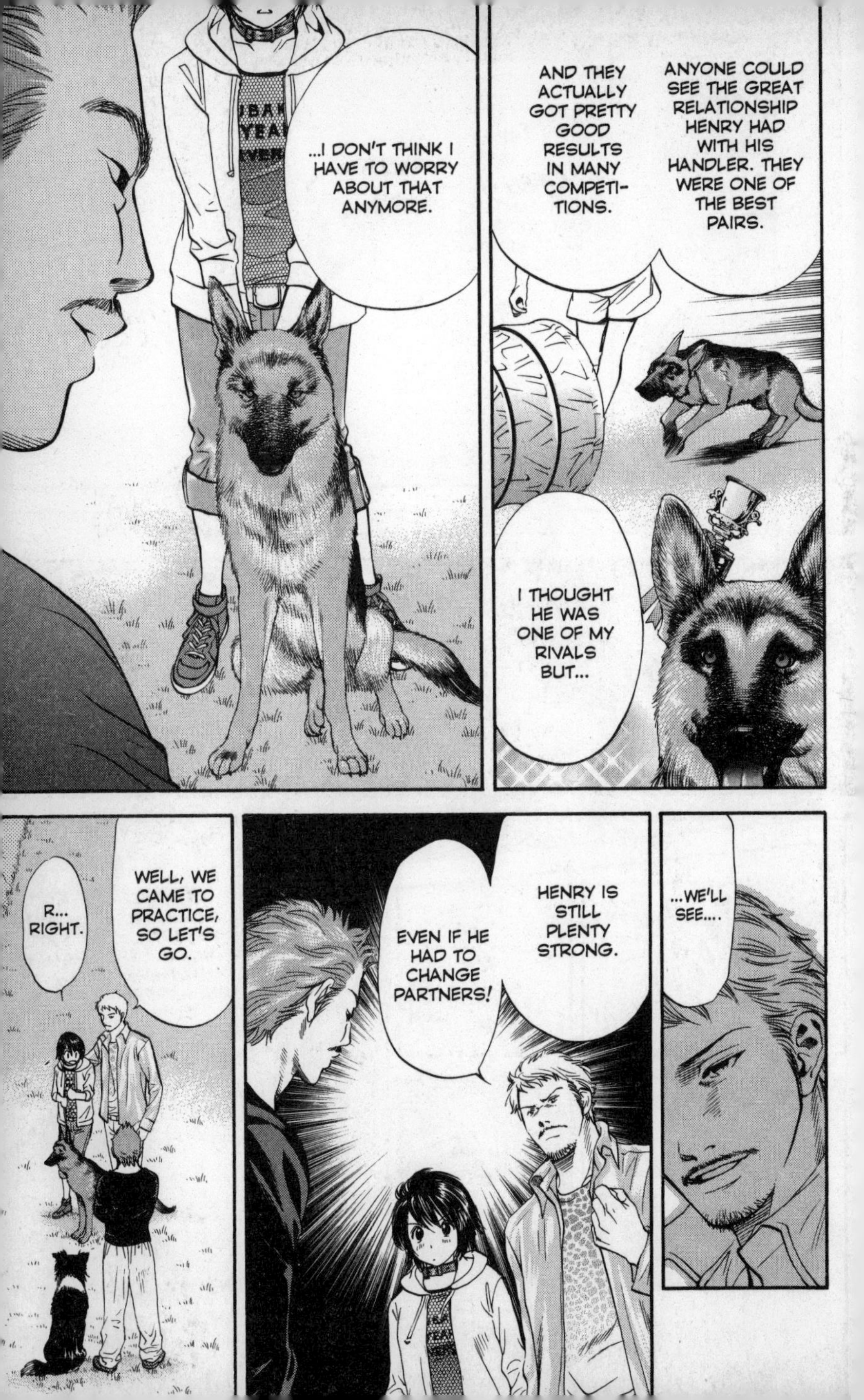
ANYONE COULD SEE THE GREAT RELATIONSHIP HENRY HAD WITH HIS HANDLER. THEY WERE ONE OF THE BEST PAIRS.
AND THEY ACTUALLY GOT PRETTY GOOD RESULTS IN MANY COMPETI-TIONS.
I THOUGHT HE WAS ONE OF MY RIVALS BUT...
...I DON'T THINK I HAVE TO WORRY ABOUT THAT ANYMORE.
...WE'LL SEE....
HENRY IS STILL PLENTY STRONG.
EVEN IF HE HAD TO CHANGE PARTNERS!
WELL, WE CAME TO PRACTICE, SO LET'S GO.
R... RIGHT.

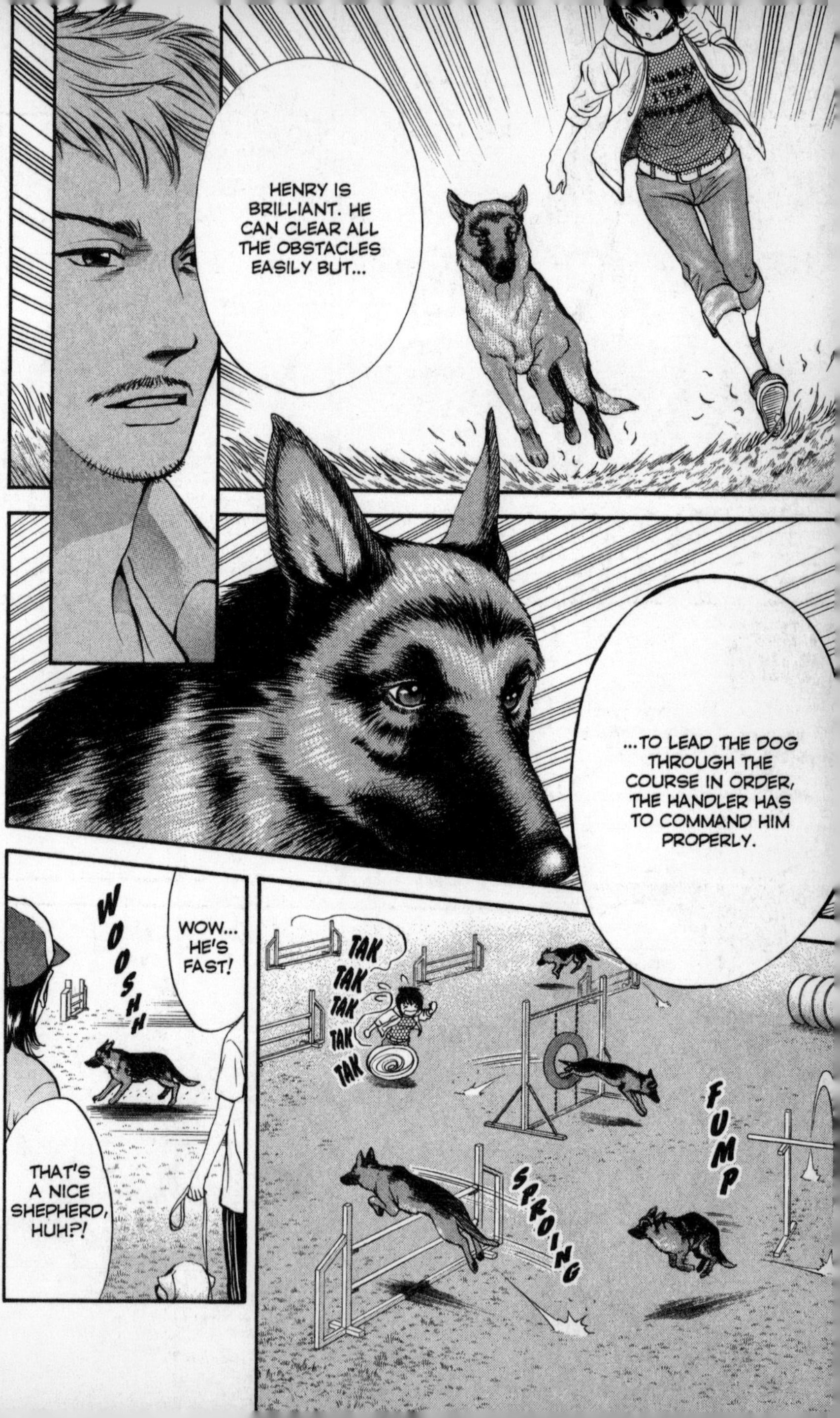
HENRY IS BRILLIANT. HE CAN CLEAR ALL THE OBSTACLES EASILY BUT...
...TO LEAD THE DOG THROUGH THE COURSE IN ORDER, THE HANDLER HAS TO COMMAND HIM PROPERLY.
TAK TAK TAK TAK TAK TAK
FUMP
SPROING
WOOSHH
WOW... HE'S FAST!
THAT'S A NICE SHEPHERD, HUH?!

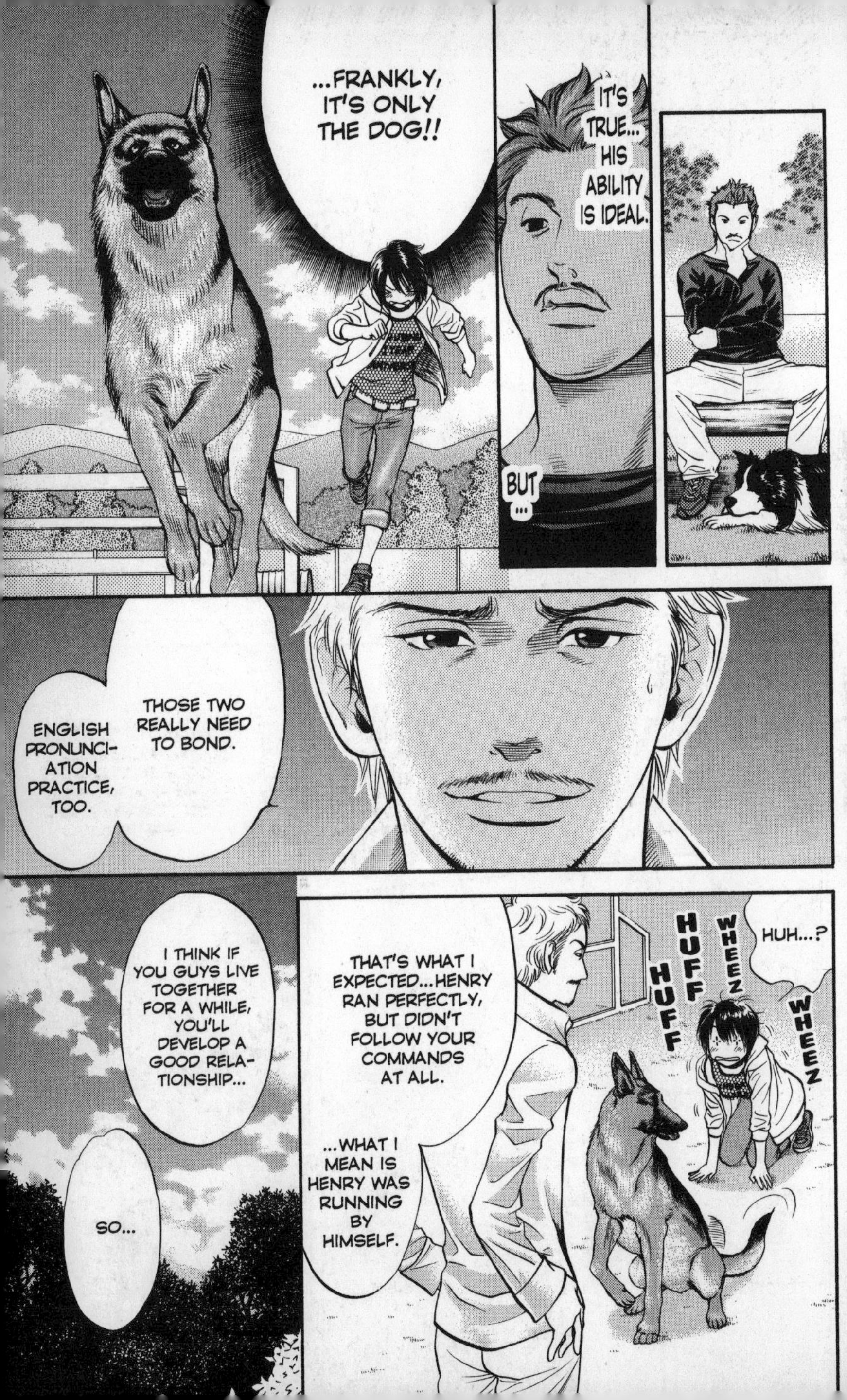
IT'S TRUE... HIS ABILITY IS IDEAL.
BUT ...
...FRANKLY, IT'S ONLY THE DOG!!
THOSE TWO REALLY NEED TO BOND.
ENGLISH PRONUNCI-ATION PRACTICE, TOO.
HUH...?
WHEEZ WHEEZ
HUFF HUFF
THAT'S WHAT I EXPECTED...HENRY RAN PERFECTLY, BUT DIDN'T FOLLOW YOUR COMMANDS AT ALL.
...WHAT I MEAN IS HENRY WAS RUNNING BY HIMSELF.
I THINK IF YOU GUYS LIVE TOGETHER FOR A WHILE, YOU'LL DEVELOP A GOOD RELA-TIONSHIP...
SO...

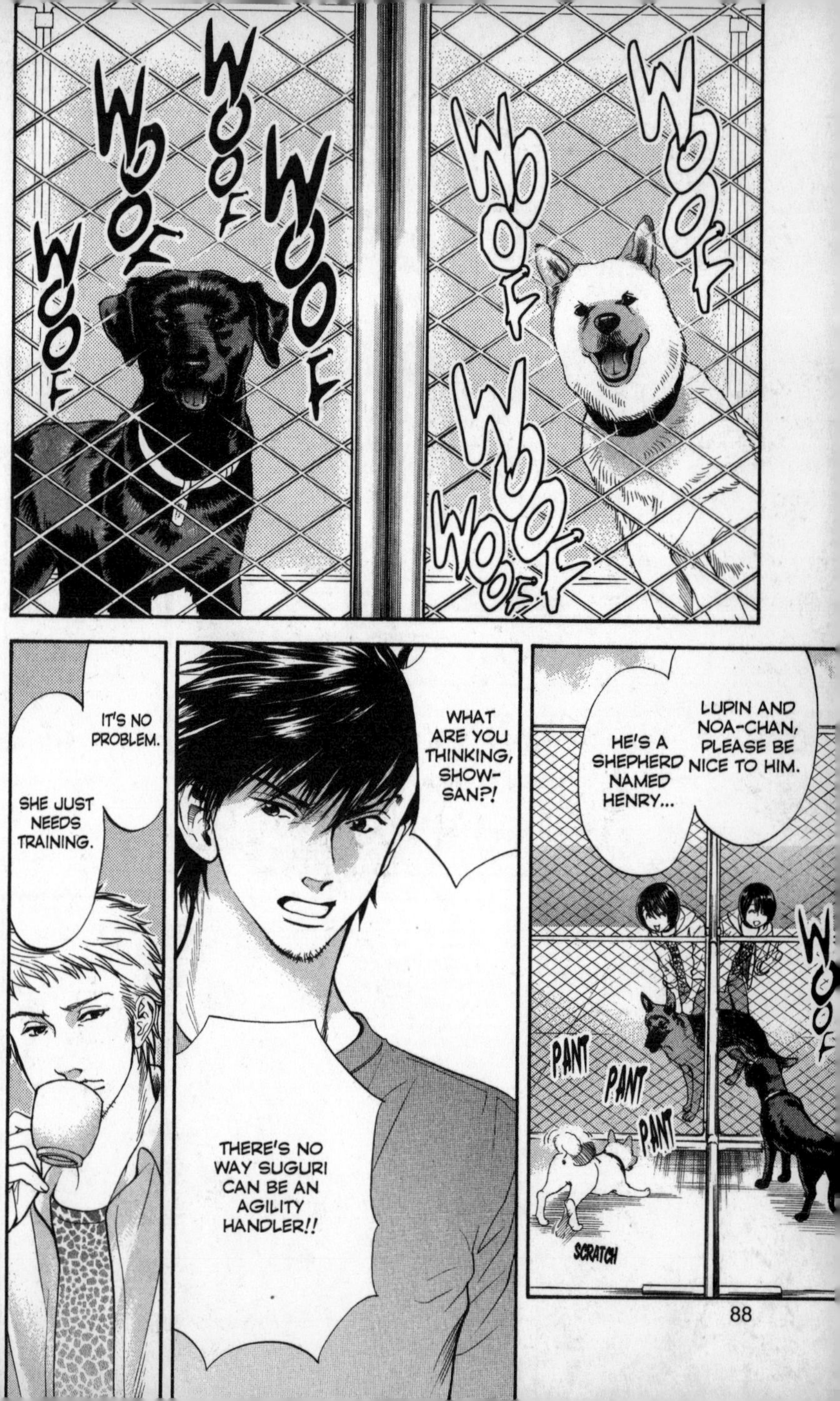
WOOF
WOOF
WOOF
WOOF
WOOF
WOOF
WOOF
WOOF
LUPIN AND NOA-CHAN, PLEASE BE NICE TO HIM.
HE'S A SHEPHERD NAMED HENRY...
WOOF
PANT
PANT
PANT
SCRATCH
WHAT ARE YOU THINKING, SHOW-SAN?!
THERE'S NO WAY SUGURI CAN BE AN AGILITY HANDLER!!
IT'S NO PROBLEM.
SHE JUST NEEDS TRAINING.

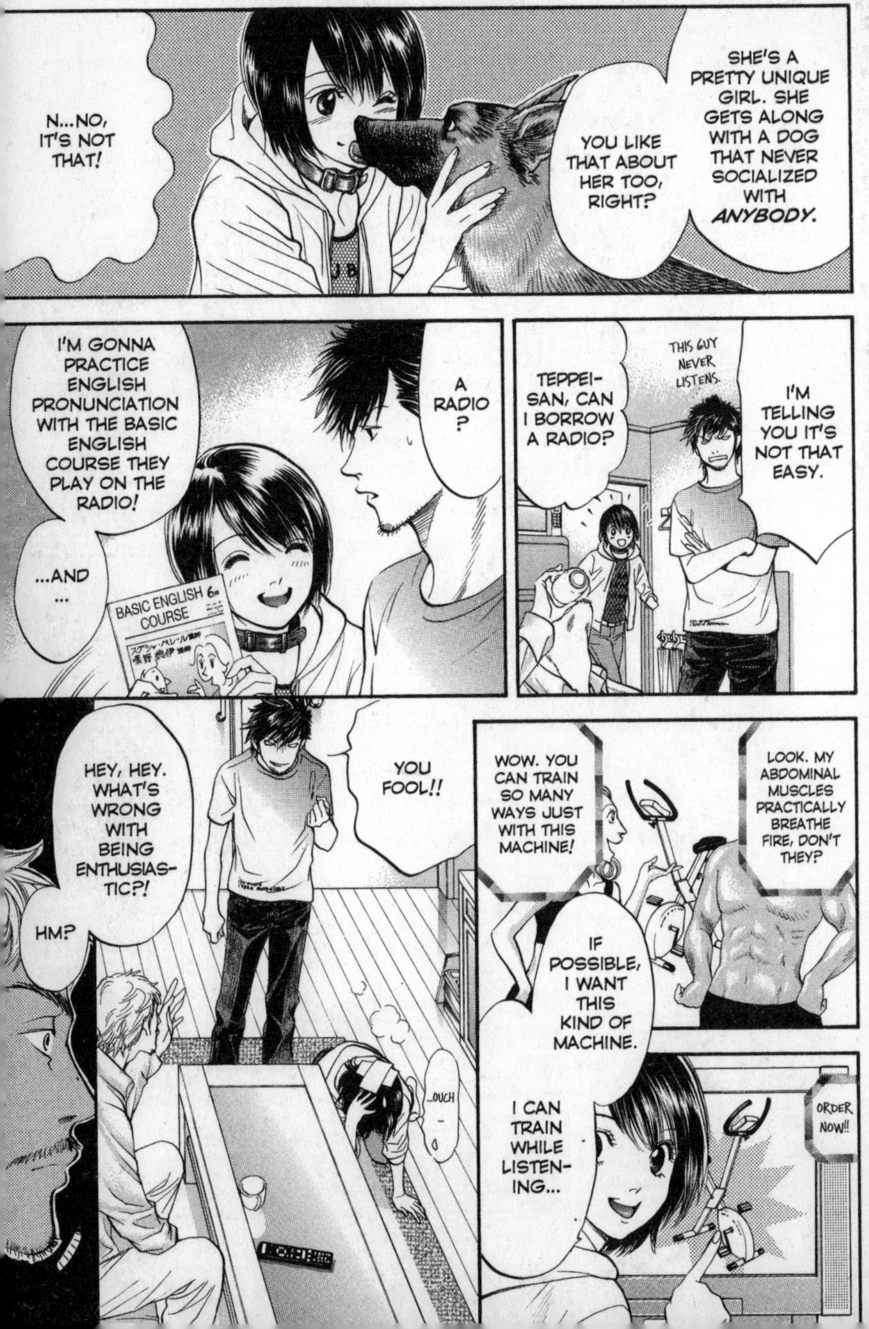
SHE'S A PRETTY UNIQUE GIRL. SHE GETS ALONG WITH A DOG THAT NEVER SOCIALIZED WITH *ANYBODY*.
YOU LIKE THAT ABOUT HER TOO, RIGHT?
N...NO, IT'S NOT THAT!
I'M TELLING YOU IT'S NOT THAT EASY.
THIS GUY NEVER LISTENS.
TEPPEI-SAN, CAN I BORROW A RADIO?
A RADIO?
I'M GONNA PRACTICE ENGLISH PRONUNCIATION WITH THE BASIC ENGLISH COURSE THEY PLAY ON THE RADIO!
...AND ...
BASIC ENGLISH COURSE 6月
LOOK. MY ABDOMINAL MUSCLES PRACTICALLY BREATHE FIRE, DON'T THEY?
WOW. YOU CAN TRAIN SO MANY WAYS JUST WITH THIS MACHINE!
IF POSSIBLE, I WANT THIS KIND OF MACHINE.
ORDER NOW!!
I CAN TRAIN WHILE LISTENING...
YOU FOOL!!
HEY, HEY. WHAT'S WRONG WITH BEING ENTHUSIASTIC?!
HM?
...OUCH ...

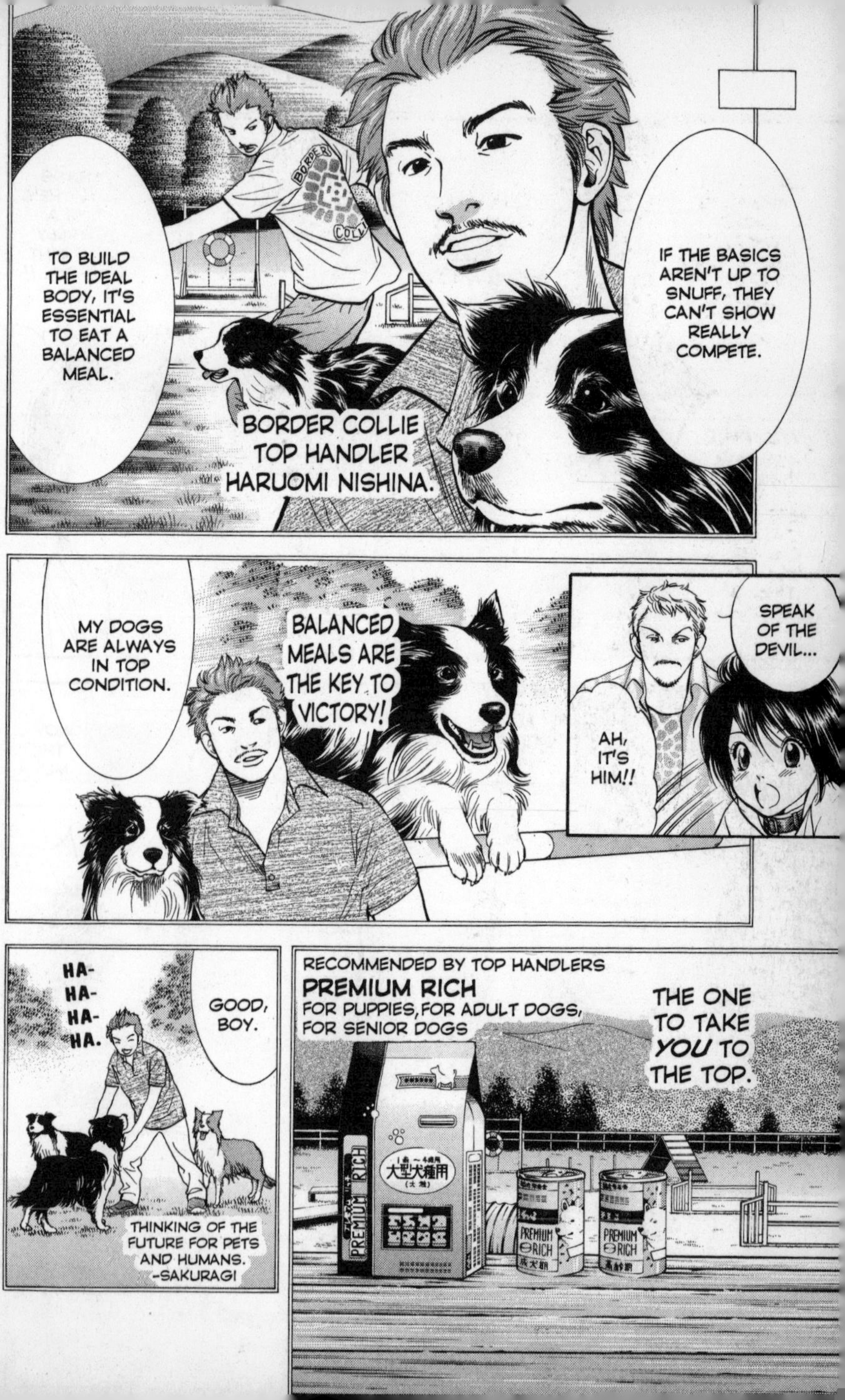
IF THE BASICS AREN'T UP TO SNUFF, THEY CAN'T SHOW REALLY COMPETE.
TO BUILD THE IDEAL BODY, IT'S ESSENTIAL TO EAT A BALANCED MEAL.
BORDER COLLIE TOP HANDLER HARUOMI NISHINA.
SPEAK OF THE DEVIL...
AH, IT'S HIM!!
BALANCED MEALS ARE THE KEY TO VICTORY!
MY DOGS ARE ALWAYS IN TOP CONDITION.
RECOMMENDED BY TOP HANDLERS
PREMIUM RICH
FOR PUPPIES, FOR ADULT DOGS, FOR SENIOR DOGS
THE ONE TO TAKE *YOU* TO THE TOP.
PREMIUM RICH
大型犬種用
PREMIUM RICH
PREMIUM RICH
GOOD, BOY.
HA-HA-HA-HA.
THINKING OF THE FUTURE FOR PETS AND HUMANS. -SAKURAGI

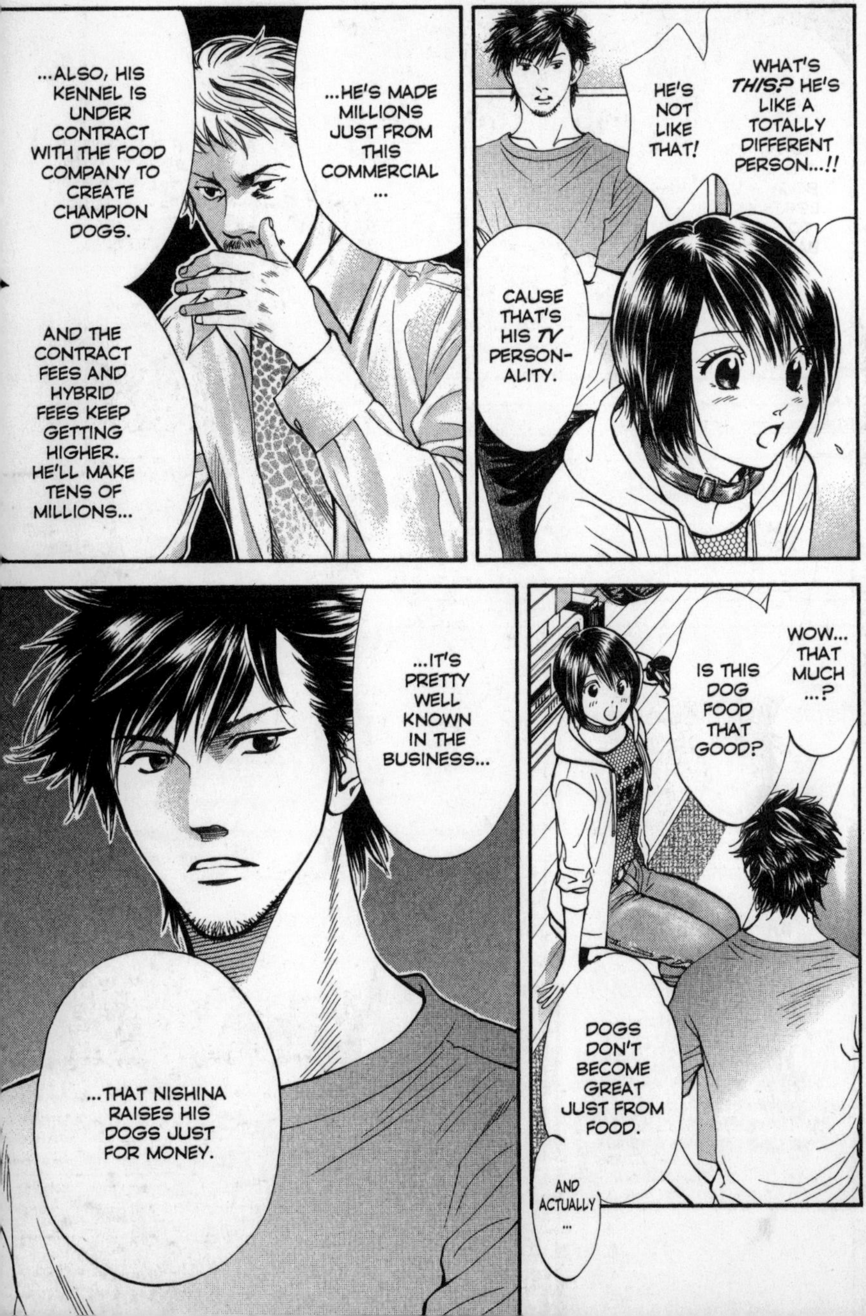
WHAT'S *THIS?* HE'S LIKE A TOTALLY DIFFERENT PERSON...!!
HE'S NOT LIKE THAT!
CAUSE THAT'S HIS *TV* PERSONALITY.
...HE'S MADE MILLIONS JUST FROM THIS COMMERCIAL ...
...ALSO, HIS KENNEL IS UNDER CONTRACT WITH THE FOOD COMPANY TO CREATE CHAMPION DOGS.
AND THE CONTRACT FEES AND HYBRID FEES KEEP GETTING HIGHER. HE'LL MAKE TENS OF MILLIONS...
WOW... THAT MUCH ...?
IS THIS DOG FOOD THAT GOOD?
DOGS DON'T BECOME GREAT JUST FROM FOOD.
AND ACTUALLY ...
...IT'S PRETTY WELL KNOWN IN THE BUSINESS...
...THAT NISHINA RAISES HIS DOGS JUST FOR MONEY.

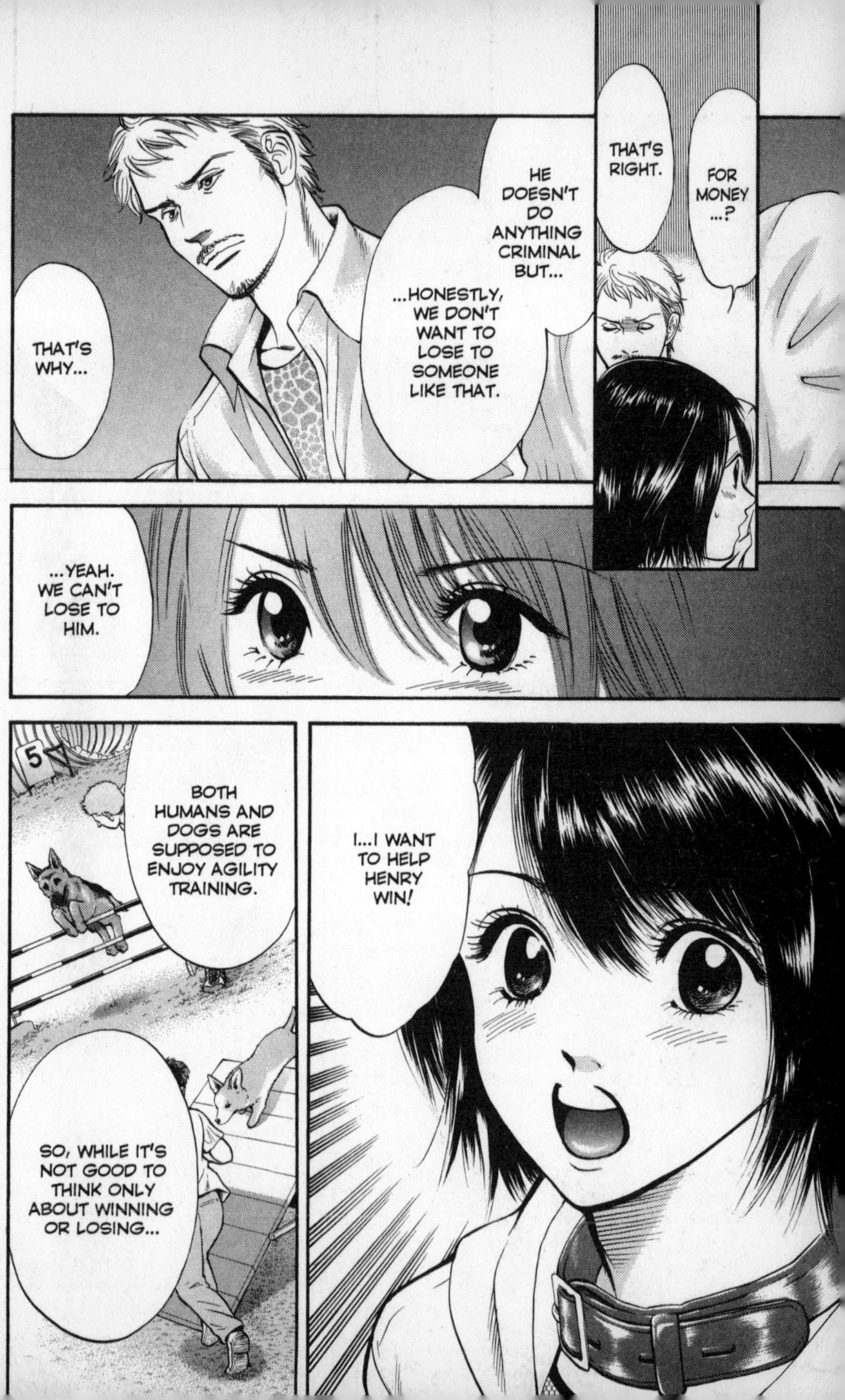
FOR MONEY ...?
THAT'S RIGHT.
HE DOESN'T DO ANYTHING CRIMINAL BUT...
...HONESTLY, WE DON'T WANT TO LOSE TO SOMEONE LIKE THAT.
THAT'S WHY...
...YEAH. WE CAN'T LOSE TO HIM.
I...I WANT TO HELP HENRY WIN!
5
BOTH HUMANS AND DOGS ARE SUPPOSED TO ENJOY AGILITY TRAINING.
SO, WHILE IT'S NOT GOOD TO THINK ONLY ABOUT WINNING OR LOSING...

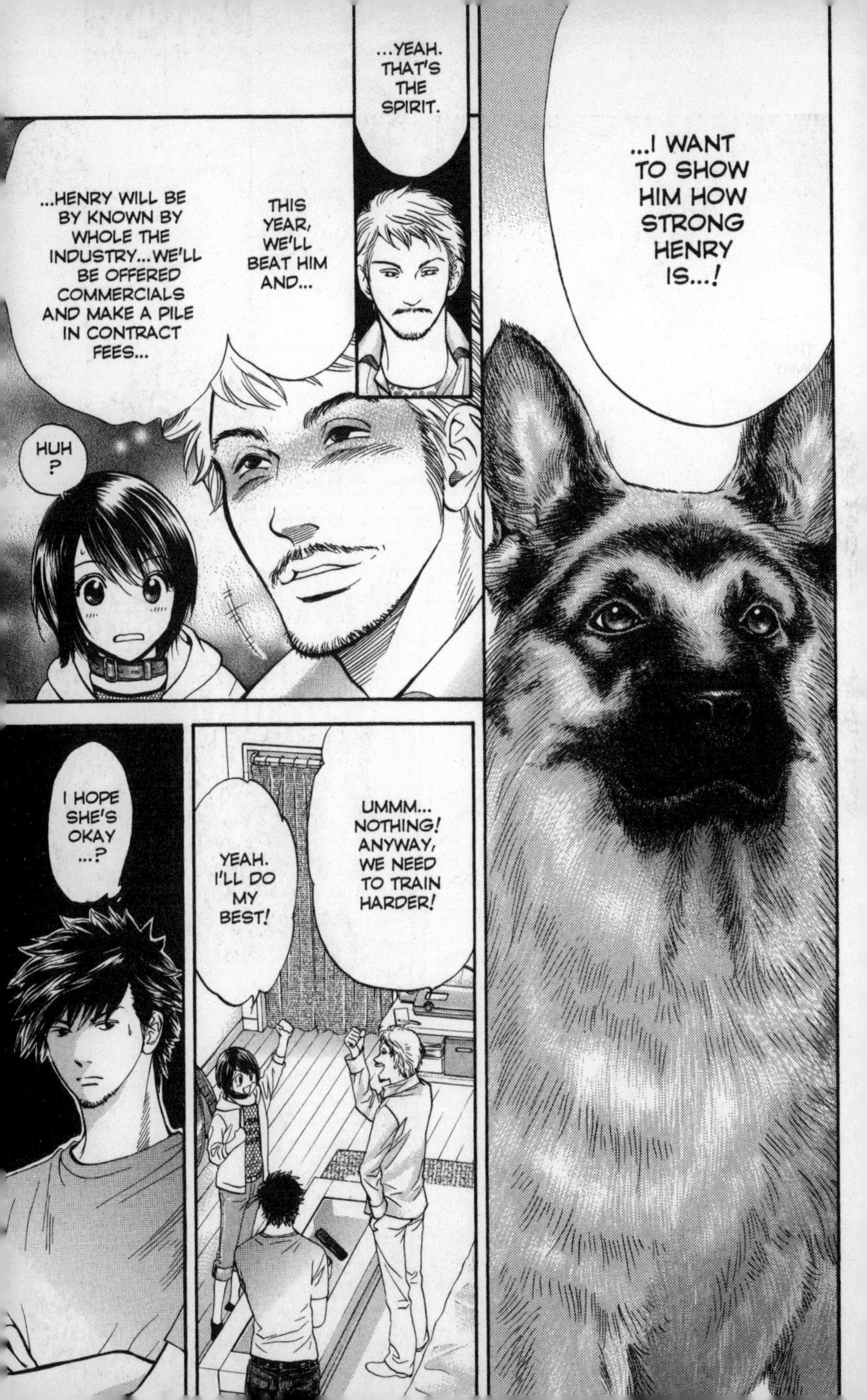
...I WANT TO SHOW HIM HOW STRONG HENRY IS...!
...YEAH. THAT'S THE SPIRIT.
THIS YEAR, WE'LL BEAT HIM AND...
...HENRY WILL BE BY KNOWN BY WHOLE THE INDUSTRY...WE'LL BE OFFERED COMMERCIALS AND MAKE A PILE IN CONTRACT FEES...
HUH?
UMMM... NOTHING! ANYWAY, WE NEED TO TRAIN HARDER!
YEAH. I'LL DO MY BEST!
I HOPE SHE'S OKAY ...?

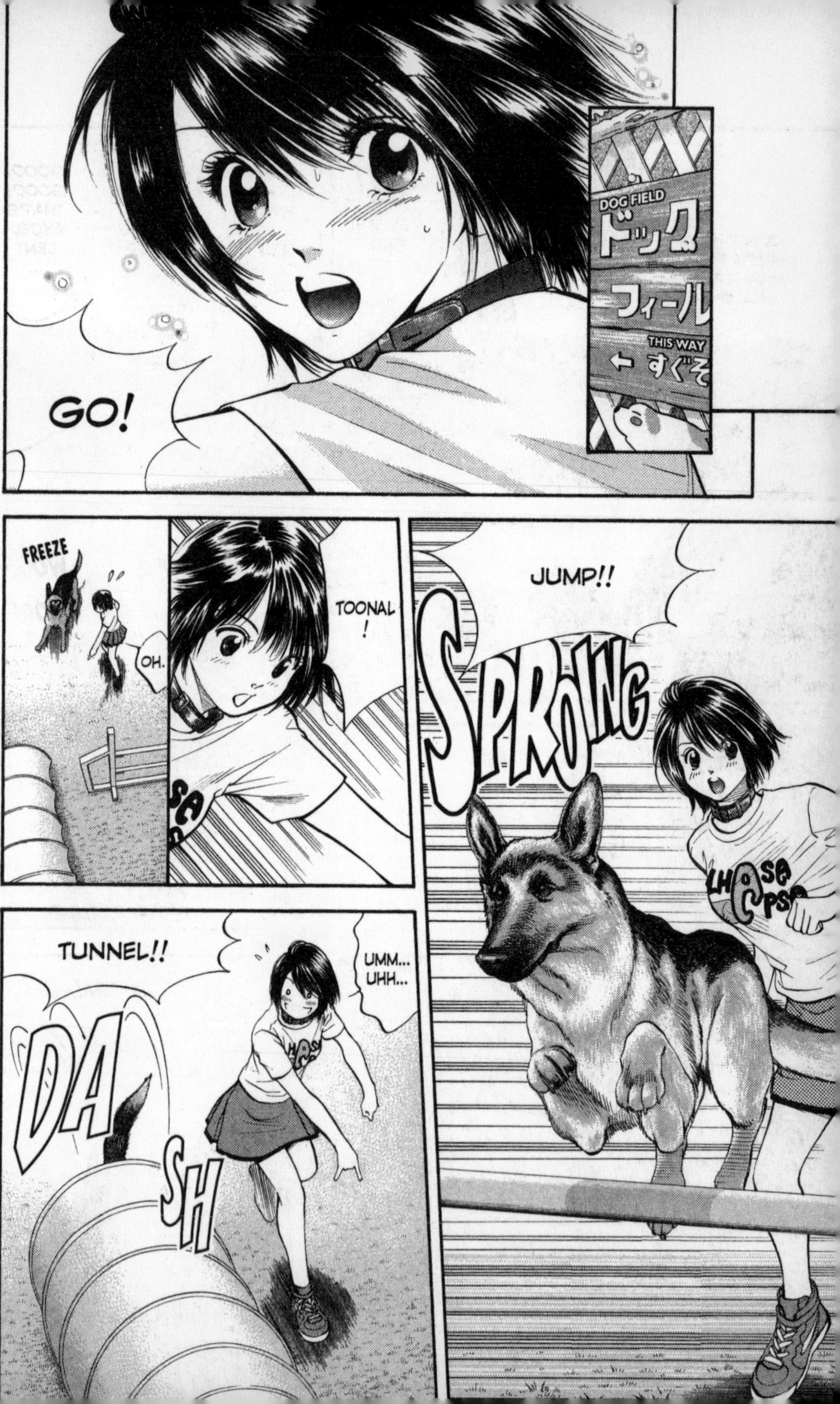
DOG FIELD
ドック
フィール
THIS WAY
← すぐそ
GO!
JUMP!!
SPROING
TOONAL
!
OH.
FREEZE
UMM... UHH...
TUNNEL!!
DASH

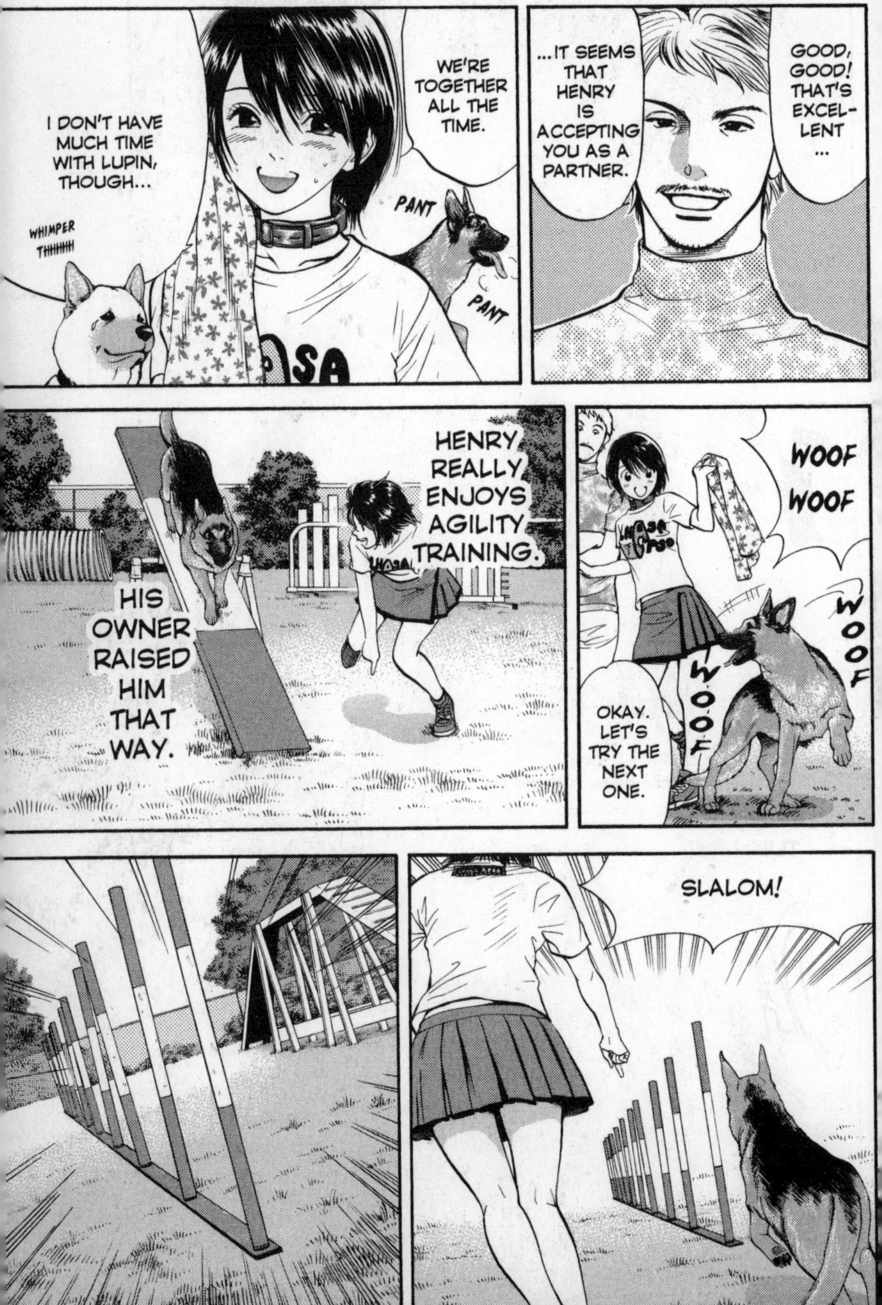
GOOD, GOOD! THAT'S EXCEL-LENT ...
...IT SEEMS THAT HENRY IS ACCEPTING YOU AS A PARTNER.
WE'RE TOGETHER ALL THE TIME.
PANT
PANT
I DON'T HAVE MUCH TIME WITH LUPIN, THOUGH...
WHIMPER
THHHHH
WOOF
WOOF
WOOF
WOOF
OKAY. LET'S TRY THE NEXT ONE.
HENRY REALLY ENJOYS AGILITY TRAINING.
HIS OWNER RAISED HIM THAT WAY.
SLALOM!

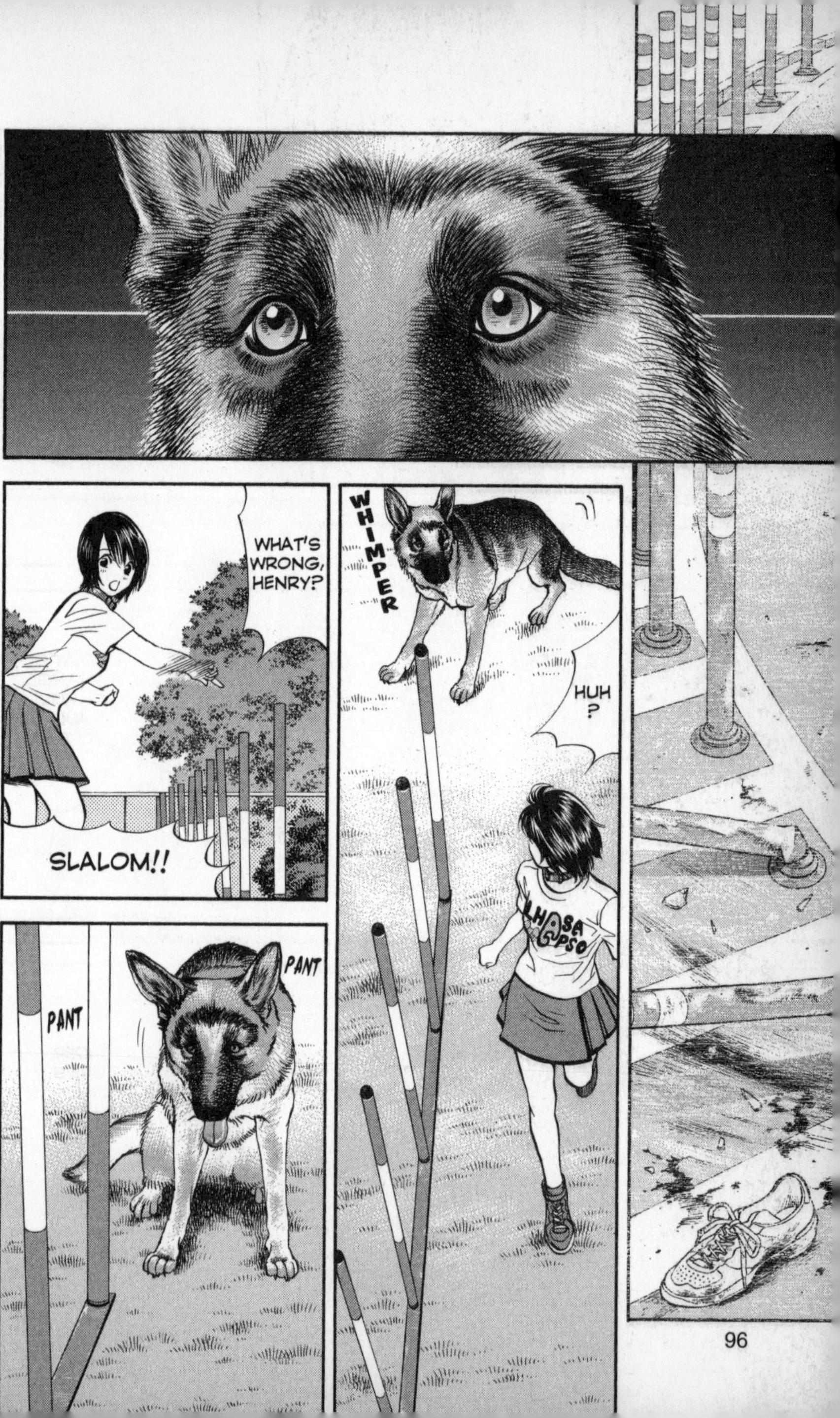
WHIMPER
HUH?
WHAT'S WRONG, HENRY?
SLALOM!!
PANT
PANT

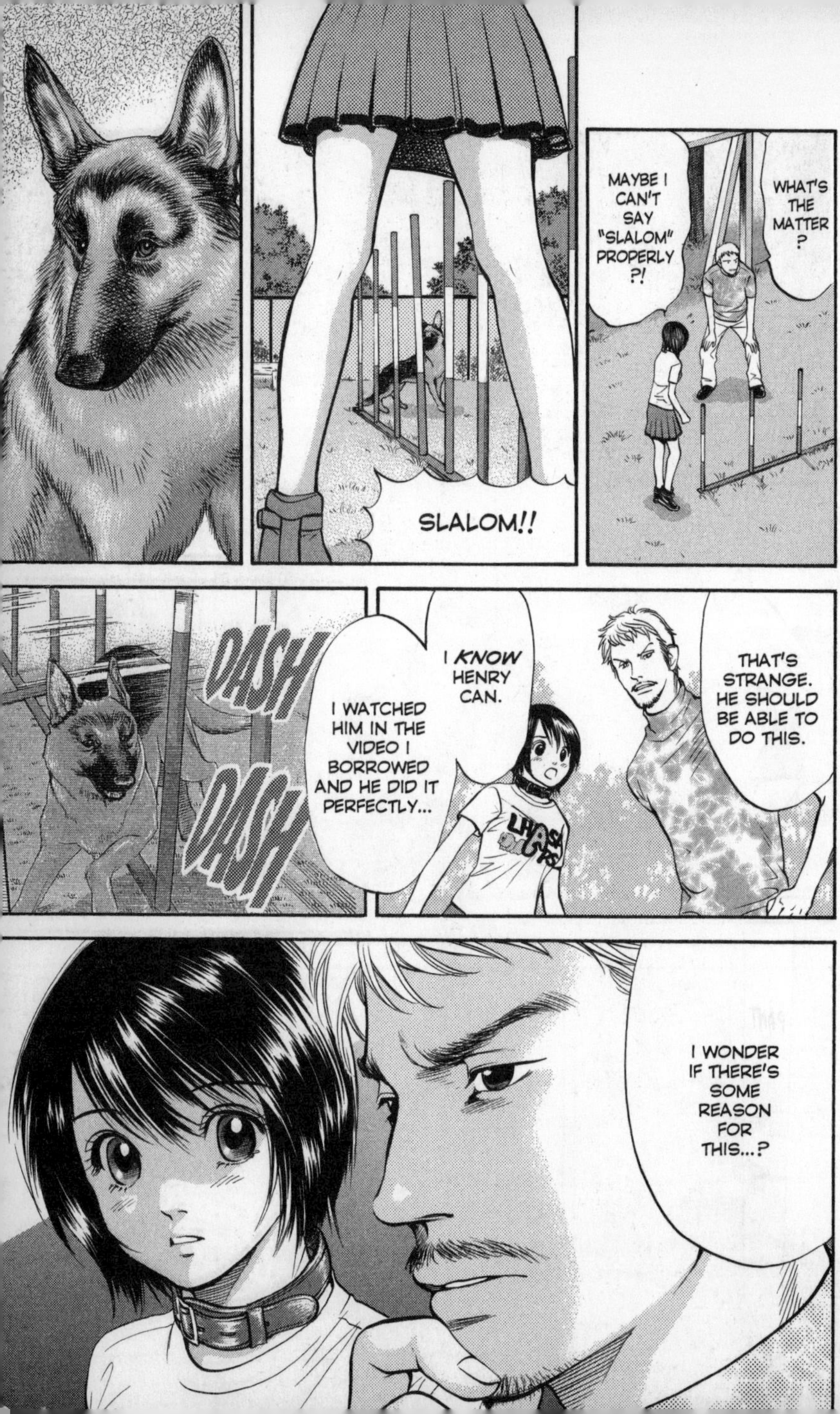
WHAT'S THE MATTER?
MAYBE I CAN'T SAY "SLALOM" PROPERLY?!
SLALOM!!
THAT'S STRANGE. HE SHOULD BE ABLE TO DO THIS.
I KNOW HENRY CAN.
I WATCHED HIM IN THE VIDEO I BORROWED AND HE DID IT PERFECTLY...
DASH
DASH
I WONDER IF THERE'S SOME REASON FOR THIS...?

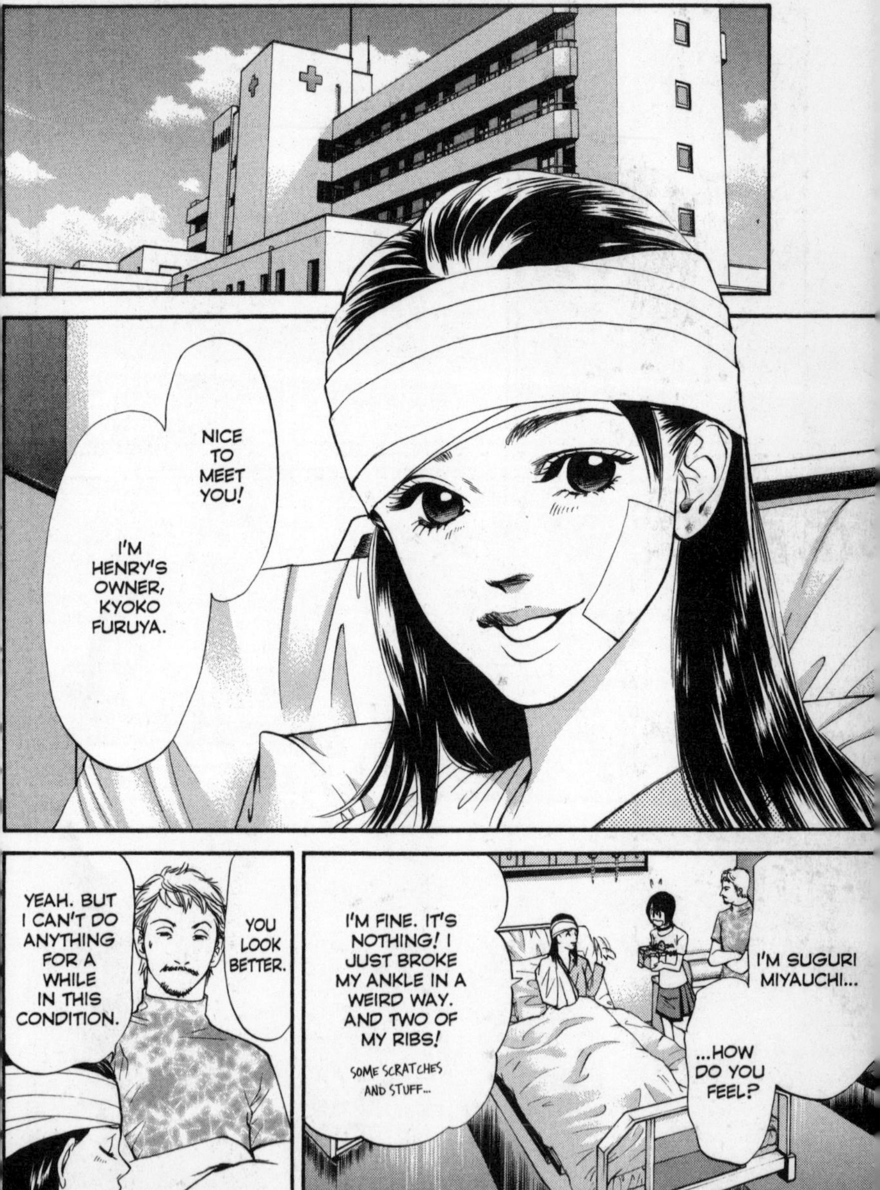
NICE TO MEET YOU!
I'M HENRY'S OWNER, KYOKO FURUYA.
I'M SUGURI MIYAUCHI...
...HOW DO YOU FEEL?
I'M FINE. IT'S NOTHING! I JUST BROKE MY ANKLE IN A WEIRD WAY. AND TWO OF MY RIBS!
SOME SCRATCHES AND STUFF...
YOU LOOK BETTER.
YEAH. BUT I CAN'T DO ANYTHING FOR A WHILE IN THIS CONDITION.

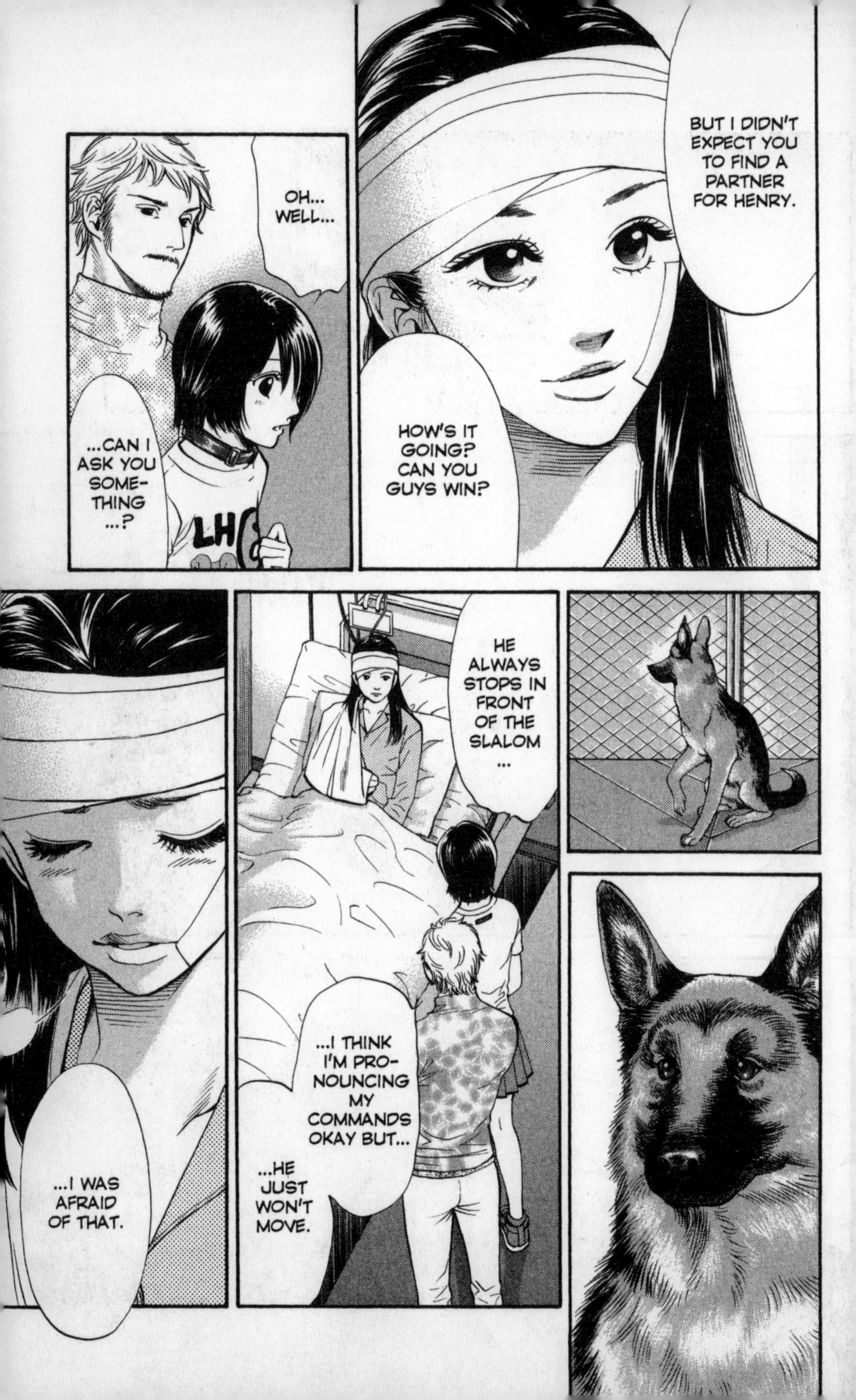
BUT I DIDN'T EXPECT YOU TO FIND A PARTNER FOR HENRY.
HOW'S IT GOING? CAN YOU GUYS WIN?
OH... WELL...
...CAN I ASK YOU SOME-THING ...?
HE ALWAYS STOPS IN FRONT OF THE SLALOM ...
...I THINK I'M PRO-NOUNCING MY COMMANDS OKAY BUT...
...HE JUST WON'T MOVE.
...I WAS AFRAID OF THAT.

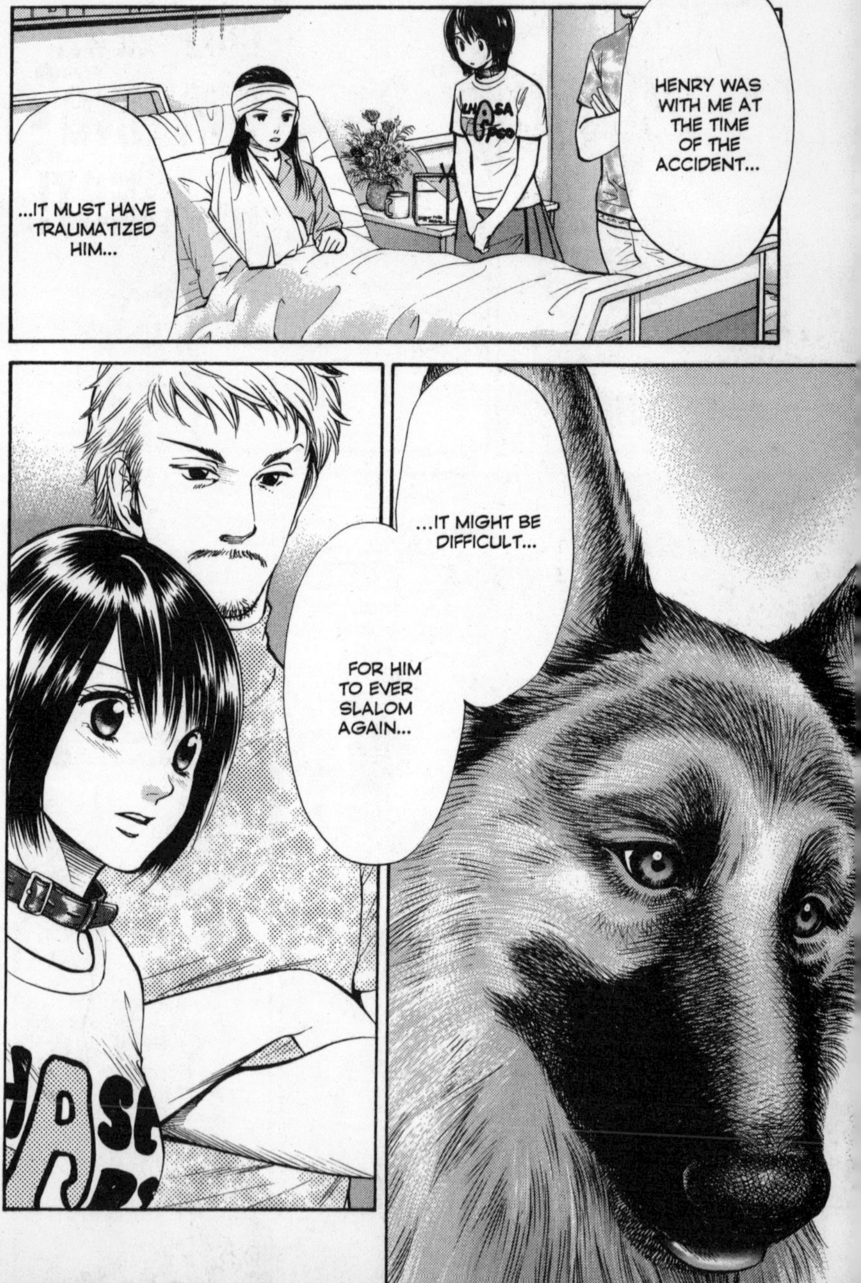
HENRY WAS WITH ME AT THE TIME OF THE ACCIDENT...
...IT MUST HAVE TRAUMATIZED HIM...
...IT MIGHT BE DIFFICULT...
FOR HIM TO EVER SLALOM AGAIN...

CHAPTER 47: STARING CONTEST!

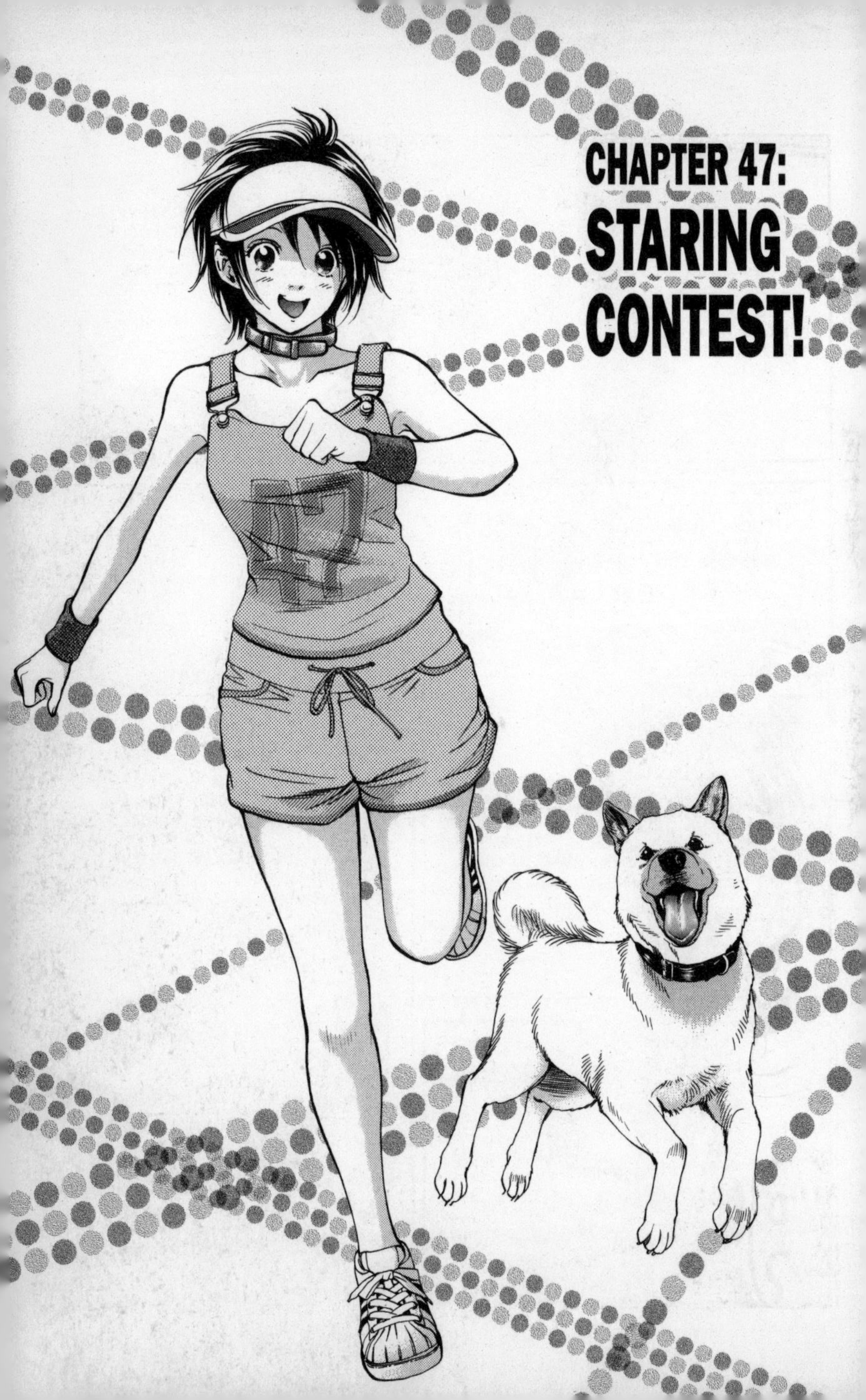

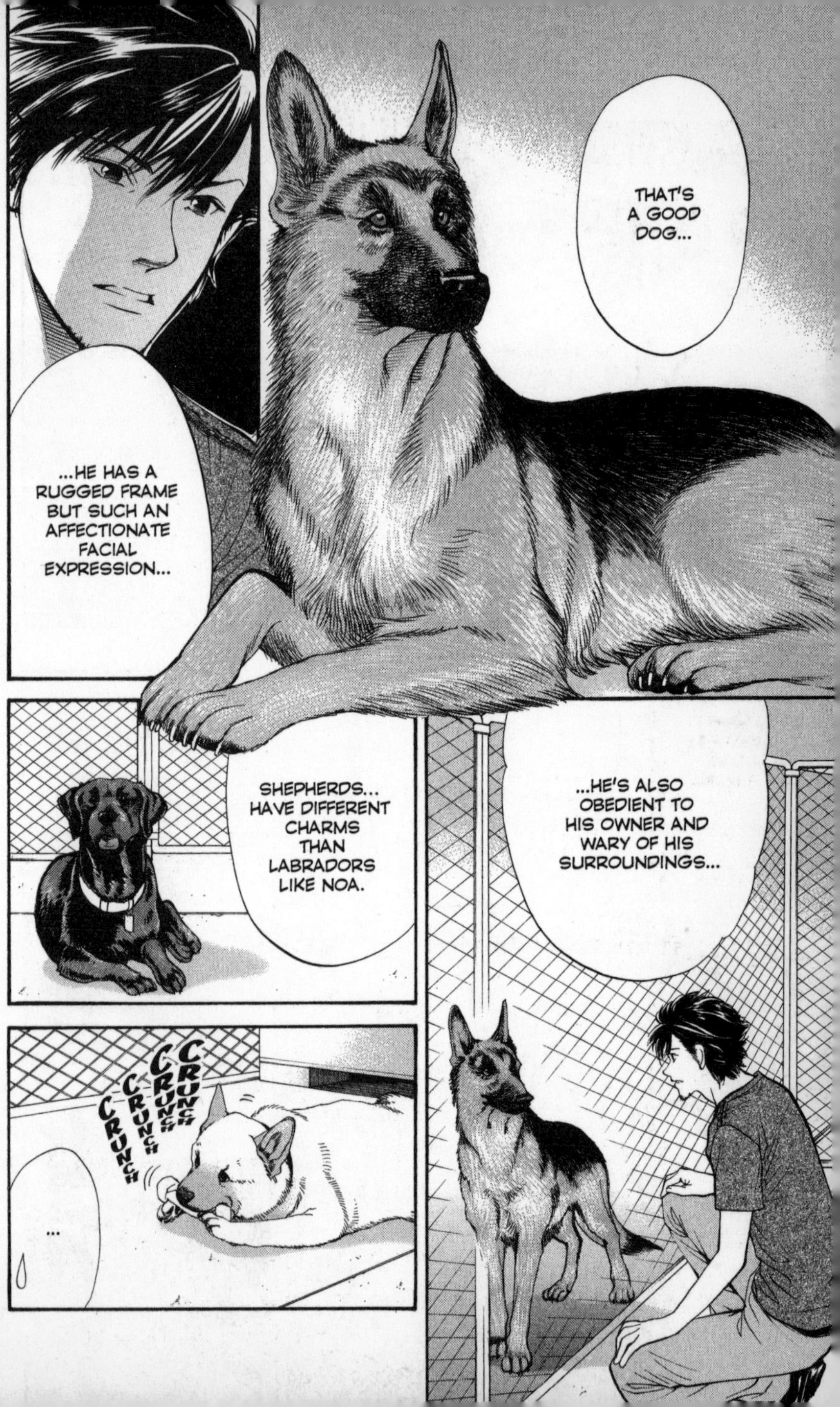
THAT'S A GOOD DOG...
...HE HAS A RUGGED FRAME BUT SUCH AN AFFECTIONATE FACIAL EXPRESSION...
...HE'S ALSO OBEDIENT TO HIS OWNER AND WARY OF HIS SURROUNDINGS...
SHEPHERDS... HAVE DIFFERENT CHARMS THAN LABRADORS LIKE NOA.
CRUNCH
CRUNCH
CRUNCH
CRUNCH
...

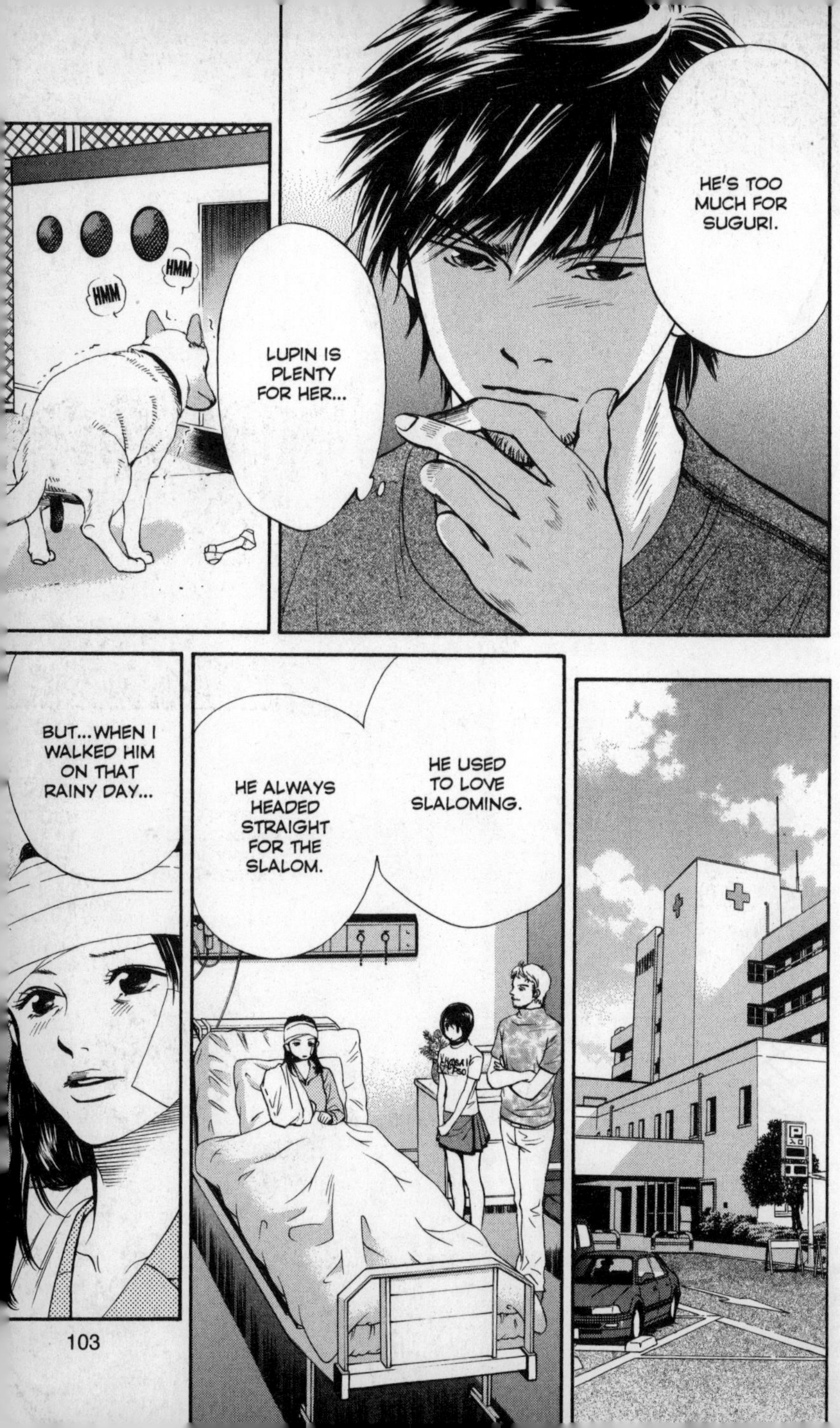
HE'S TOO MUCH FOR SUGURI.
LUPIN IS PLENTY FOR HER...
HMM
HMM
HE USED TO LOVE SLALOMING.
HE ALWAYS HEADED STRAIGHT FOR THE SLALOM.
BUT...WHEN I WALKED HIM ON THAT RAINY DAY...

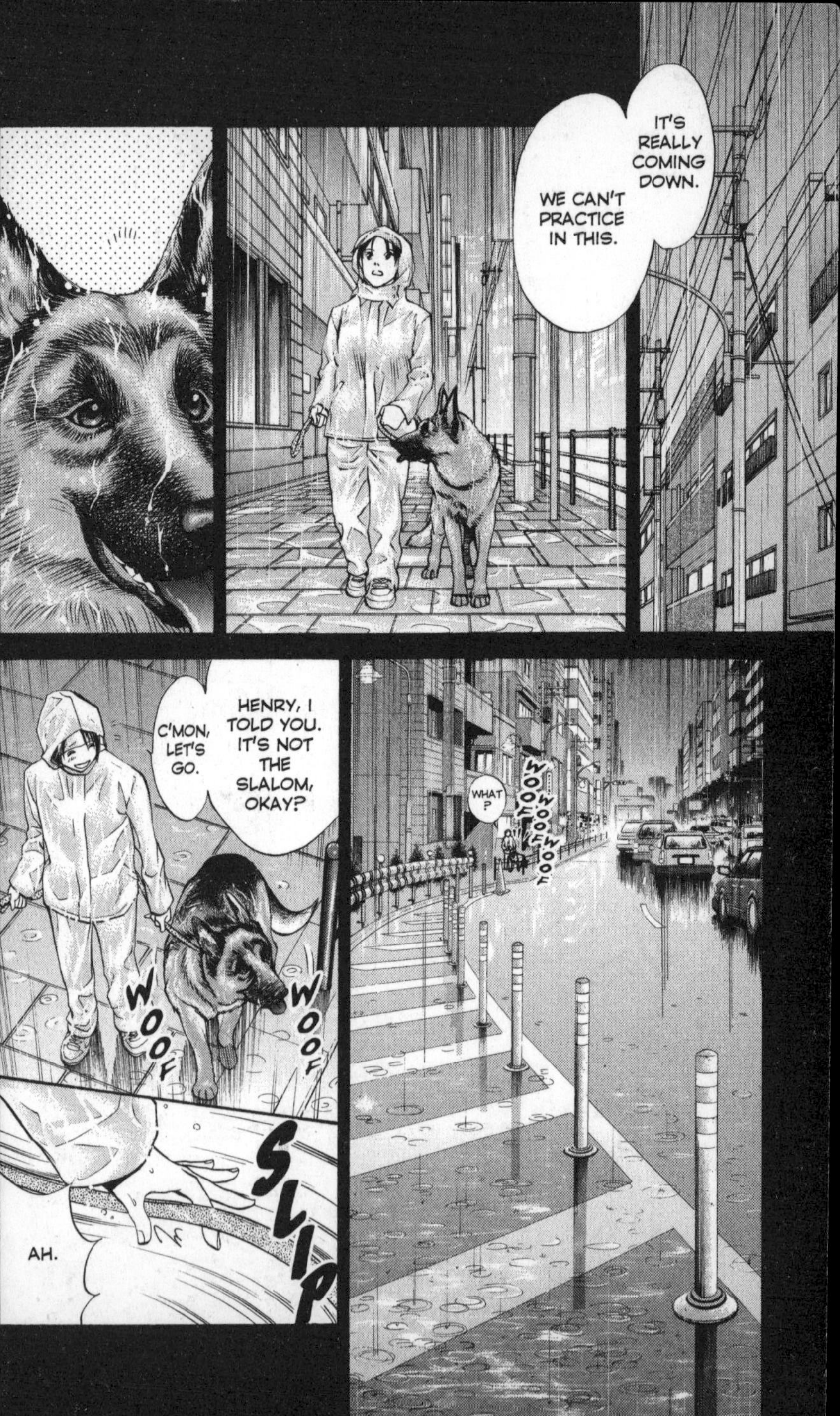
IT'S REALLY COMING DOWN.
WE CAN'T PRACTICE IN THIS.
WHAT?
WOOF WOOF WOOF
HENRY, I TOLD YOU. IT'S NOT THE SLALOM, OKAY?
C'MON, LET'S GO.
WOOF
WOOF
SLIP
AH.

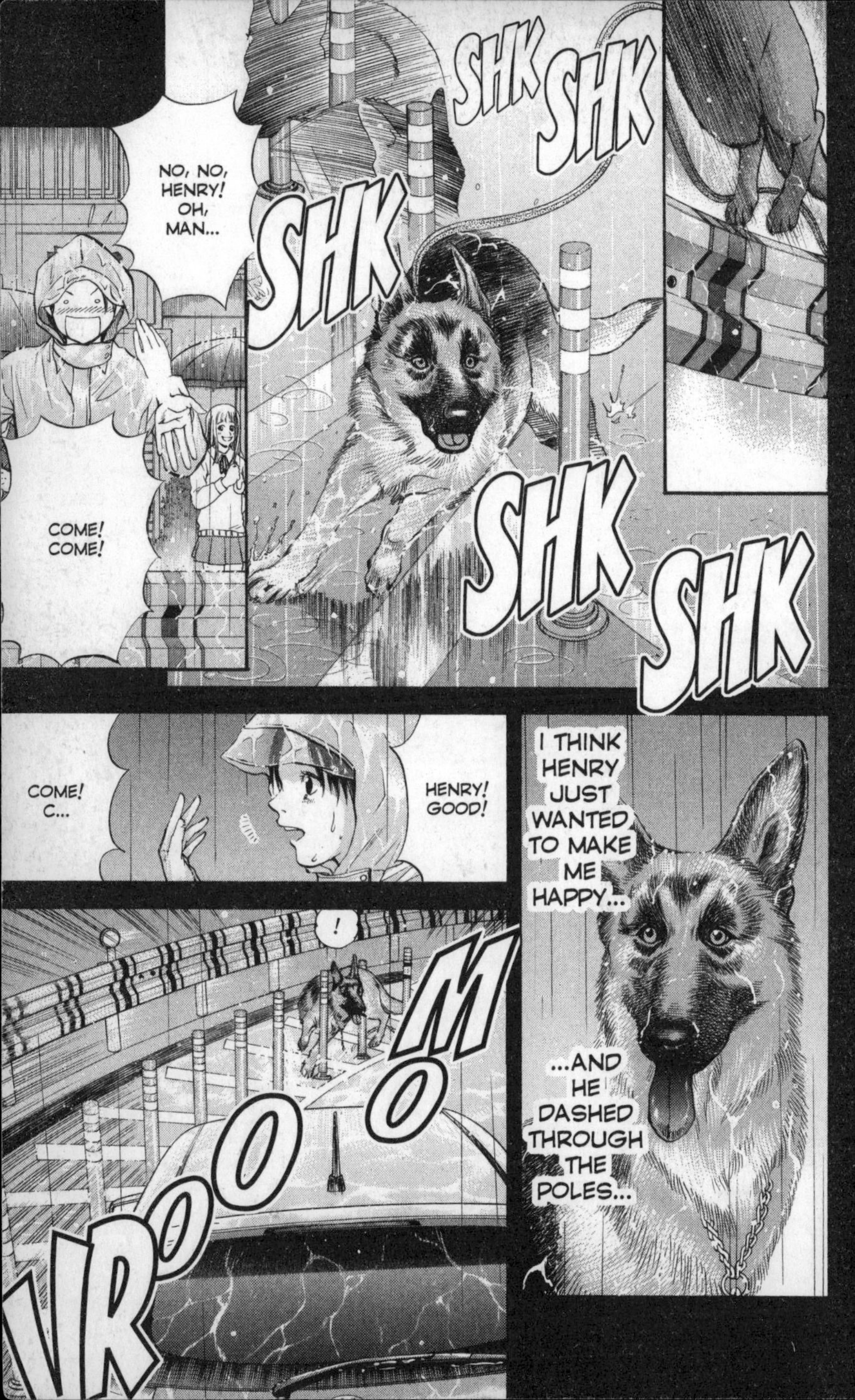
SHK SHK
SHK
SHK SHK
SHK
NO, NO, HENRY! OH, MAN...
COME! COME!
I THINK HENRY JUST WANTED TO MAKE ME HAPPY...
...AND HE DASHED THROUGH THE POLES...
HENRY! GOOD!
COME! C...
!
VROOOOM

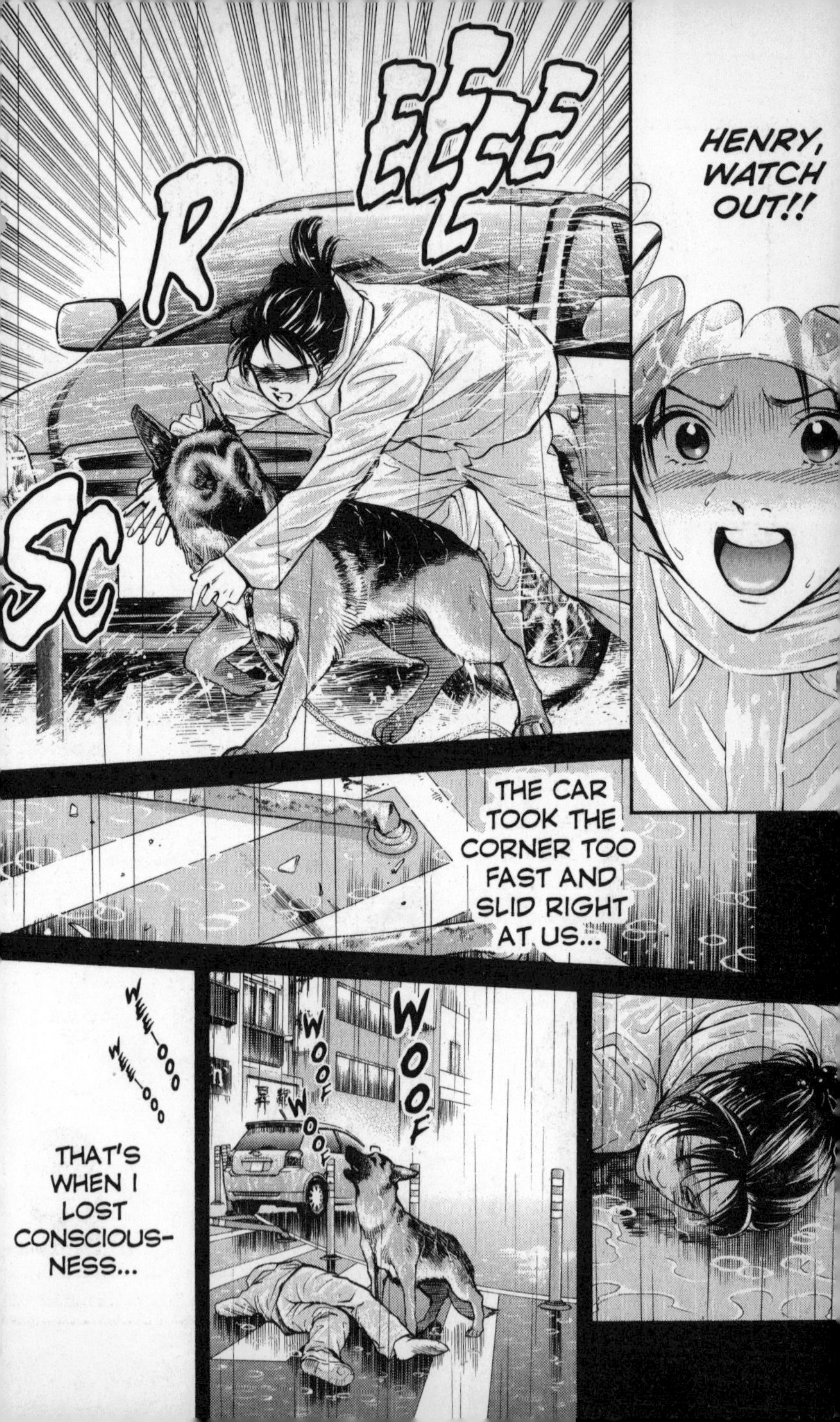
HENRY, WATCH OUT!!
R
SC
THE CAR TOOK THE CORNER TOO FAST AND SLID RIGHT AT US...
WOOF
WOOF
WOOF
WWW—OOO
WWW—OOO
THAT'S WHEN I LOST CONSCIOUS-NESS...

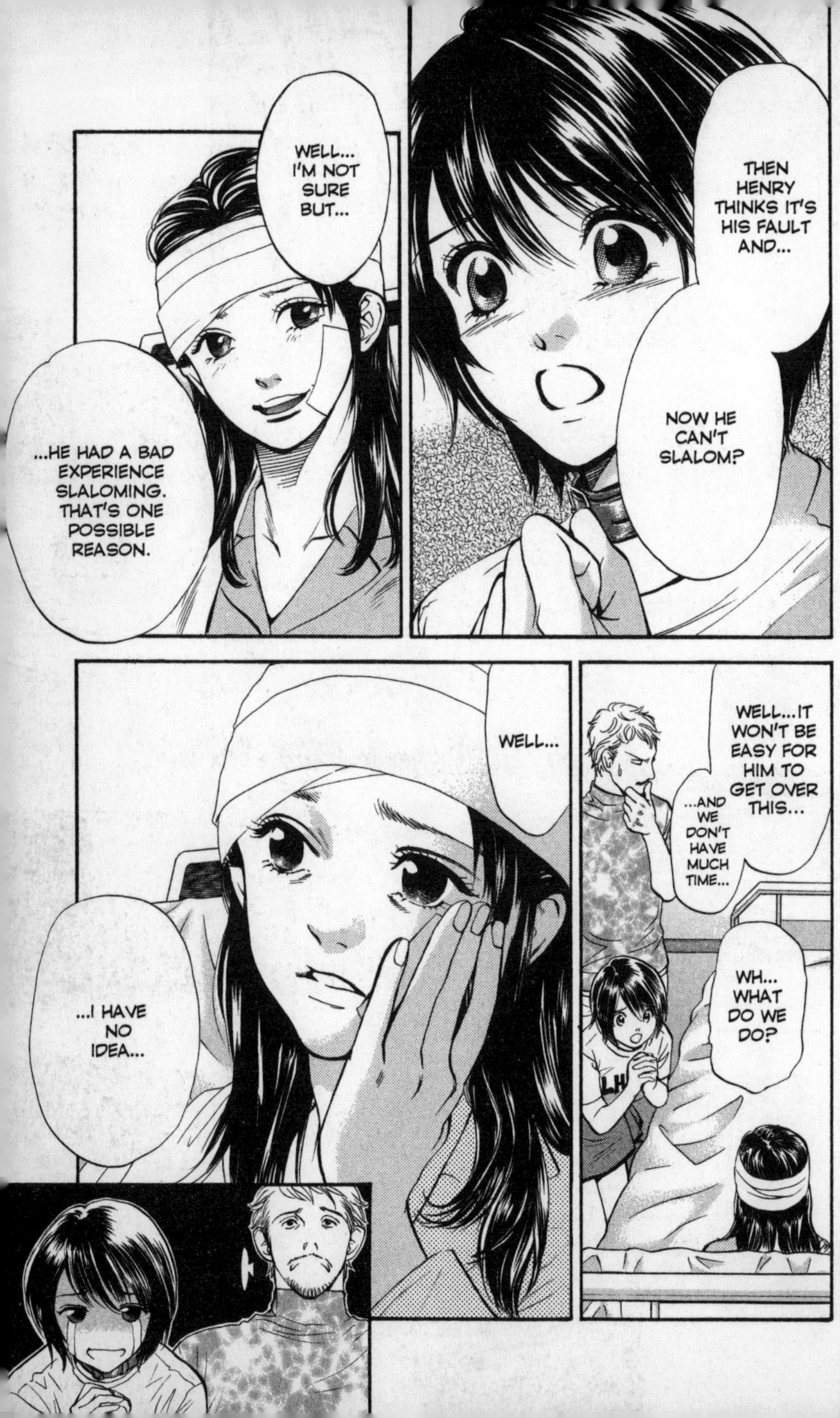
THEN HENRY THINKS IT'S HIS FAULT AND...
NOW HE CAN'T SLALOM?
WELL... I'M NOT SURE BUT...
...HE HAD A BAD EXPERIENCE SLALOMING. THAT'S ONE POSSIBLE REASON.
WELL...IT WON'T BE EASY FOR HIM TO GET OVER THIS...
...AND WE DON'T HAVE MUCH TIME...
WH... WHAT DO WE DO?
WELL...
...I HAVE NO IDEA...

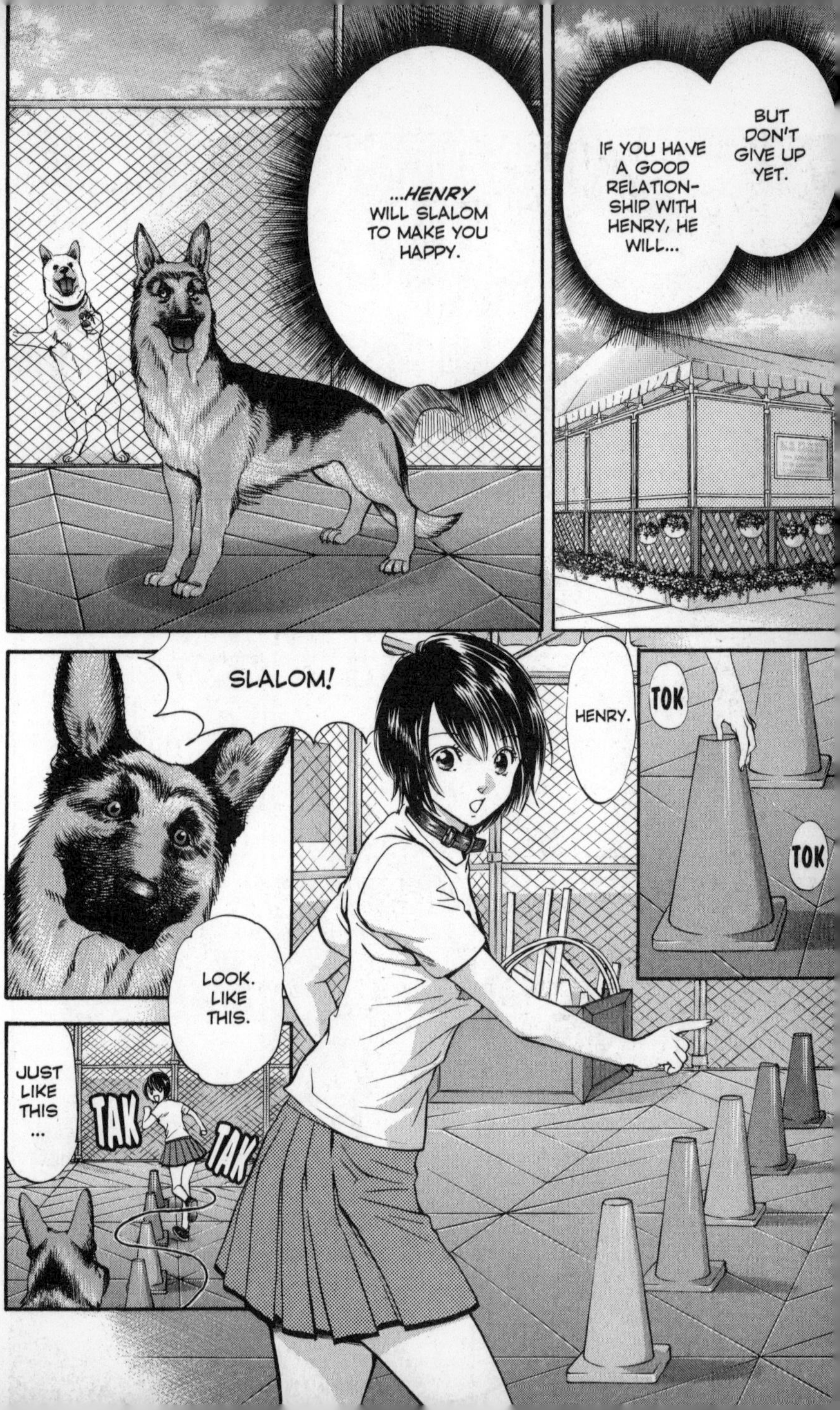
BUT DON'T GIVE UP YET.
IF YOU HAVE A GOOD RELATIONSHIP WITH HENRY, HE WILL...
...HENRY WILL SLALOM TO MAKE YOU HAPPY.
TOK
HENRY.
TOK
SLALOM!
LOOK. LIKE THIS.
JUST LIKE THIS ...
TAK
TAK

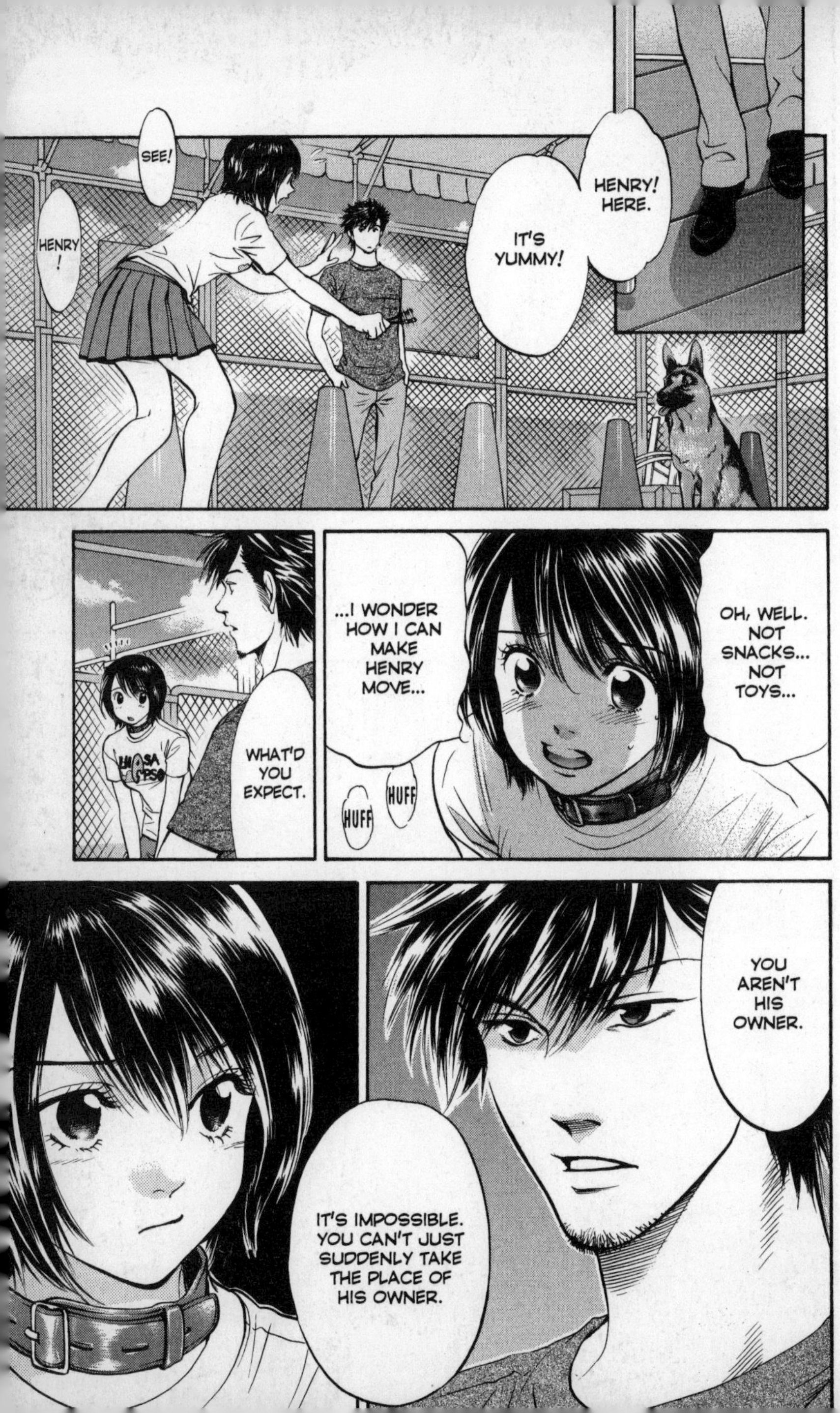
HENRY! HERE.
IT'S YUMMY!
SEE!
HENRY!
OH, WELL. NOT SNACKS... NOT TOYS...
...I WONDER HOW I CAN MAKE HENRY MOVE...
HUFF
HUFF
WHAT'D YOU EXPECT.
YOU AREN'T HIS OWNER.
IT'S IMPOSSIBLE. YOU CAN'T JUST SUDDENLY TAKE THE PLACE OF HIS OWNER.

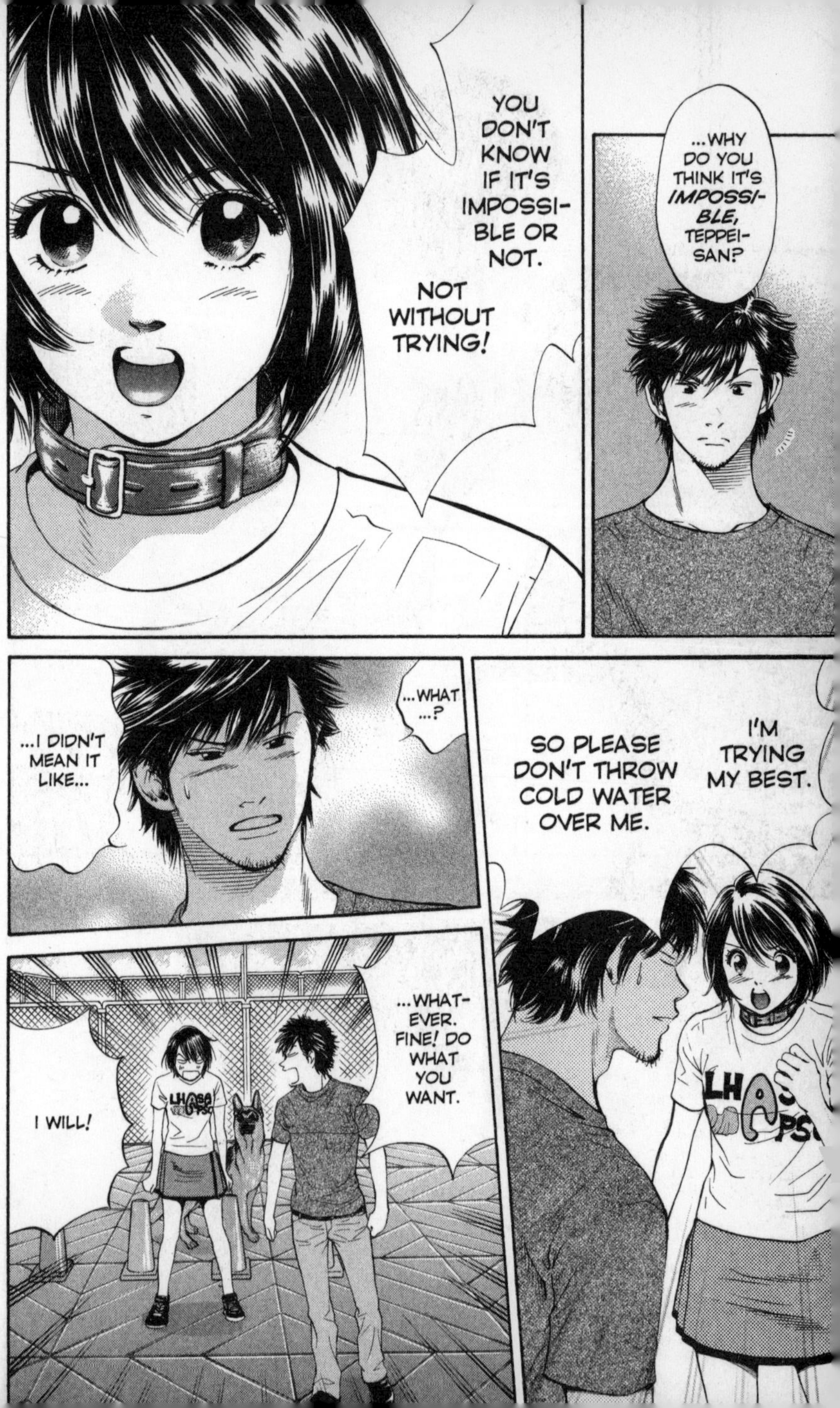
...WHY DO YOU THINK IT'S *IMPOSSIBLE,* TEPPEI-SAN?
YOU DON'T KNOW IF IT'S IMPOSSIBLE OR NOT.
NOT WITHOUT TRYING!
I'M TRYING MY BEST.
SO PLEASE DON'T THROW COLD WATER OVER ME.
...WHAT ...?
...I DIDN'T MEAN IT LIKE...
...WHATEVER. FINE! DO WHAT YOU WANT.
I WILL!

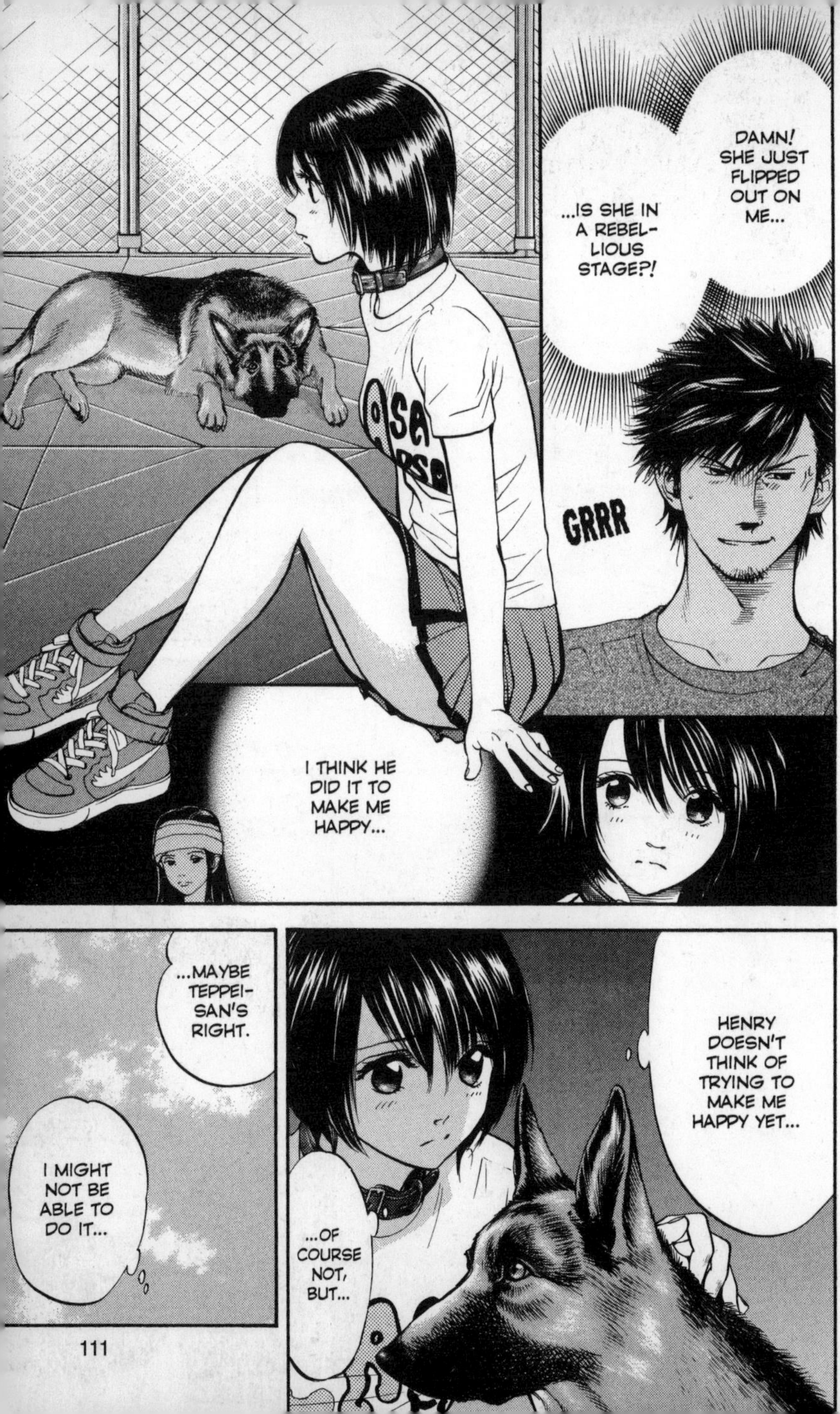
DAMN! SHE JUST FLIPPED OUT ON ME...
...IS SHE IN A REBEL-LIOUS STAGE?!
GRRR
I THINK HE DID IT TO MAKE ME HAPPY...
HENRY DOESN'T THINK OF TRYING TO MAKE ME HAPPY YET...
...OF COURSE NOT, BUT...
...MAYBE TEPPEI-SAN'S RIGHT.
I MIGHT NOT BE ABLE TO DO IT...

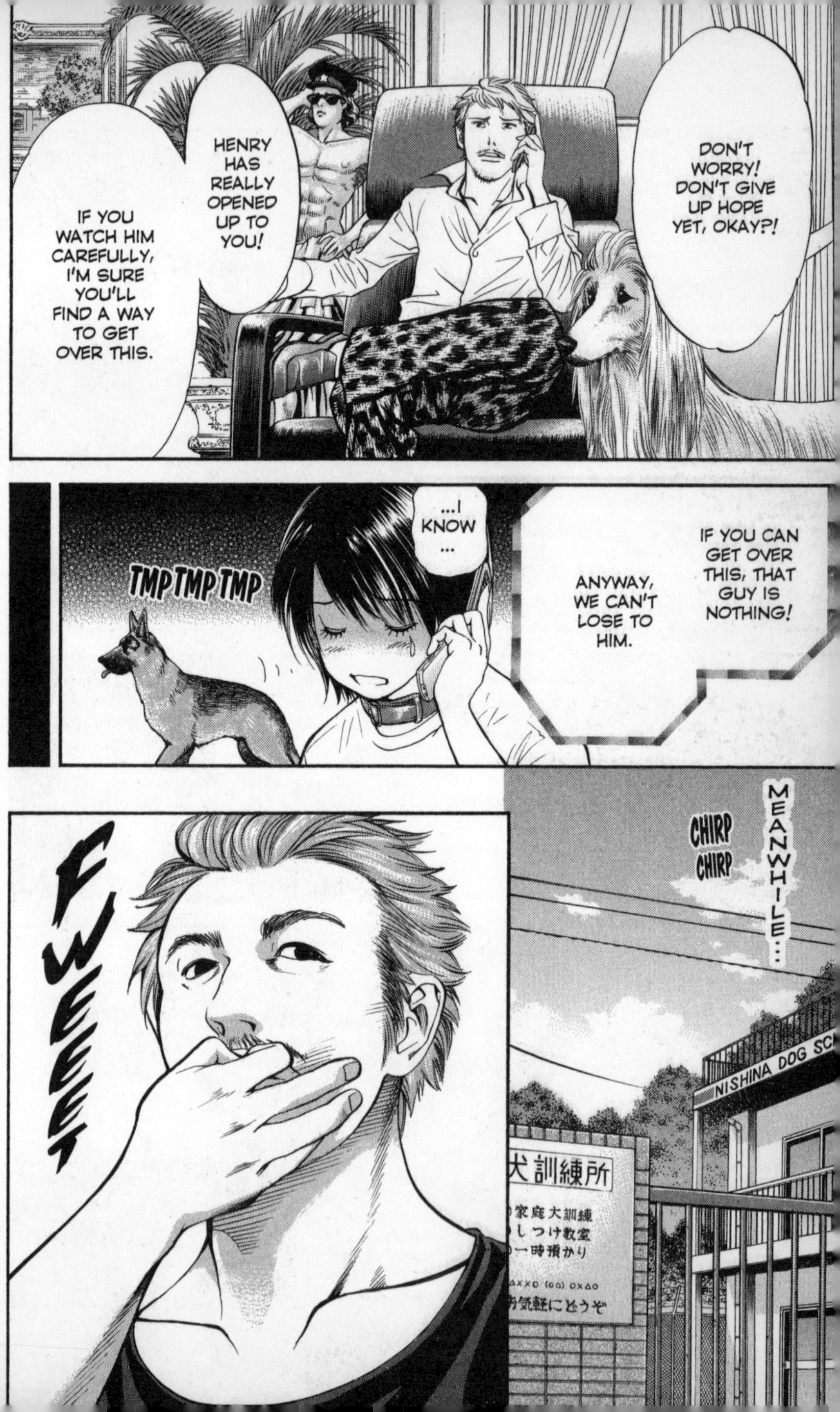
DON'T WORRY! DON'T GIVE UP HOPE YET, OKAY?!
HENRY HAS REALLY OPENED UP TO YOU!
IF YOU WATCH HIM CAREFULLY, I'M SURE YOU'LL FIND A WAY TO GET OVER THIS.
IF YOU CAN GET OVER THIS, THAT GUY IS NOTHING!
ANYWAY, WE CAN'T LOSE TO HIM.
...I KNOW ...
TMP TMP TMP
MEANWHILE...
CHIRP CHIRP
NISHINA DOG SC
犬訓練所
一時預かり
FWEEEET

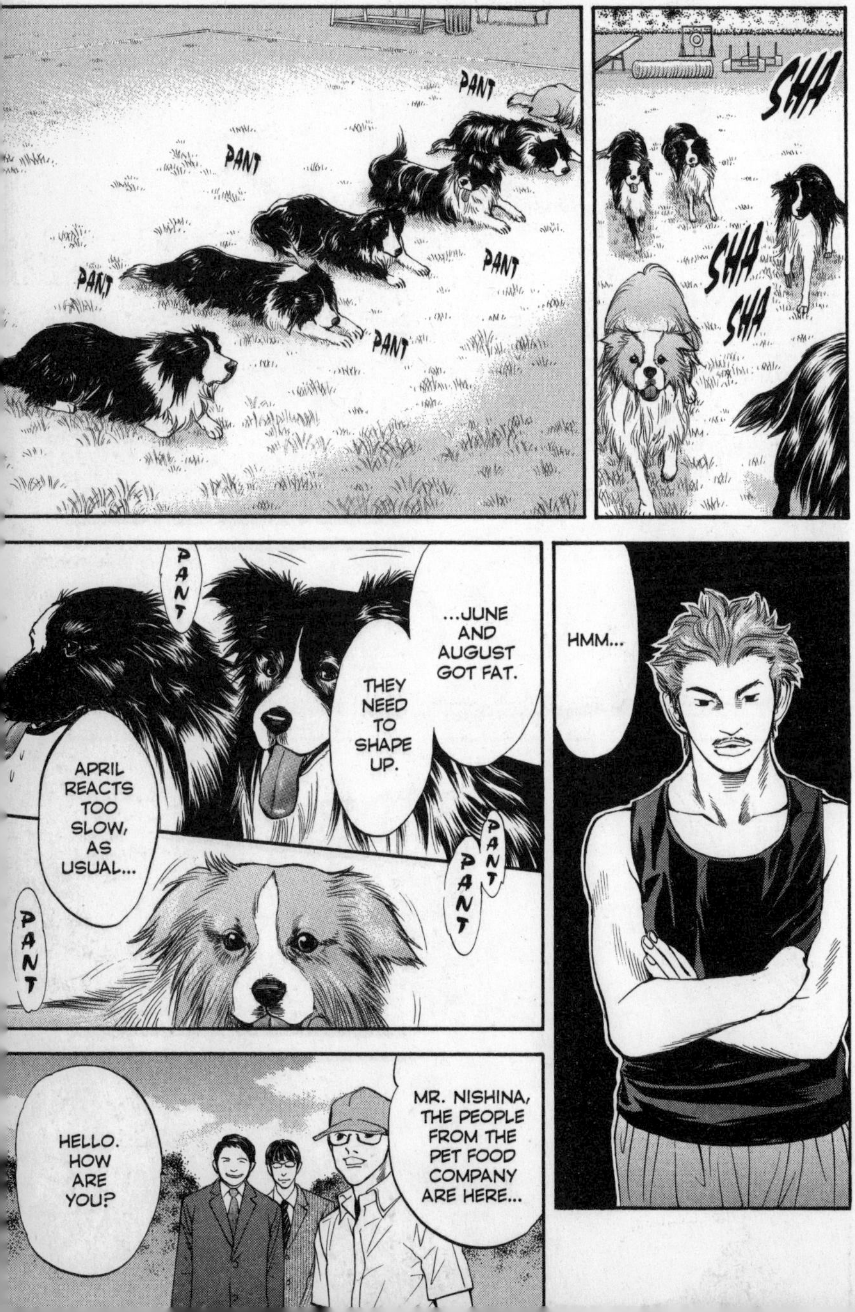
SHA
SHA
SHA
PANT
PANT
PANT
PANT
PANT
HMM...
...JUNE AND AUGUST GOT FAT.
THEY NEED TO SHAPE UP.
PANT
PANT
PANT
APRIL REACTS TOO SLOW, AS USUAL...
PANT
MR. NISHINA, THE PEOPLE FROM THE PET FOOD COMPANY ARE HERE...
HELLO. HOW ARE YOU?

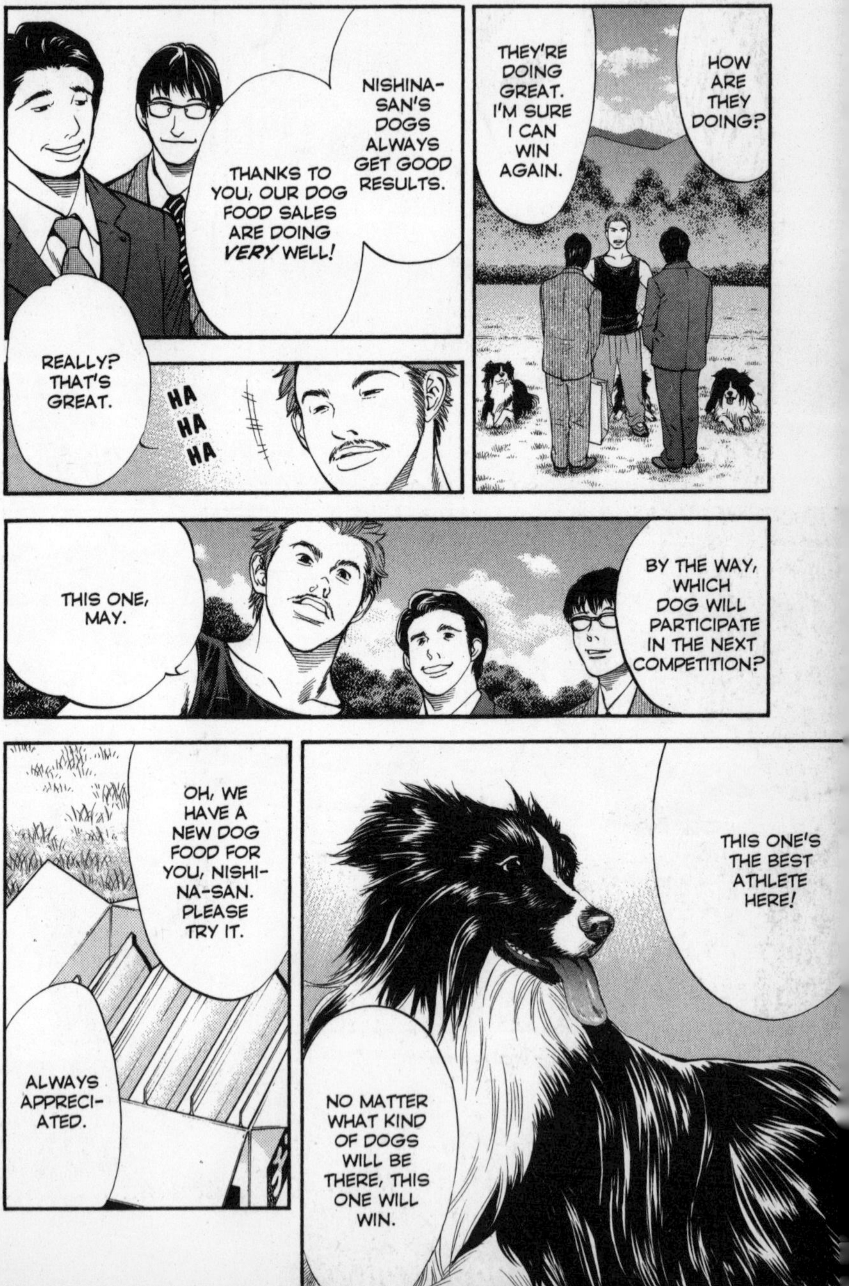
HOW ARE THEY DOING?
THEY'RE DOING GREAT. I'M SURE I CAN WIN AGAIN.
NISHINA-SAN'S DOGS ALWAYS GET GOOD RESULTS.
THANKS TO YOU, OUR DOG FOOD SALES ARE DOING *VERY* WELL!
HA HA HA
REALLY? THAT'S GREAT.
BY THE WAY, WHICH DOG WILL PARTICIPATE IN THE NEXT COMPETITION?
THIS ONE, MAY.
THIS ONE'S THE BEST ATHLETE HERE!
NO MATTER WHAT KIND OF DOGS WILL BE THERE, THIS ONE WILL WIN.
OH, WE HAVE A NEW DOG FOOD FOR YOU, NISHI-NA-SAN. PLEASE TRY IT.
ALWAYS APPRECI-ATED.

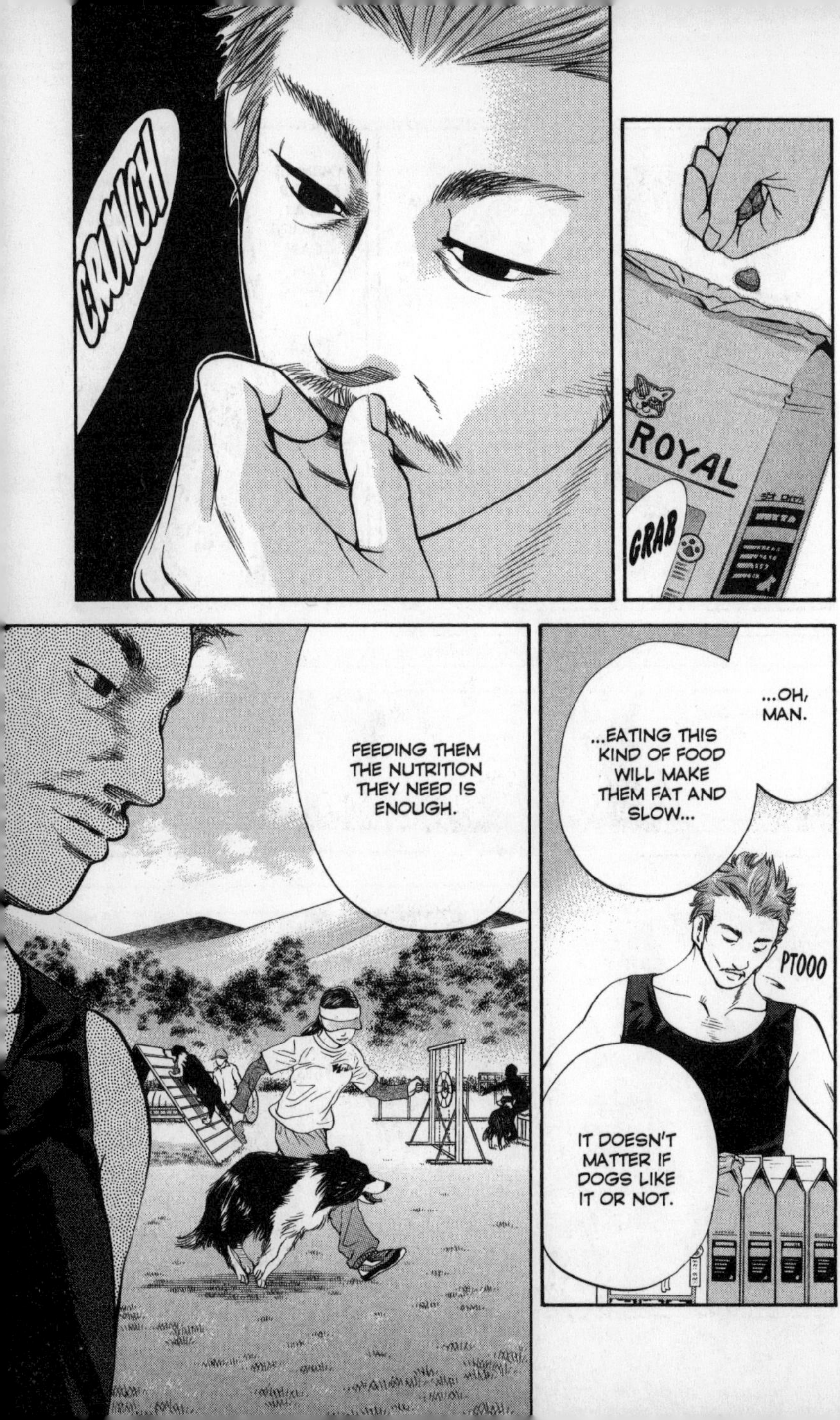
ROYAL
GRAB
CRUNCH
...OH, MAN.
...EATING THIS KIND OF FOOD WILL MAKE THEM FAT AND SLOW...
PTOOO
IT DOESN'T MATTER IF DOGS LIKE IT OR NOT.
FEEDING THEM THE NUTRITION THEY NEED IS ENOUGH.

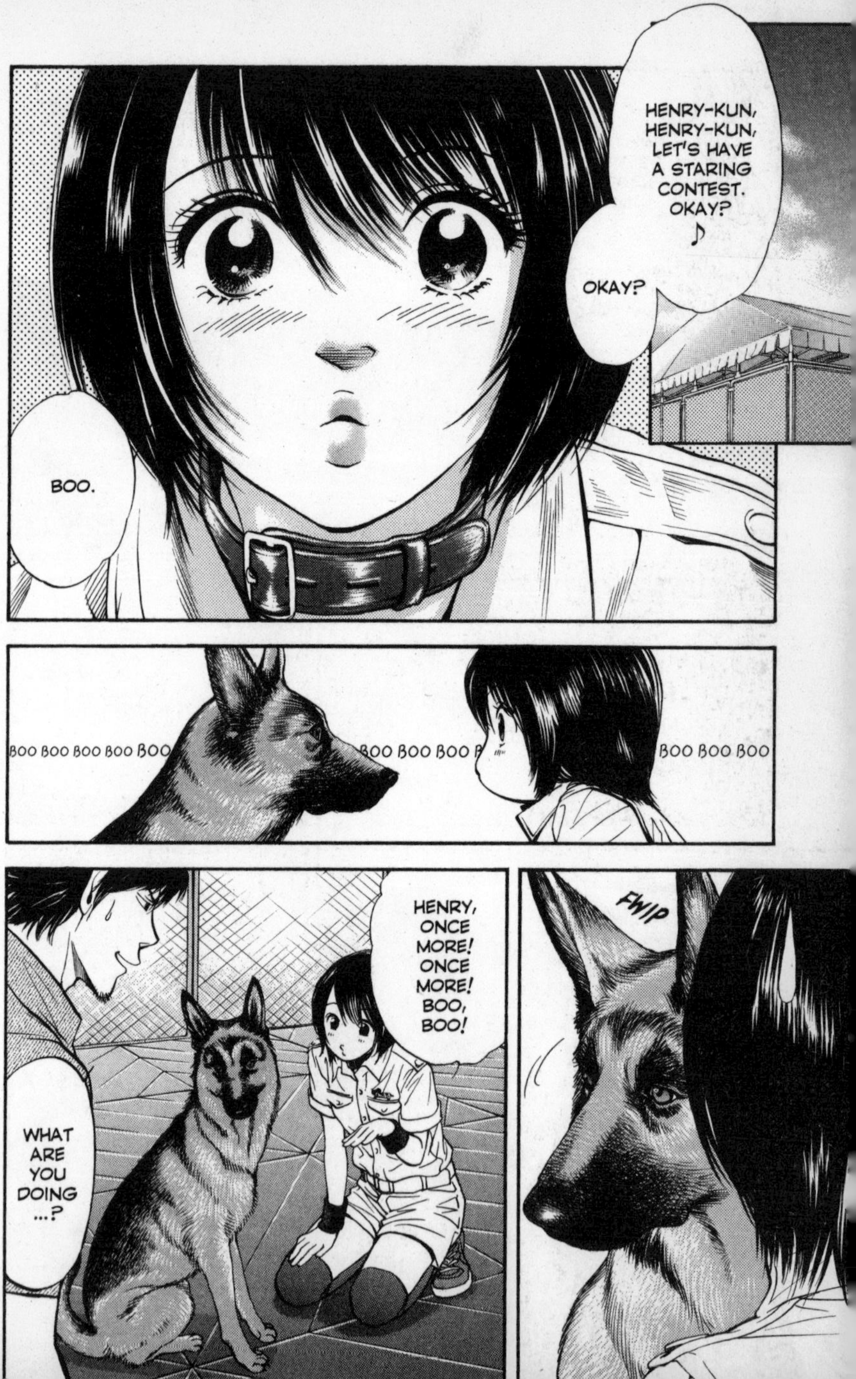
HENRY-KUN, HENRY-KUN, LET'S HAVE A STARING CONTEST. OKAY? ♪
OKAY?
BOO.
BOO BOO BOO
BOO BOO BOO
BOO BOO BOO BOO BOO
FWIP
HENRY, ONCE MORE! ONCE MORE! BOO, BOO!
WHAT ARE YOU DOING ...?

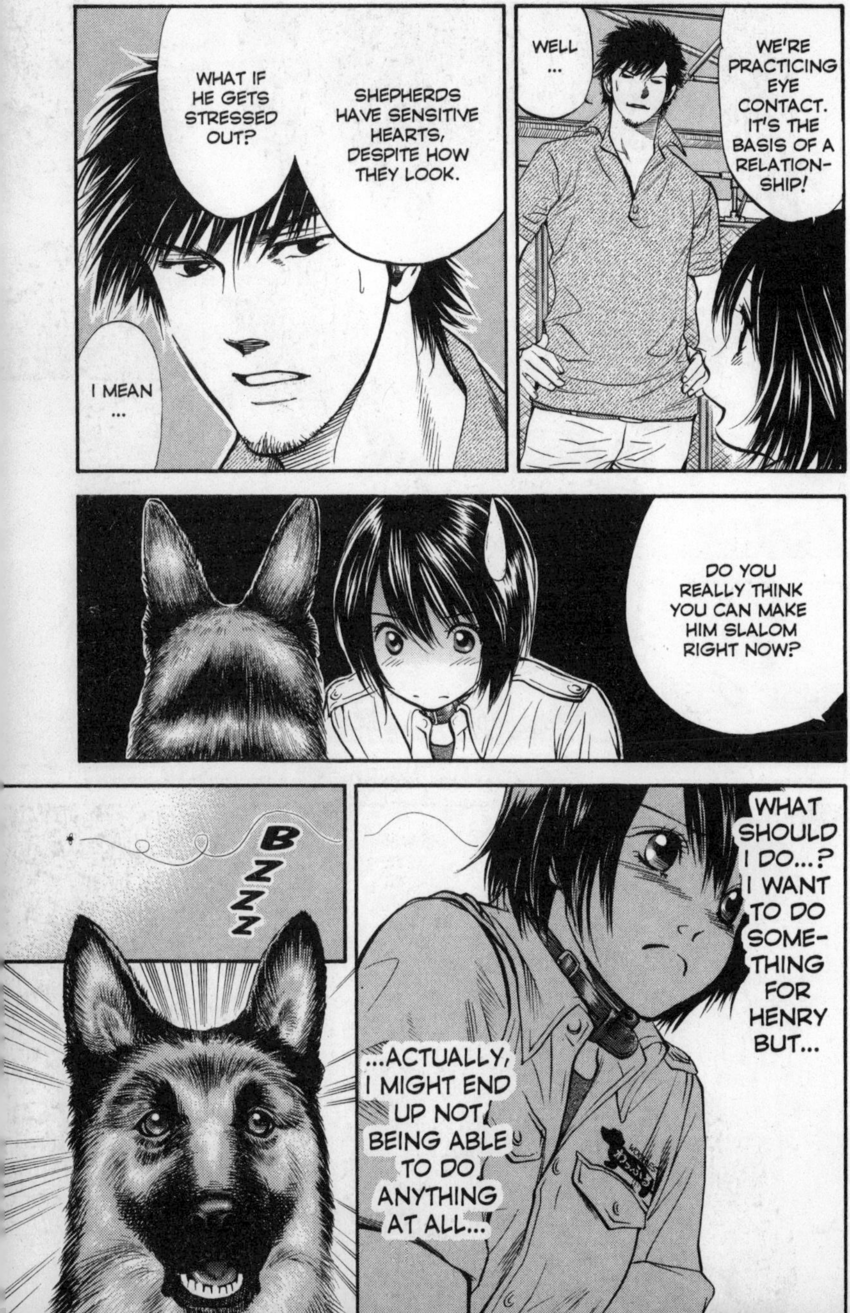
WE'RE PRACTICING EYE CONTACT. IT'S THE BASIS OF A RELATION-SHIP!
WELL ...
SHEPHERDS HAVE SENSITIVE HEARTS, DESPITE HOW THEY LOOK.
WHAT IF HE GETS STRESSED OUT?
I MEAN ...
DO YOU REALLY THINK YOU CAN MAKE HIM SLALOM RIGHT NOW?
WHAT SHOULD I DO...? I WANT TO DO SOME-THING FOR HENRY BUT...
...ACTUALLY, I MIGHT END UP NOT BEING ABLE TO DO ANYTHING AT ALL...
BZZZ

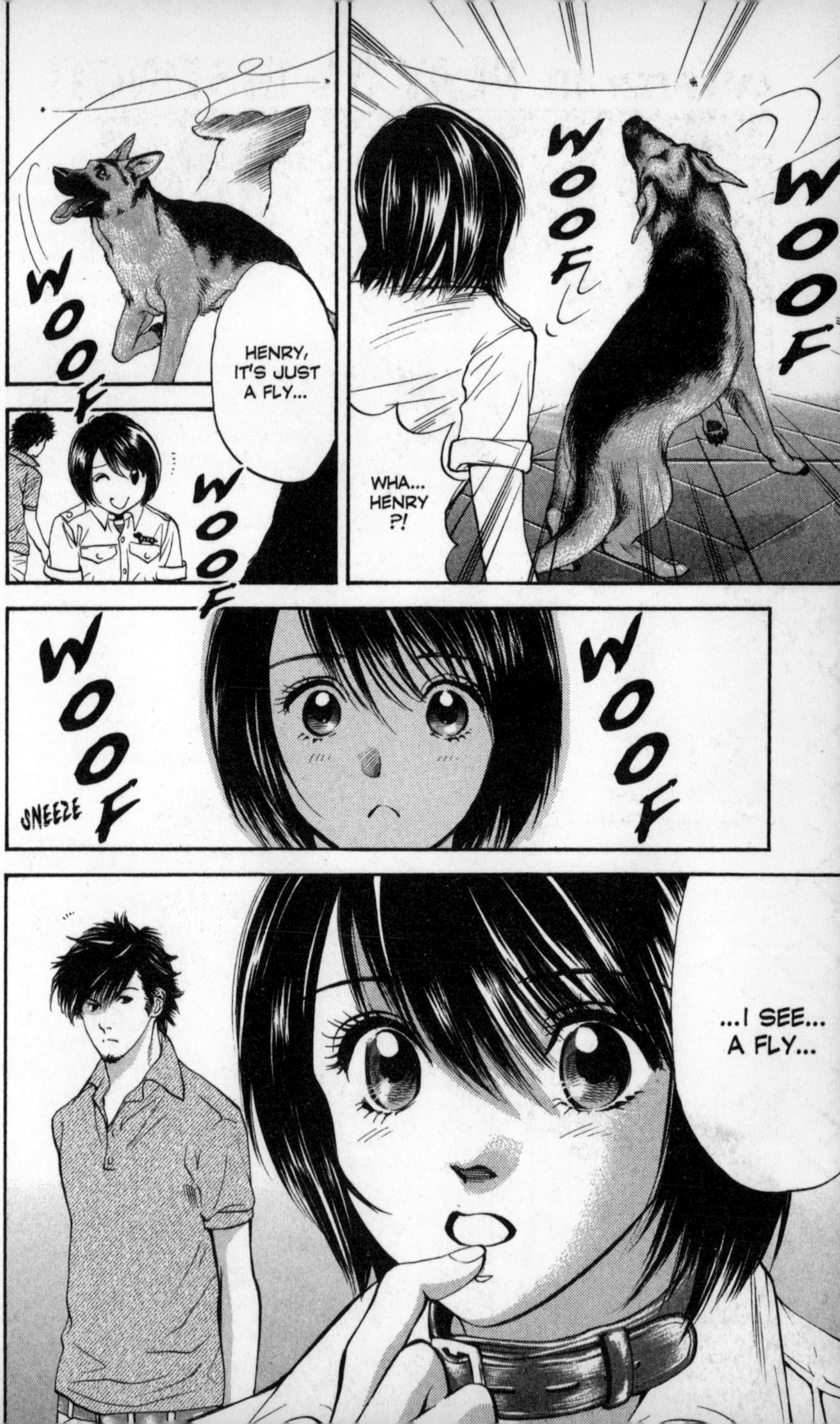
WOOF
WOOF
WHA... HENRY ?!
WOOF
HENRY, IT'S JUST A FLY...
WOOF
WOOF
WOOF
SNEEZE
...I SEE... A FLY...

CHAPTER 48: PLAY ON INSTINCT!

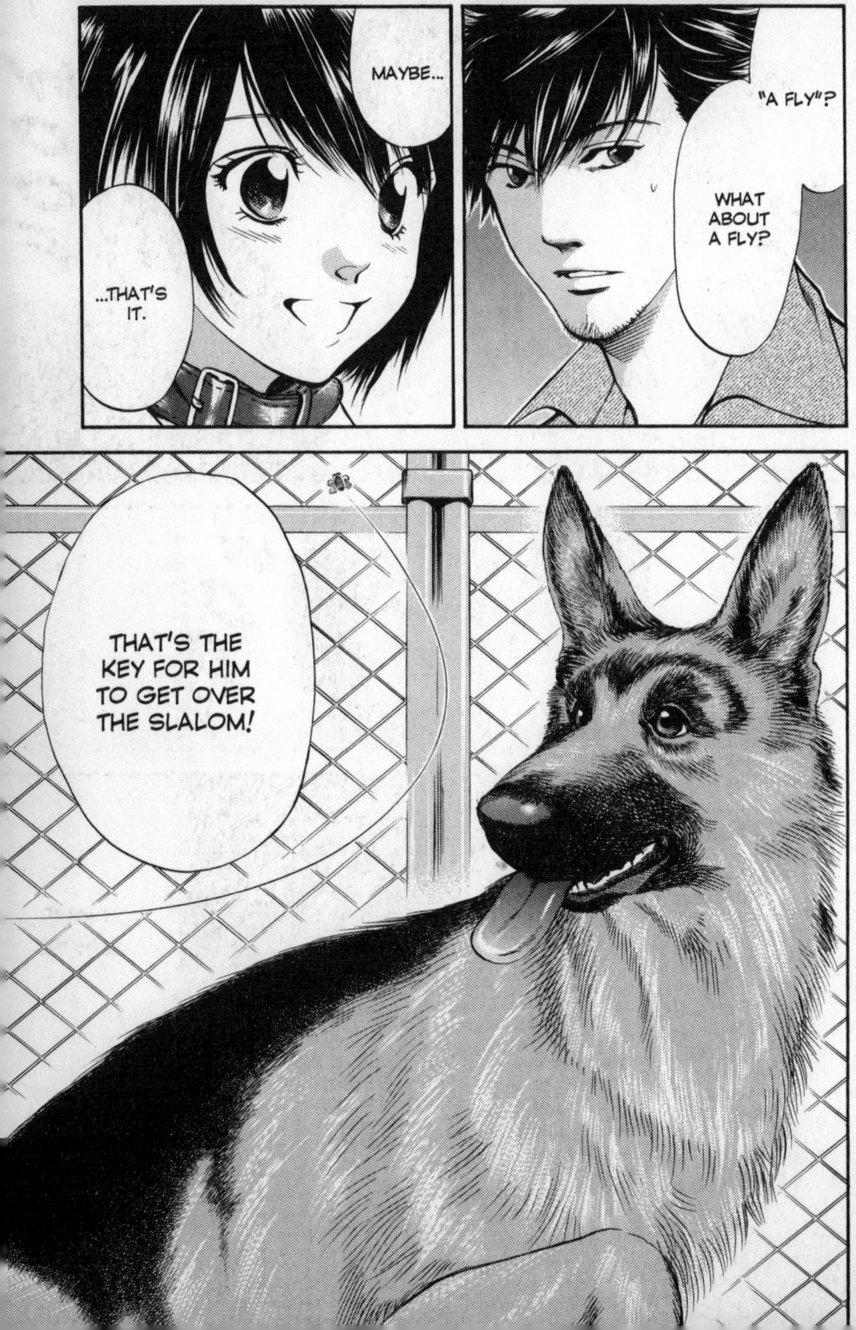
"A FLY"?
WHAT ABOUT A FLY?
MAYBE...
...THAT'S IT.
THAT'S THE KEY FOR HIM TO GET OVER THE SLALOM!

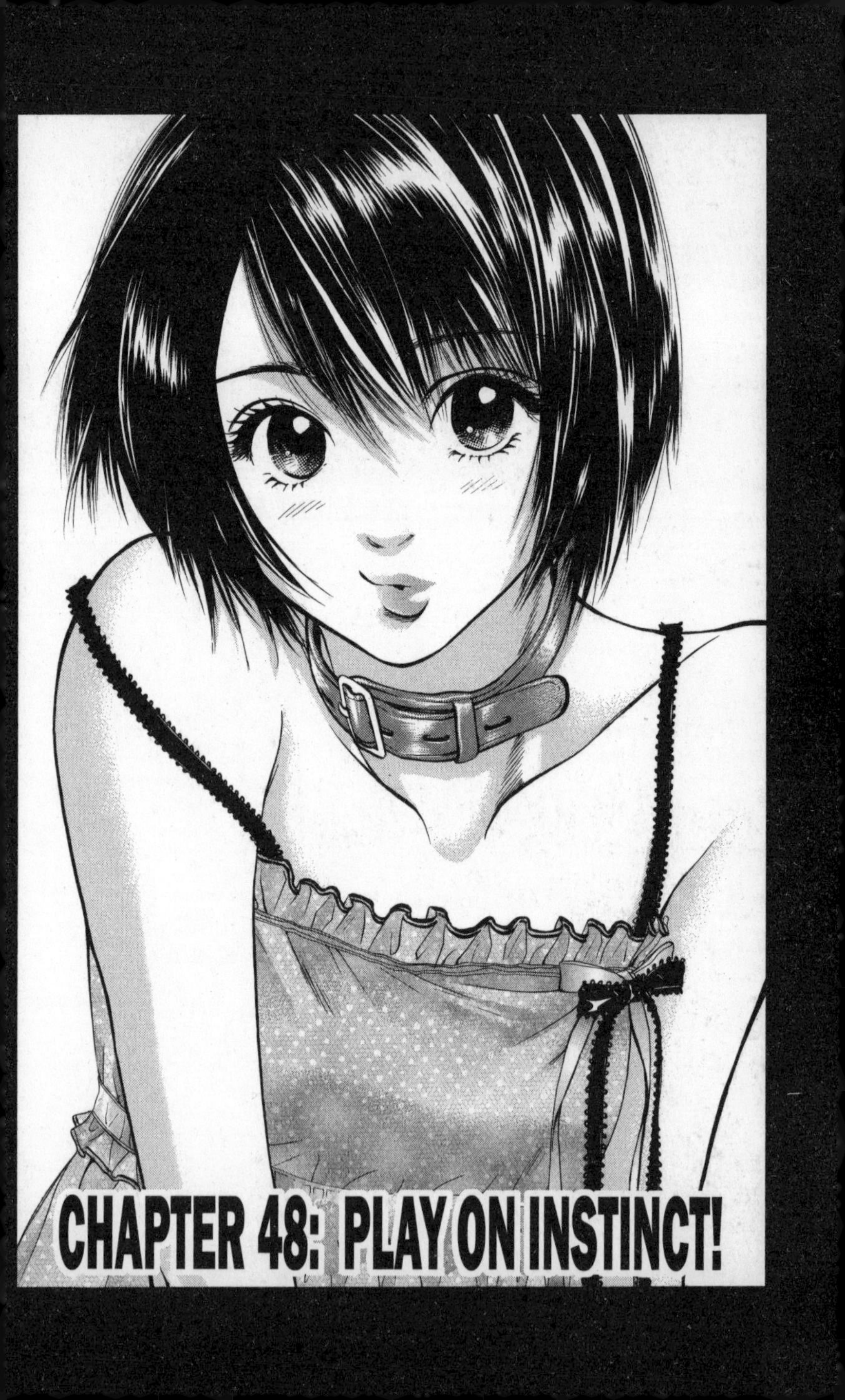
CHAPTER 48: PLAY ON INSTINCT!

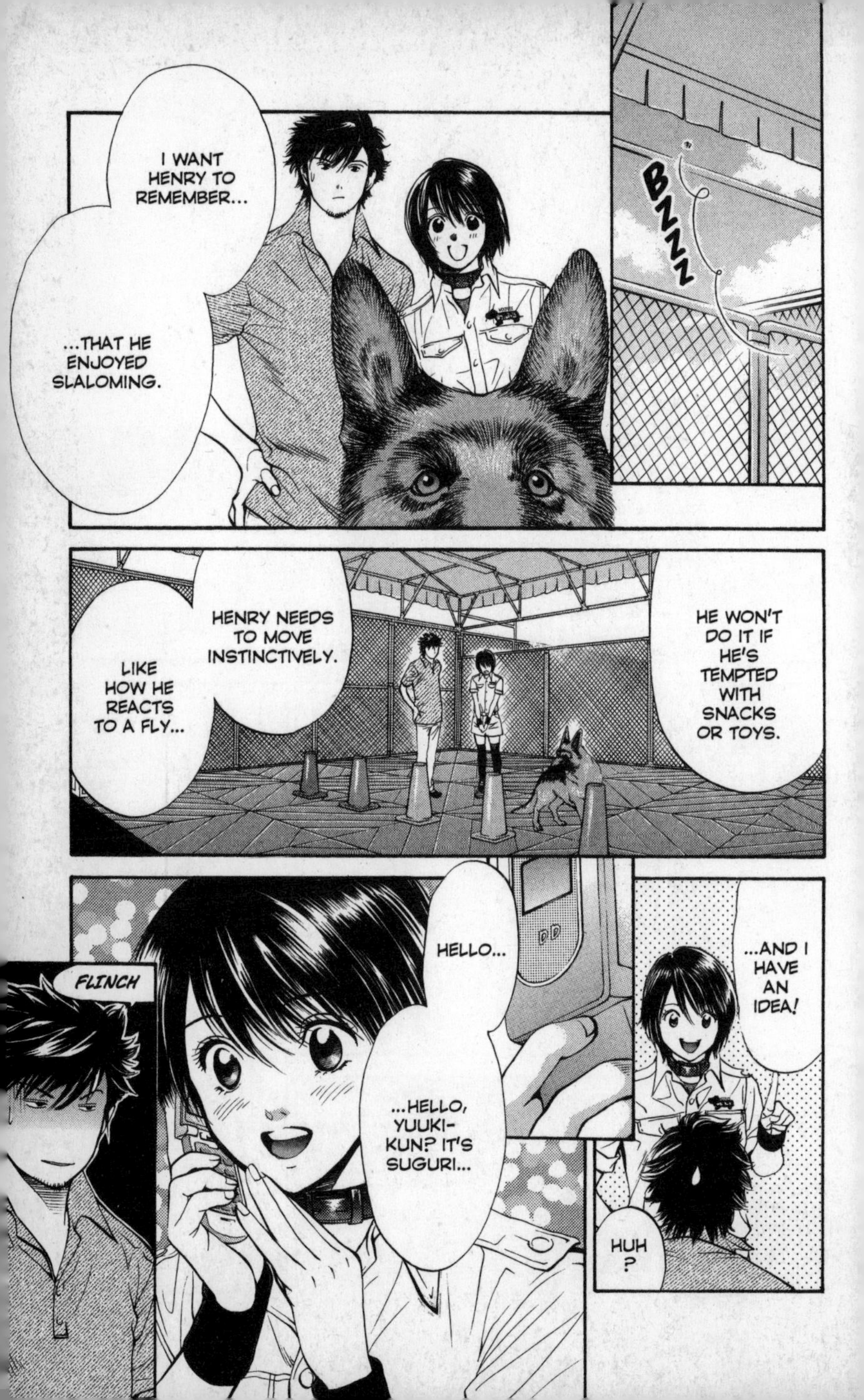
BZZZZ
I WANT HENRY TO REMEMBER...
...THAT HE ENJOYED SLALOMING.
HE WON'T DO IT IF HE'S TEMPTED WITH SNACKS OR TOYS.
HENRY NEEDS TO MOVE INSTINCTIVELY.
LIKE HOW HE REACTS TO A FLY...
...AND I HAVE AN IDEA!
HUH?
HELLO...
...HELLO, YUUKI-KUN? IT'S SUGURI...
FLINCH

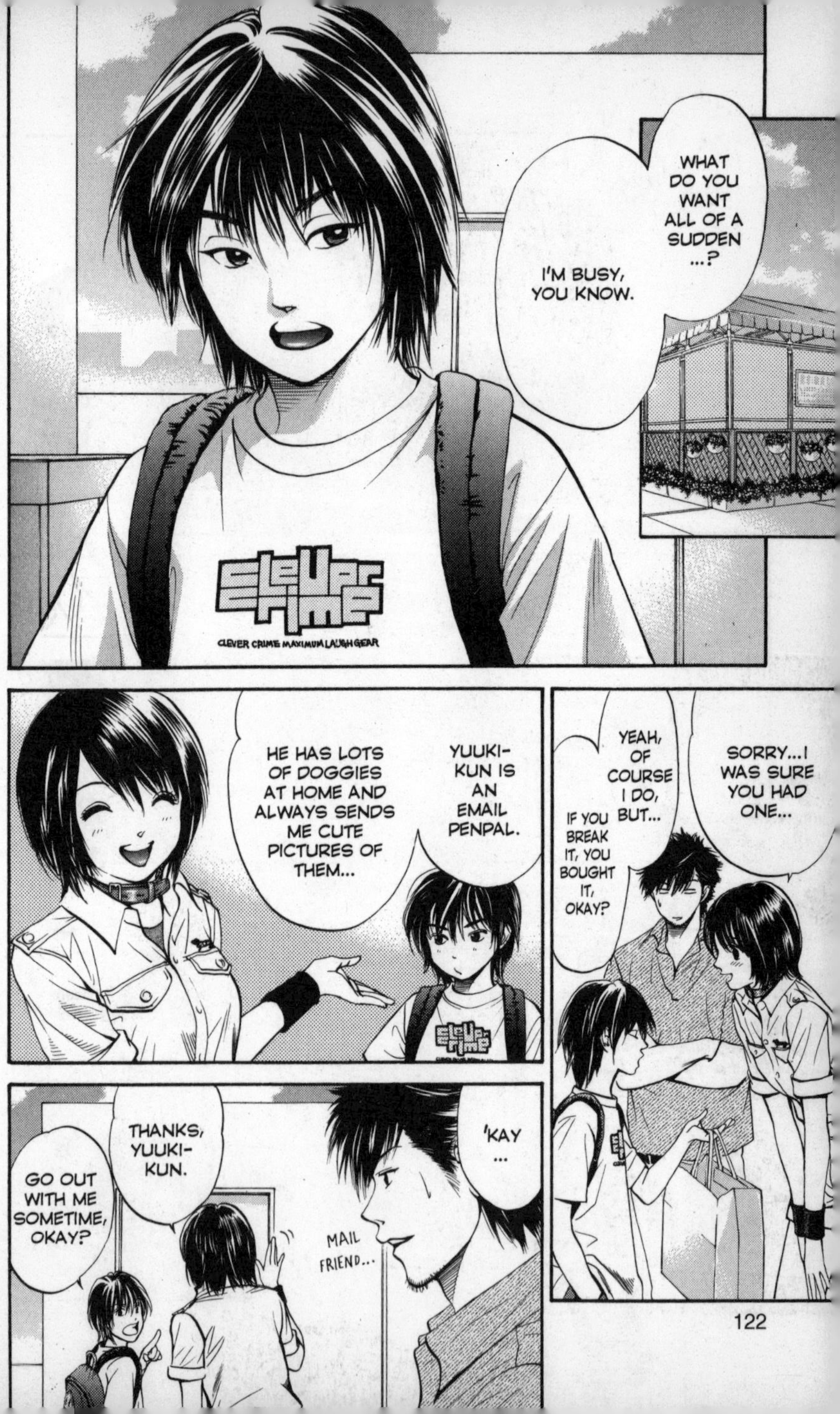
WHAT DO YOU WANT ALL OF A SUDDEN ...?
I'M BUSY, YOU KNOW.
CLEVER CRIME MAXIMUM LAUGH GEAR
SORRY...I WAS SURE YOU HAD ONE...
YEAH, OF COURSE I DO, BUT...
IF YOU BREAK IT, YOU BOUGHT IT, OKAY?
YUUKI-KUN IS AN EMAIL PENPAL.
HE HAS LOTS OF DOGGIES AT HOME AND ALWAYS SENDS ME CUTE PICTURES OF THEM...
'KAY ...
THANKS, YUUKI-KUN.
GO OUT WITH ME SOMETIME, OKAY?
MAIL FRIEND...

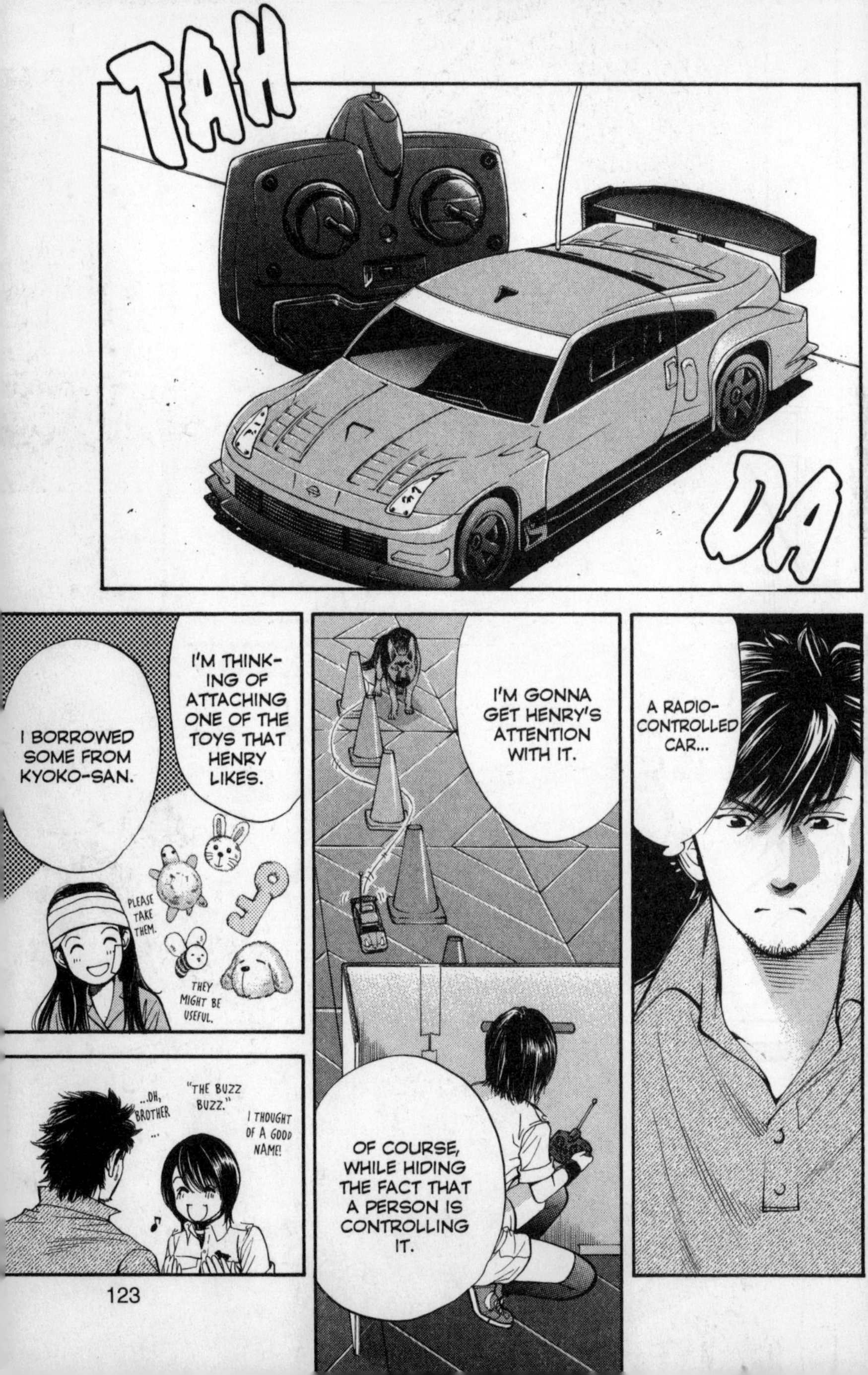
TAH
DA
A RADIO-CONTROLLED CAR...
I'M GONNA GET HENRY'S ATTENTION WITH IT.
OF COURSE, WHILE HIDING THE FACT THAT A PERSON IS CONTROLLING IT.
I'M THINKING OF ATTACHING ONE OF THE TOYS THAT HENRY LIKES.
I BORROWED SOME FROM KYOKO-SAN.
PLEASE TAKE THEM.
THEY MIGHT BE USEFUL.
I THOUGHT OF A GOOD NAME!
"THE BUZZ BUZZ."
...OH, BROTHER...

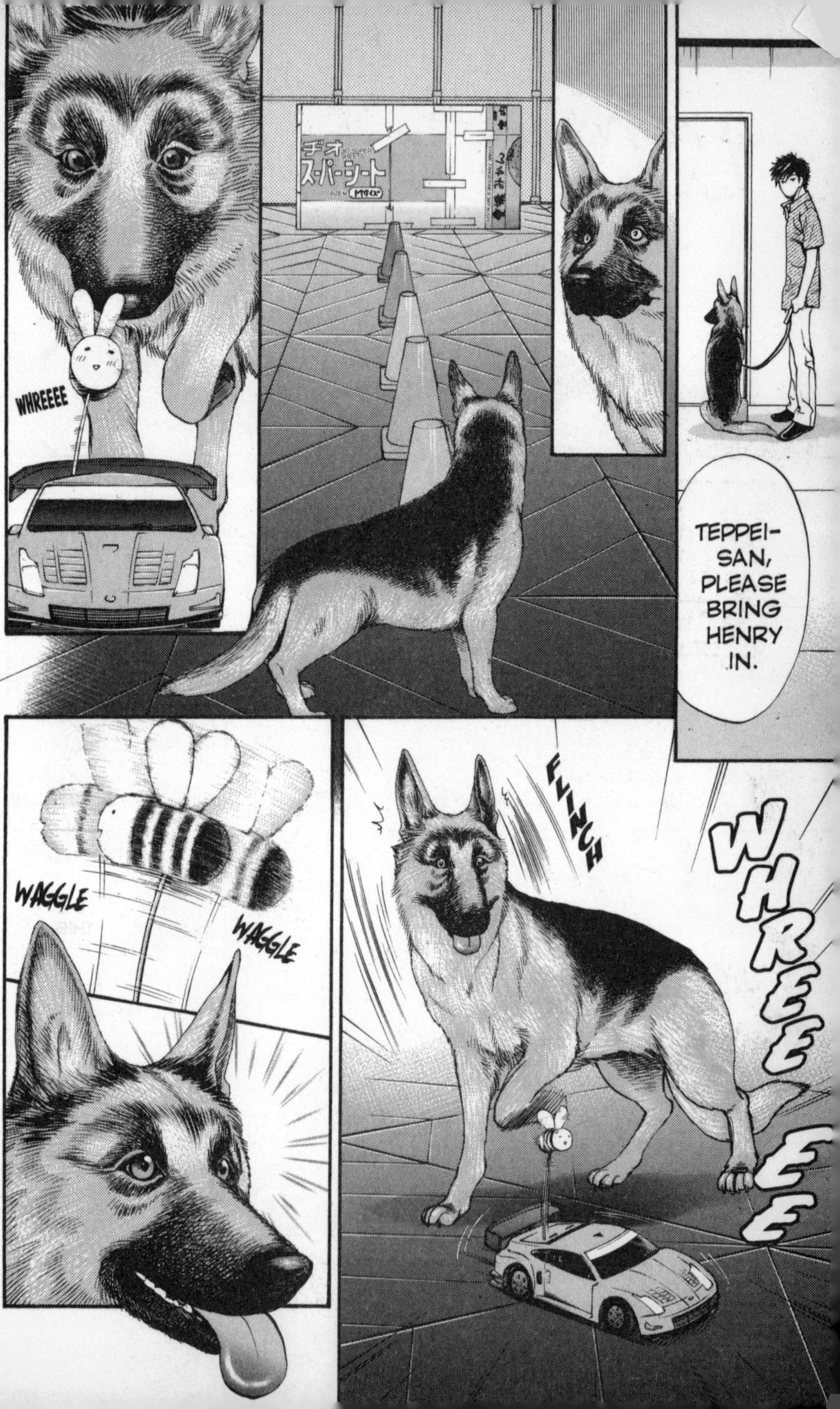
TEPPEI-SAN, PLEASE BRING HENRY IN.
WHREEEE
WHREEEEE
FLINCH
WAGGLE
WAGGLE

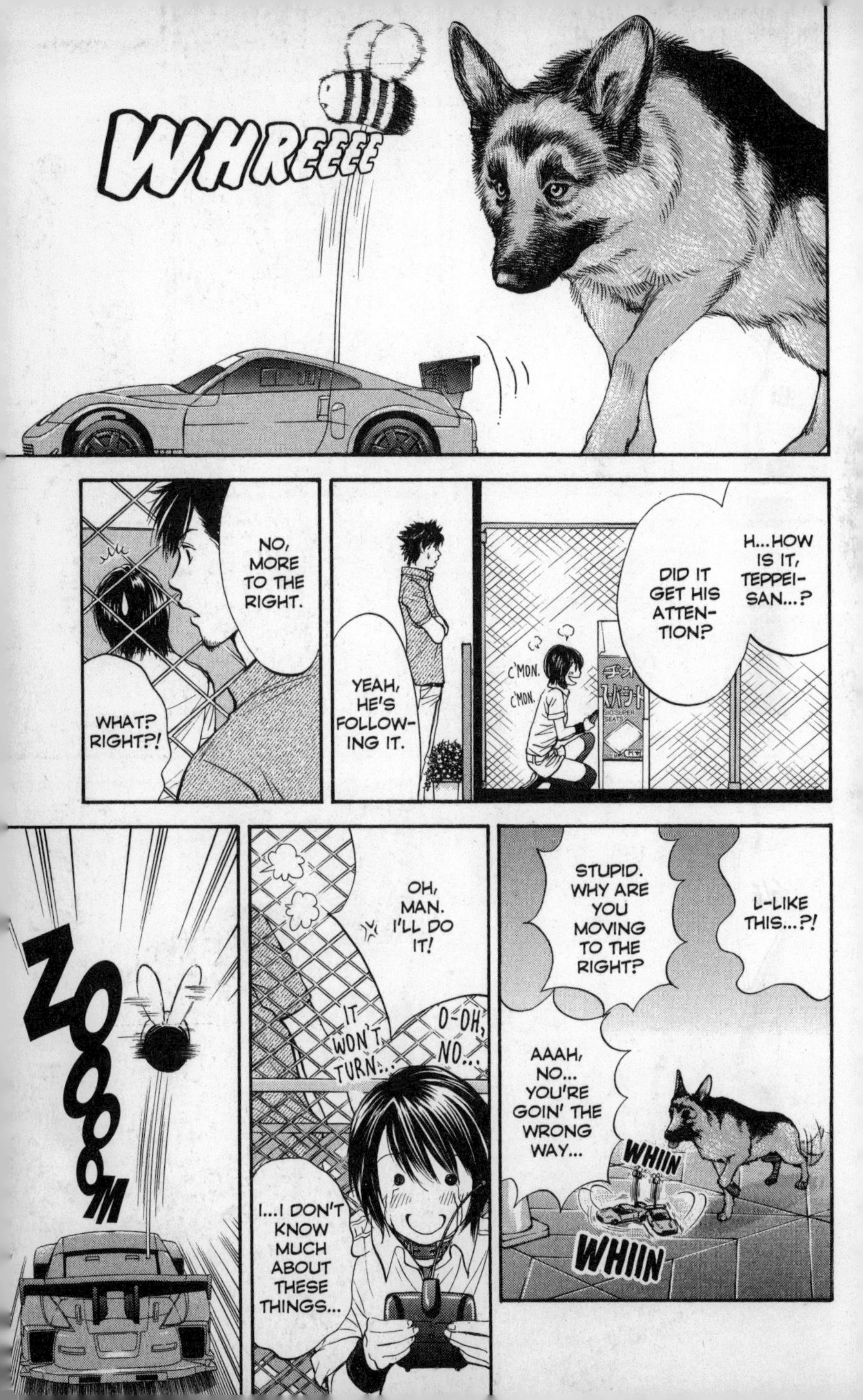
WHREEEE
H...HOW IS IT, TEPPEI-SAN...?
DID IT GET HIS ATTENTION?
C'MON.
C'MON.
YEAH, HE'S FOLLOWING IT.
NO, MORE TO THE RIGHT.
WHAT? RIGHT?!
L-LIKE THIS...?!
STUPID. WHY ARE YOU MOVING TO THE RIGHT?
AAAH, NO... YOU'RE GOIN' THE WRONG WAY...
WHIIN
WHIIN
OH, MAN. I'LL DO IT!
O-OH, NO...
IT WON'T TURN...
I...I DON'T KNOW MUCH ABOUT THESE THINGS...
ZOOOOM

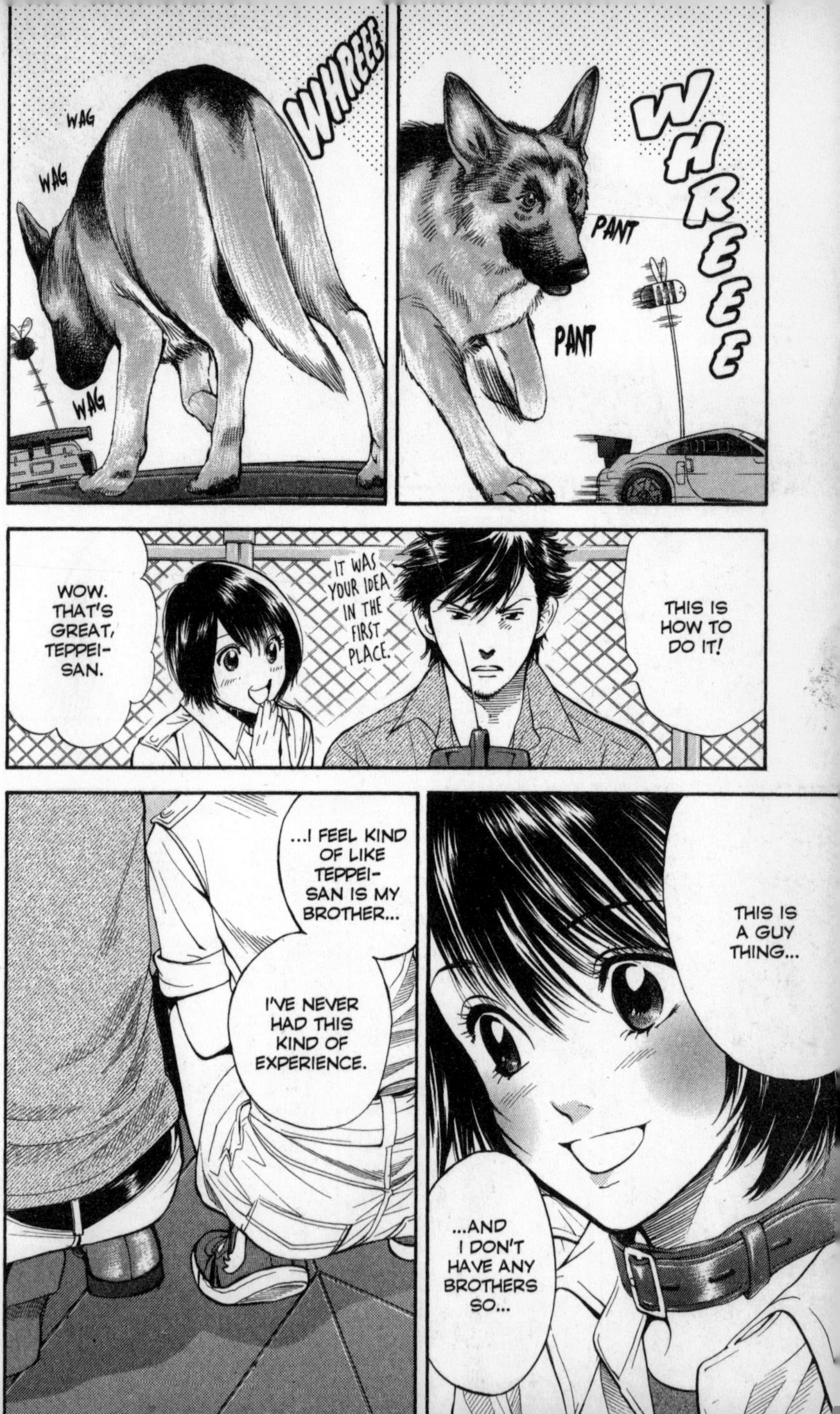
WHREEE
PANT
PANT
WHREEE
WAG
WAG
WAG
THIS IS HOW TO DO IT!
IT WAS YOUR IDEA IN THE FIRST PLACE.
WOW. THAT'S GREAT, TEPPEI-SAN.
THIS IS A GUY THING...
...AND I DON'T HAVE ANY BROTHERS SO...
...I FEEL KIND OF LIKE TEPPEI-SAN IS MY BROTHER...
I'VE NEVER HAD THIS KIND OF EXPERIENCE.

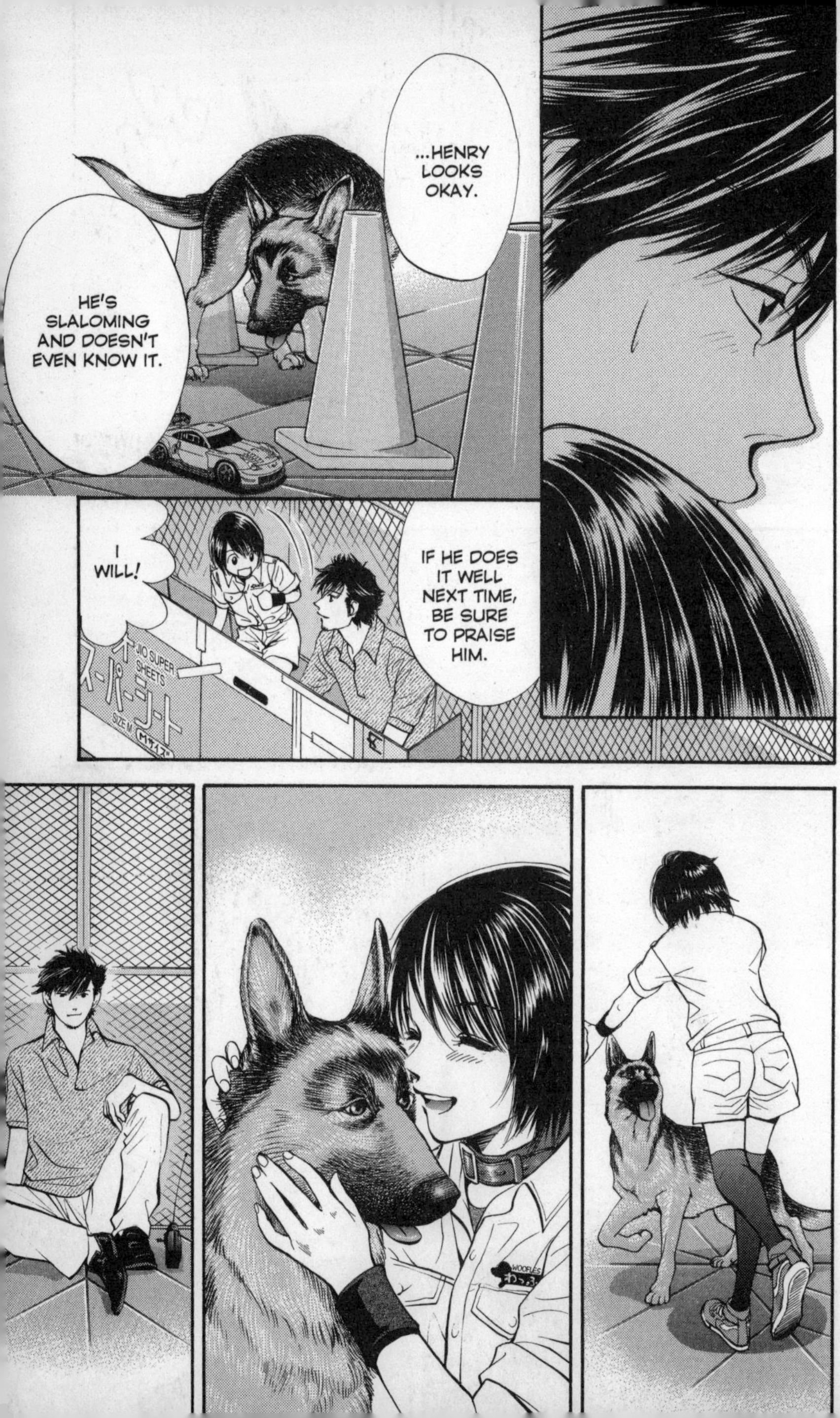
...HENRY LOOKS OKAY.
HE'S SLALOMING AND DOESN'T EVEN KNOW IT.
IF HE DOES IT WELL NEXT TIME, BE SURE TO PRAISE HIM.
I WILL!
JIO SUPER SHEETS
SIZE M
WOOFLES

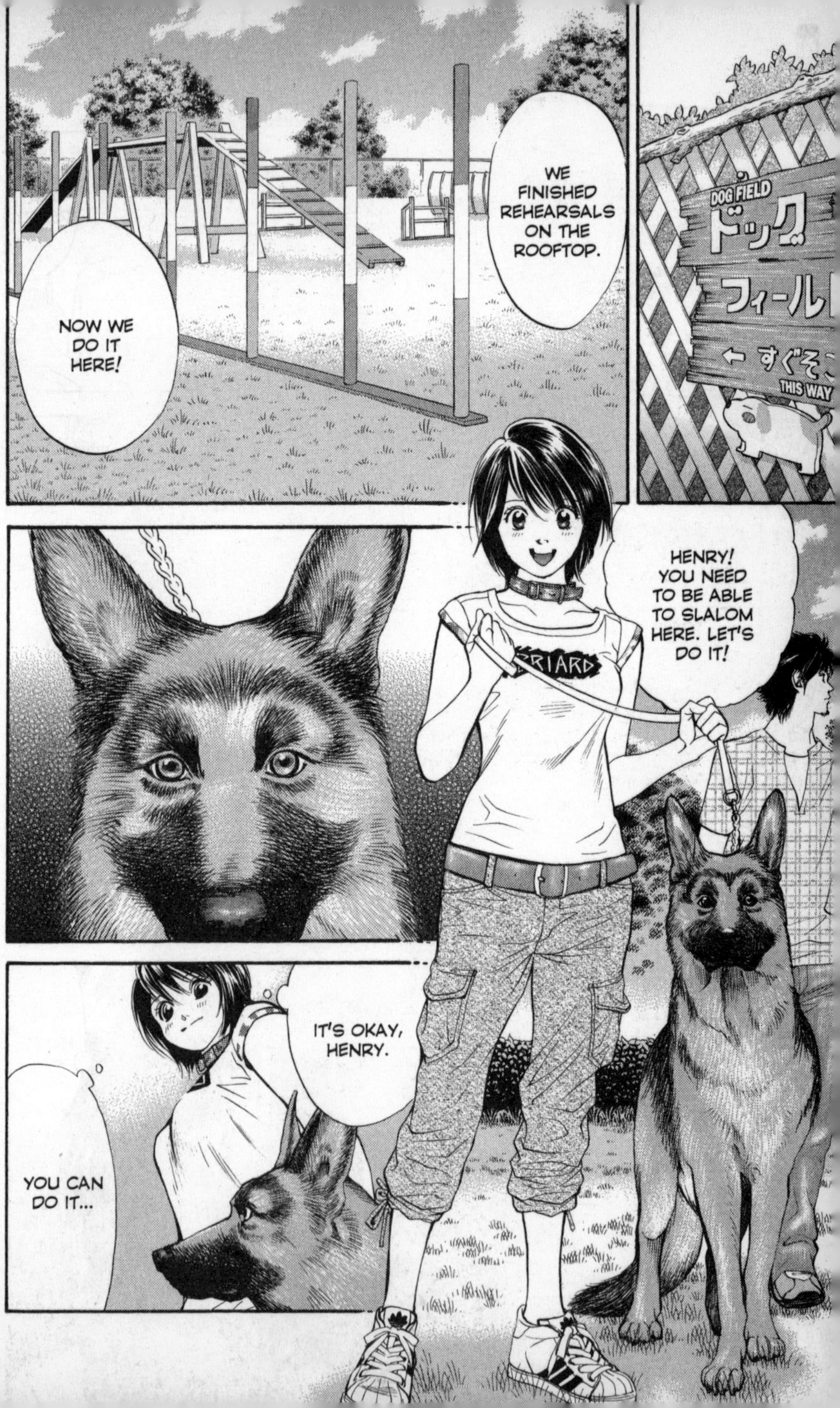
DOG FIELD
ドッグ
THIS WAY
WE FINISHED REHEARSALS ON THE ROOFTOP.
NOW WE DO IT HERE!
HENRY! YOU NEED TO BE ABLE TO SLALOM HERE. LET'S DO IT!
IT'S OKAY, HENRY.
YOU CAN DO IT...

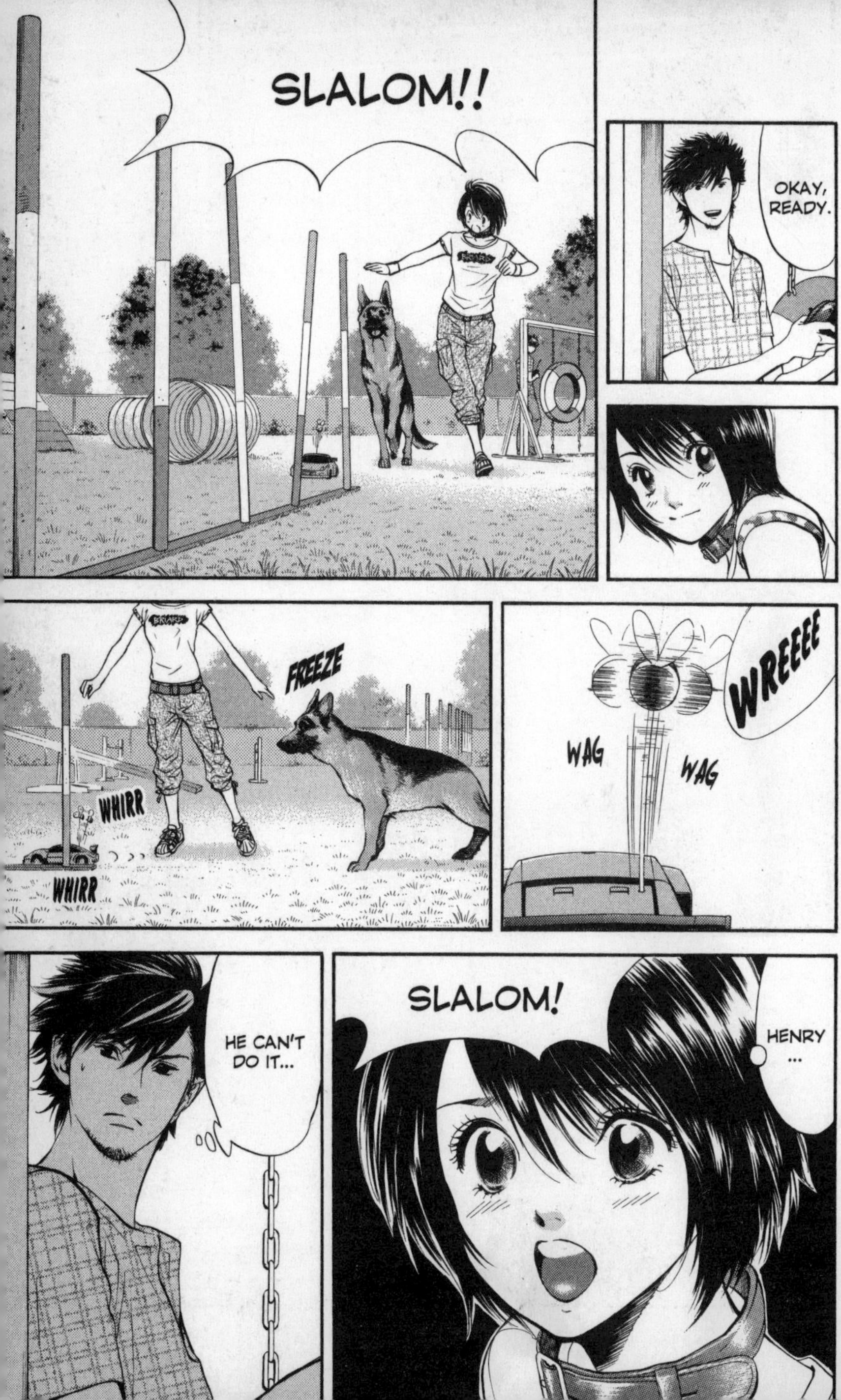
OKAY, READY.
SLALOM!!
WREEEE
WAG
WAG
FREEZE
WHIRR
WHIRR
HENRY ...
SLALOM!
HE CAN'T DO IT...

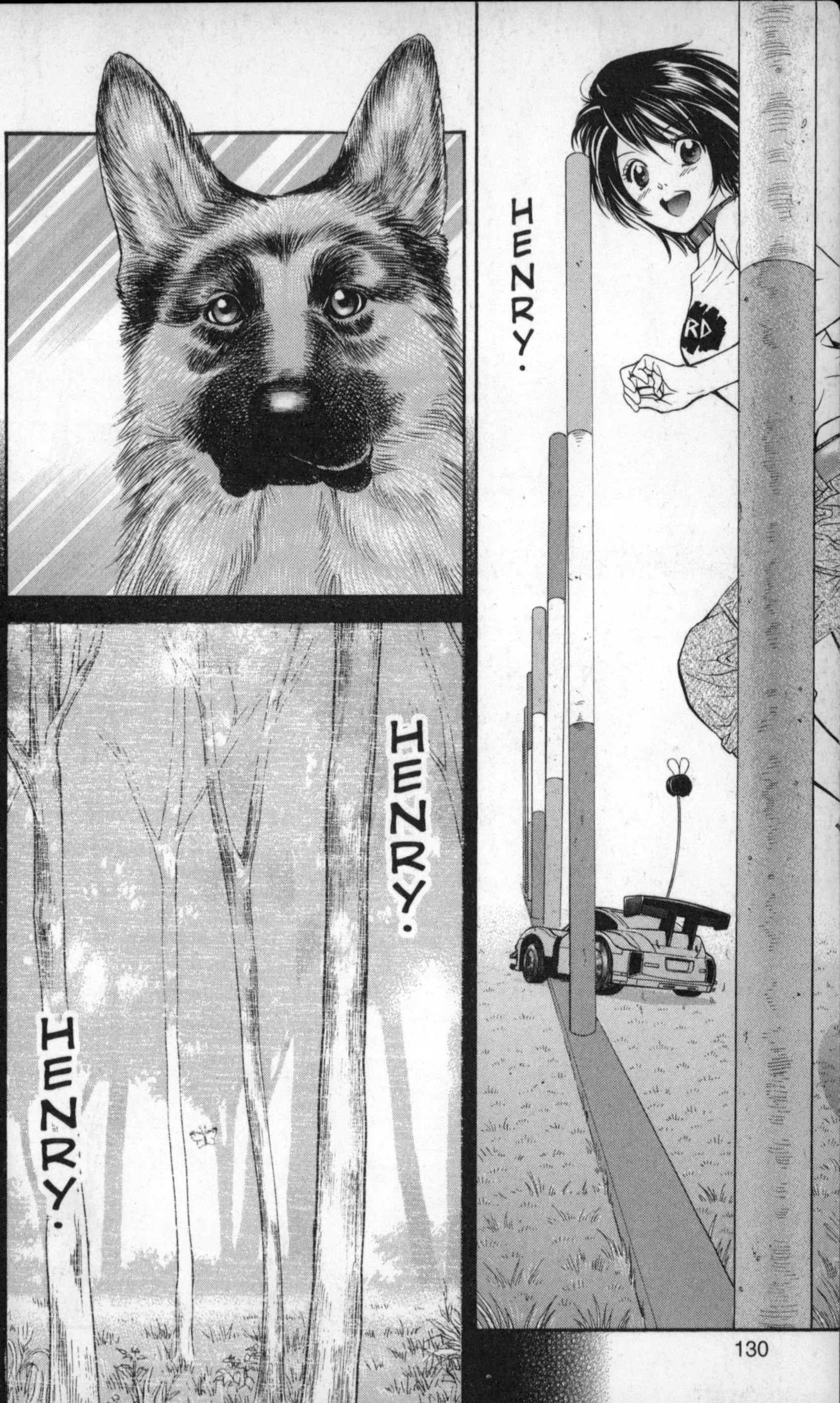
HENRY.
HENRY.
HENRY.

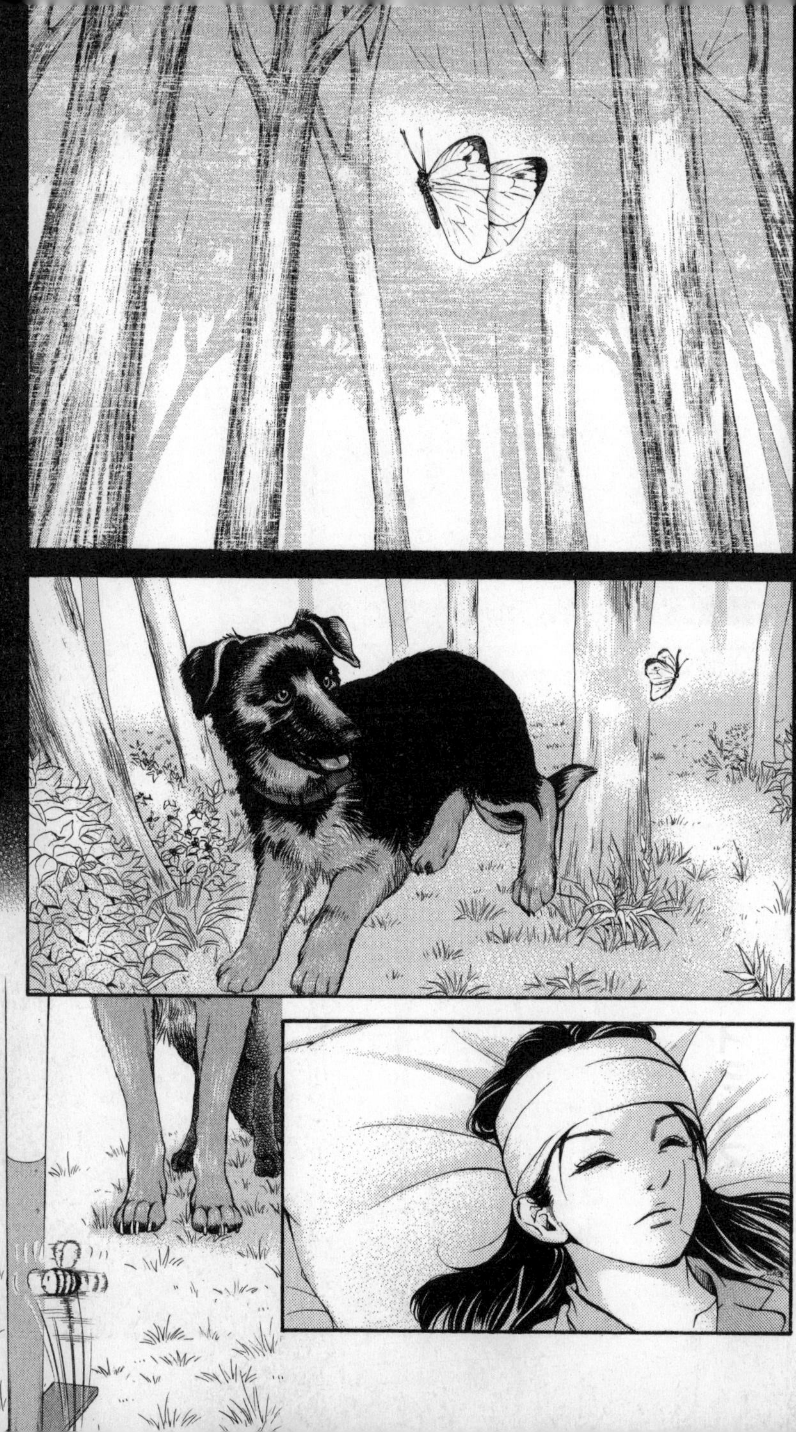

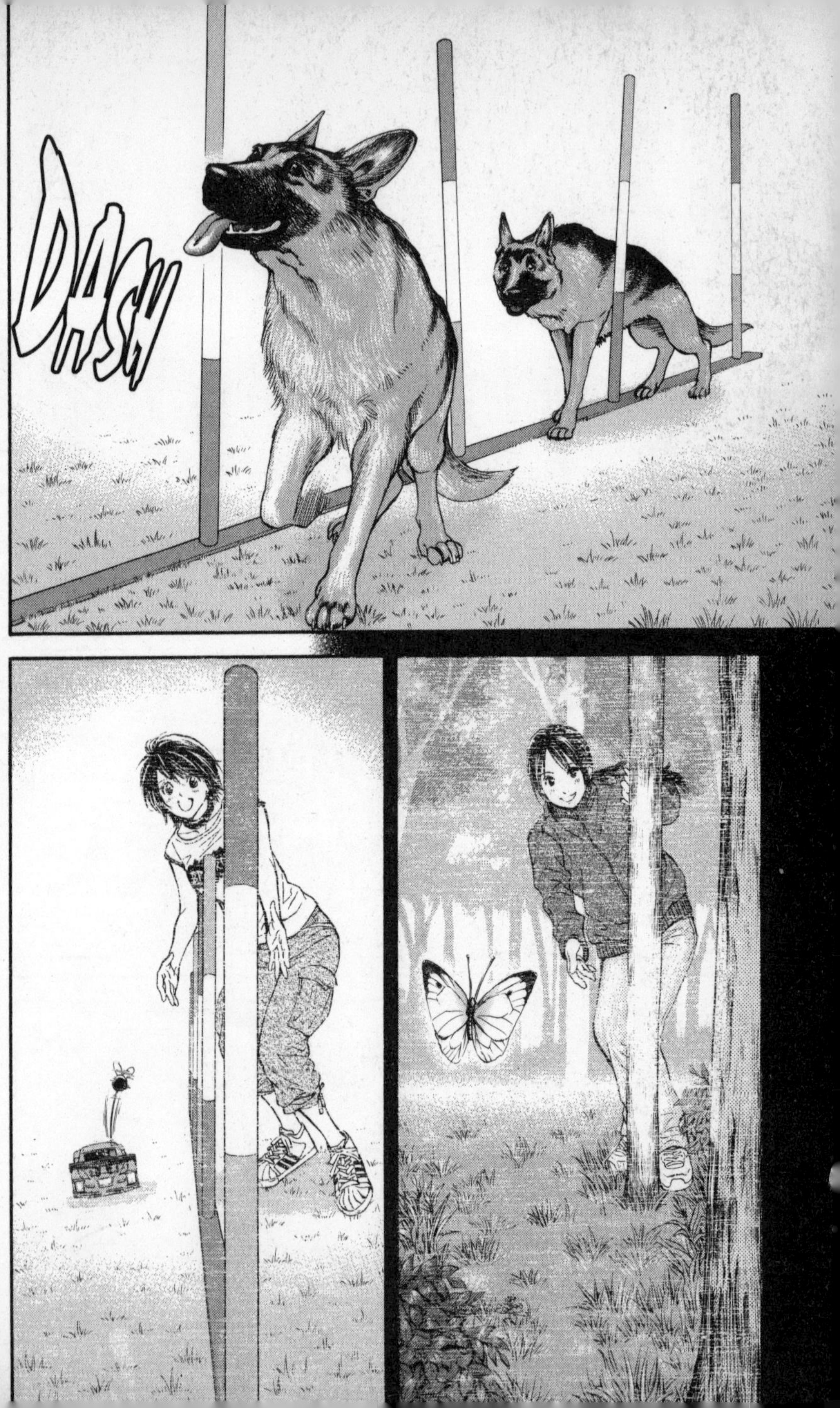
DASH

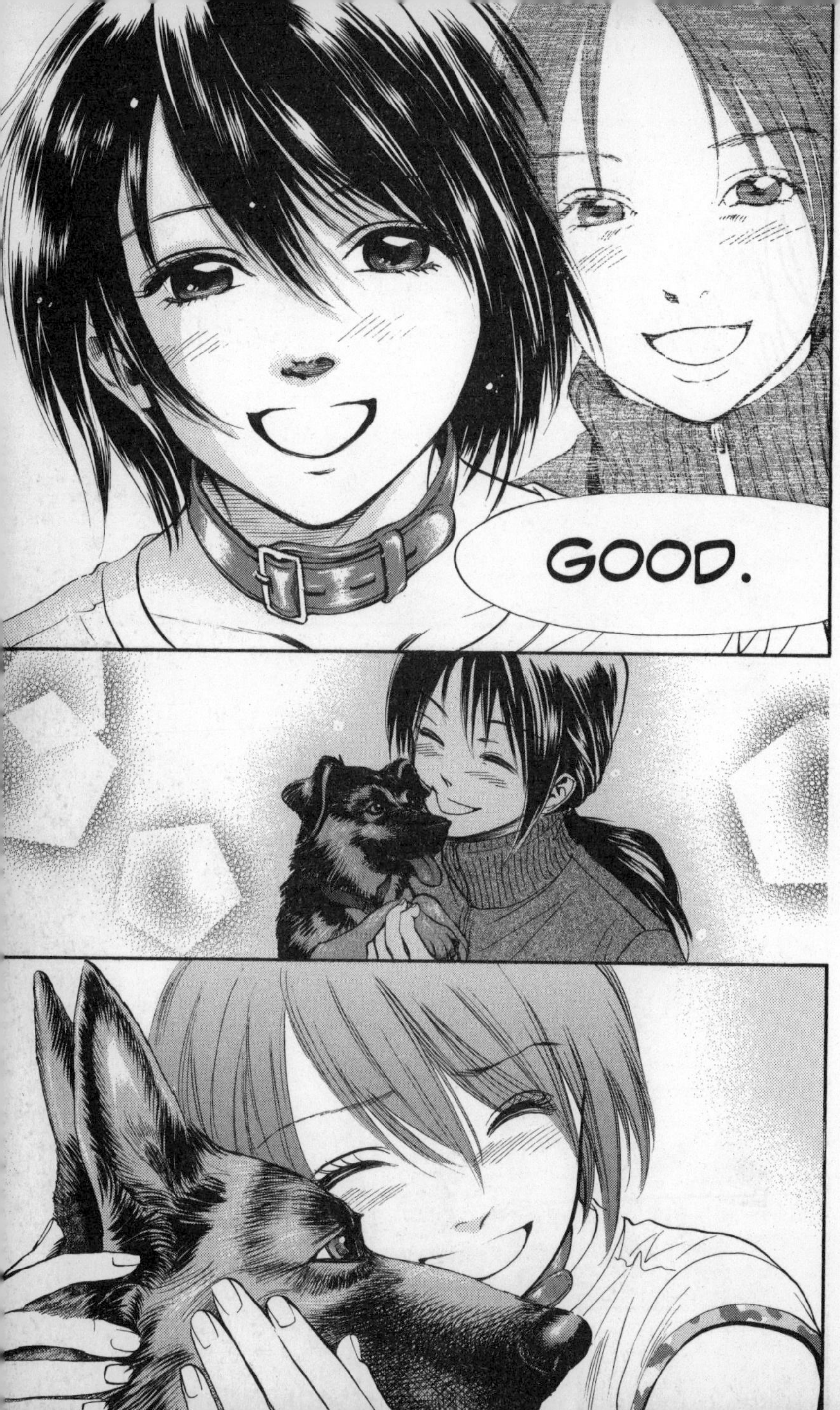
GOOD.

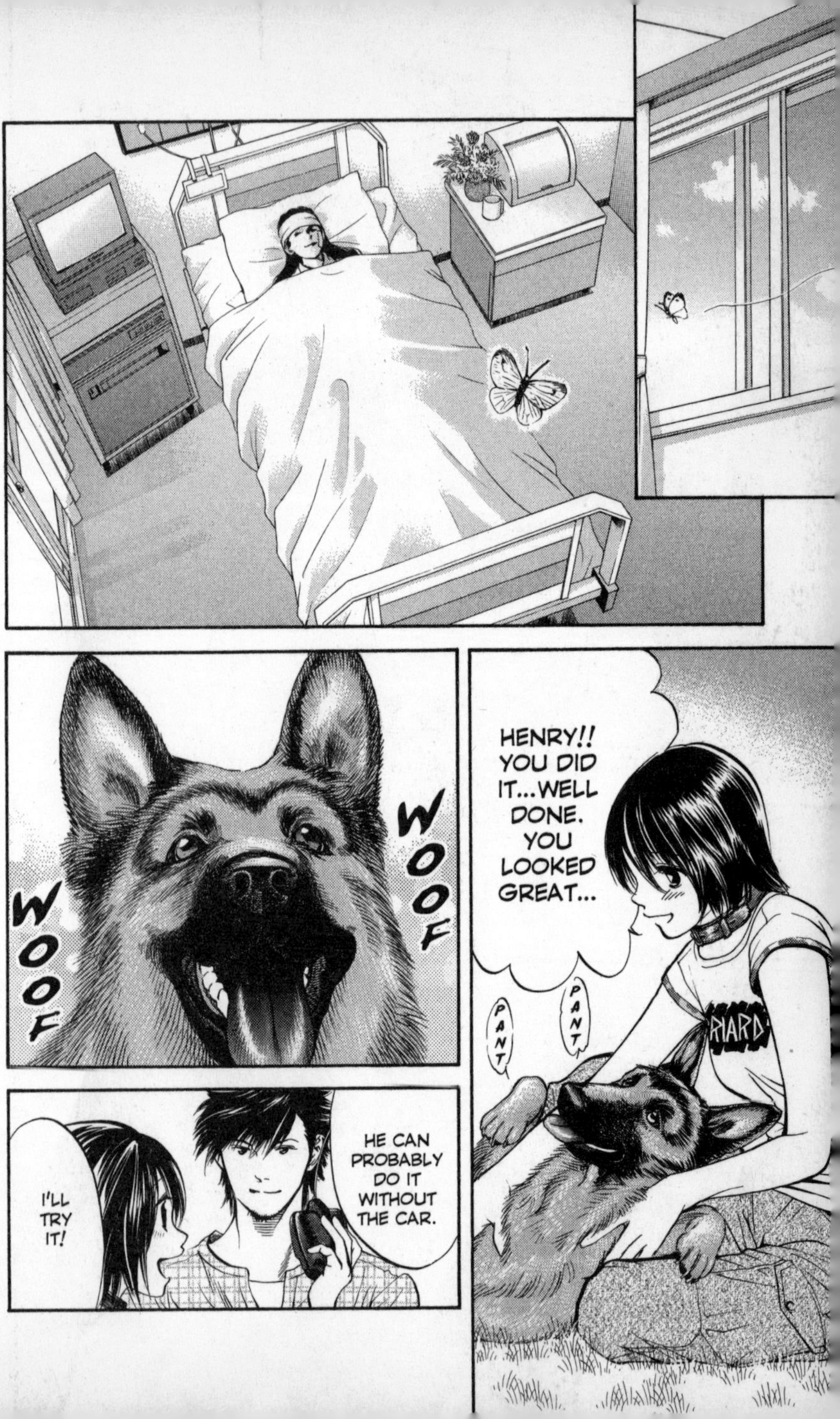
HENRY!! YOU DID IT...WELL DONE. YOU LOOKED GREAT...
PANT
PANT
WOOF
WOOF
HE CAN PROBABLY DO IT WITHOUT THE CAR.
I'LL TRY IT!

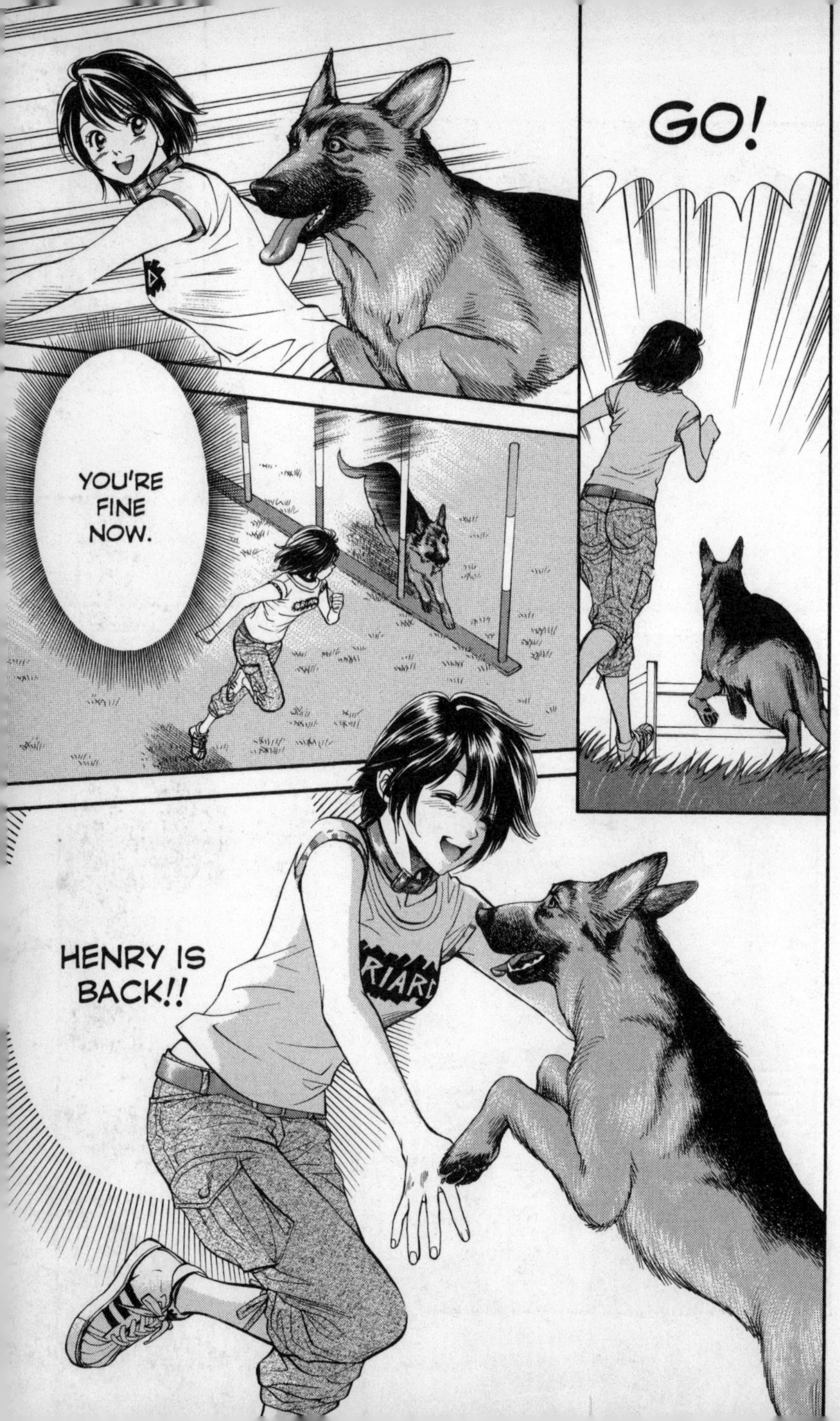
GO!
YOU'RE FINE NOW.
HENRY IS BACK!!

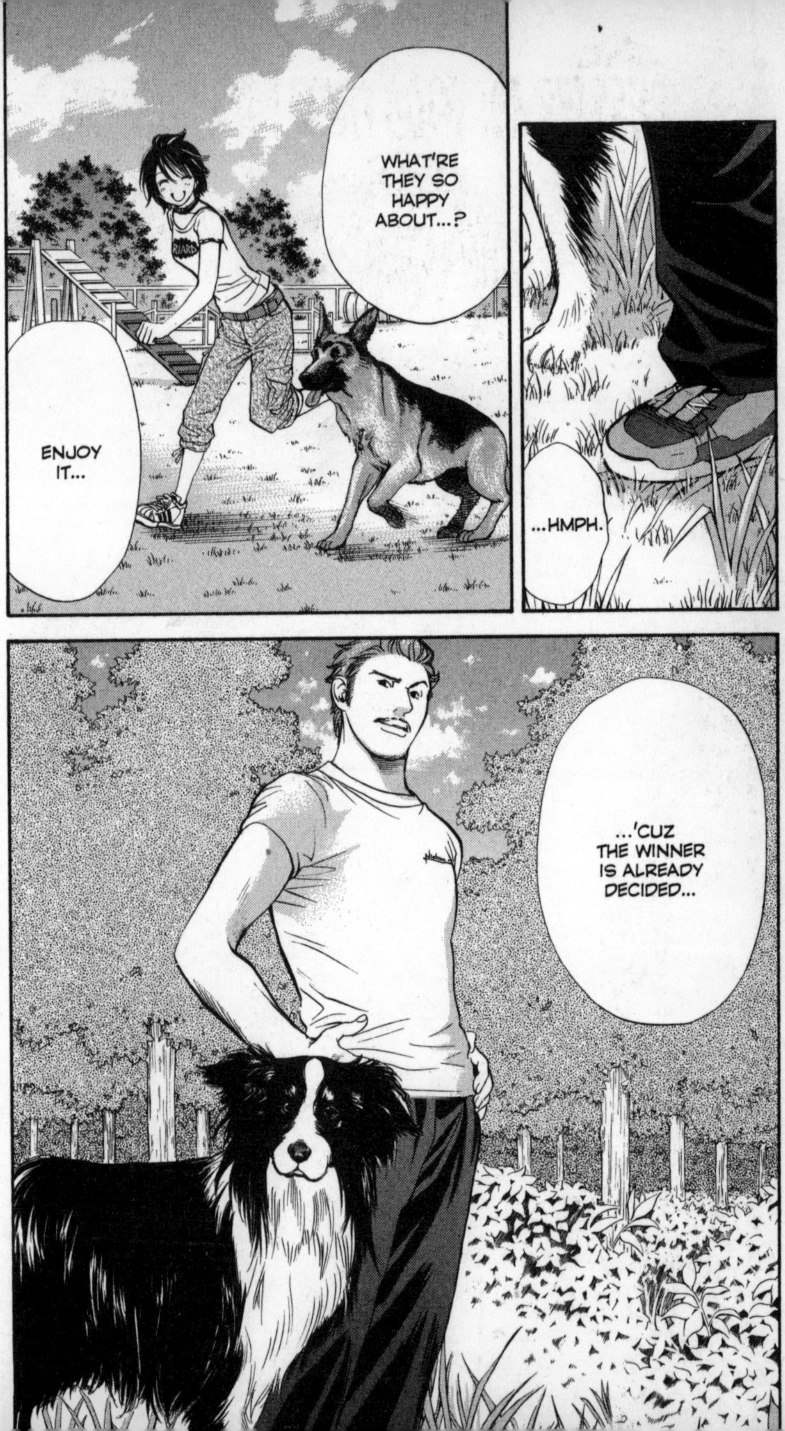
...HMPH.
WHAT'RE THEY SO HAPPY ABOUT...?
ENJOY IT...
...'CUZ THE WINNER IS ALREADY DECIDED...

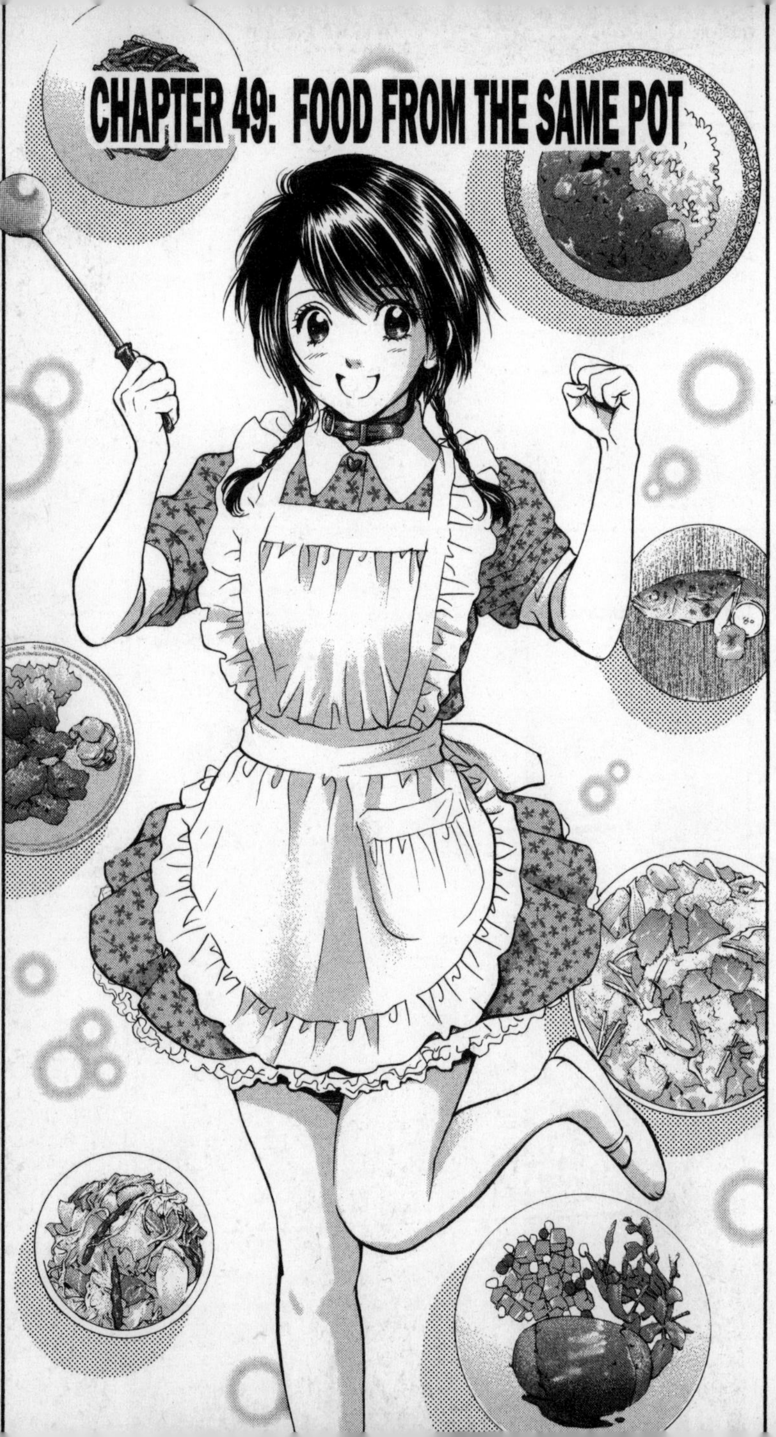
CHAPTER 49: FOOD FROM THE SAME POT

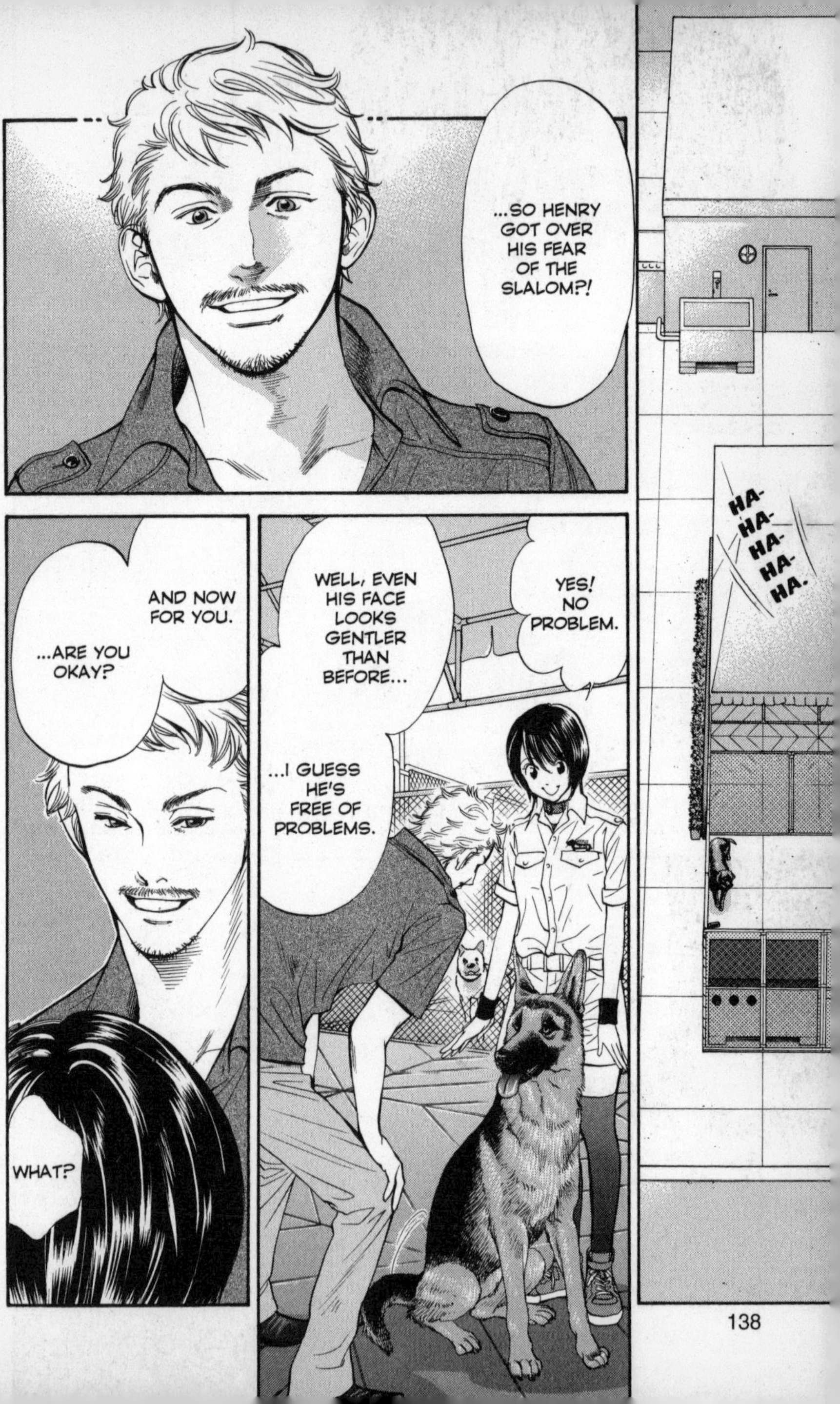
HA-HA-HA-HA-HA.
...SO HENRY GOT OVER HIS FEAR OF THE SLALOM?!
YES! NO PROBLEM.
WELL, EVEN HIS FACE LOOKS GENTLER THAN BEFORE...
...I GUESS HE'S FREE OF PROBLEMS.
AND NOW FOR YOU.
...ARE YOU OKAY?
WHAT?

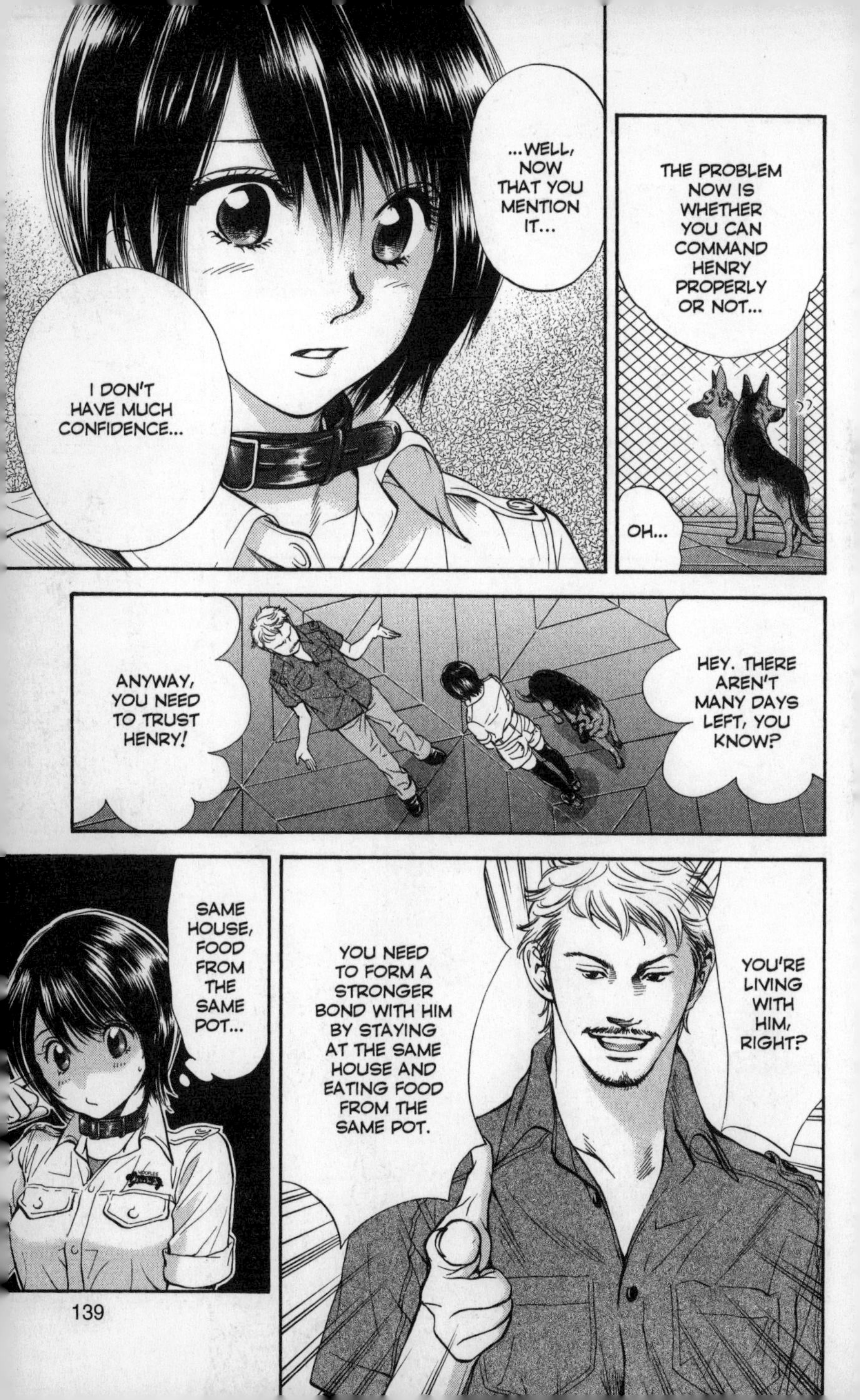
THE PROBLEM NOW IS WHETHER YOU CAN COMMAND HENRY PROPERLY OR NOT...
OH...
...WELL, NOW THAT YOU MENTION IT...
I DON'T HAVE MUCH CONFIDENCE...
HEY. THERE AREN'T MANY DAYS LEFT, YOU KNOW?
ANYWAY, YOU NEED TO TRUST HENRY!
YOU'RE LIVING WITH HIM, RIGHT?
YOU NEED TO FORM A STRONGER BOND WITH HIM BY STAYING AT THE SAME HOUSE AND EATING FOOD FROM THE SAME POT.
SAME HOUSE, FOOD FROM THE SAME POT...

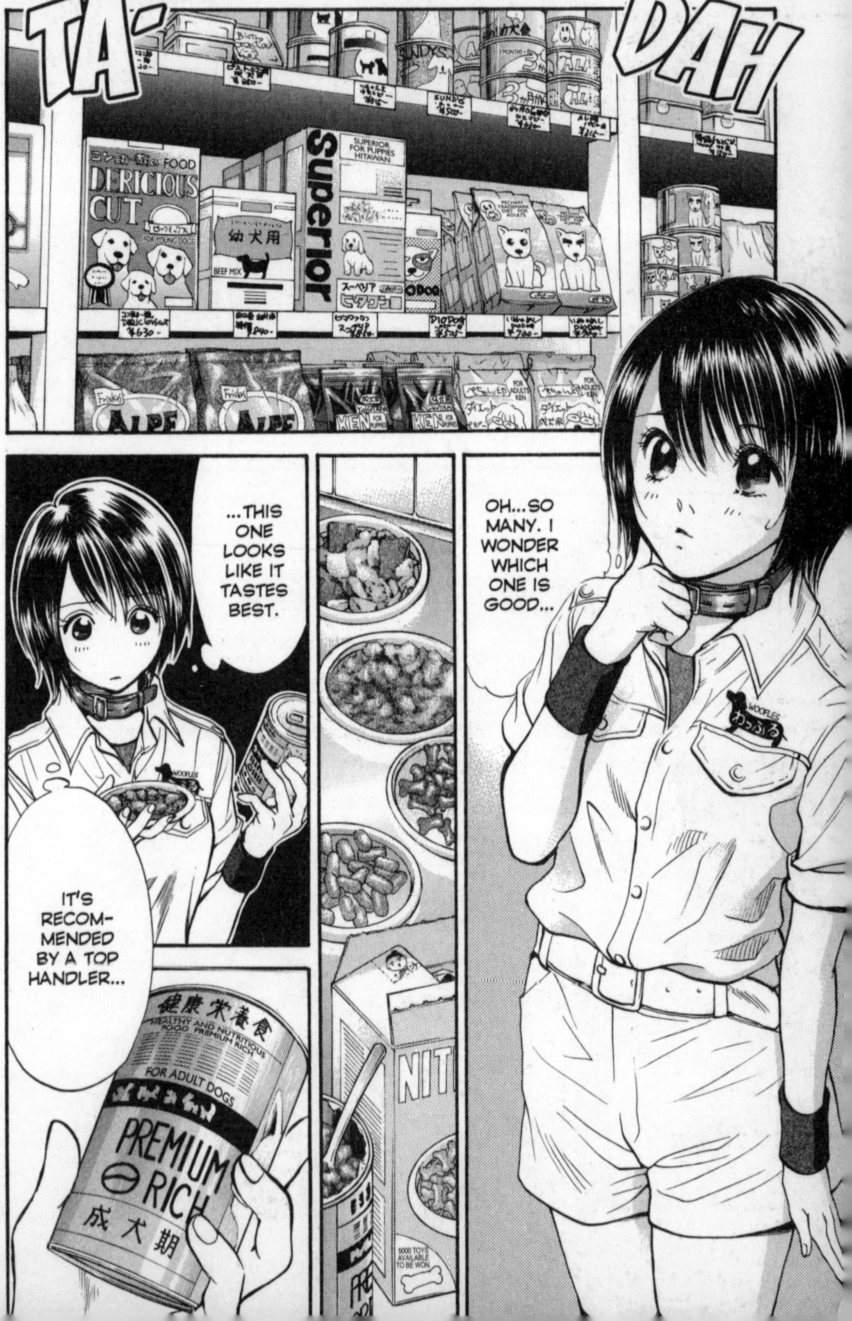
TA-
DAH
DERICIOUS CUT
FOR YOUNG DOGS
幼犬用
BEEF MIX
SUPERIOR FOR PUPPIES HITAWAN
Superior
スーペリア
KEN FOR PUPPIES
FOR ADULT KEN
OH... SO MANY. I WONDER WHICH ONE IS GOOD...
WOOFLES
わっふる
...THIS ONE LOOKS LIKE IT TASTES BEST.
IT'S RECOMMENDED BY A TOP HANDLER...
健康栄養食
HEALTHY AND NUTRITIOUS FOOD PREMIUM RICH
FOR ADULT DOGS
PREMIUM RICH
成犬期
NITI
5000 TOYS AVAILABLE TO BE WON

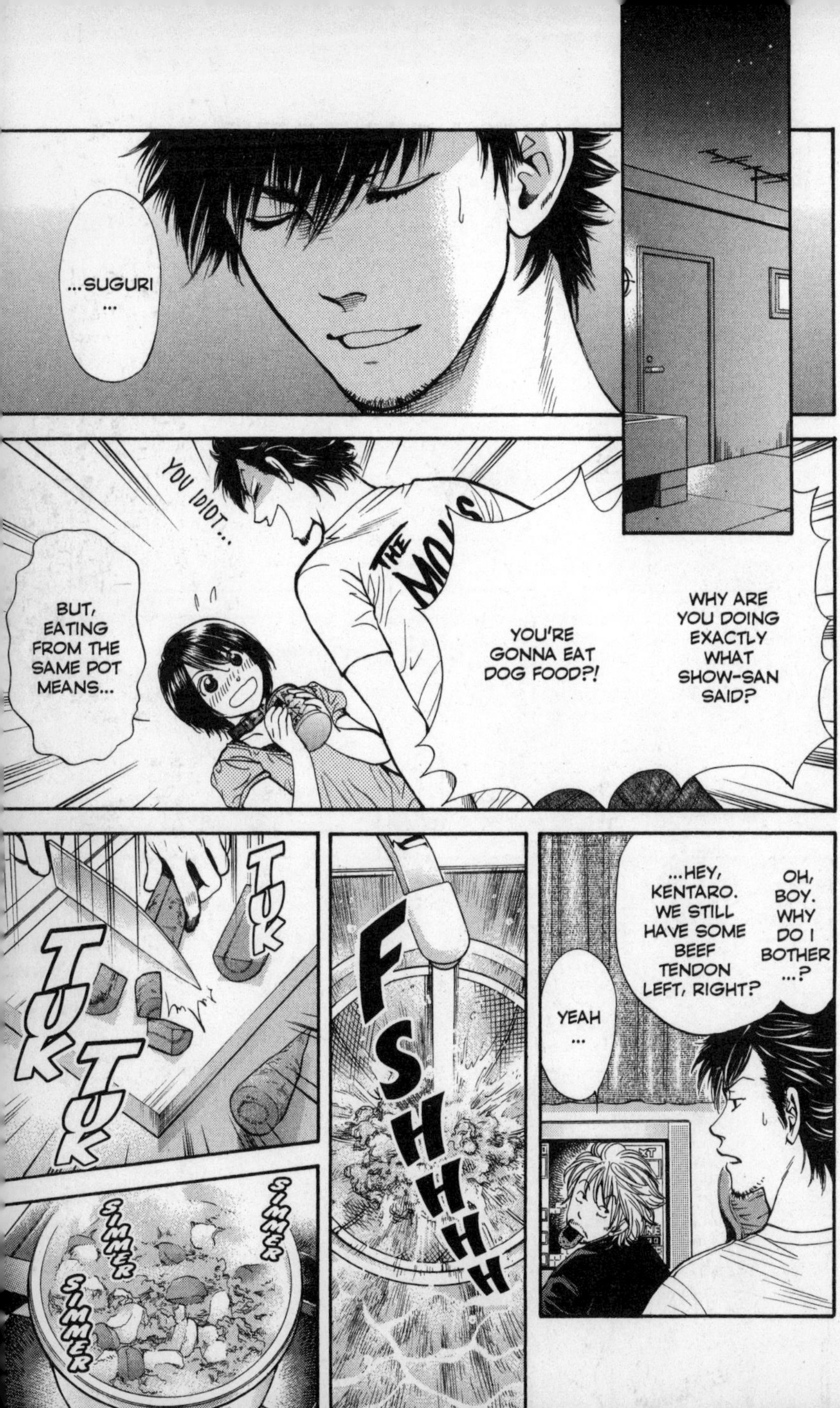
...SUGURI ...
WHY ARE YOU DOING EXACTLY WHAT SHOW-SAN SAID?
YOU'RE GONNA EAT DOG FOOD?!
YOU IDIOT...
BUT, EATING FROM THE SAME POT MEANS...
OH, BOY. WHY DO I BOTHER ...?
...HEY, KENTARO. WE STILL HAVE SOME BEEF TENDON LEFT, RIGHT?
YEAH ...
FSHHHH
TUK
TUK
TUK
SIMMER
SIMMER
SIMMER

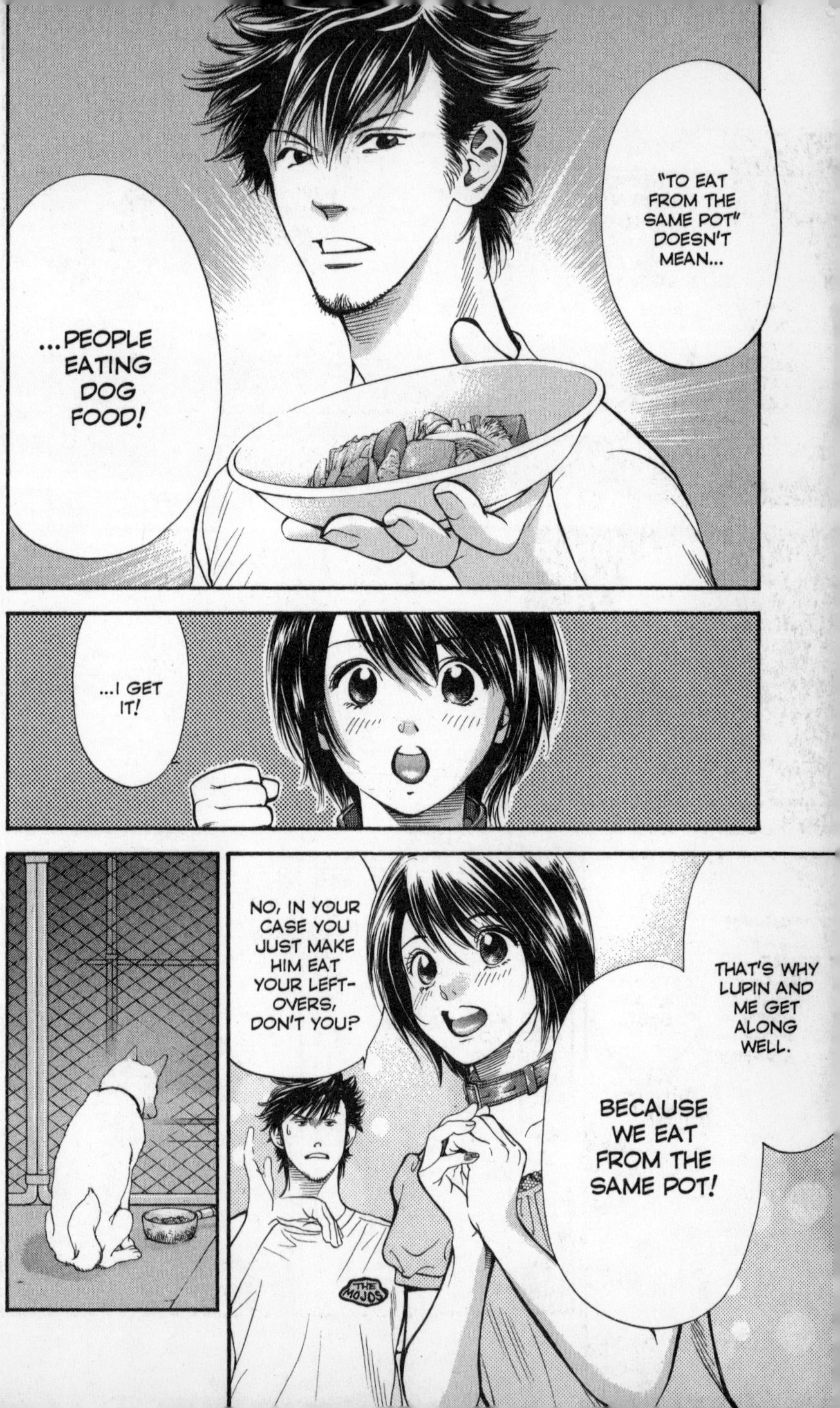
"TO EAT FROM THE SAME POT" DOESN'T MEAN...
...PEOPLE EATING DOG FOOD!
...I GET IT!
THAT'S WHY LUPIN AND ME GET ALONG WELL.
BECAUSE WE EAT FROM THE SAME POT!
NO, IN YOUR CASE YOU JUST MAKE HIM EAT YOUR LEFT-OVERS, DON'T YOU?
THE MOJOS

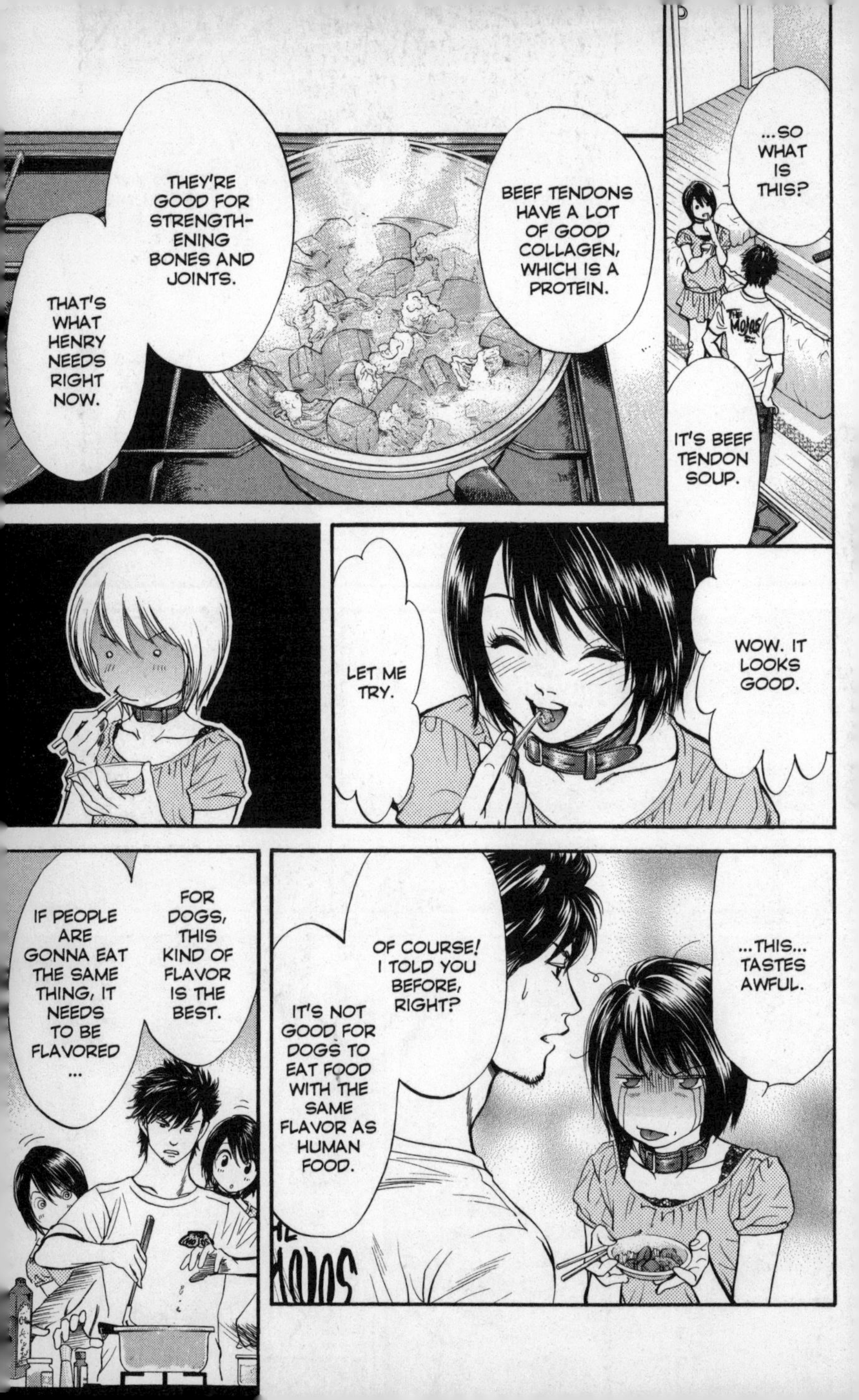
...SO WHAT IS THIS?
IT'S BEEF TENDON SOUP.
BEEF TENDONS HAVE A LOT OF GOOD COLLAGEN, WHICH IS A PROTEIN.
THEY'RE GOOD FOR STRENGTH-ENING BONES AND JOINTS.
THAT'S WHAT HENRY NEEDS RIGHT NOW.
WOW. IT LOOKS GOOD.
LET ME TRY.
...THIS... TASTES AWFUL.
OF COURSE! I TOLD YOU BEFORE, RIGHT?
IT'S NOT GOOD FOR DOGS TO EAT FOOD WITH THE SAME FLAVOR AS HUMAN FOOD.
FOR DOGS, THIS KIND OF FLAVOR IS THE BEST.
IF PEOPLE ARE GONNA EAT THE SAME THING, IT NEEDS TO BE FLAVORED ...

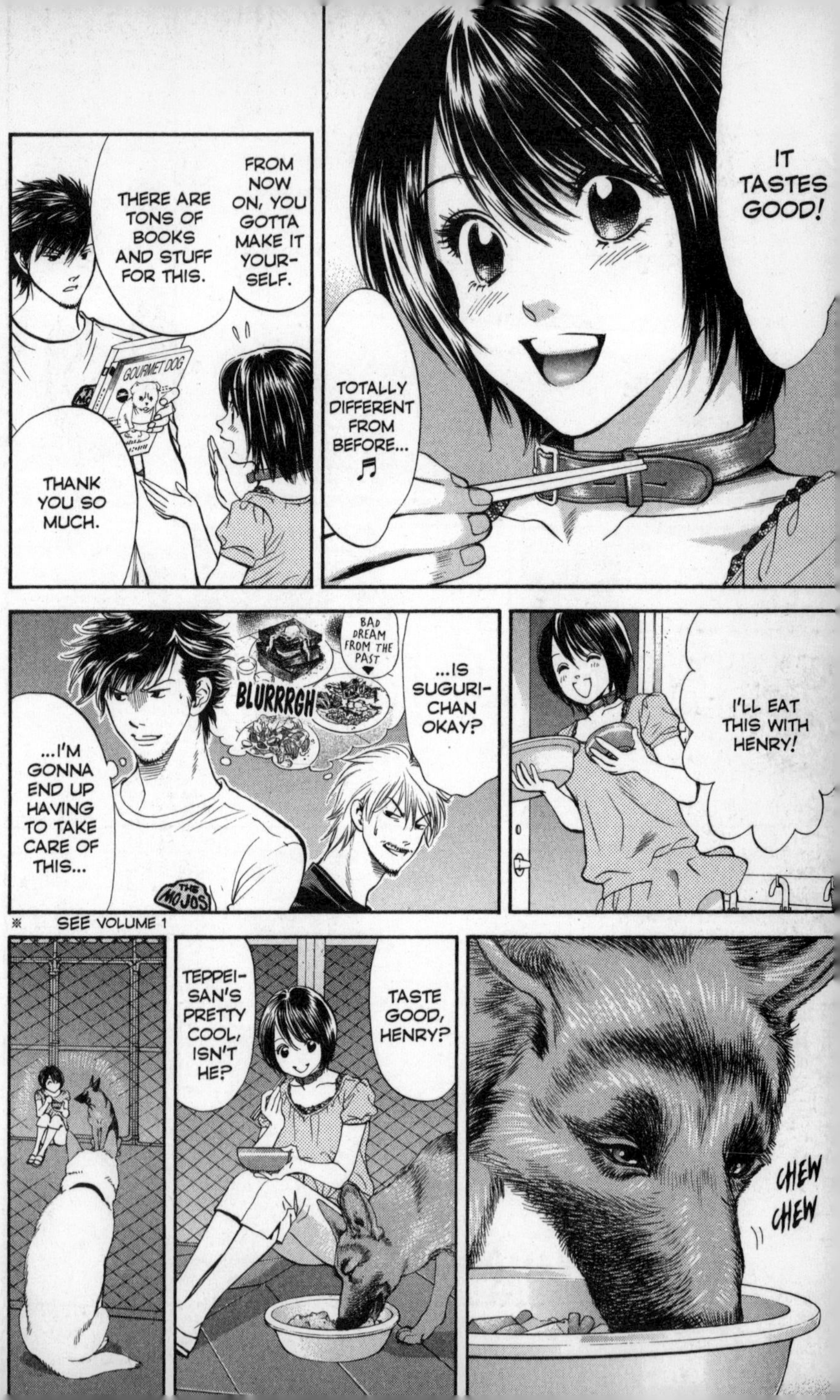
IT TASTES GOOD!
TOTALLY DIFFERENT FROM BEFORE... ♬
FROM NOW ON, YOU GOTTA MAKE IT YOURSELF.
THERE ARE TONS OF BOOKS AND STUFF FOR THIS.
GOURMET DOG
THANK YOU SO MUCH.
I'LL EAT THIS WITH HENRY!
...IS SUGURI-CHAN OKAY?
BAD DREAM FROM THE PAST
BLURRRGH
...I'M GONNA END UP HAVING TO TAKE CARE OF THIS...
THE MOJOS
※ SEE VOLUME 1
CHEW CHEW
TASTE GOOD, HENRY?
TEPPEI-SAN'S PRETTY COOL, ISN'T HE?

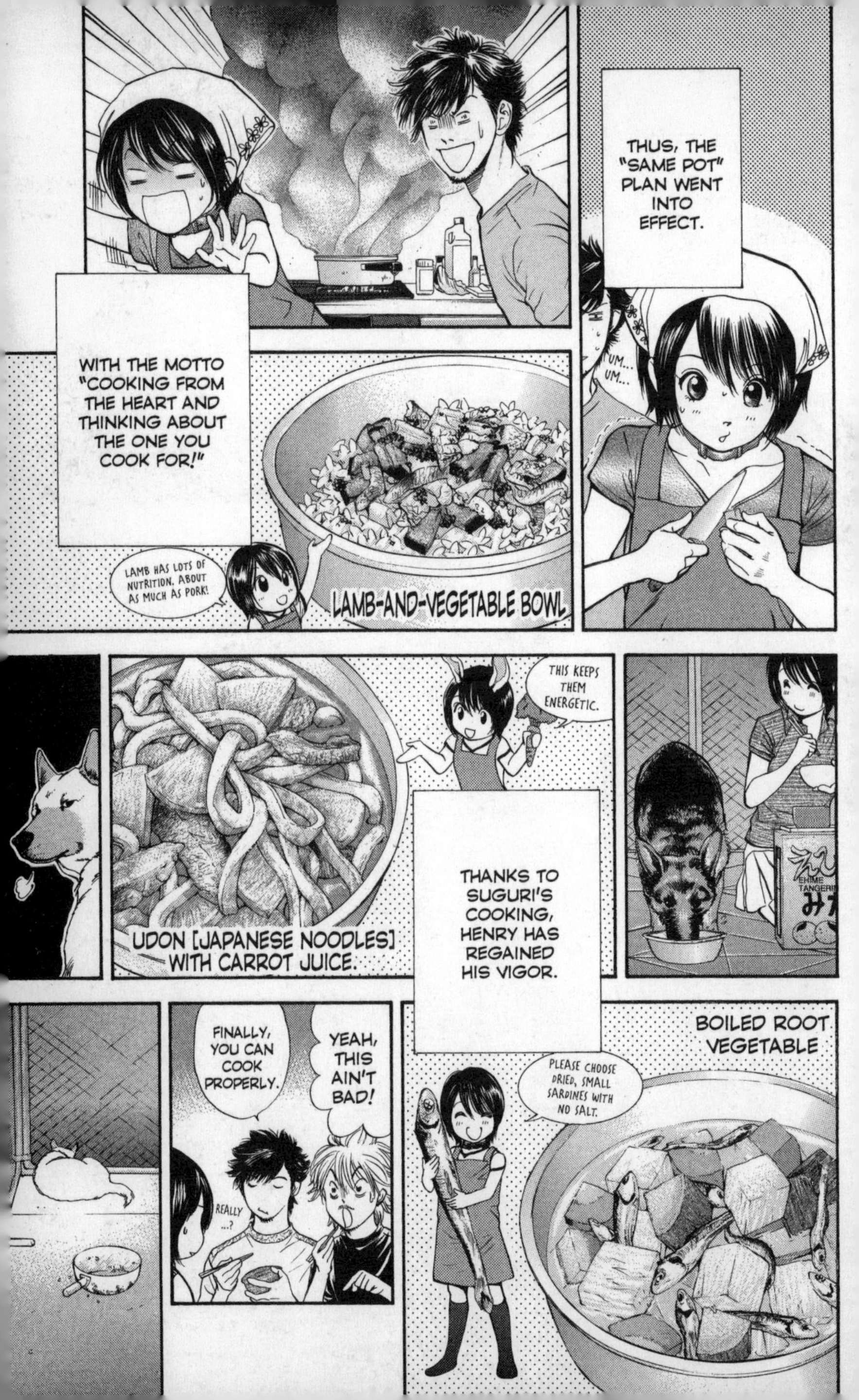
THUS, THE "SAME POT" PLAN WENT INTO EFFECT.
UM... UM...
WITH THE MOTTO "COOKING FROM THE HEART AND THINKING ABOUT THE ONE YOU COOK FOR!"
LAMB HAS LOTS OF NUTRITION. ABOUT AS MUCH AS PORK!
LAMB-AND-VEGETABLE BOWL
THIS KEEPS THEM ENERGETIC.
UDON [JAPANESE NOODLES] WITH CARROT JUICE.
THANKS TO SUGURI'S COOKING, HENRY HAS REGAINED HIS VIGOR.
BOILED ROOT VEGETABLE
PLEASE CHOOSE DRIED, SMALL SARDINES WITH NO SALT.
YEAH, THIS AIN'T BAD!
FINALLY, YOU CAN COOK PROPERLY.
REALLY ...?

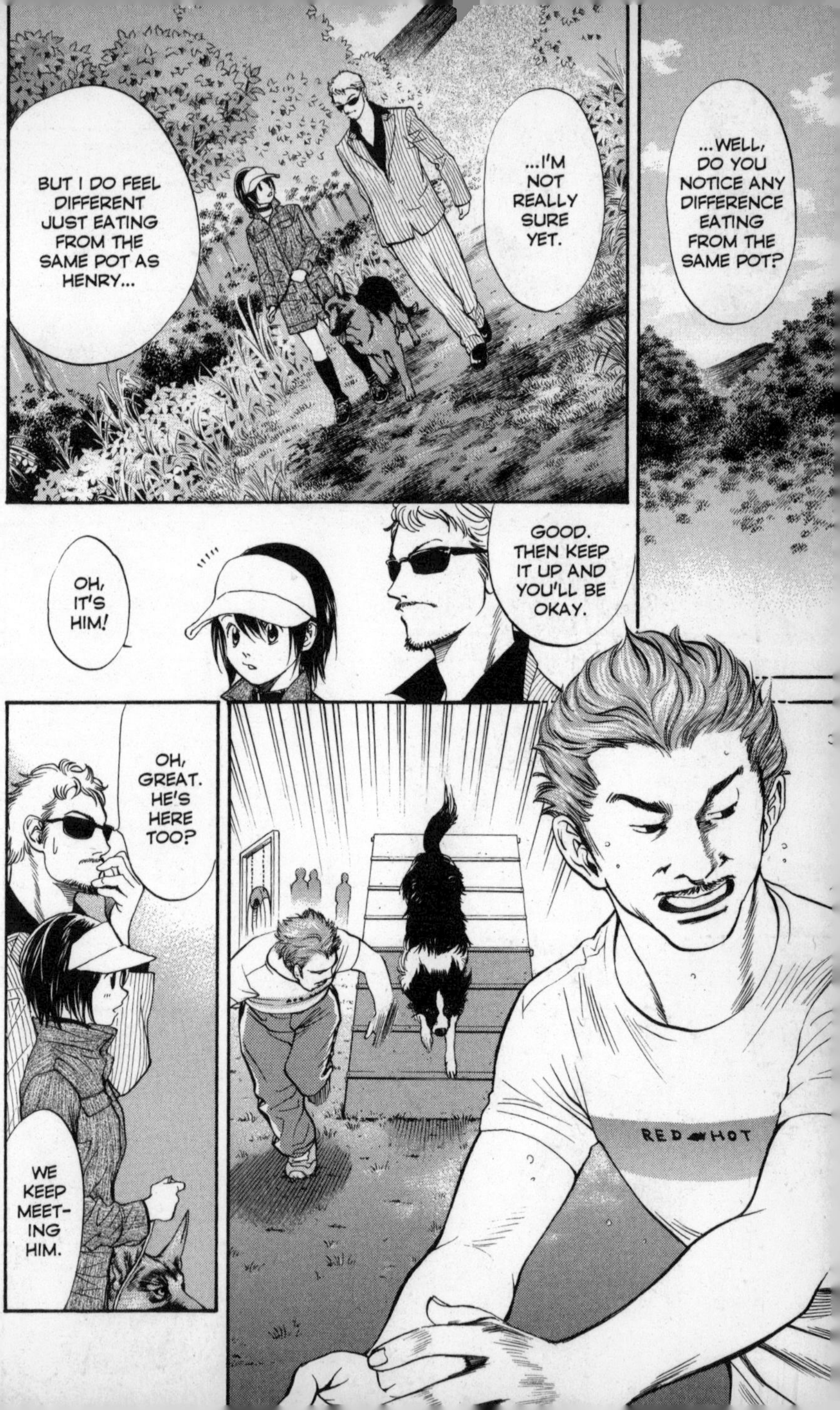
...WELL, DO YOU NOTICE ANY DIFFERENCE EATING FROM THE SAME POT?
...I'M NOT REALLY SURE YET.
BUT I DO FEEL DIFFERENT JUST EATING FROM THE SAME POT AS HENRY...
GOOD. THEN KEEP IT UP AND YOU'LL BE OKAY.
OH, IT'S HIM!
RED HOT
OH, GREAT. HE'S HERE TOO?
WE KEEP MEETING HIM.

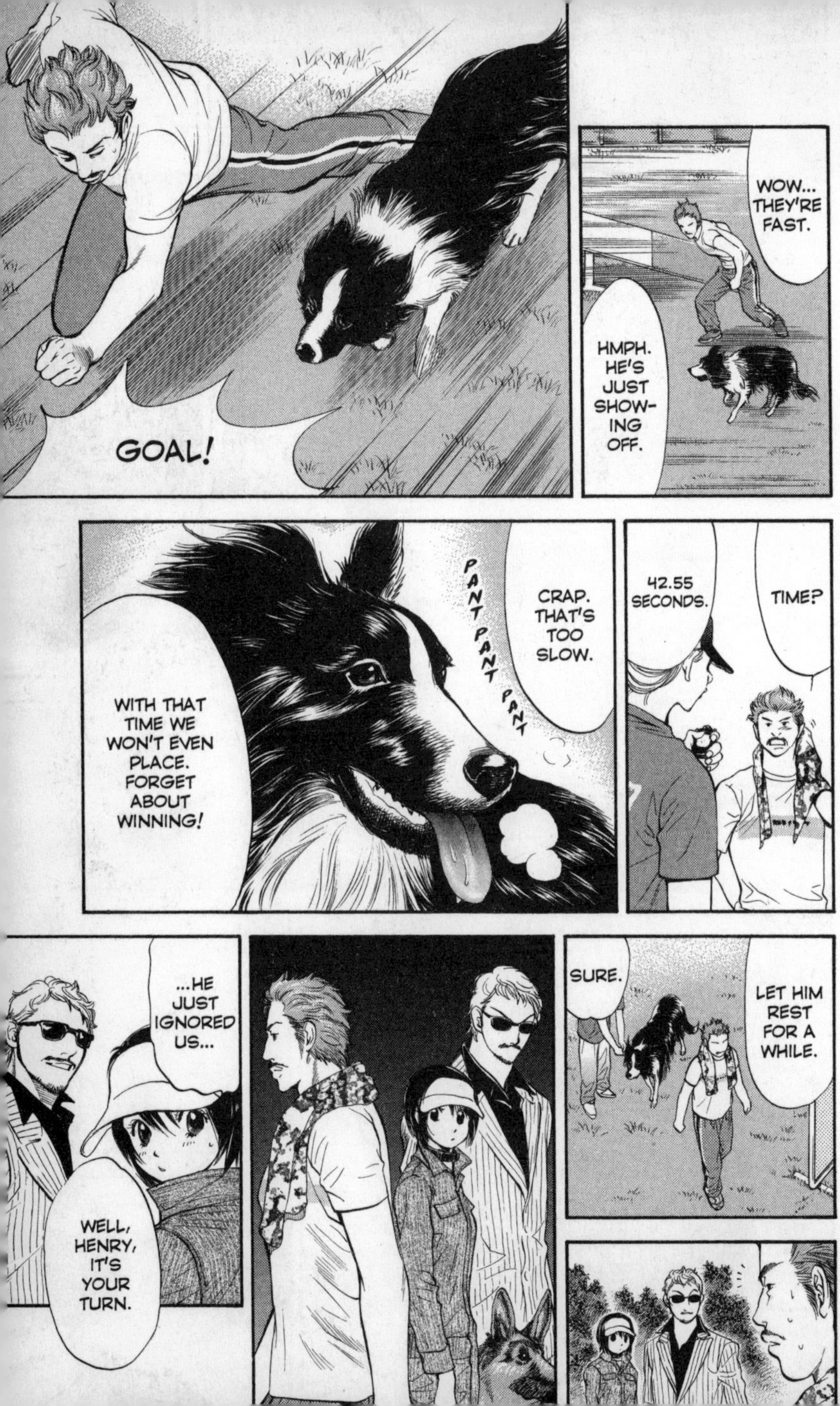
WOW... THEY'RE FAST.
HMPH. HE'S JUST SHOWING-OFF.
GOAL!
TIME?
42.55 SECONDS.
CRAP. THAT'S TOO SLOW.
PANT PANT PANT
WITH THAT TIME WE WON'T EVEN PLACE. FORGET ABOUT WINNING!
LET HIM REST FOR A WHILE.
SURE.
...HE JUST IGNORED US...
WELL, HENRY, IT'S YOUR TURN.

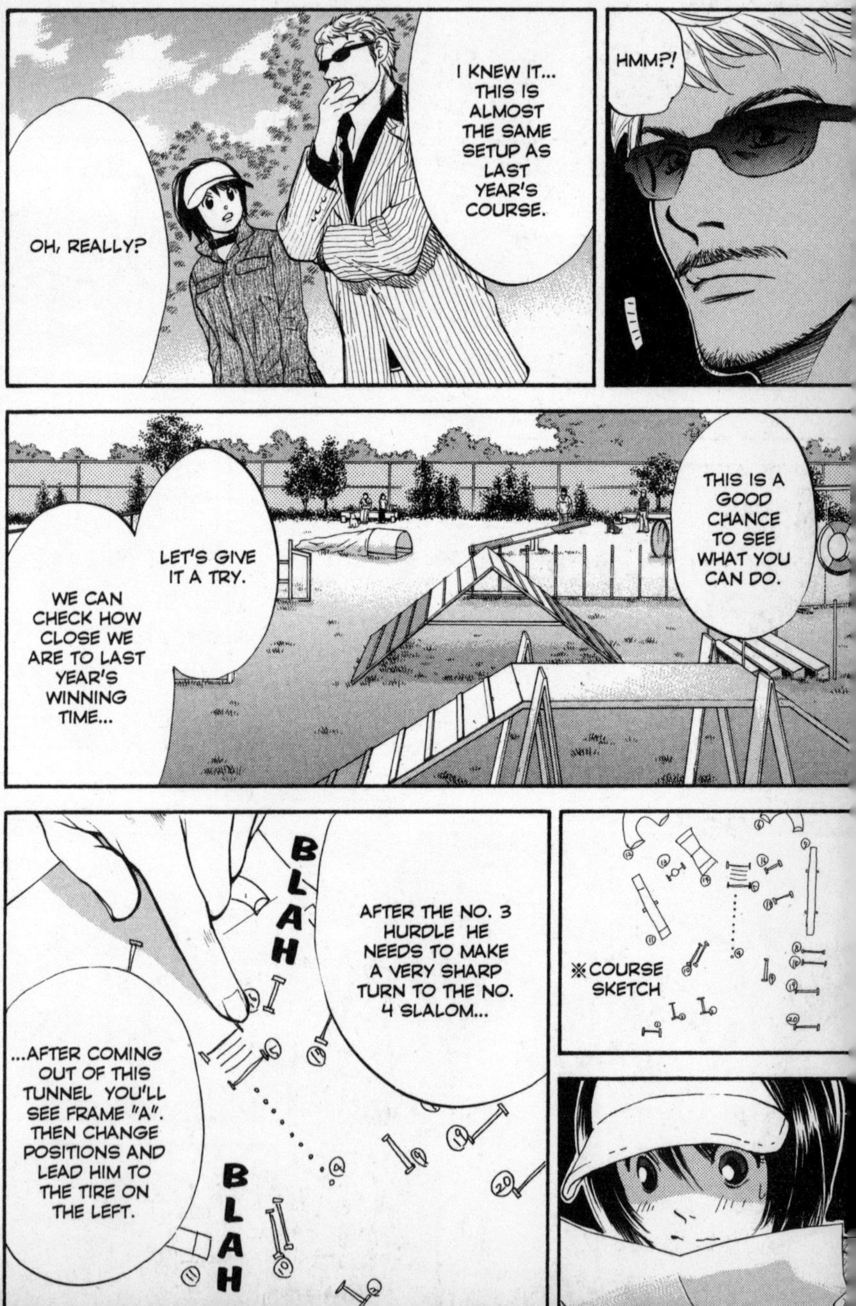
HMM?!
I KNEW IT... THIS IS ALMOST THE SAME SETUP AS LAST YEAR'S COURSE.
OH, REALLY?
THIS IS A GOOD CHANCE TO SEE WHAT YOU CAN DO.
LET'S GIVE IT A TRY.
WE CAN CHECK HOW CLOSE WE ARE TO LAST YEAR'S WINNING TIME...
※COURSE SKETCH
AFTER THE NO. 3 HURDLE HE NEEDS TO MAKE A VERY SHARP TURN TO THE NO. 4 SLALOM...
BLAH
...AFTER COMING OUT OF THIS TUNNEL YOU'LL SEE FRAME "A". THEN CHANGE POSITIONS AND LEAD HIM TO THE TIRE ON THE LEFT.
BLAH

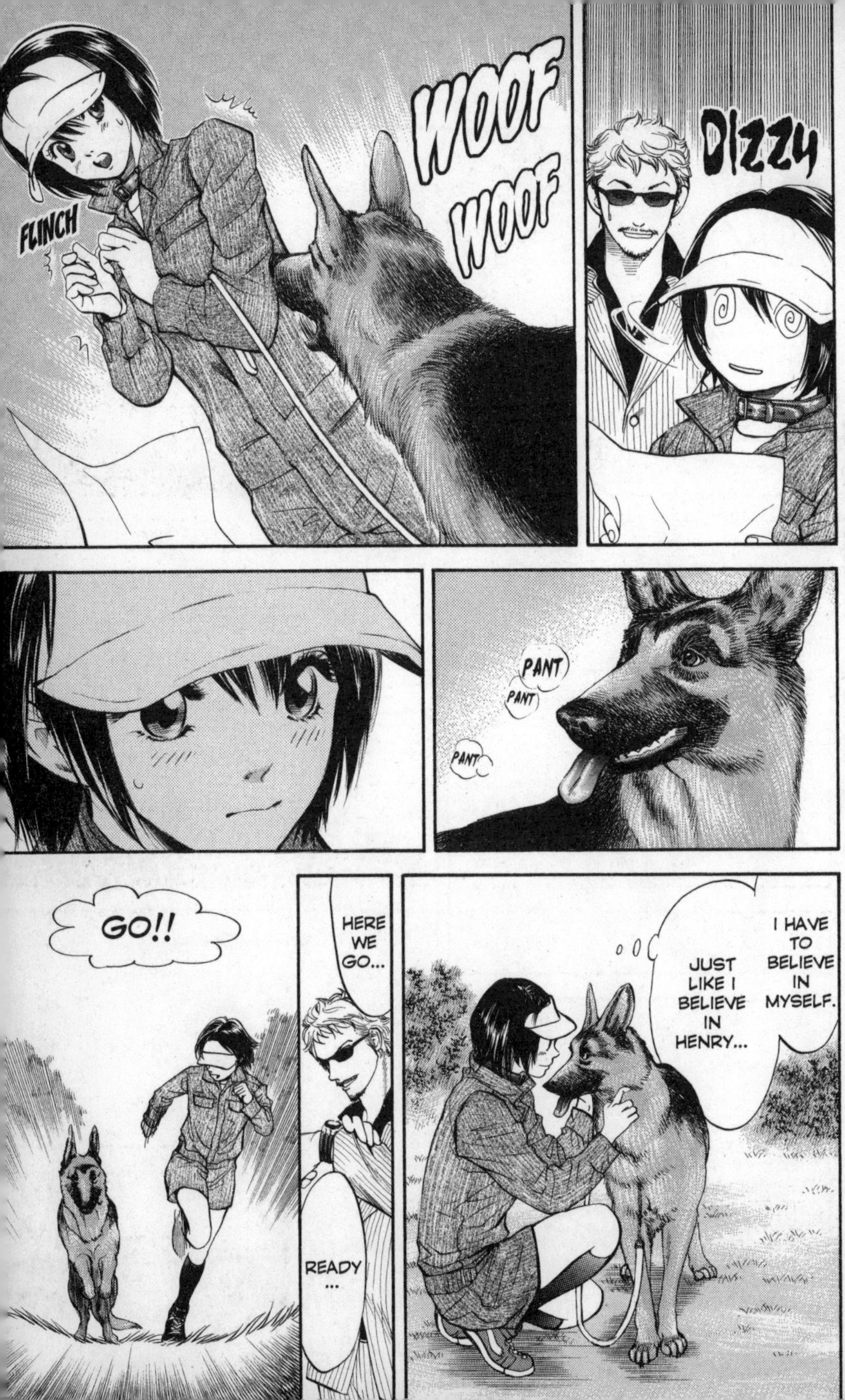
DIZZY
WOOF
WOOF
FLINCH
PANT
PANT
PANT
JUST LIKE I BELIEVE IN HENRY... I HAVE TO BELIEVE IN MYSELF.
HERE WE GO...
READY...
GO!!

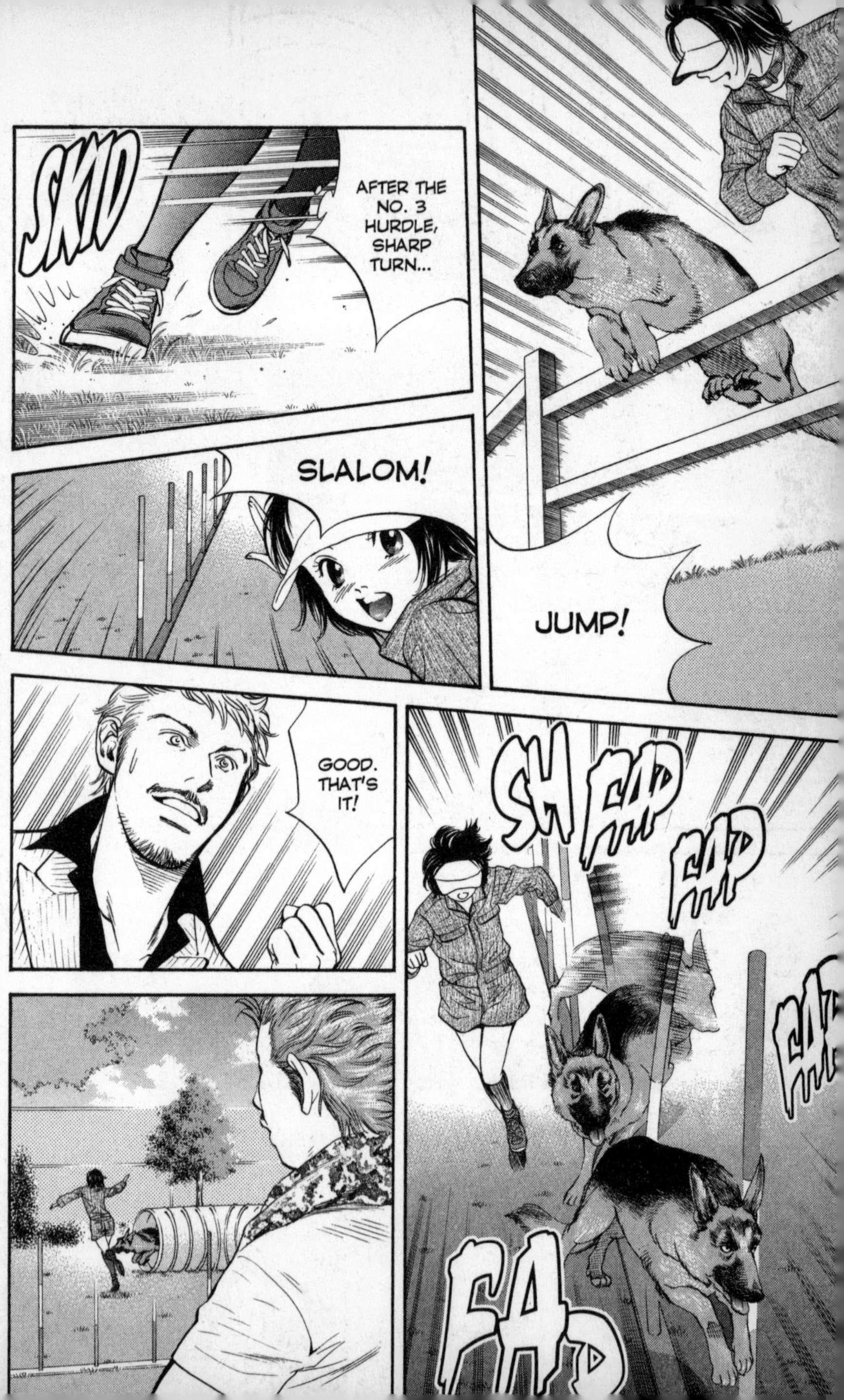
JUMP!
SKID
AFTER THE NO. 3 HURDLE, SHARP TURN...
SLALOM!
SH
FAP
FAP
FAP
GOOD. THAT'S IT!

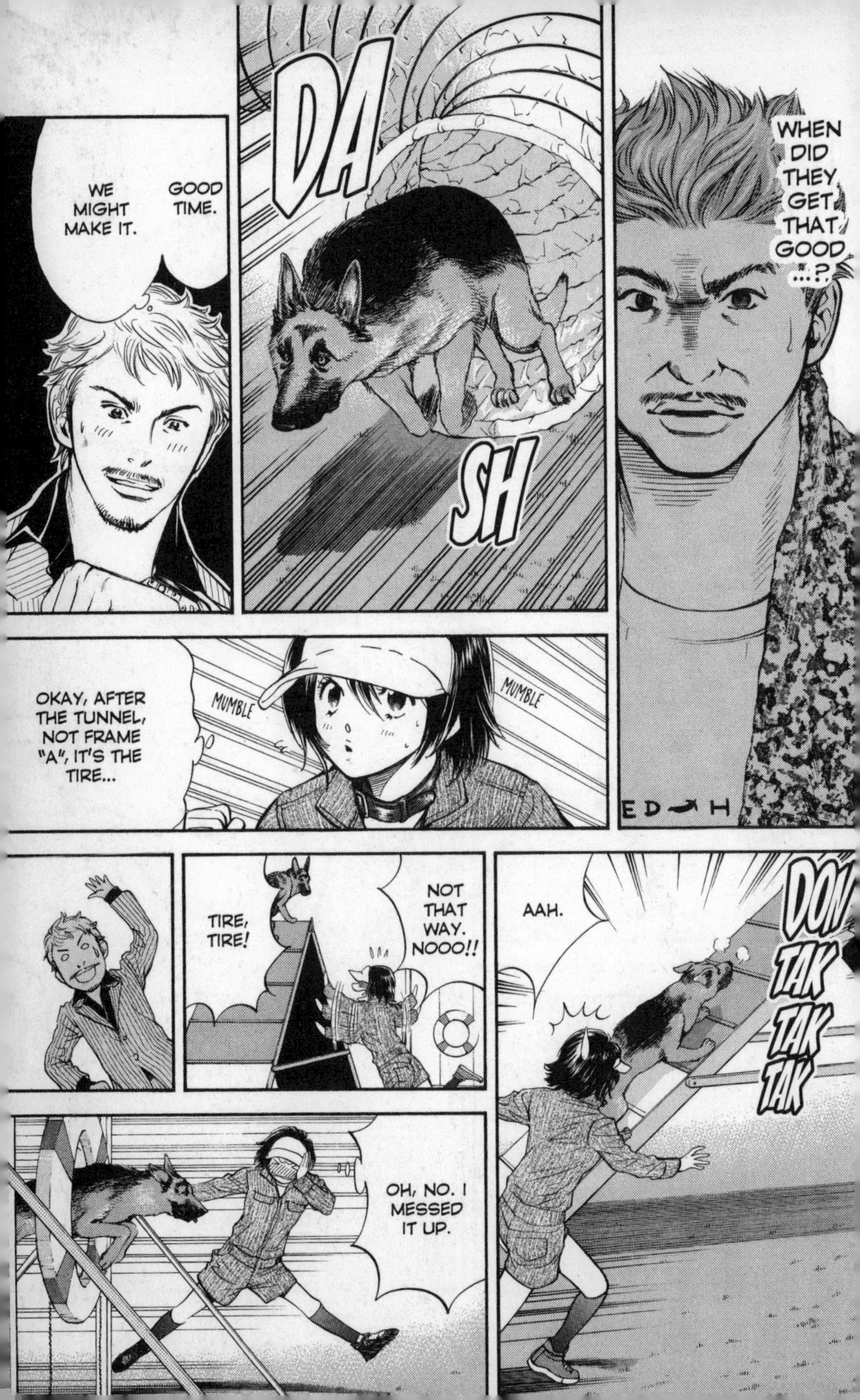
WHEN DID THEY GET THAT GOOD ...?
DA
SH
GOOD TIME.
WE MIGHT MAKE IT.
MUMBLE
MUMBLE
OKAY, AFTER THE TUNNEL, NOT FRAME "A", IT'S THE TIRE...
DON
TAK TAK TAK
AAH.
NOT THAT WAY. NOOO!!
TIRE, TIRE!
OH, NO. I MESSED IT UP.

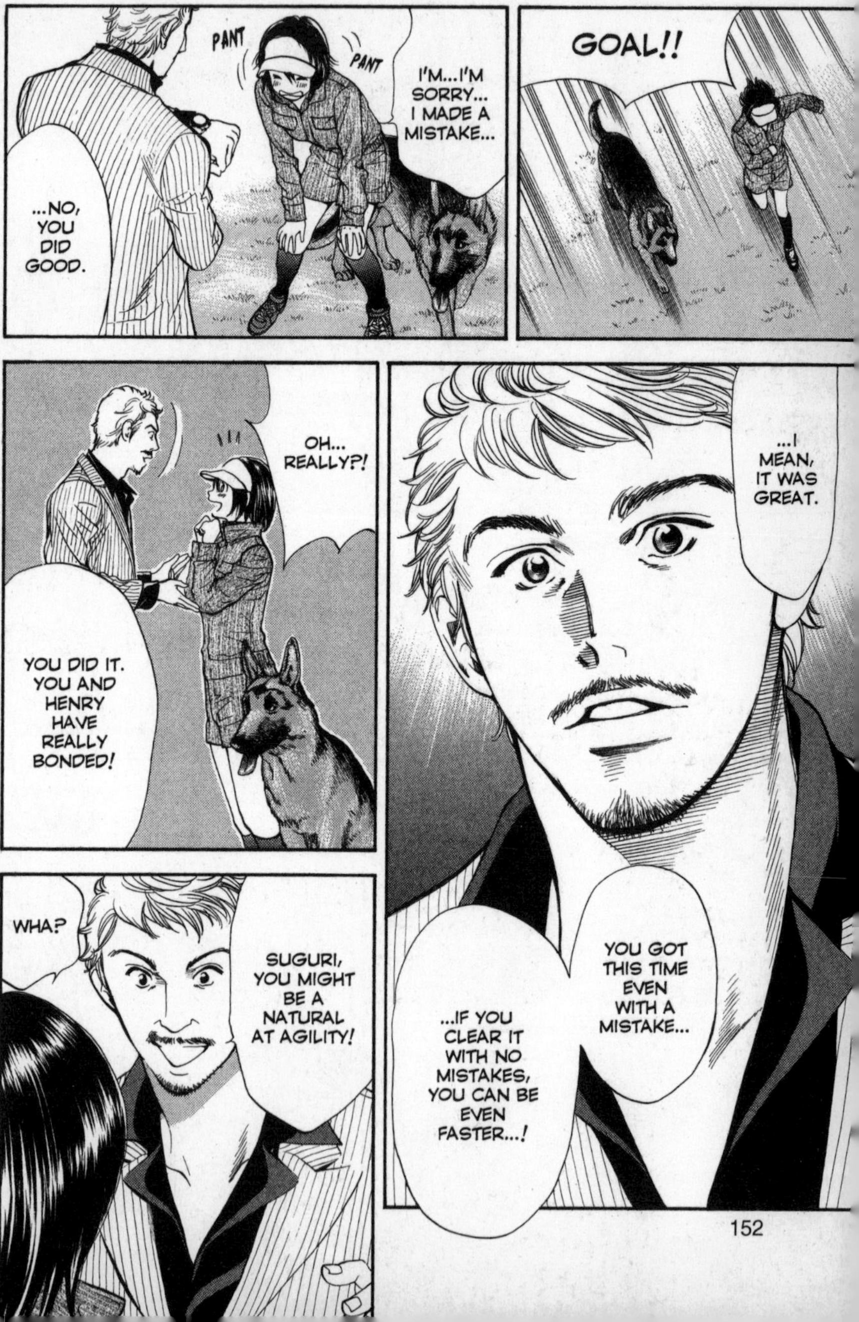
GOAL!!
PANT
PANT
I'M...I'M SORRY... I MADE A MISTAKE...
...NO, YOU DID GOOD.
...I MEAN, IT WAS GREAT.
YOU GOT THIS TIME EVEN WITH A MISTAKE...
...IF YOU CLEAR IT WITH NO MISTAKES, YOU CAN BE EVEN FASTER...!
OH... REALLY?!
YOU DID IT. YOU AND HENRY HAVE REALLY BONDED!
SUGURI, YOU MIGHT BE A NATURAL AT AGILITY!
WHA?

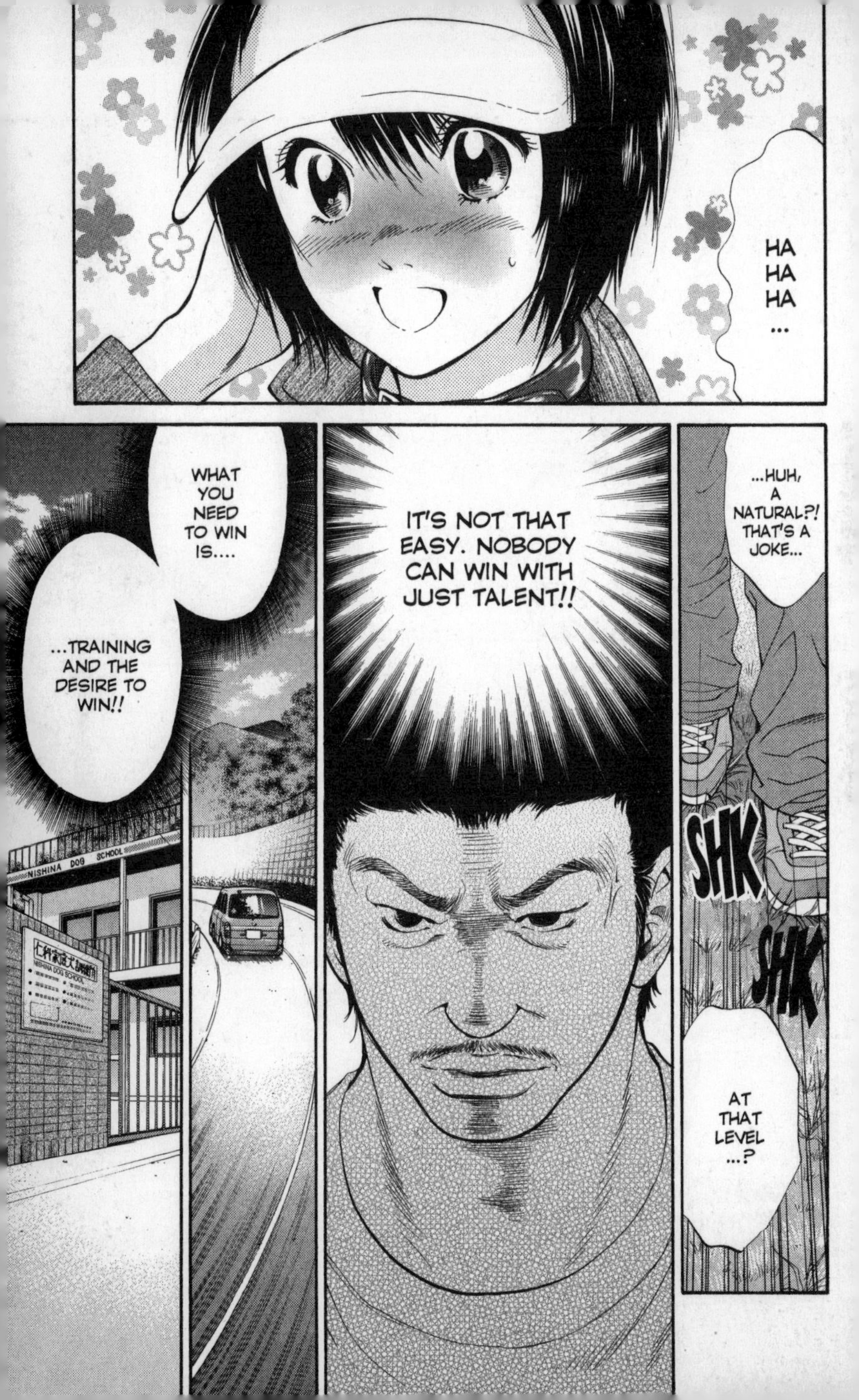
HA HA HA ...
...HUH, A NATURAL?! THAT'S A JOKE...
SHK
SHK
AT THAT LEVEL ...?
IT'S NOT THAT EASY. NOBODY CAN WIN WITH JUST TALENT!!
WHAT YOU NEED TO WIN IS....
...TRAINING AND THE DESIRE TO WIN!!
NISHINA DOG SCHOOL

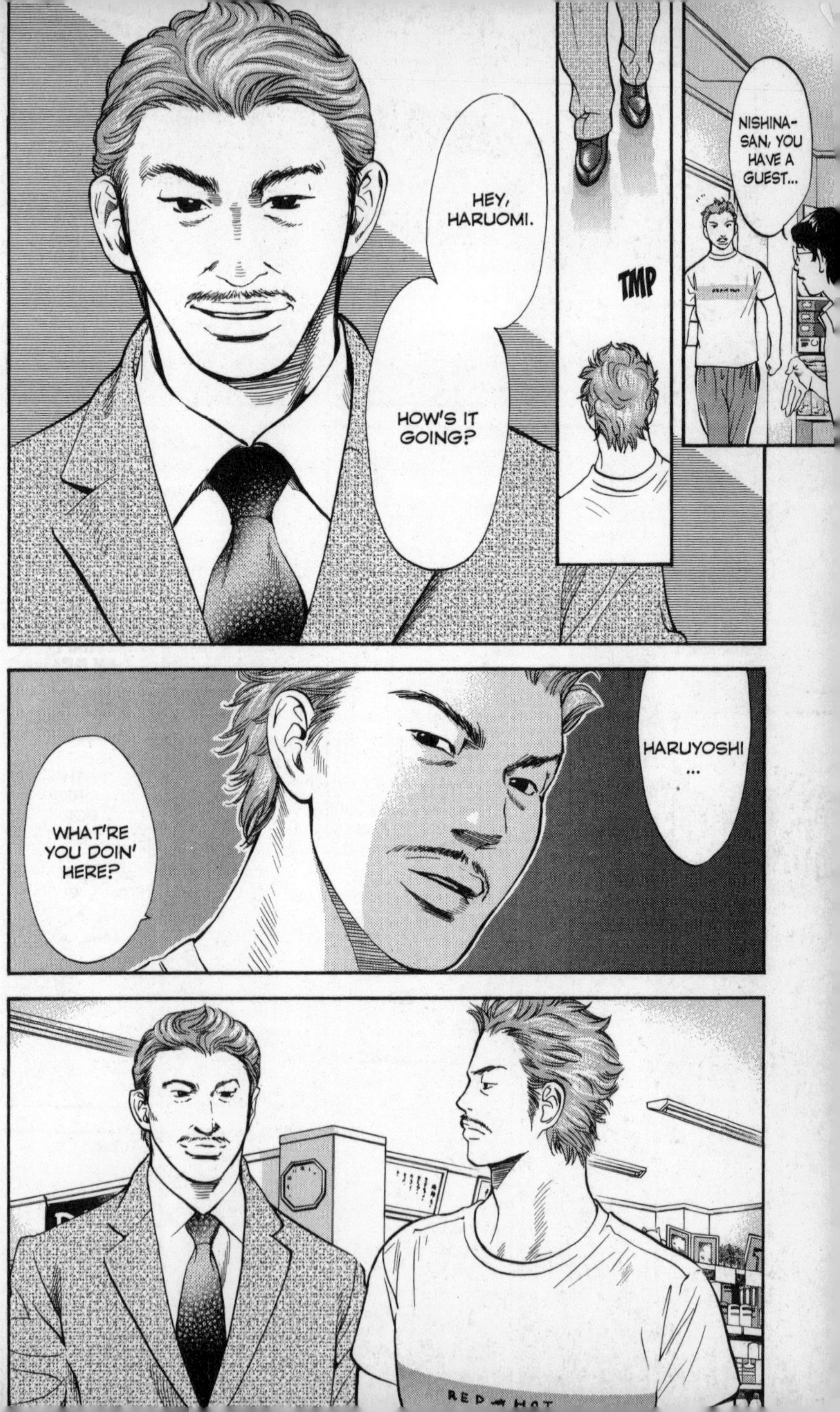
NISHINA-SAN, YOU HAVE A GUEST...
TMP
HEY, HARUOMI.
HOW'S IT GOING?
HARUYOSHI ...
WHAT'RE YOU DOIN' HERE?

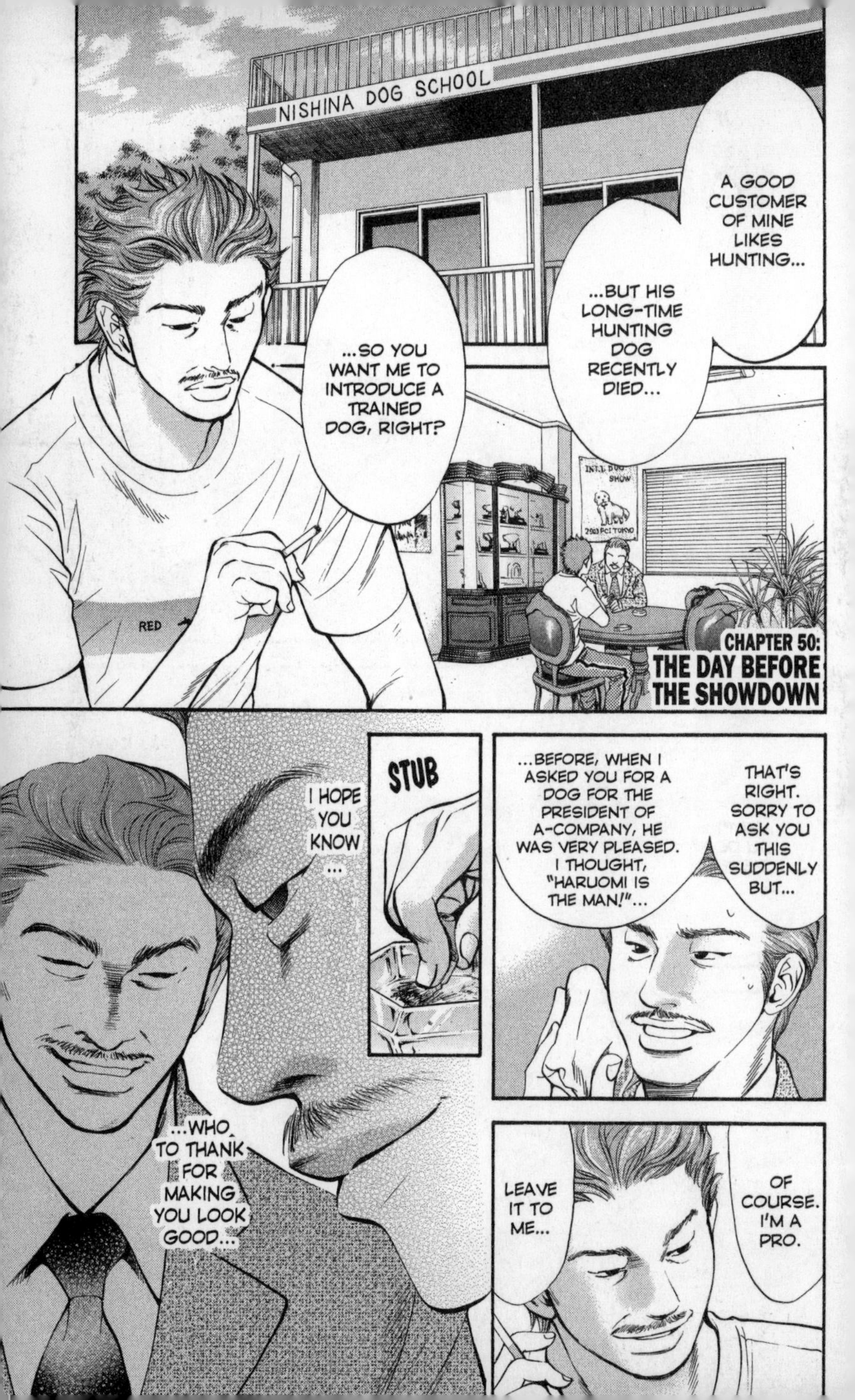
NISHINA DOG SCHOOL
A GOOD CUSTOMER OF MINE LIKES HUNTING...
...BUT HIS LONG-TIME HUNTING DOG RECENTLY DIED...
...SO YOU WANT ME TO INTRODUCE A TRAINED DOG, RIGHT?
INT'L DOG SHOW
2003 FCI TOKYO
RED
CHAPTER 50: THE DAY BEFORE THE SHOWDOWN
THAT'S RIGHT. SORRY TO ASK YOU THIS SUDDENLY BUT...
...BEFORE, WHEN I ASKED YOU FOR A DOG FOR THE PRESIDENT OF A-COMPANY, HE WAS VERY PLEASED. I THOUGHT, "HARUOMI IS THE MAN!"...
STUB
I HOPE YOU KNOW ...
...WHO TO THANK FOR MAKING YOU LOOK GOOD...
OF COURSE. I'M A PRO.
LEAVE IT TO ME...

CHAPTER 50: THE DAY BEFORE THE SHOWDOWN

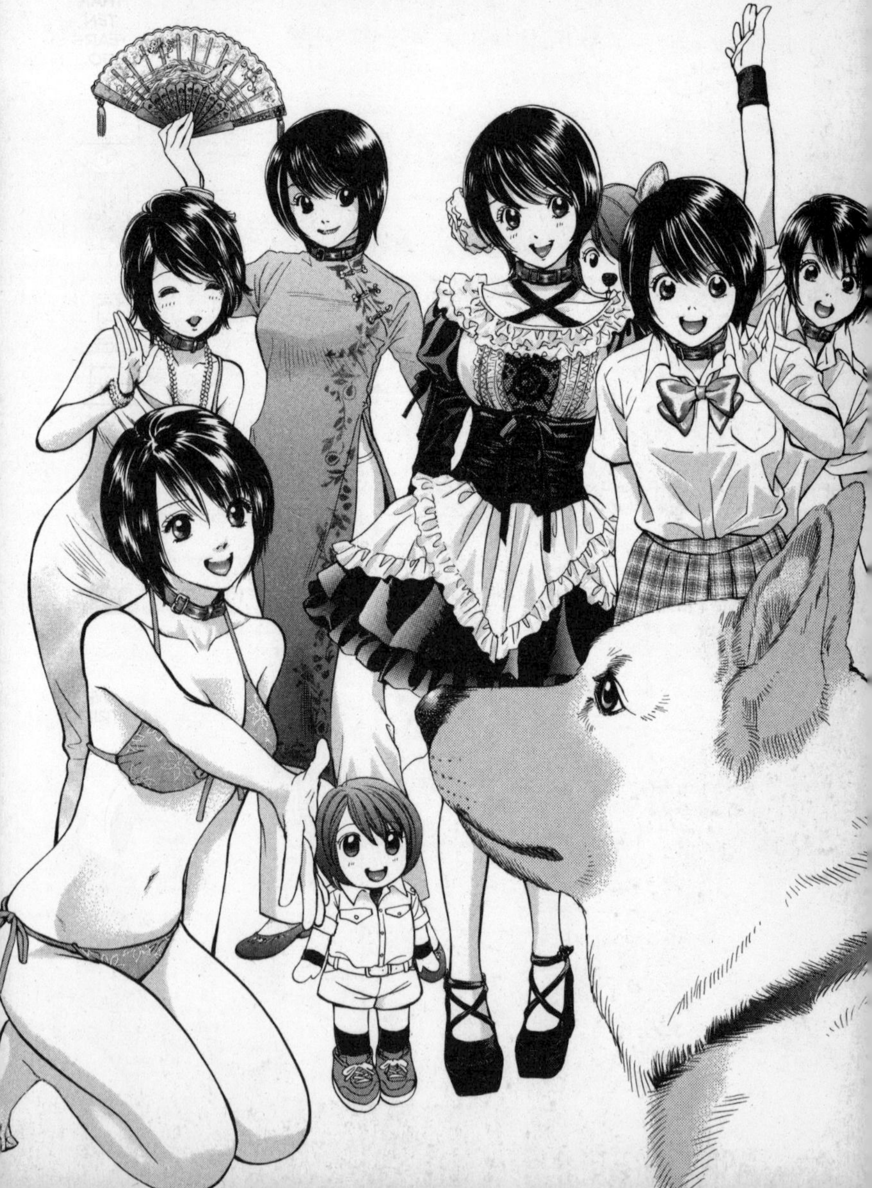

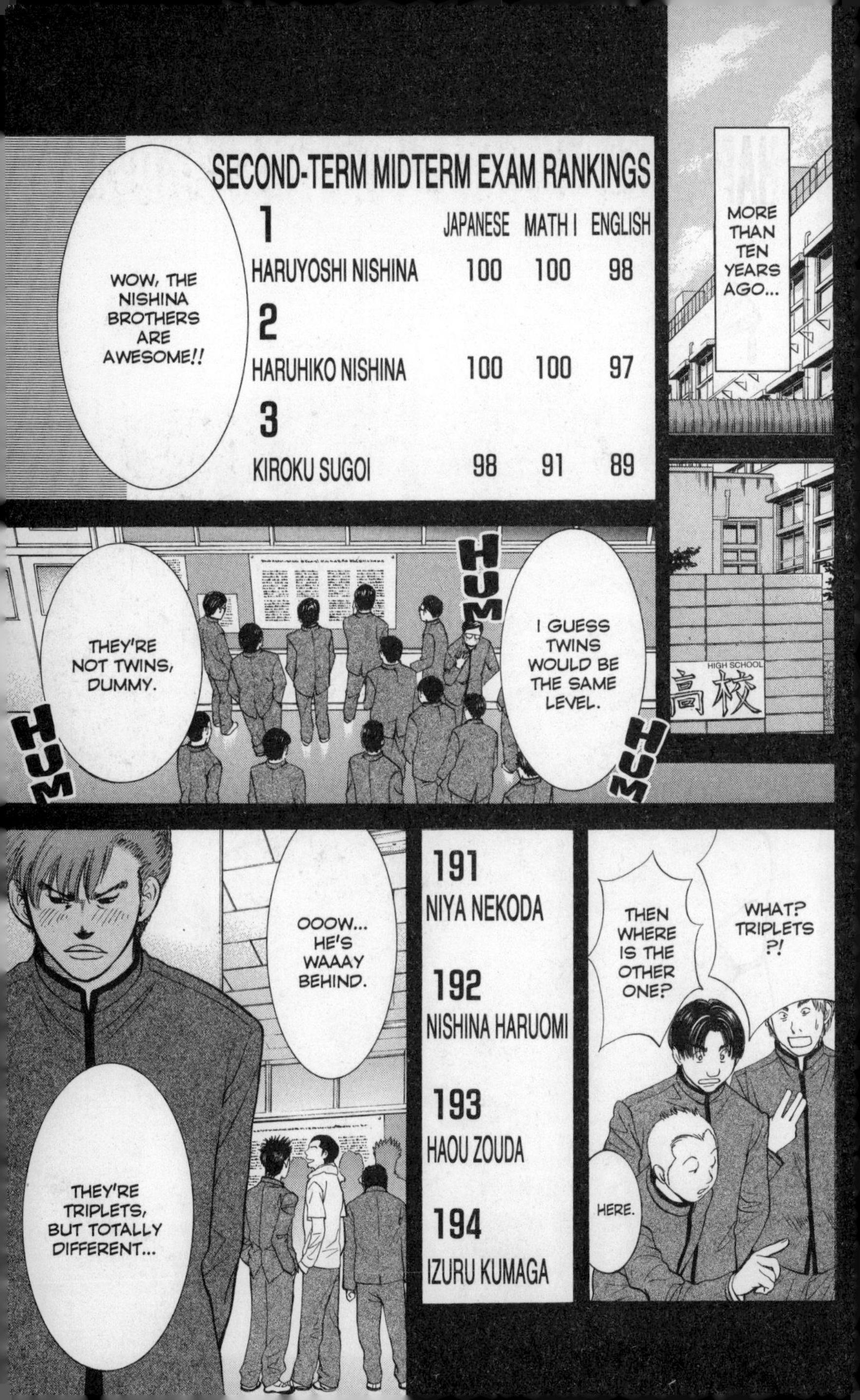
MORE THAN TEN YEARS AGO...
SECOND-TERM MIDTERM EXAM RANKINGS
1 JAPANESE MATH I ENGLISH
HARUYOSHI NISHINA 100 100 98
2
HARUHIKO NISHINA 100 100 97
3
KIROKU SUGOI 98 91 89
WOW, THE NISHINA BROTHERS ARE AWESOME!!
HIGH SCHOOL
高校
HUM
I GUESS TWINS WOULD BE THE SAME LEVEL.
THEY'RE NOT TWINS, DUMMY.
HUM
HUM
WHAT? TRIPLETS?!
THEN WHERE IS THE OTHER ONE?
HERE.
191
NIYA NEKODA
192
NISHINA HARUOMI
193
HAOU ZOUDA
194
IZURU KUMAGA
OOOW... HE'S WAAAY BEHIND.
THEY'RE TRIPLETS, BUT TOTALLY DIFFERENT...

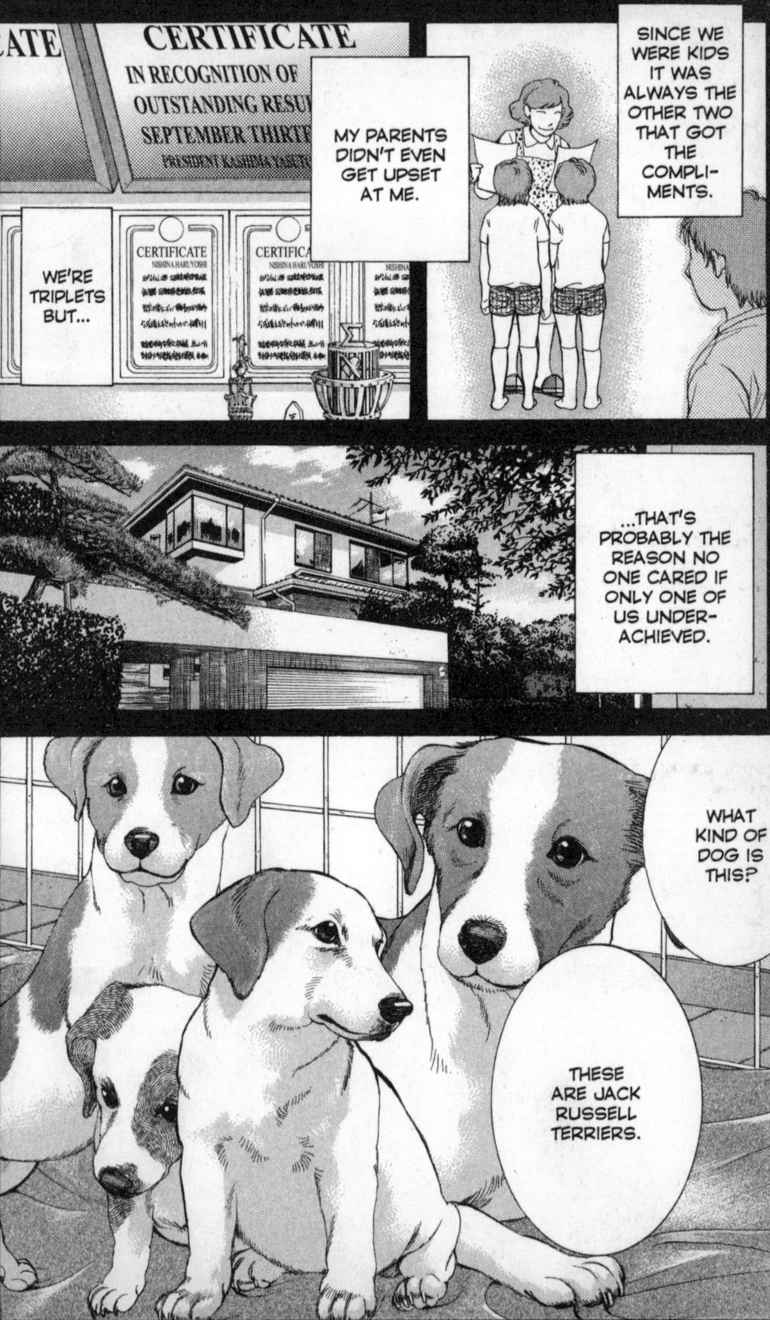
SINCE WE WERE KIDS IT WAS ALWAYS THE OTHER TWO THAT GOT THE COMPLI-MENTS.
MY PARENTS DIDN'T EVEN GET UPSET AT ME.
CERTIFICATE
IN RECOGNITION OF
CERTIFICATE
NISHINA HARUYOSHI
WE'RE TRIPLETS BUT...
...THAT'S PROBABLY THE REASON NO ONE CARED IF ONLY ONE OF US UNDER-ACHIEVED.
WHAT KIND OF DOG IS THIS?
THESE ARE JACK RUSSELL TERRIERS.

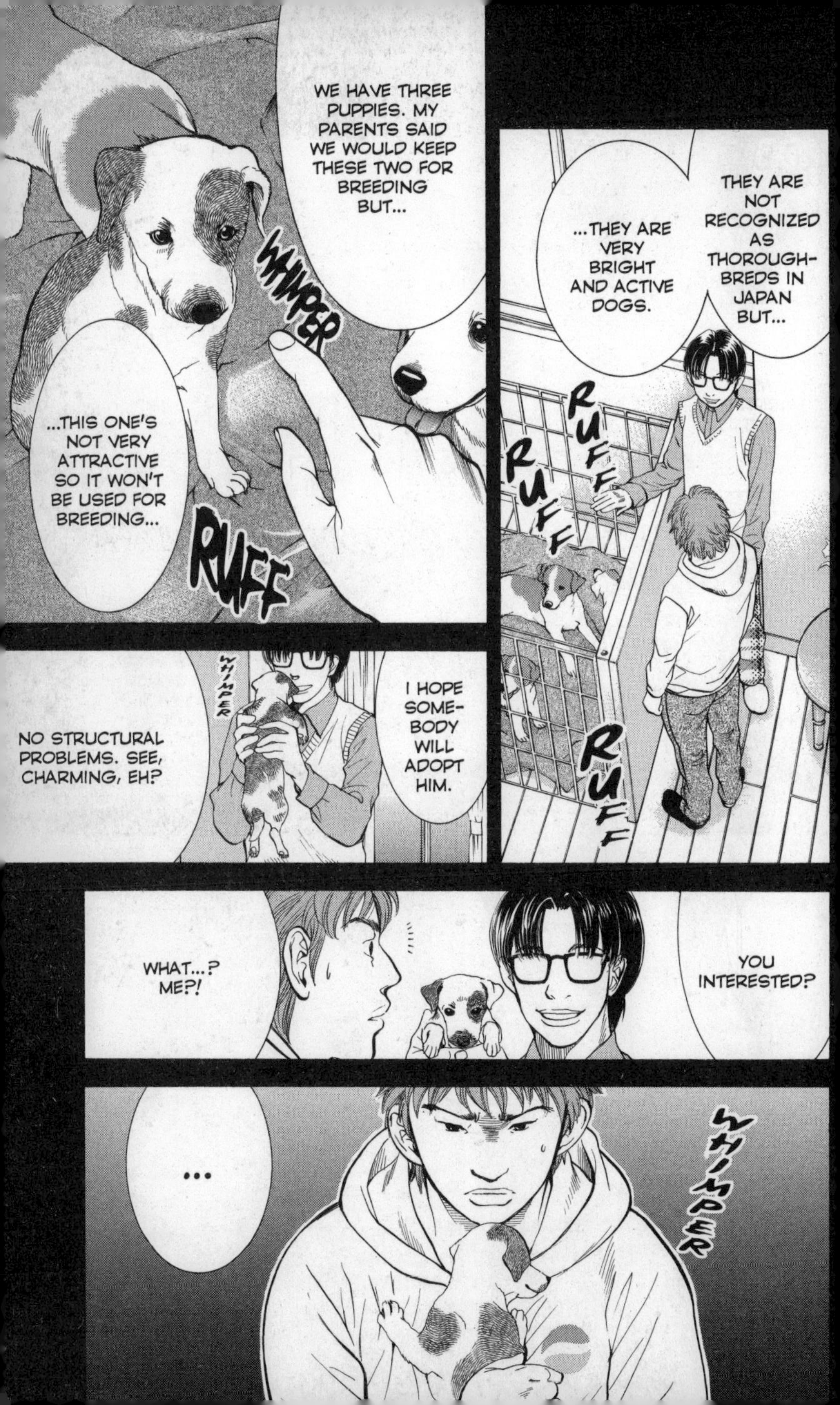
THEY ARE NOT RECOGNIZED AS THOROUGH-BREDS IN JAPAN BUT...
...THEY ARE VERY BRIGHT AND ACTIVE DOGS.
RUFF RUFF
RUFF
RUFF
WE HAVE THREE PUPPIES. MY PARENTS SAID WE WOULD KEEP THESE TWO FOR BREEDING BUT...
WHIMPER
...THIS ONE'S NOT VERY ATTRACTIVE SO IT WON'T BE USED FOR BREEDING...
RUFF
I HOPE SOMEBODY WILL ADOPT HIM.
WHIMPER
NO STRUCTURAL PROBLEMS. SEE, CHARMING, EH?
YOU INTERESTED?
WHAT...? ME?!
WHIMPER
...

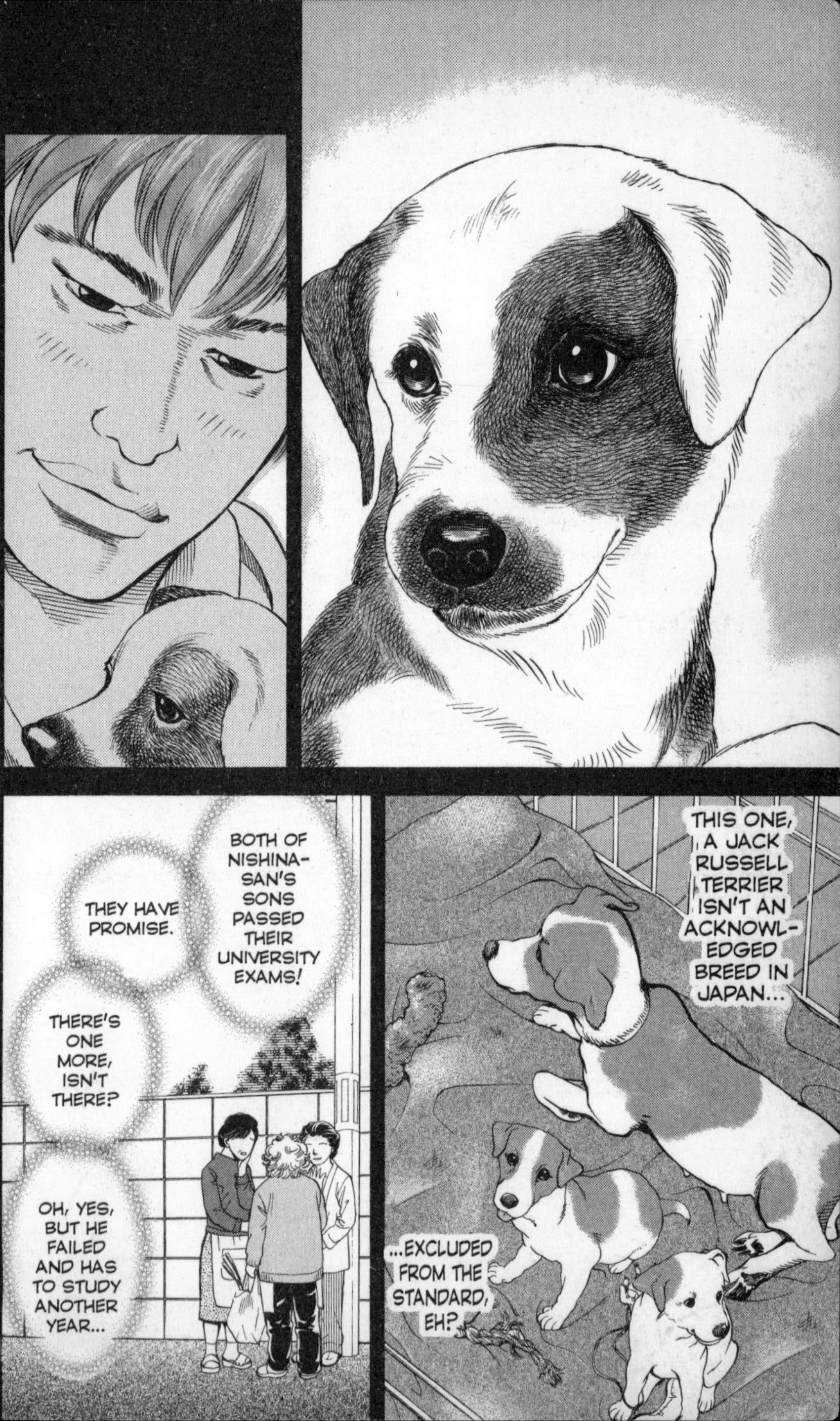
THIS ONE, A JACK RUSSELL TERRIER ISN'T AN ACKNOWL-EDGED BREED IN JAPAN...
...EXCLUDED FROM THE STANDARD, EH?
BOTH OF NISHINA-SAN'S SONS PASSED THEIR UNIVERSITY EXAMS!
THEY HAVE PROMISE.
THERE'S ONE MORE, ISN'T THERE?
OH, YES, BUT HE FAILED AND HAS TO STUDY ANOTHER YEAR...

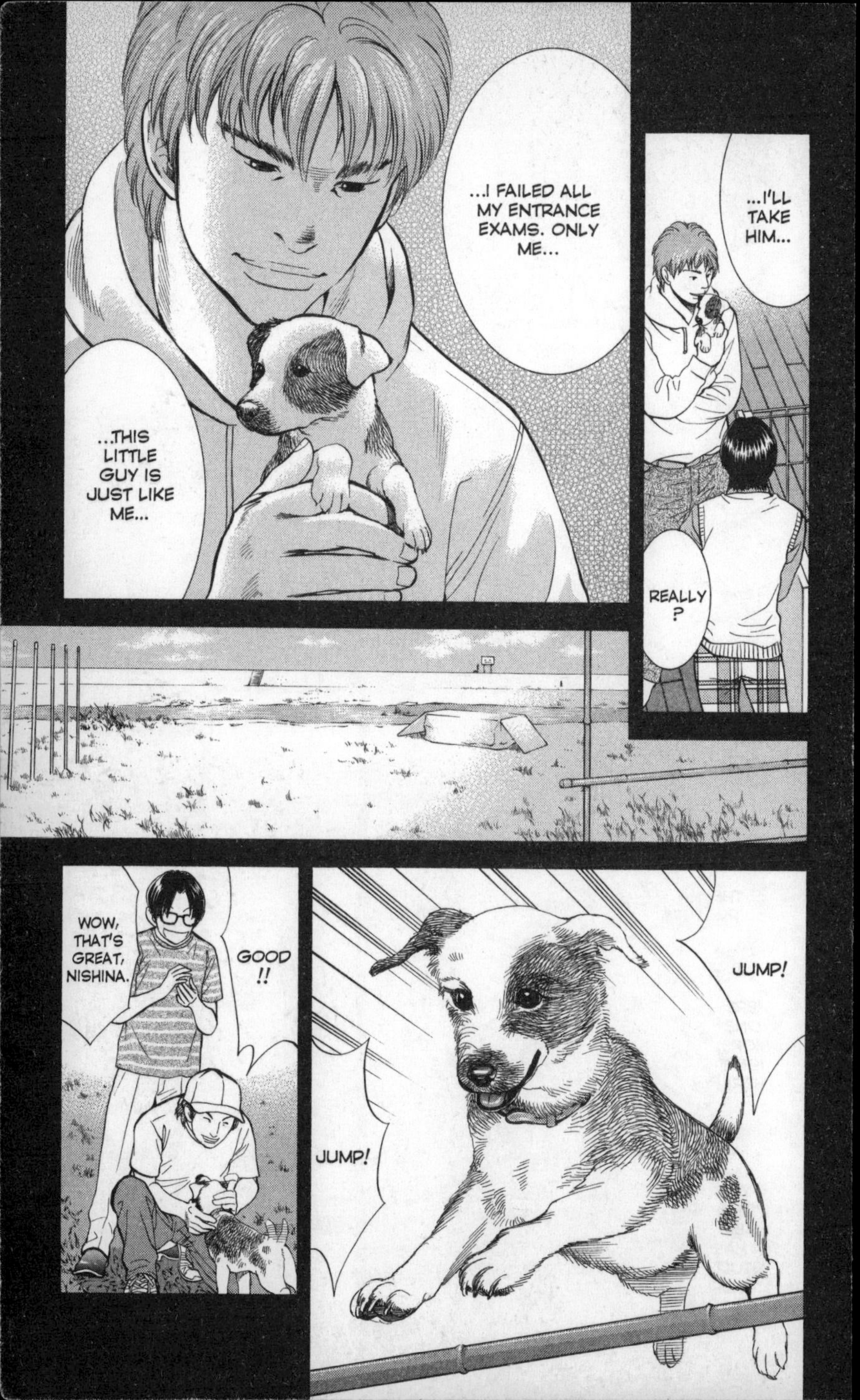
...I FAILED ALL MY ENTRANCE EXAMS. ONLY ME...
...THIS LITTLE GUY IS JUST LIKE ME...
...I'LL TAKE HIM...
REALLY ?
JUMP!
JUMP!
GOOD !!
WOW, THAT'S GREAT, NISHINA.

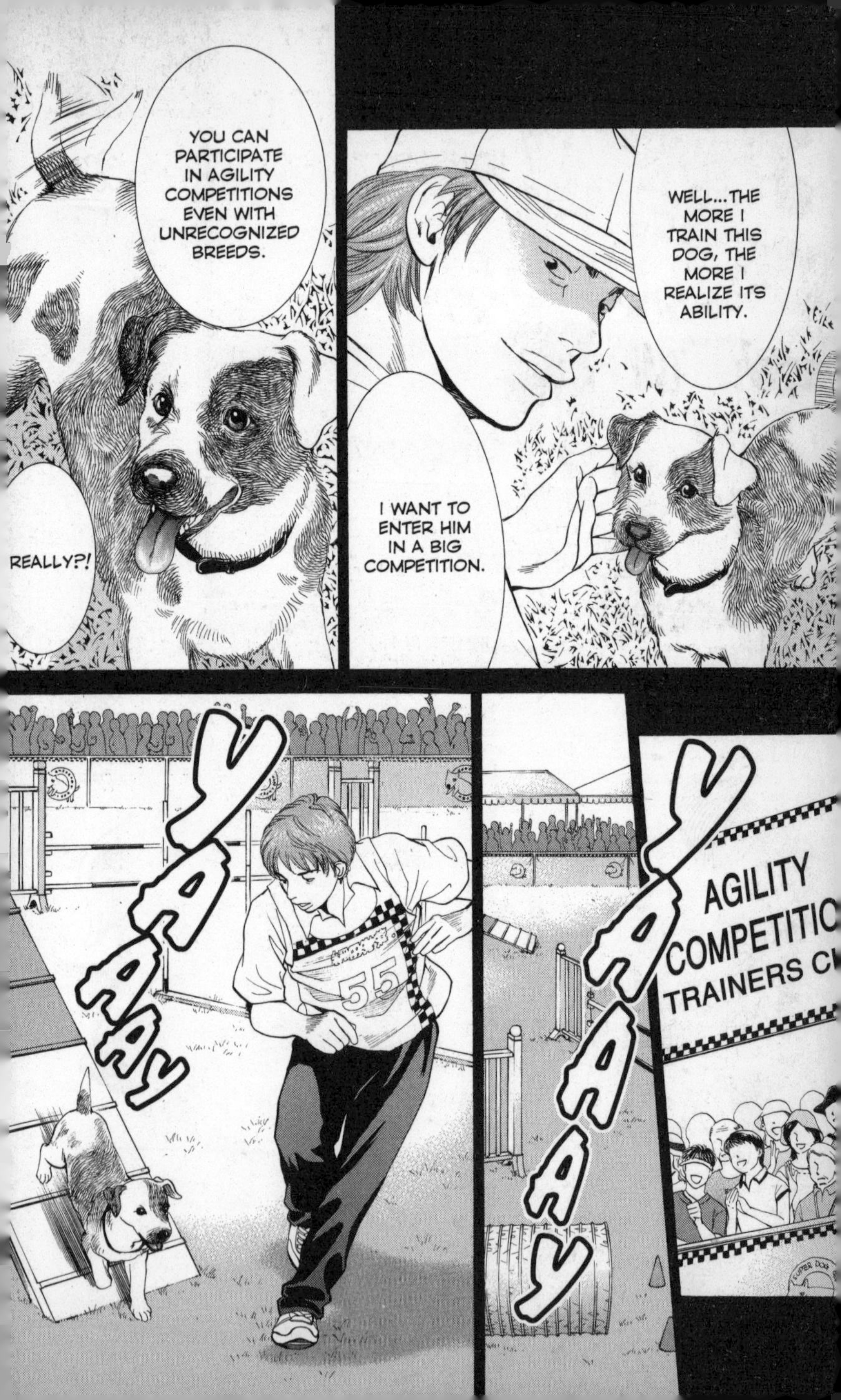
WELL...THE MORE I TRAIN THIS DOG, THE MORE I REALIZE ITS ABILITY.
I WANT TO ENTER HIM IN A BIG COMPETITION.
YOU CAN PARTICIPATE IN AGILITY COMPETITIONS EVEN WITH UNRECOGNIZED BREEDS.
REALLY?!
YAAAAY
AGILITY
COMPETITIO
TRAINERS C
55
YAAAY

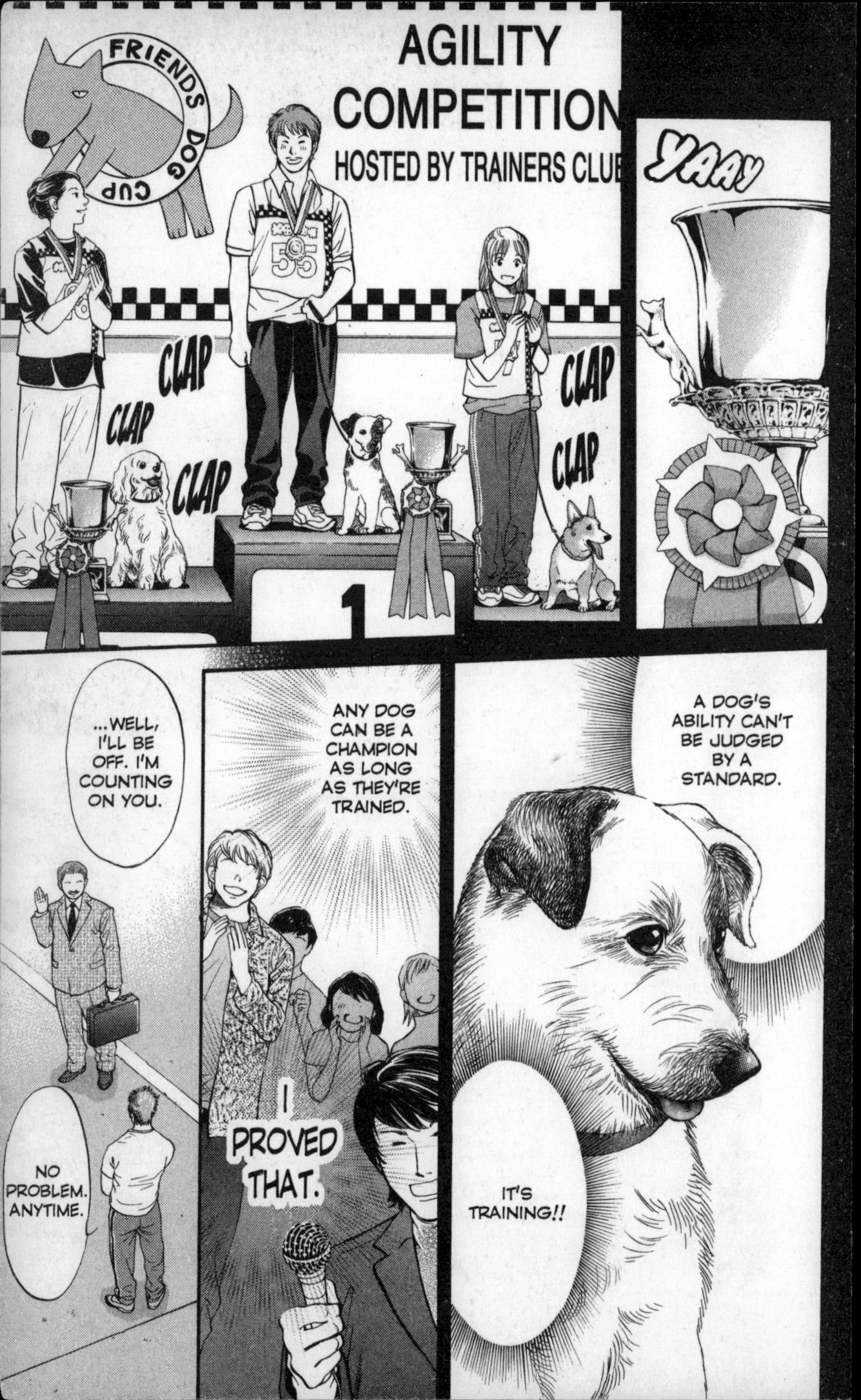
YAAY
AGILITY COMPETITION
HOSTED BY TRAINERS CLUB
FRIENDS DOG CUP
CLAP
CLAP
CLAP
CLAP
CLAP
1
A DOG'S ABILITY CAN'T BE JUDGED BY A STANDARD.
IT'S TRAINING!!
ANY DOG CAN BE A CHAMPION AS LONG AS THEY'RE TRAINED.
I PROVED THAT.
...WELL, I'LL BE OFF. I'M COUNTING ON YOU.
NO PROBLEM. ANYTIME.

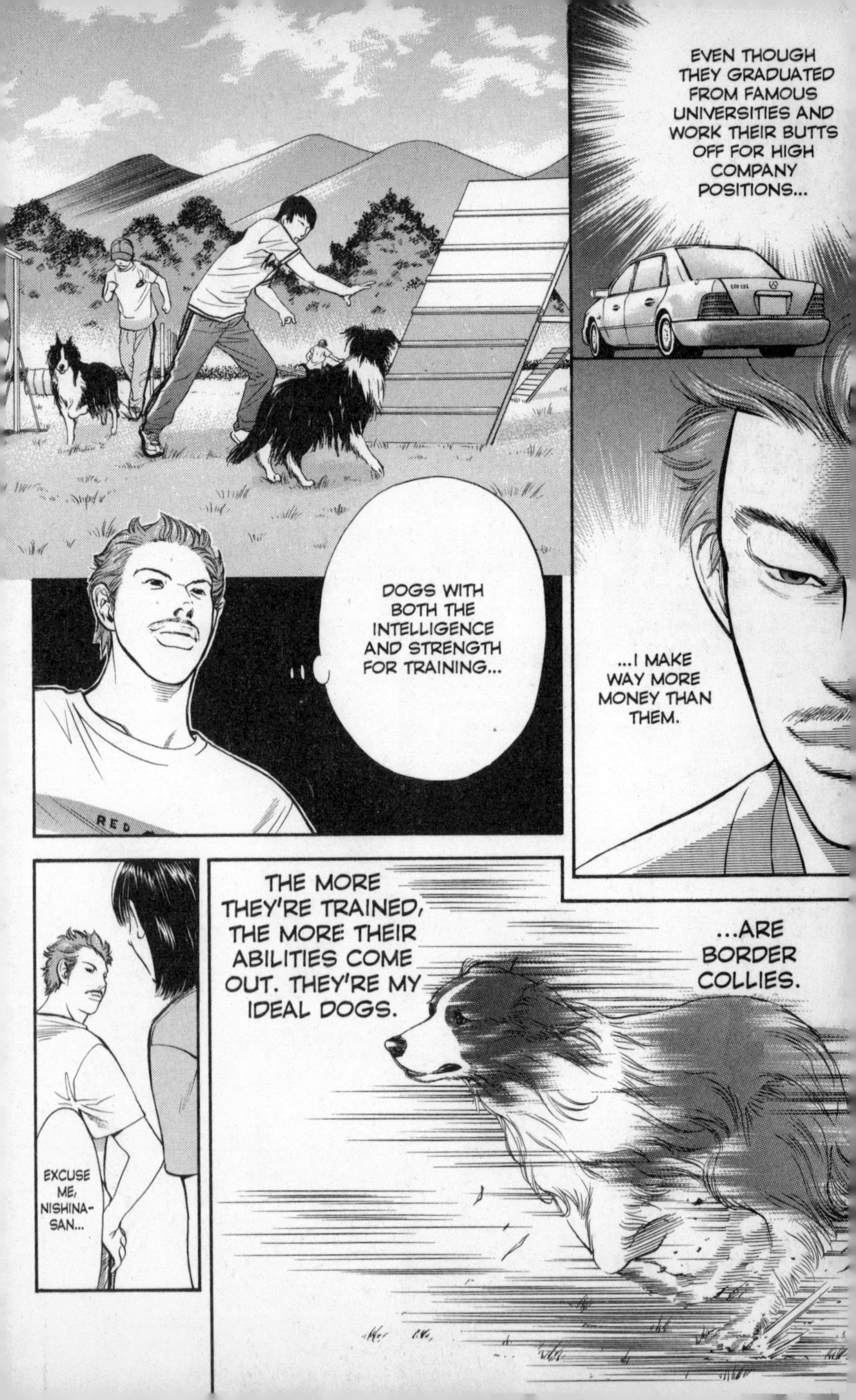
EVEN THOUGH THEY GRADUATED FROM FAMOUS UNIVERSITIES AND WORK THEIR BUTTS OFF FOR HIGH COMPANY POSITIONS...
...I MAKE WAY MORE MONEY THAN THEM.
DOGS WITH BOTH THE INTELLIGENCE AND STRENGTH FOR TRAINING...
...ARE BORDER COLLIES.
THE MORE THEY'RE TRAINED, THE MORE THEIR ABILITIES COME OUT. THEY'RE MY IDEAL DOGS.
EXCUSE ME, NISHINA-SAN...

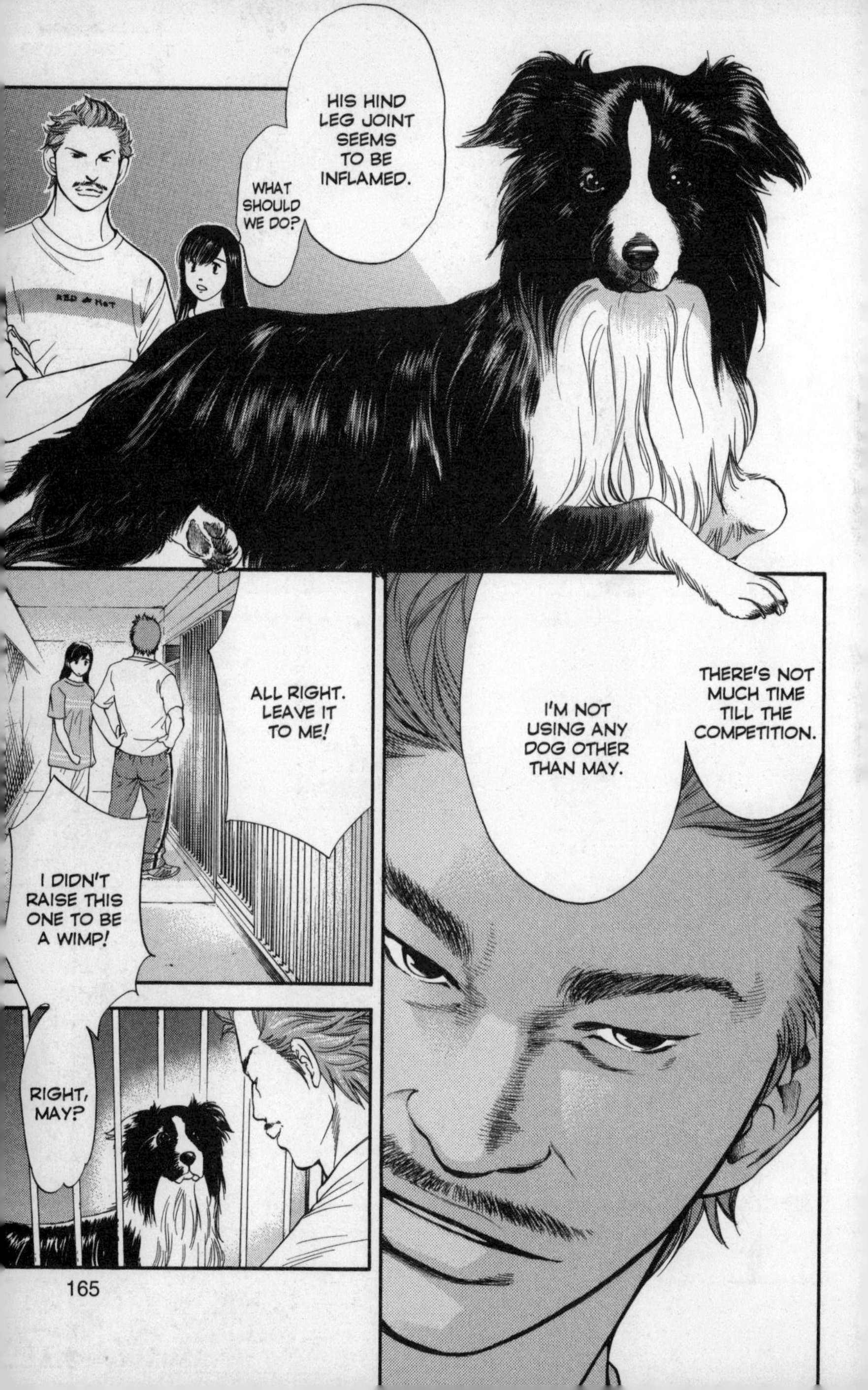
HIS HIND LEG JOINT SEEMS TO BE INFLAMED.
WHAT SHOULD WE DO?
THERE'S NOT MUCH TIME TILL THE COMPETITION.
I'M NOT USING ANY DOG OTHER THAN MAY.
ALL RIGHT. LEAVE IT TO ME!
I DIDN'T RAISE THIS ONE TO BE A WIMP!
RIGHT, MAY?

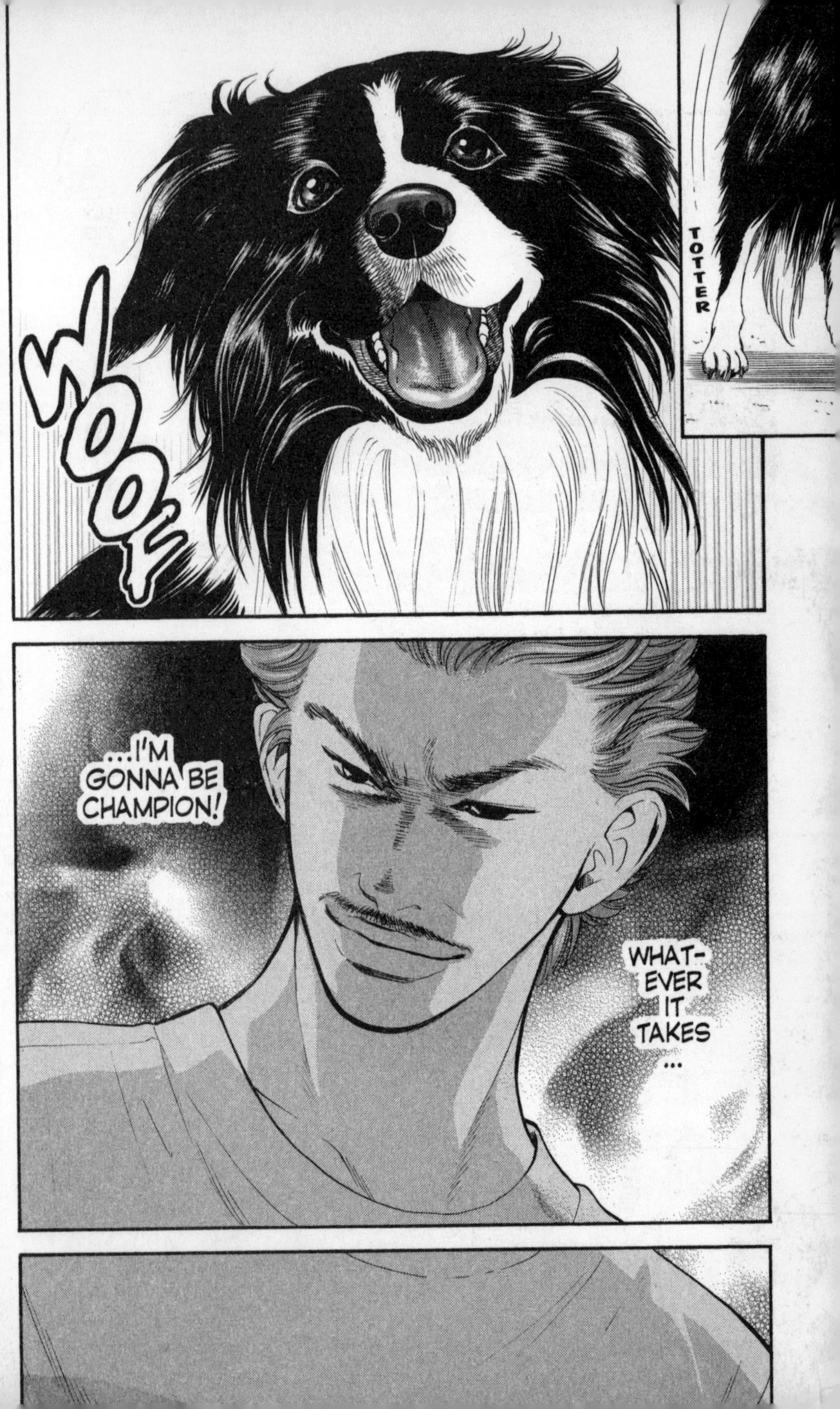
TOTTER
WOOOF
...I'M GONNA BE CHAMPION!
WHAT-EVER IT TAKES ...

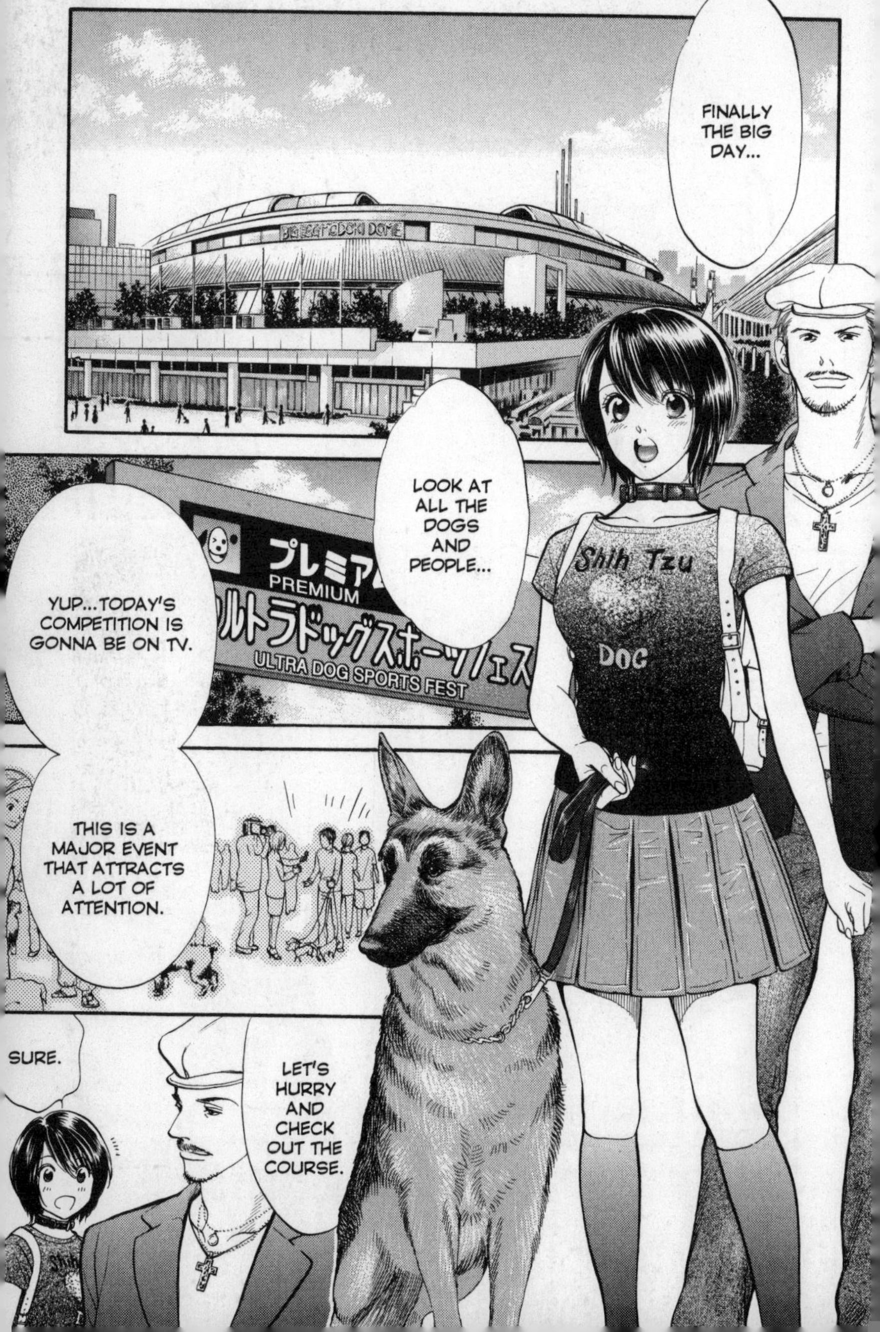
FINALLY THE BIG DAY...
LOOK AT ALL THE DOGS AND PEOPLE...
PREMIUM
ULTRA DOG SPORTS FEST
YUP...TODAY'S COMPETITION IS GONNA BE ON TV.
Shih Tzu
DOG
THIS IS A MAJOR EVENT THAT ATTRACTS A LOT OF ATTENTION.
LET'S HURRY AND CHECK OUT THE COURSE.
SURE.

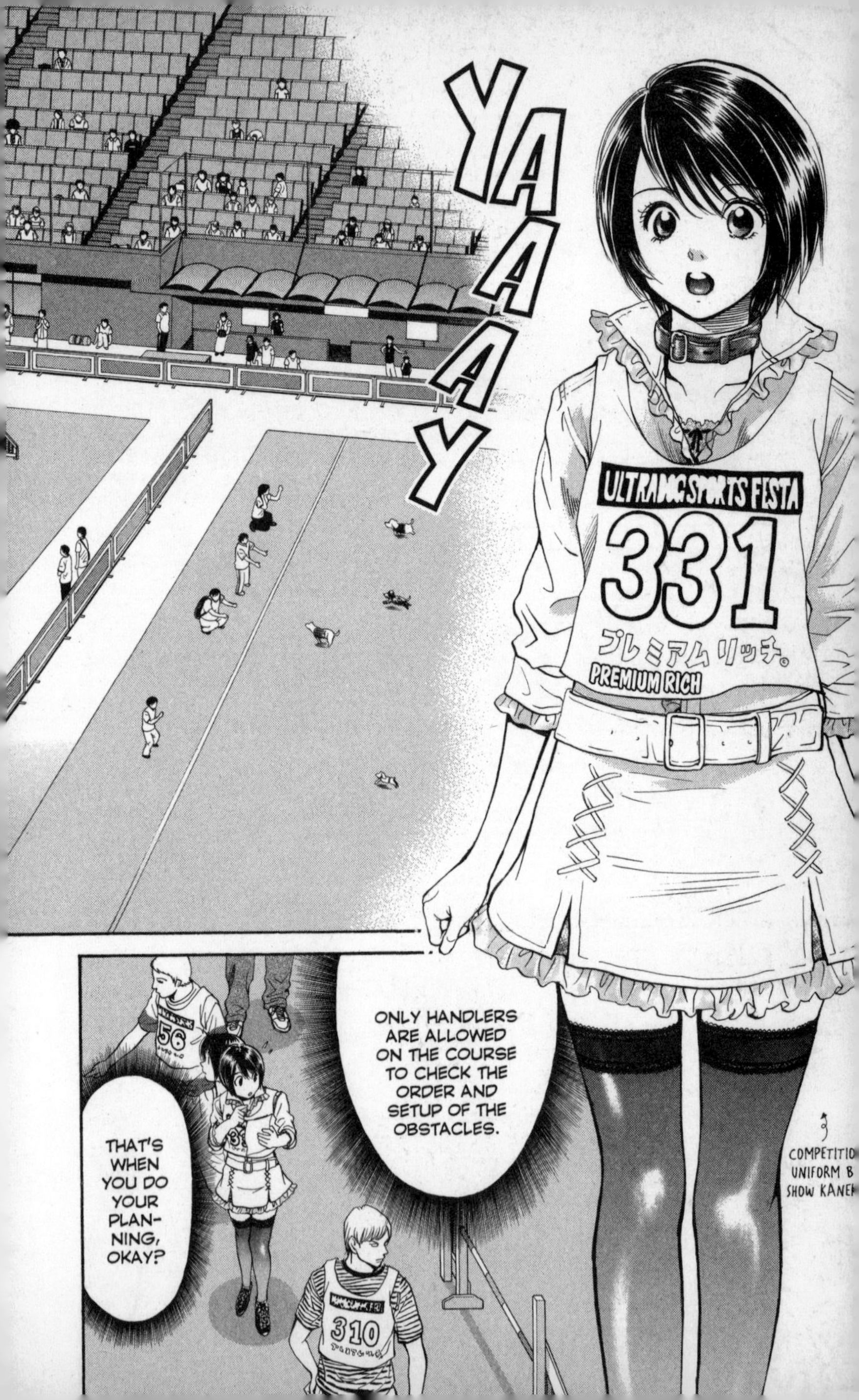
ULTRADOG SPORTS FESTA
331
プレミアムリッチ。
PREMIUM RICH
COMPETITIO UNIFORM B SHOW KANE
YAAAAAY
ONLY HANDLERS ARE ALLOWED ON THE COURSE TO CHECK THE ORDER AND SETUP OF THE OBSTACLES.
THAT'S WHEN YOU DO YOUR PLAN-NING, OKAY?

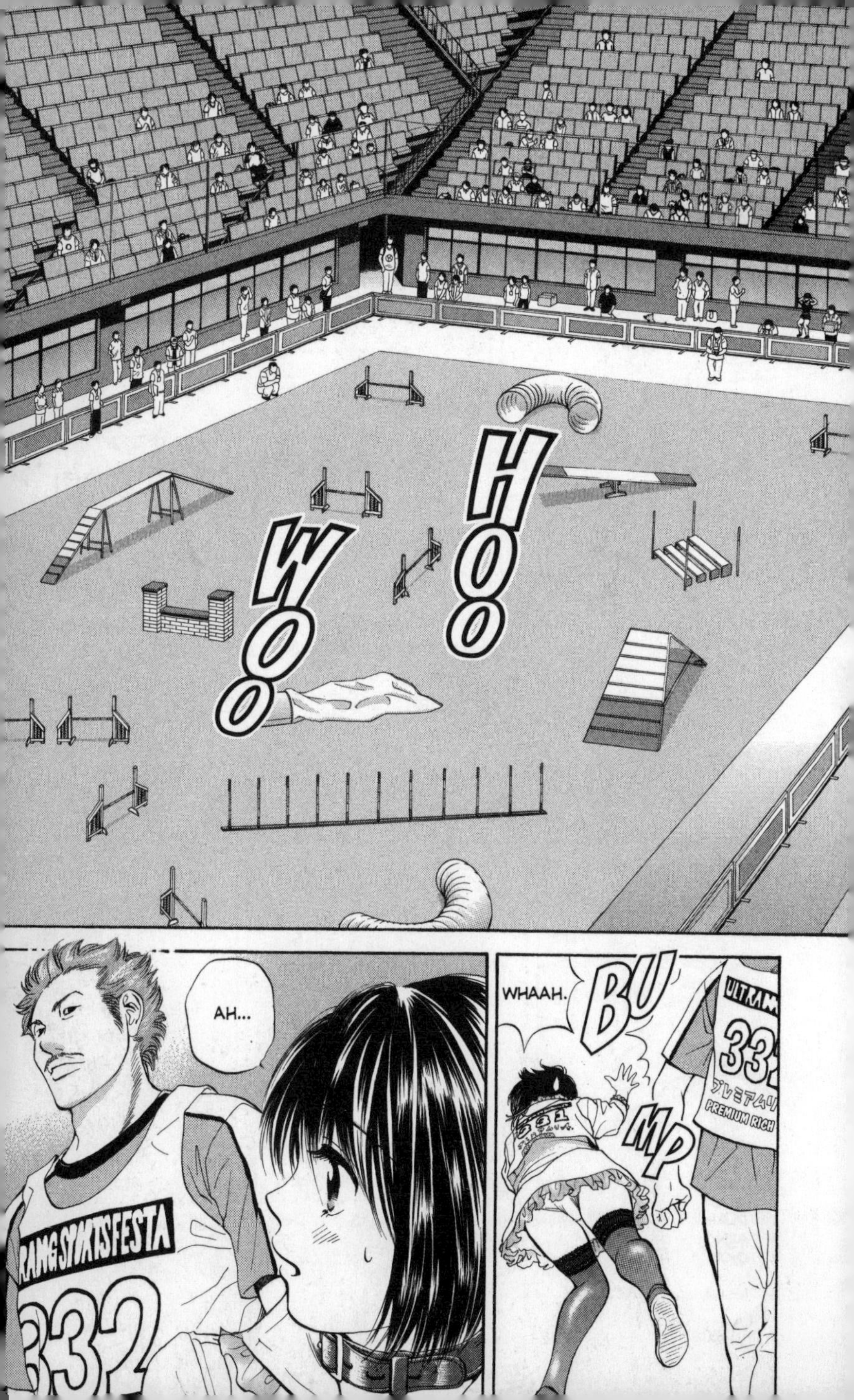
WOOO HOOO
WHAAH.
BUMP
ULTRAM
332
プレミアムリ
PREMIUM RICH
AH...
332

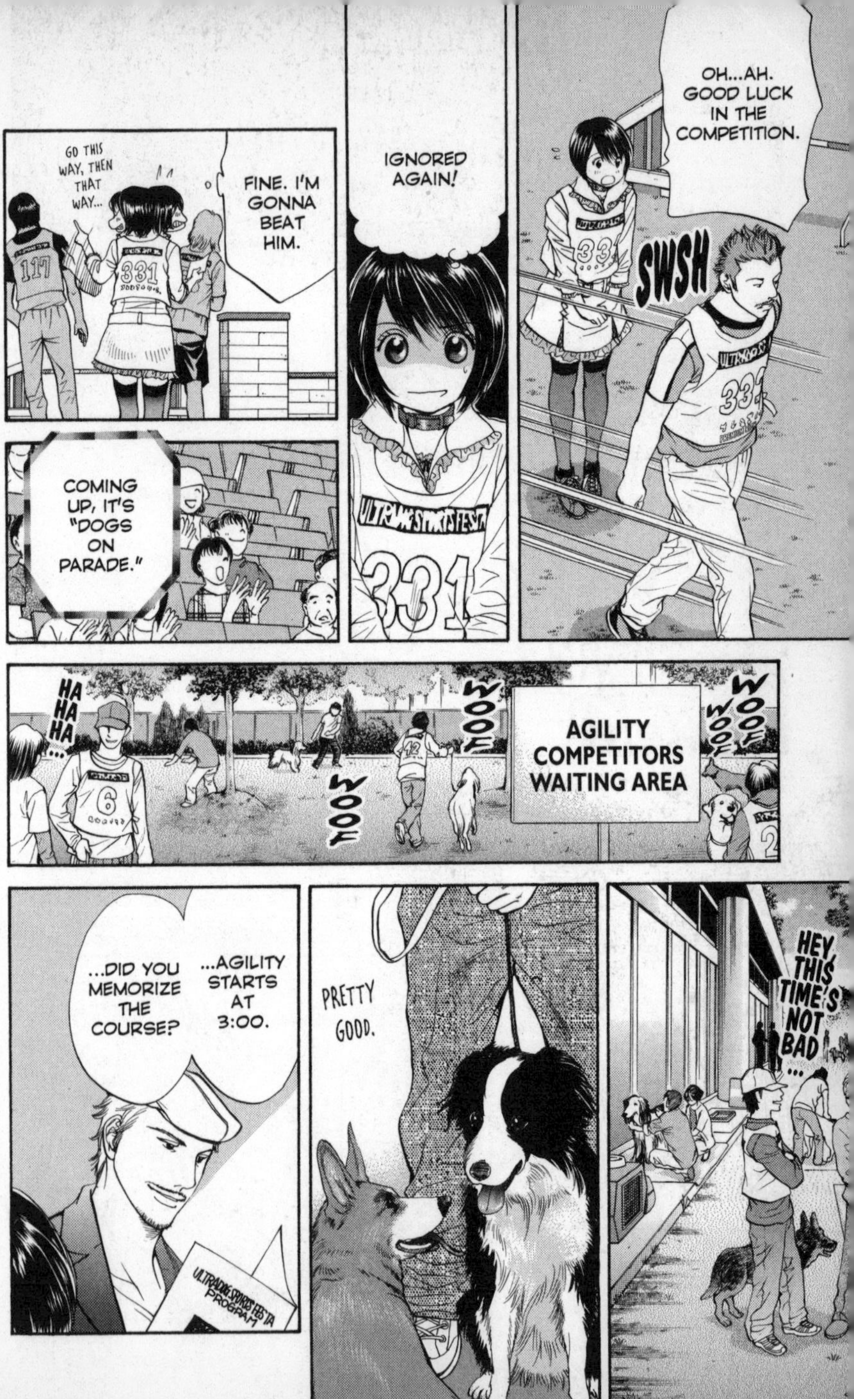
OH...AH. GOOD LUCK IN THE COMPETITION.
SWSH
IGNORED AGAIN!
ULTRADOG SPORTS FESTA
331
FINE. I'M GONNA BEAT HIM.
GO THIS WAY, THEN THAT WAY...
COMING UP, IT'S "DOGS ON PARADE."
WOOF WOOF
AGILITY COMPETITORS WAITING AREA
WOOF
WOOF
HA HA HA...
HEY, THIS TIME'S NOT BAD...
PRETTY GOOD.
...AGILITY STARTS AT 3:00.
...DID YOU MEMORIZE THE COURSE?
ULTRADOG SPORTS FESTA PROGRAM

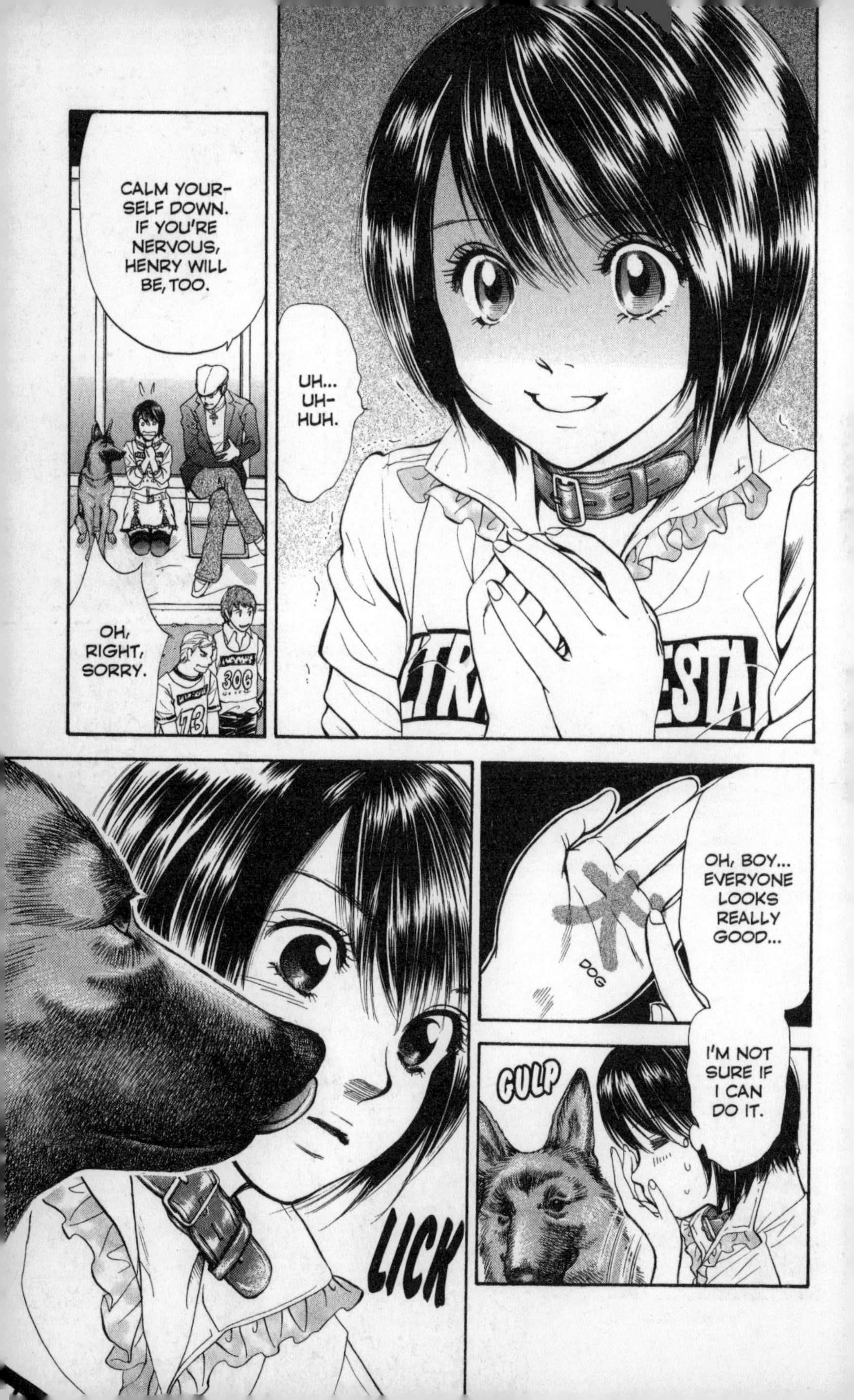
UH... UH-HUH.
CALM YOURSELF DOWN. IF YOU'RE NERVOUS, HENRY WILL BE, TOO.
OH, RIGHT, SORRY.
OH, BOY... EVERYONE LOOKS REALLY GOOD...
DOG
I'M NOT SURE IF I CAN DO IT.
GULP
LICK

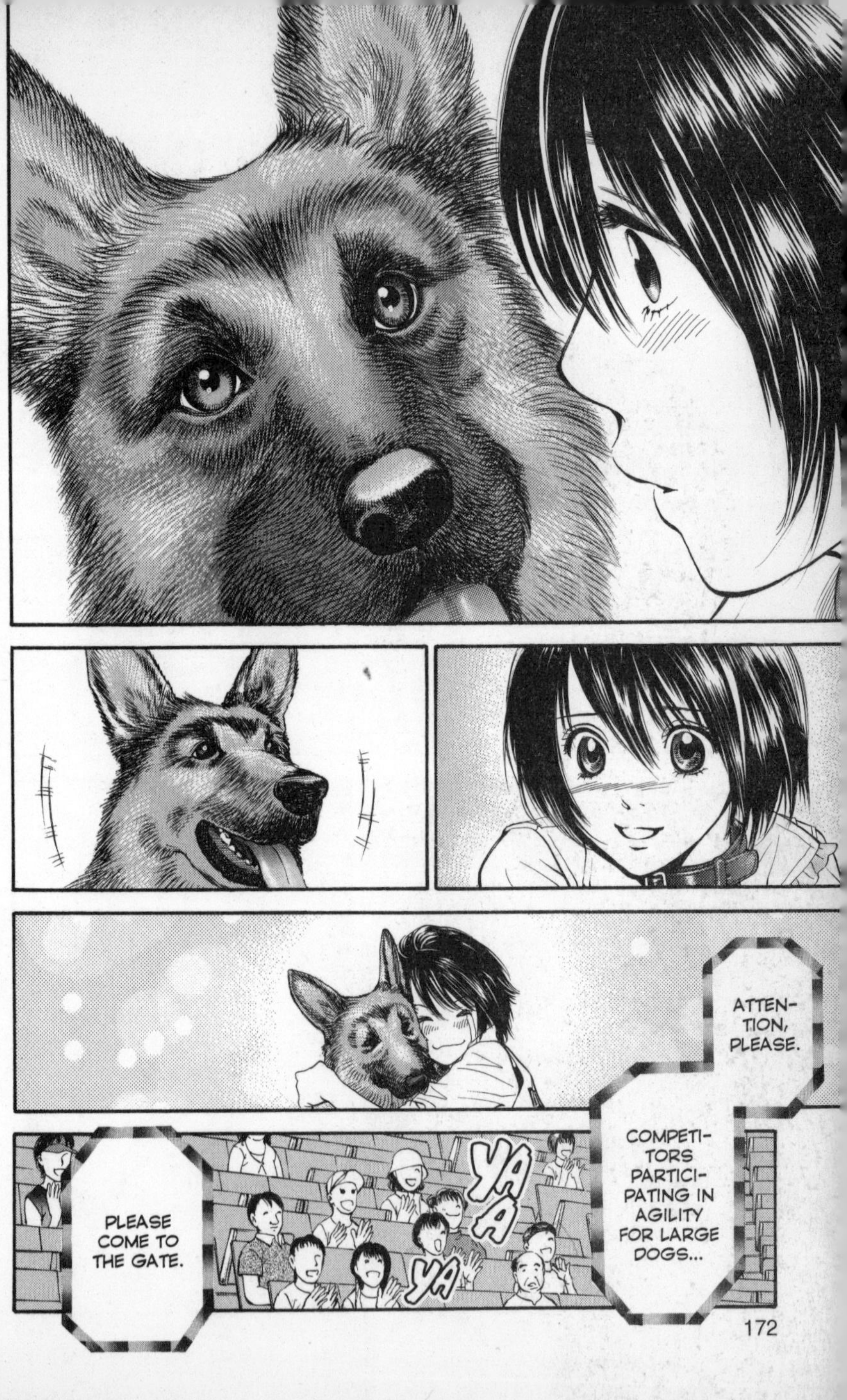
ATTENTION, PLEASE.
COMPETITORS PARTICIPATING IN AGILITY FOR LARGE DOGS...
YA A YA
PLEASE COME TO THE GATE.

CHAPTER 51: THE BOND BETWEEN THEM

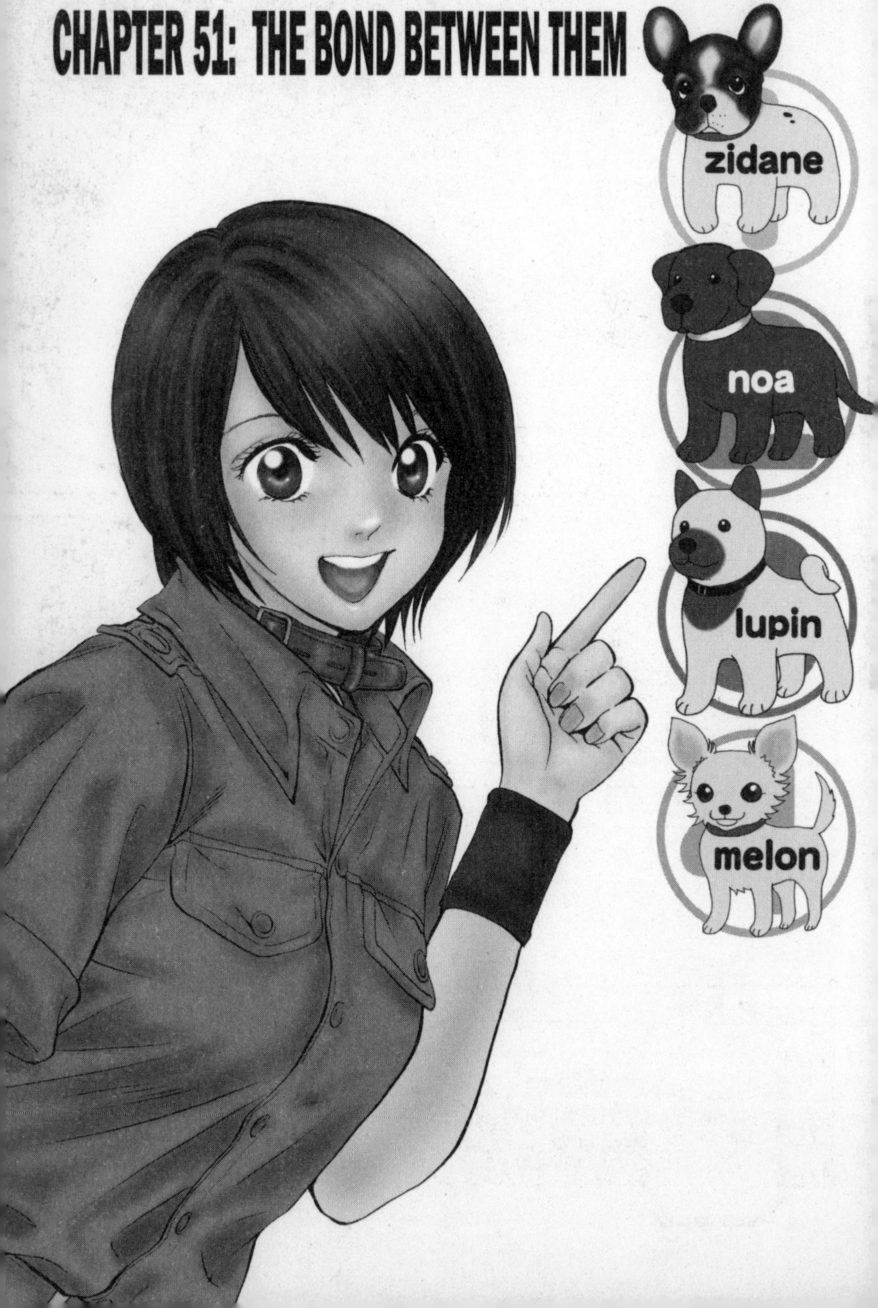
zidane
noa
lupin
melon

いぬばか

CRAZY FOR DOGS!

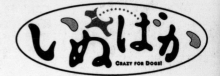

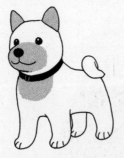

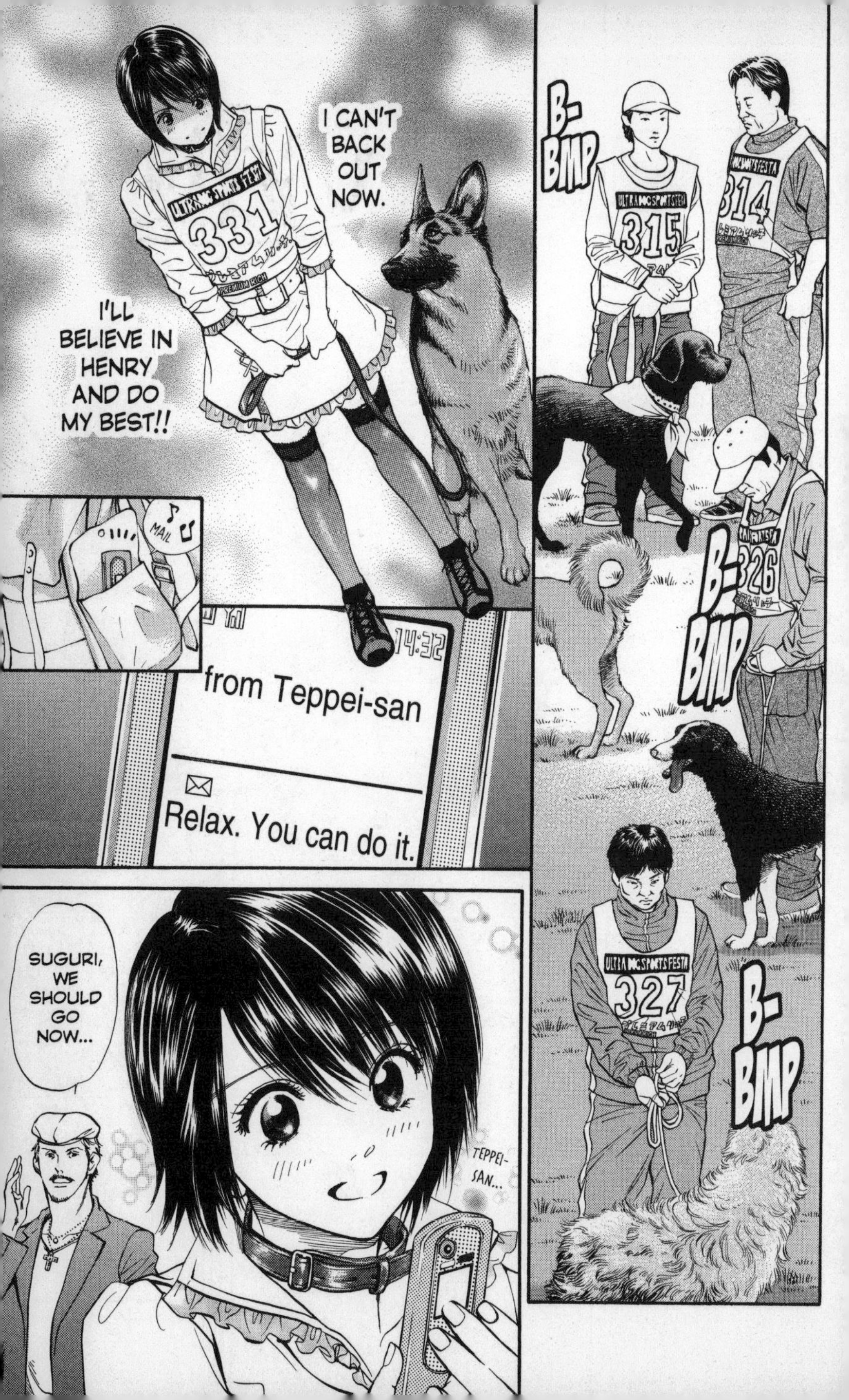
B-BMP
B-BMP
B-BMP
I CAN'T BACK OUT NOW.
I'LL BELIEVE IN HENRY AND DO MY BEST!!
MAIL
14:32
from Teppei-san
Relax. You can do it.
TEPPEI-SAN...
SUGURI, WE SHOULD GO NOW...

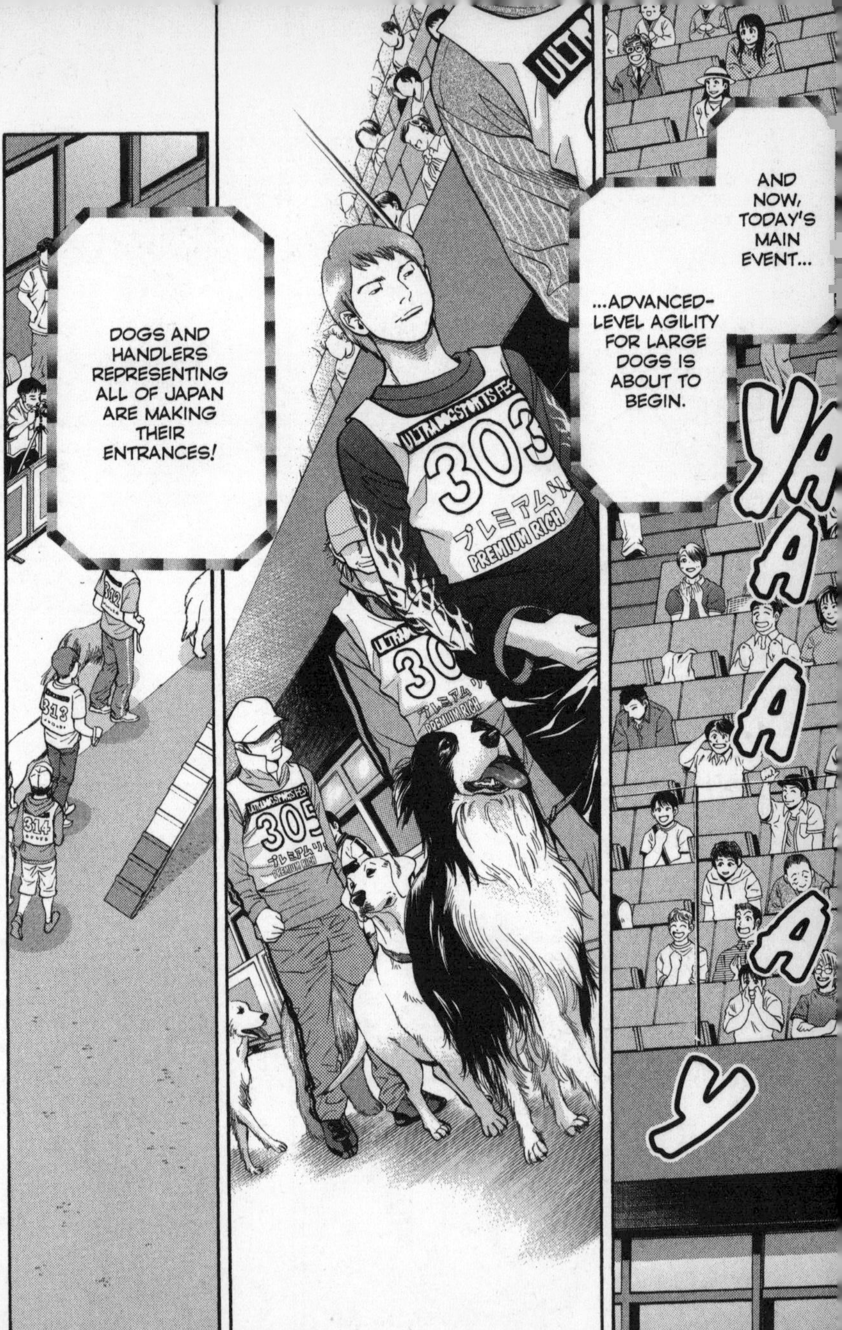
AND NOW, TODAY'S MAIN EVENT...
...ADVANCED-LEVEL AGILITY FOR LARGE DOGS IS ABOUT TO BEGIN.
YAAAAY
303
PREMIUM RICH
305
PREMIUM RICH
DOGS AND HANDLERS REPRESENTING ALL OF JAPAN ARE MAKING THEIR ENTRANCES!
313
314

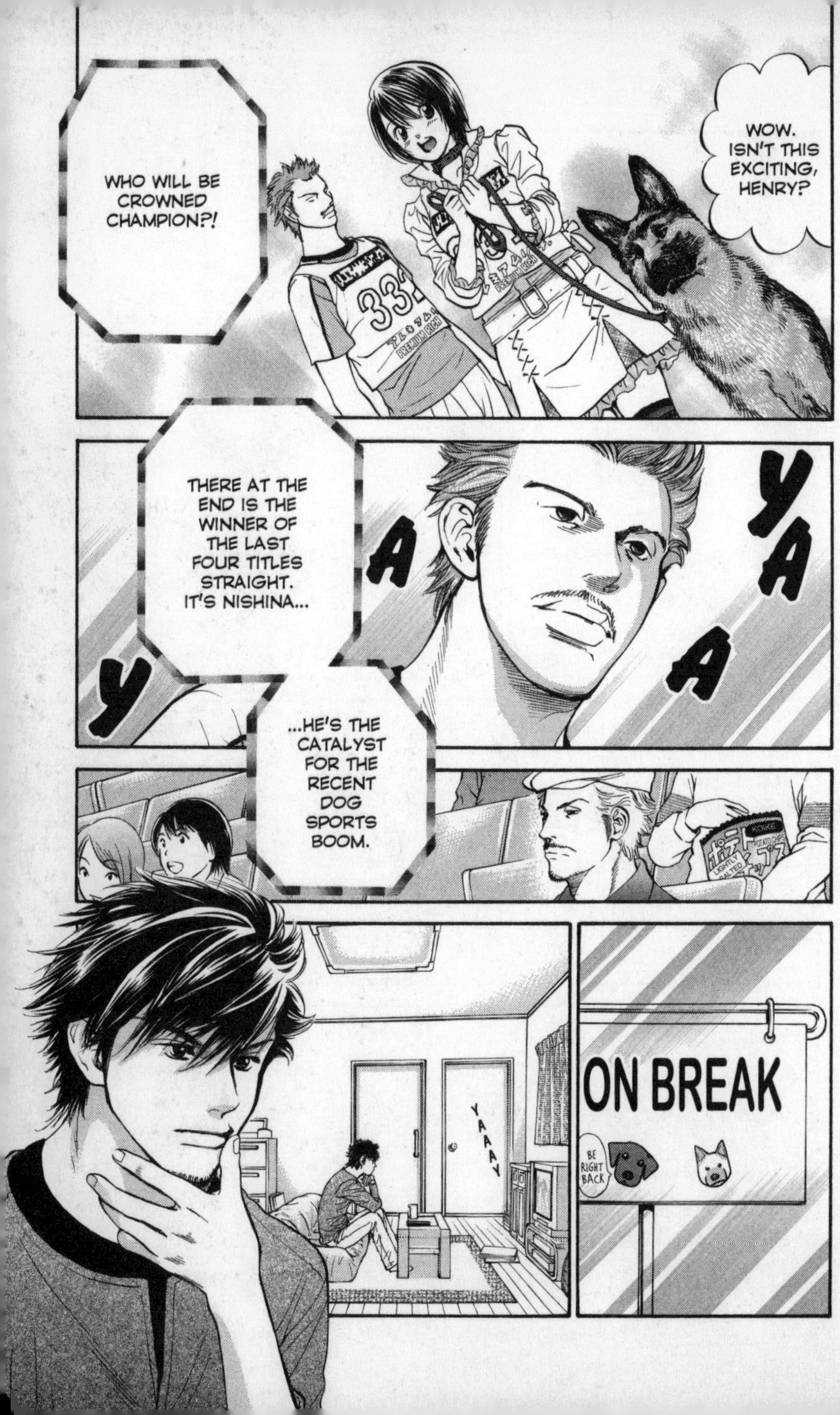
WOW. ISN'T THIS EXCITING, HENRY?
WHO WILL BE CROWNED CHAMPION?!
YAAAY
THERE AT THE END IS THE WINNER OF THE LAST FOUR TITLES STRAIGHT. IT'S NISHINA...
...HE'S THE CATALYST FOR THE RECENT DOG SPORTS BOOM.
KOIKE
POTATO CHIPS
LIGHTLY SALTED
ON BREAK
BE RIGHT BACK
YAAAY

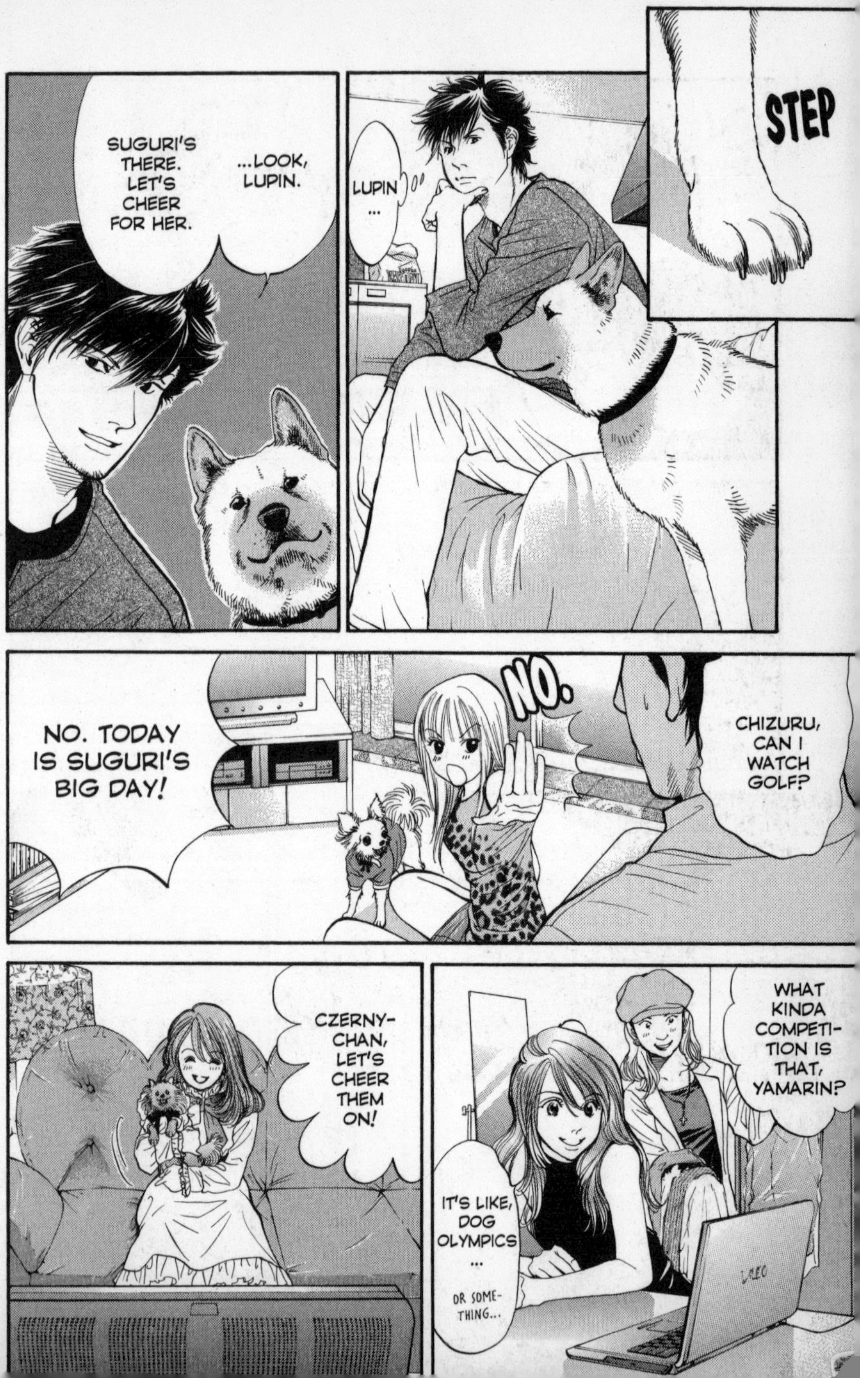
STEP
LUPIN ...
...LOOK, LUPIN.
SUGURI'S THERE. LET'S CHEER FOR HER.
CHIZURU, CAN I WATCH GOLF?
NO.
NO. TODAY IS SUGURI'S BIG DAY!
WHAT KINDA COMPETITION IS THAT, YAMARIN?
IT'S LIKE, DOG OLYMPICS ...
OR SOMETHING...
CZERNY-CHAN, LET'S CHEER THEM ON!

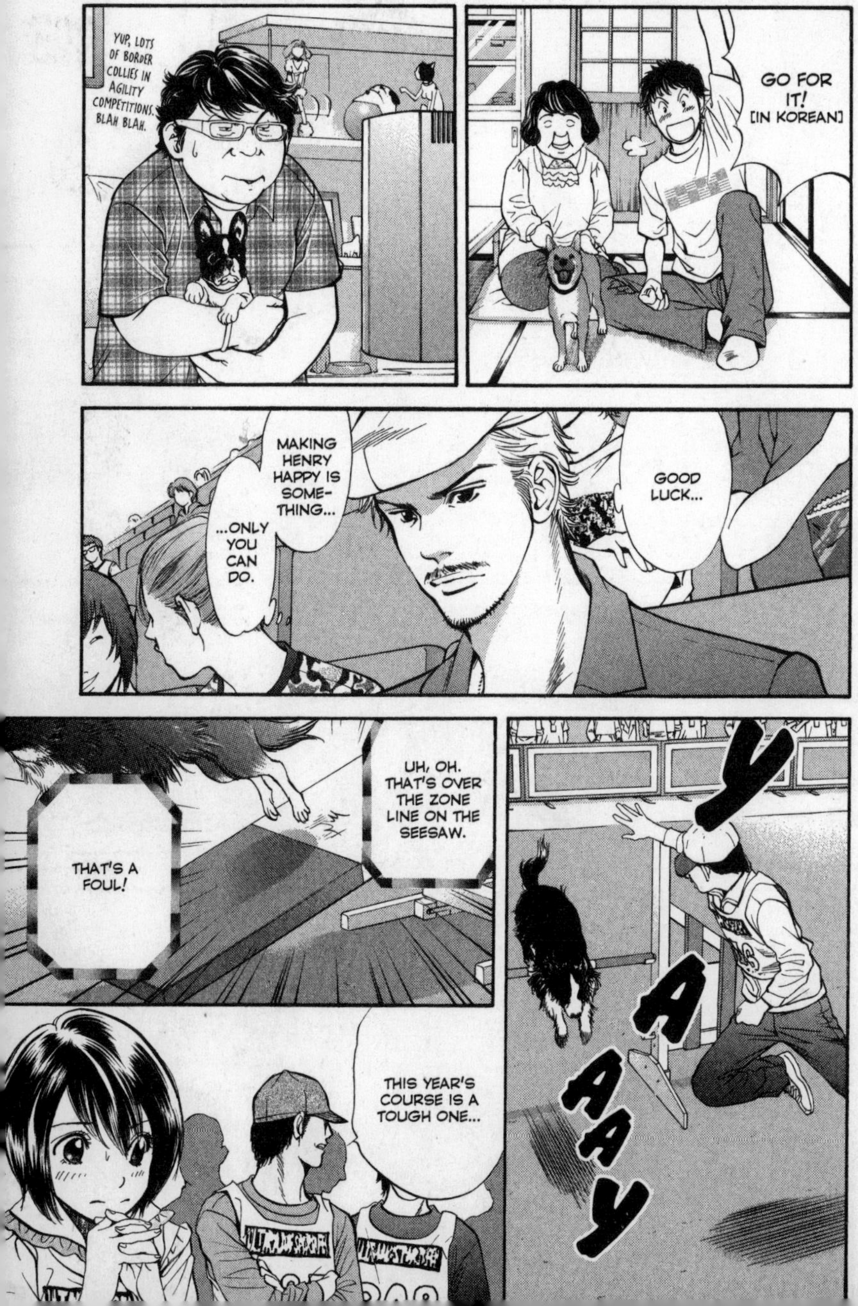
GO FOR IT! [IN KOREAN]
YUP, LOTS OF BORDER COLLIES IN AGILITY COMPETITIONS. BLAH BLAH.
GOOD LUCK...
MAKING HENRY HAPPY IS SOMETHING...
...ONLY YOU CAN DO.
YAAAY
UH, OH. THAT'S OVER THE ZONE LINE ON THE SEESAW.
THAT'S A FOUL!
THIS YEAR'S COURSE IS A TOUGH ONE...

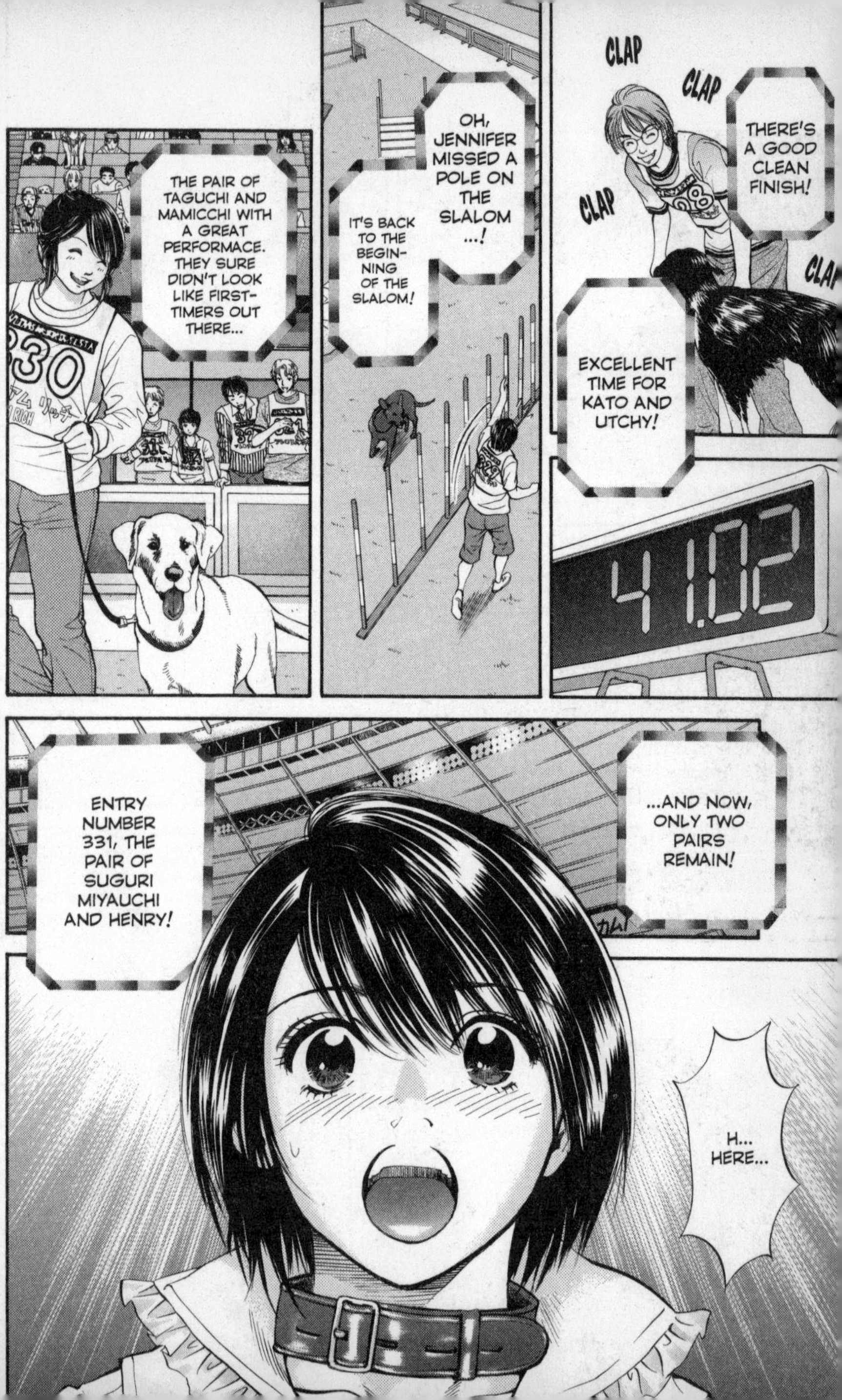
CLAP
CLAP
THERE'S A GOOD CLEAN FINISH!
CLAP
CLAP
EXCELLENT TIME FOR KATO AND UTCHY!
41.02
OH, JENNIFER MISSED A POLE ON THE SLALOM ...!
IT'S BACK TO THE BEGIN-NING OF THE SLALOM!
THE PAIR OF TAGUCHI AND MAMICCHI WITH A GREAT PERFORMACE. THEY SURE DIDN'T LOOK LIKE FIRST-TIMERS OUT THERE...
...AND NOW, ONLY TWO PAIRS REMAIN!
ENTRY NUMBER 331, THE PAIR OF SUGURI MIYAUCHI AND HENRY!
H... HERE...

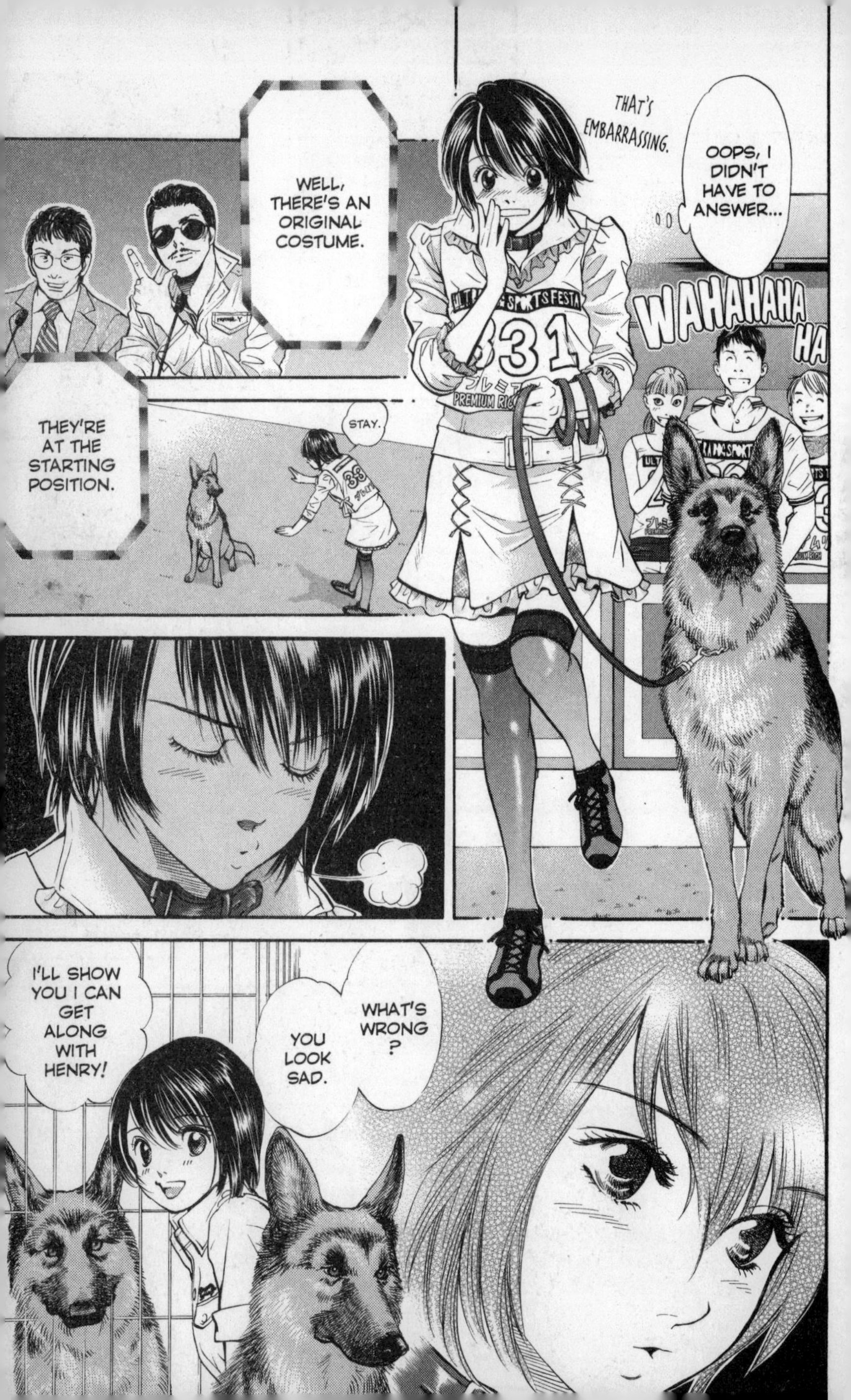
OOPS, I DIDN'T HAVE TO ANSWER...
THAT'S EMBARRASSING.
WAHAHAHA HA
WELL, THERE'S AN ORIGINAL COSTUME.
THEY'RE AT THE STARTING POSITION.
STAY.
WHAT'S WRONG?
YOU LOOK SAD.
I'LL SHOW YOU I CAN GET ALONG WITH HENRY!

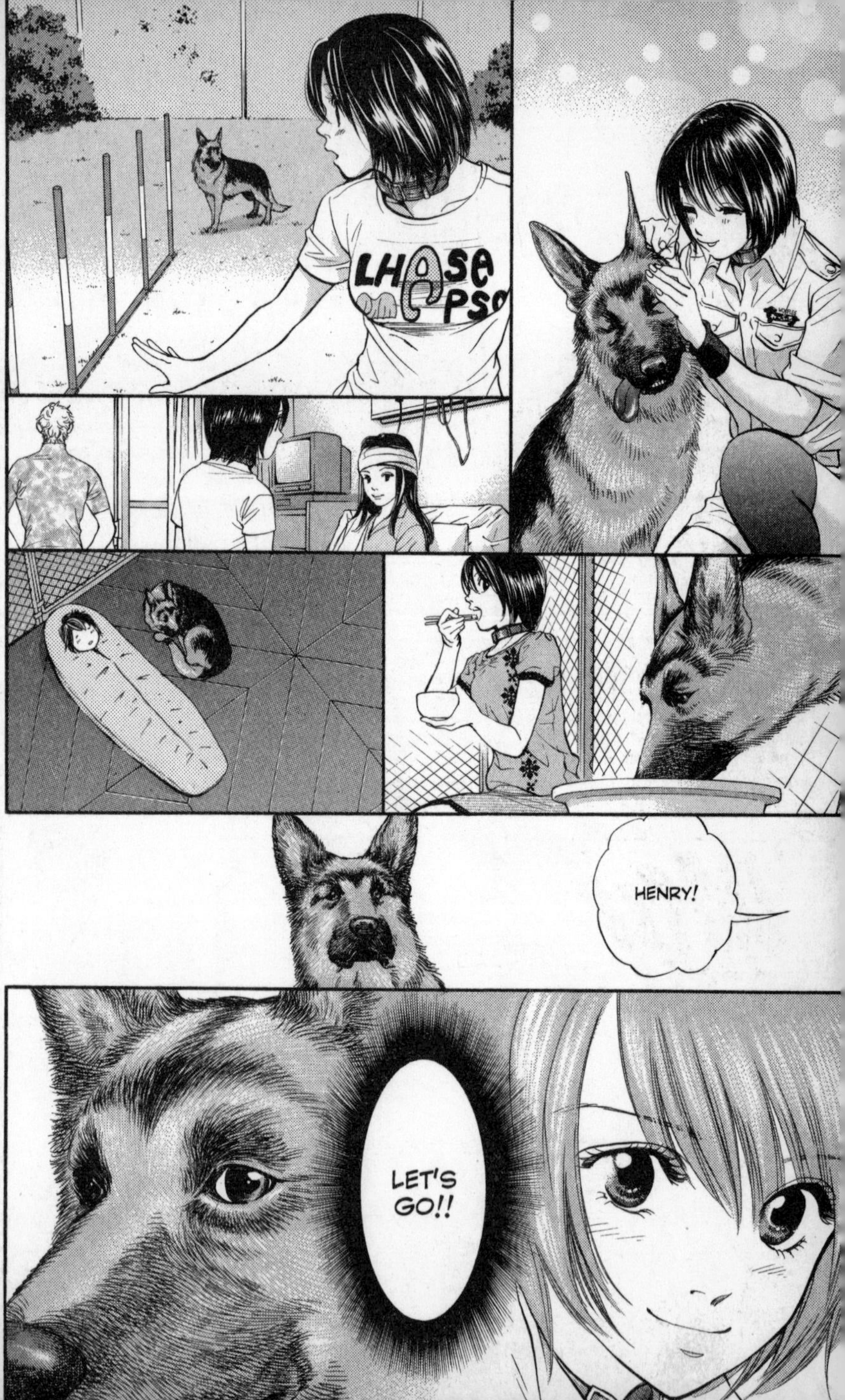
HENRY!
LET'S GO!!

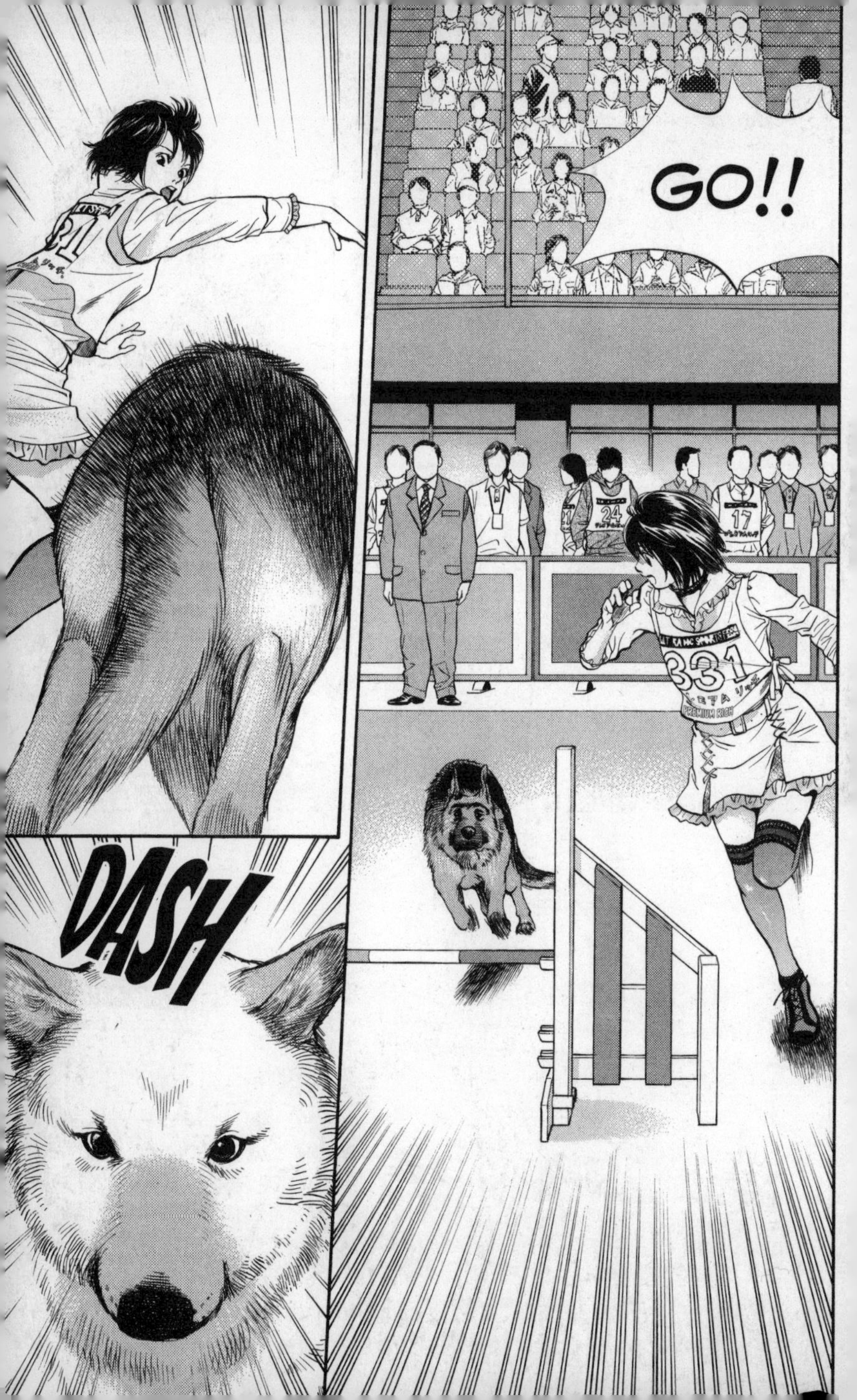
GO!!
DASH

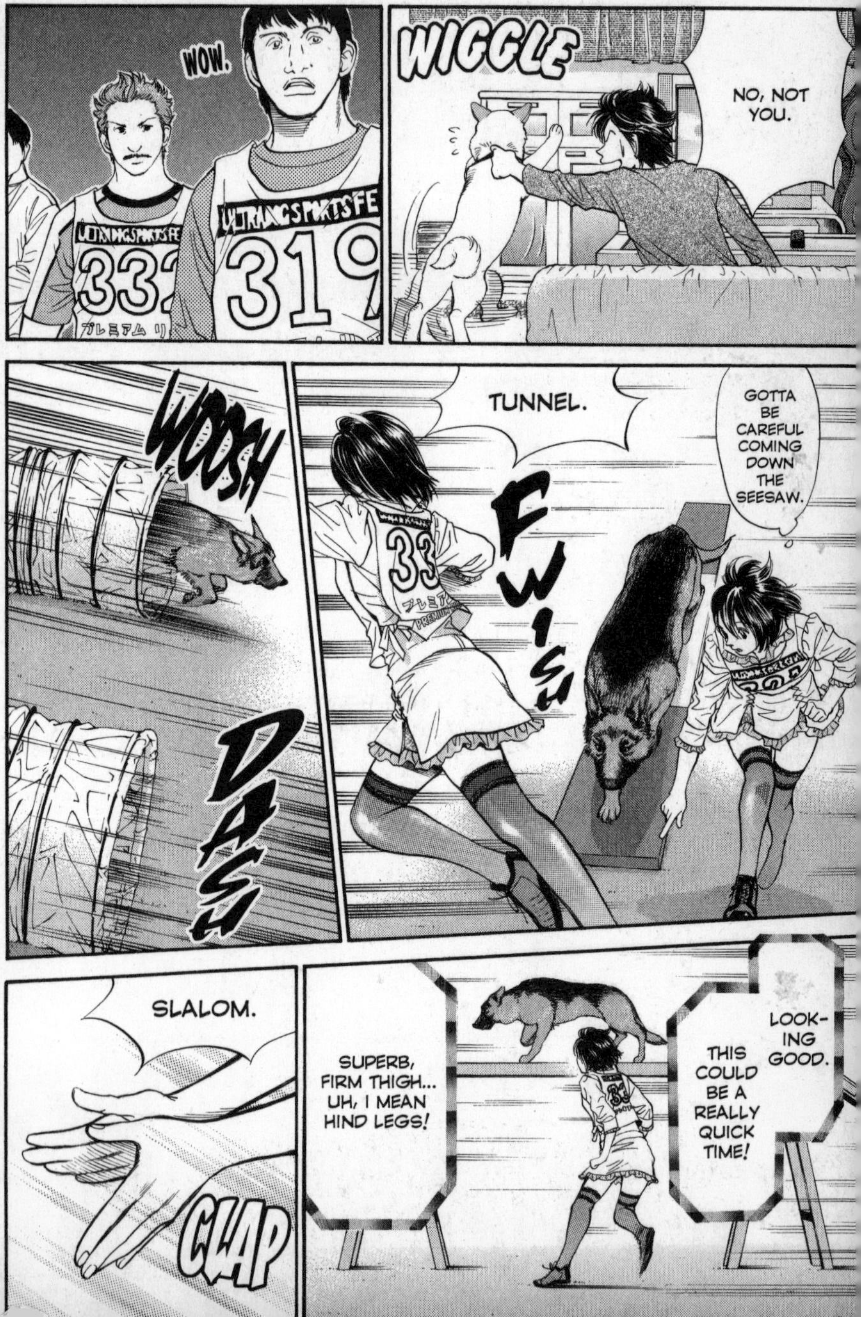
WIGGLE
NO, NOT YOU.
WOW.
GOTTA BE CAREFUL COMING DOWN THE SEESAW.
TUNNEL.
FWISH
WOOSH
DASH
LOOKING GOOD.
THIS COULD BE A REALLY QUICK TIME!
SUPERB, FIRM THIGH... UH, I MEAN HIND LEGS!
SLALOM.
CLAP

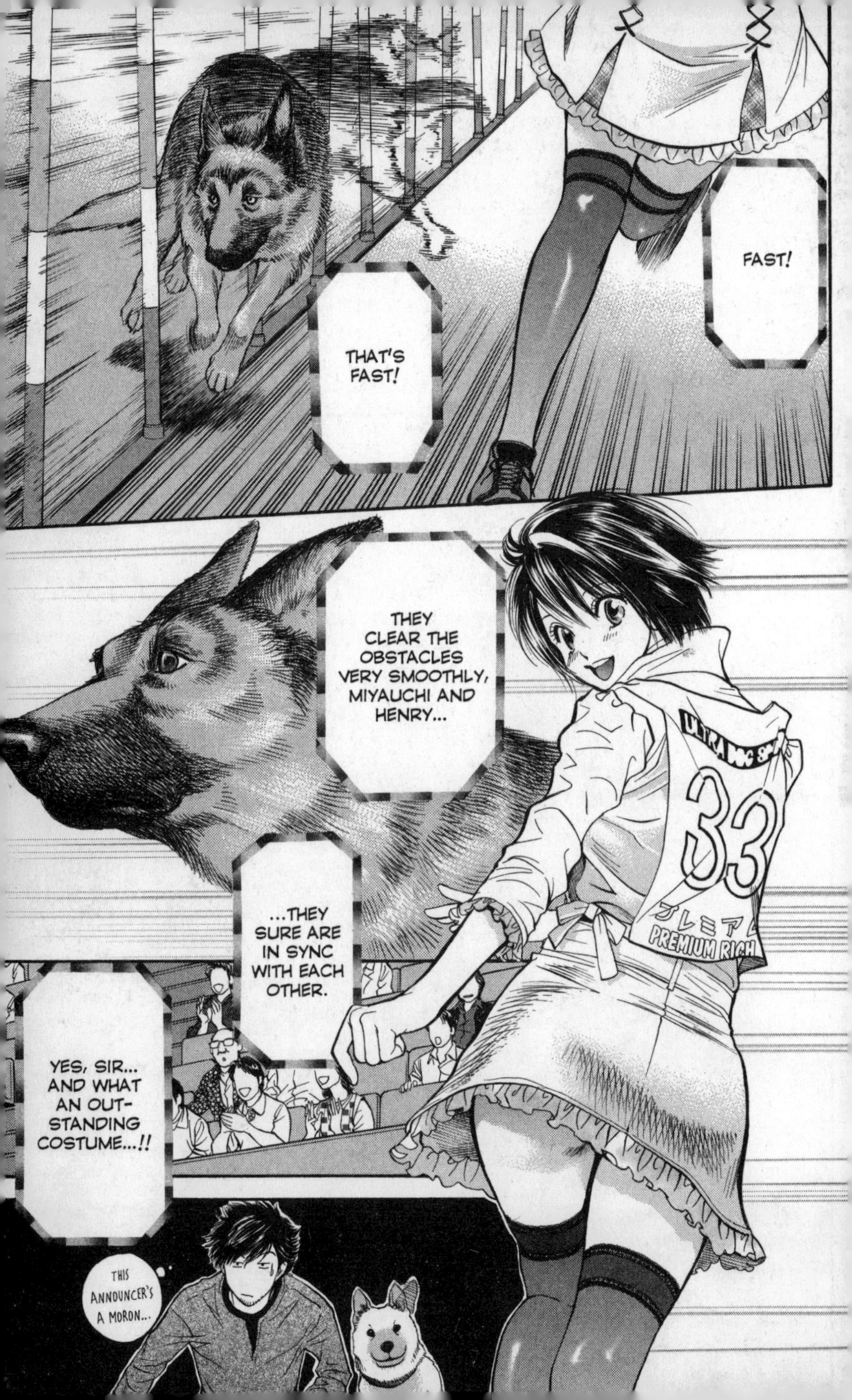
FAST!
THAT'S FAST!
THEY CLEAR THE OBSTACLES VERY SMOOTHLY, MIYAUCHI AND HENRY...
...THEY SURE ARE IN SYNC WITH EACH OTHER.
YES, SIR... AND WHAT AN OUT-STANDING COSTUME...!!
THIS ANNOUNCER'S A MORON...

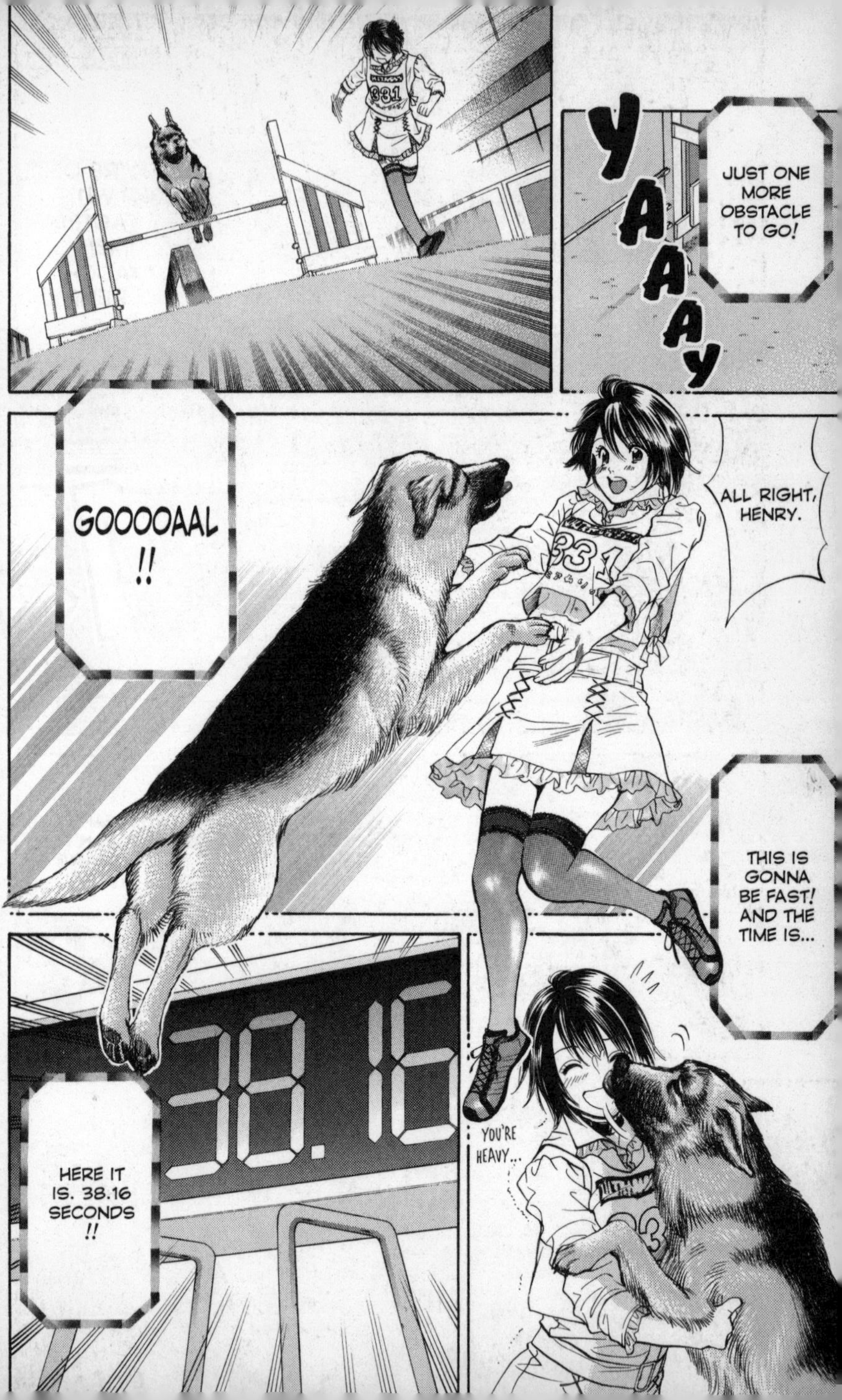
JUST ONE MORE OBSTACLE TO GO!
YAAAAY
331
ALL RIGHT, HENRY.
GOOOOAAL !!
THIS IS GONNA BE FAST! AND THE TIME IS...
YOU'RE HEAVY...
38.16
HERE IT IS. 38.16 SECONDS !!

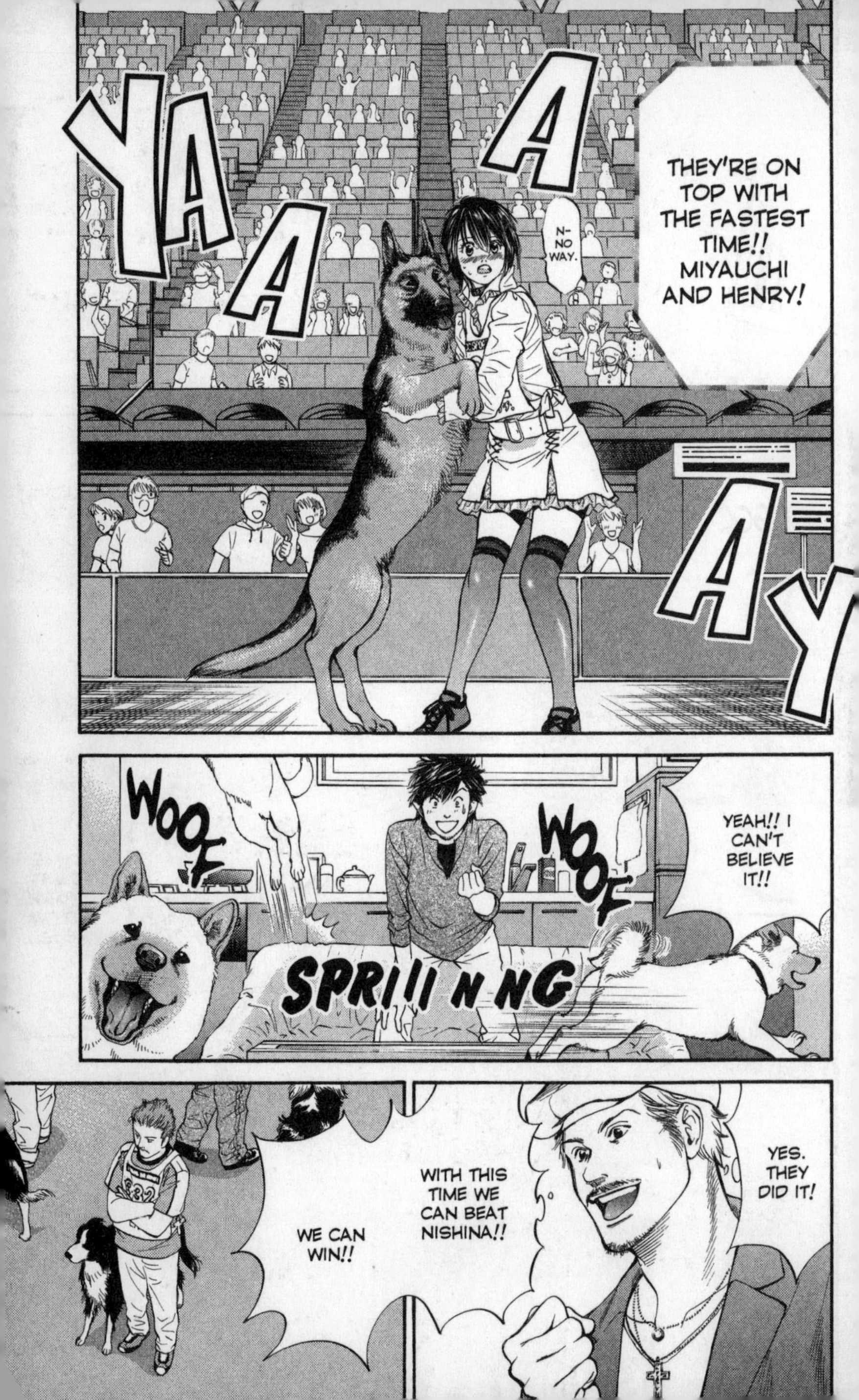
THEY'RE ON TOP WITH THE FASTEST TIME!! MIYAUCHI AND HENRY!
N-NO WAY.
YAAA
A
AY
YEAH!! I CAN'T BELIEVE IT!!
WOOF
WOOF
SPRIIING
YES. THEY DID IT!
WITH THIS TIME WE CAN BEAT NISHINA!!
WE CAN WIN!!

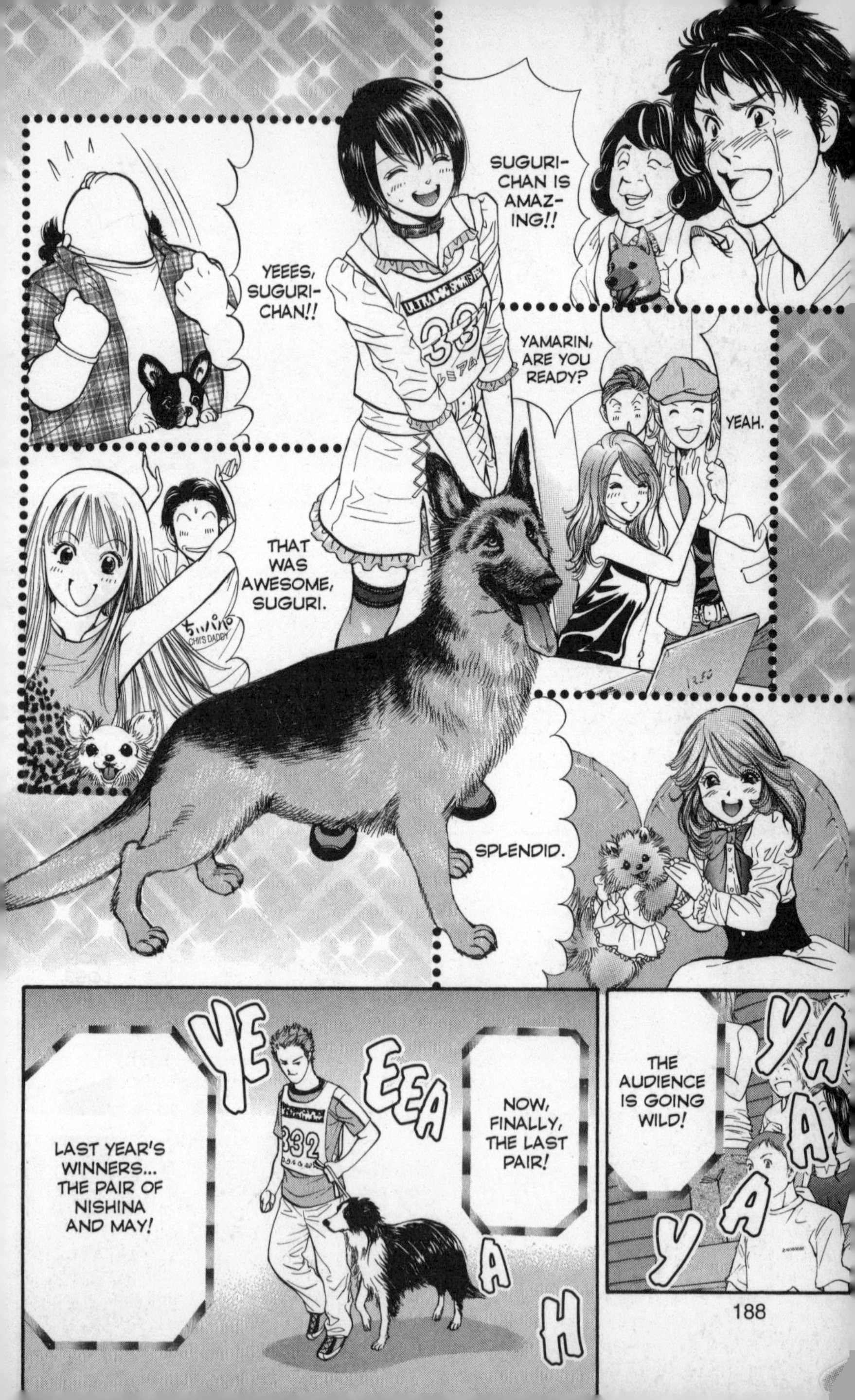
SUGURI-CHAN IS AMAZ-ING!!
YEEES, SUGURI-CHAN!!
YAMARIN, ARE YOU READY?
YEAH.
THAT WAS AWESOME, SUGURI.
CHII'S DADDY
SPLENDID.
THE AUDIENCE IS GOING WILD!
YA YA A Y
NOW, FINALLY, THE LAST PAIR!
YEEEAAH
LAST YEAR'S WINNERS... THE PAIR OF NISHINA AND MAY!

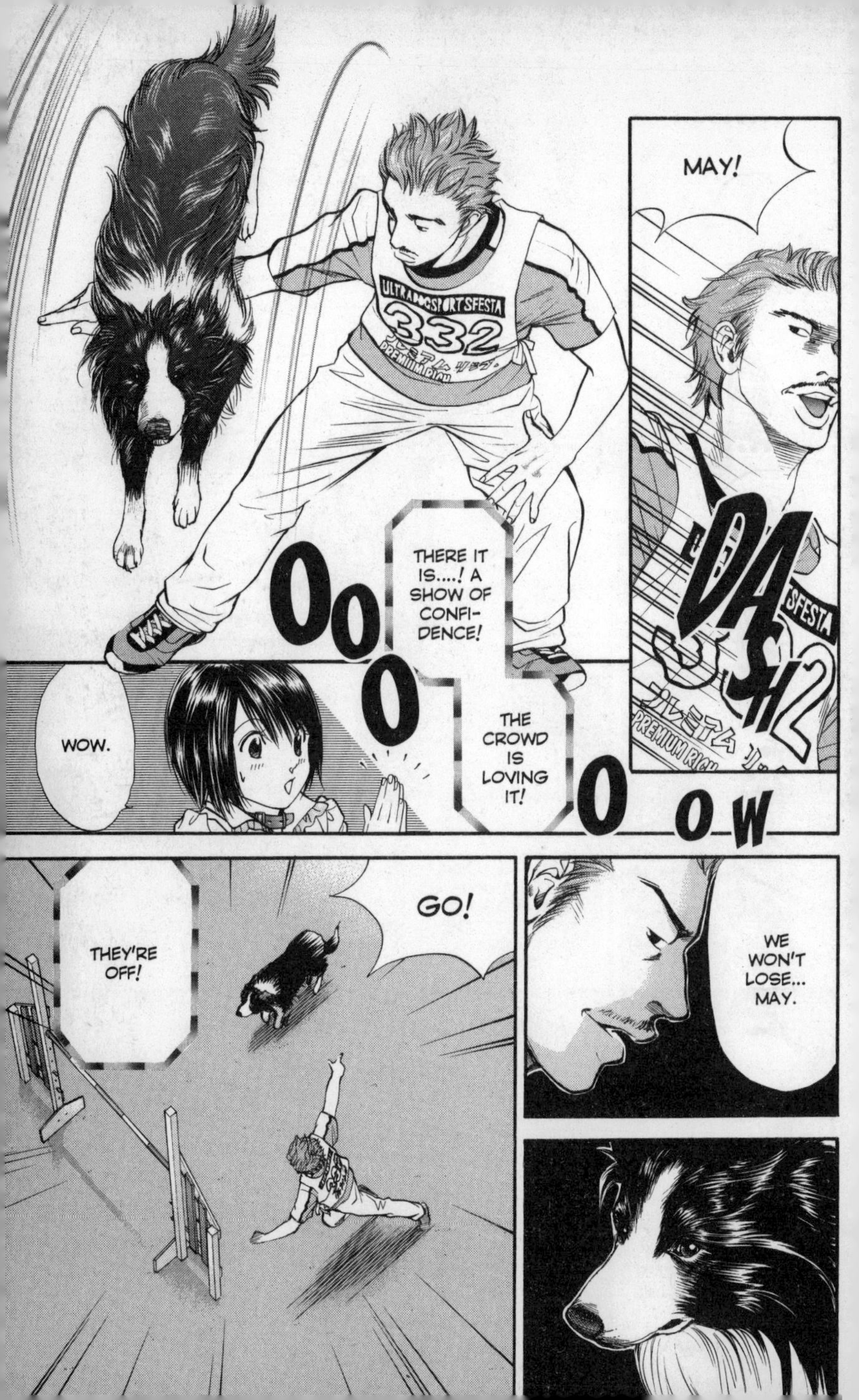
MAY!
DASH
THERE IT IS....! A SHOW OF CONFIDENCE!
THE CROWD IS LOVING IT!
OOOOOOW
WOW.
WE WON'T LOSE... MAY.
GO!
THEY'RE OFF!

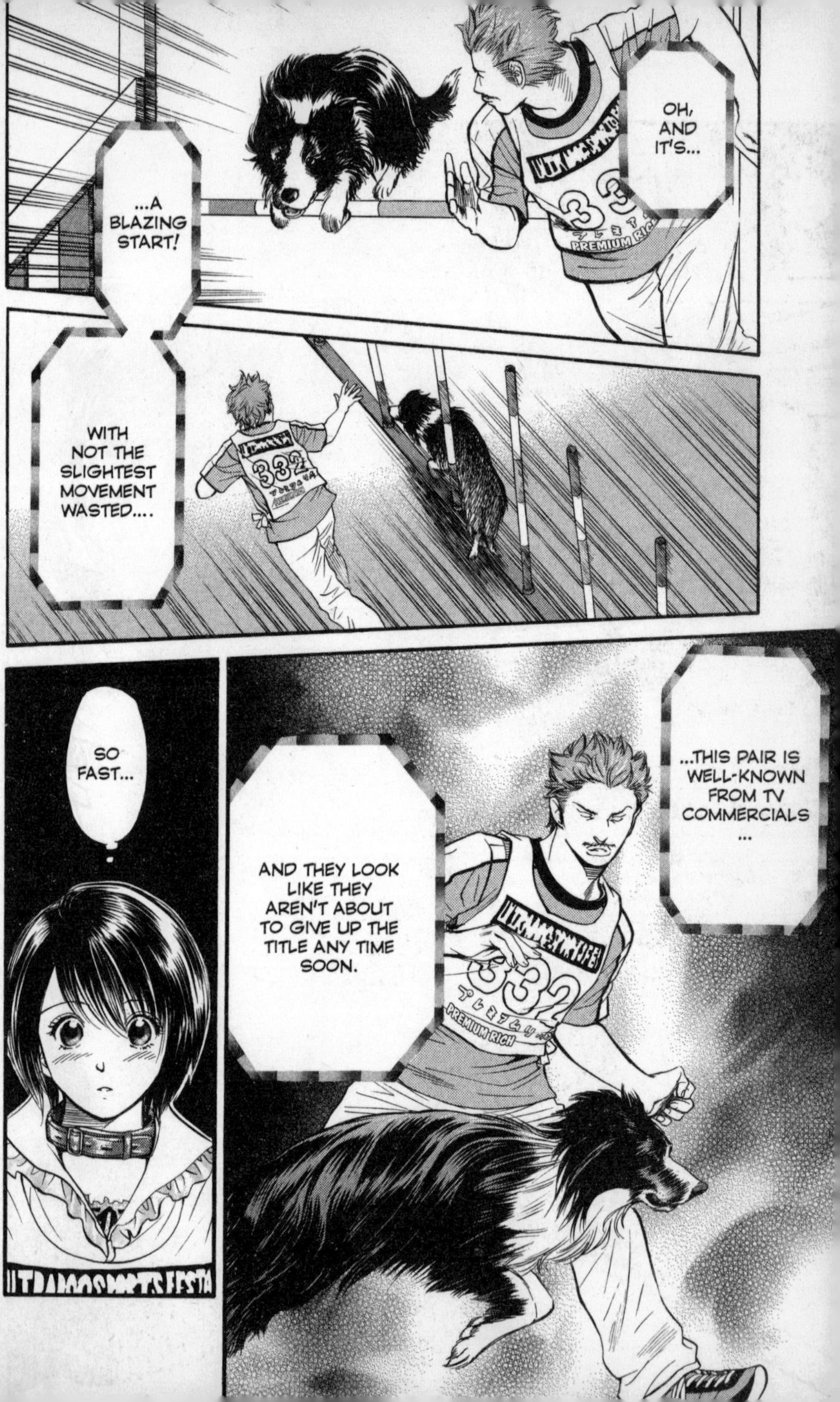
OH, AND IT'S...
...A BLAZING START!
WITH NOT THE SLIGHTEST MOVEMENT WASTED....
...THIS PAIR IS WELL-KNOWN FROM TV COMMERCIALS ...
AND THEY LOOK LIKE THEY AREN'T ABOUT TO GIVE UP THE TITLE ANY TIME SOON.
SO FAST...

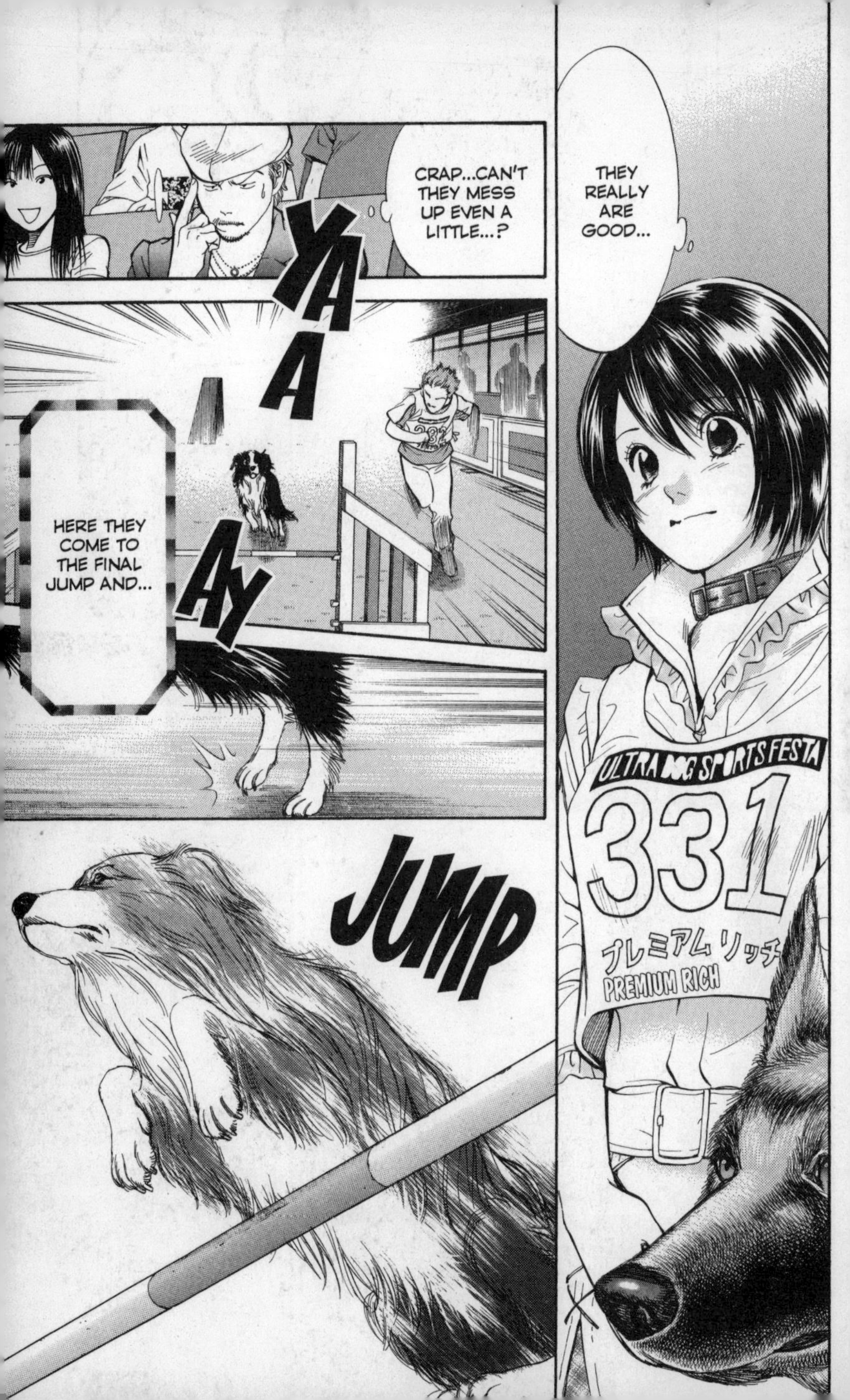
THEY REALLY ARE GOOD...
ULTRA DOG SPORTS FESTA
331
プレミアム リッチ
PREMIUM RICH
CRAP...CAN'T THEY MESS UP EVEN A LITTLE...?
YAAAY
HERE THEY COME TO THE FINAL JUMP AND...
JUMP

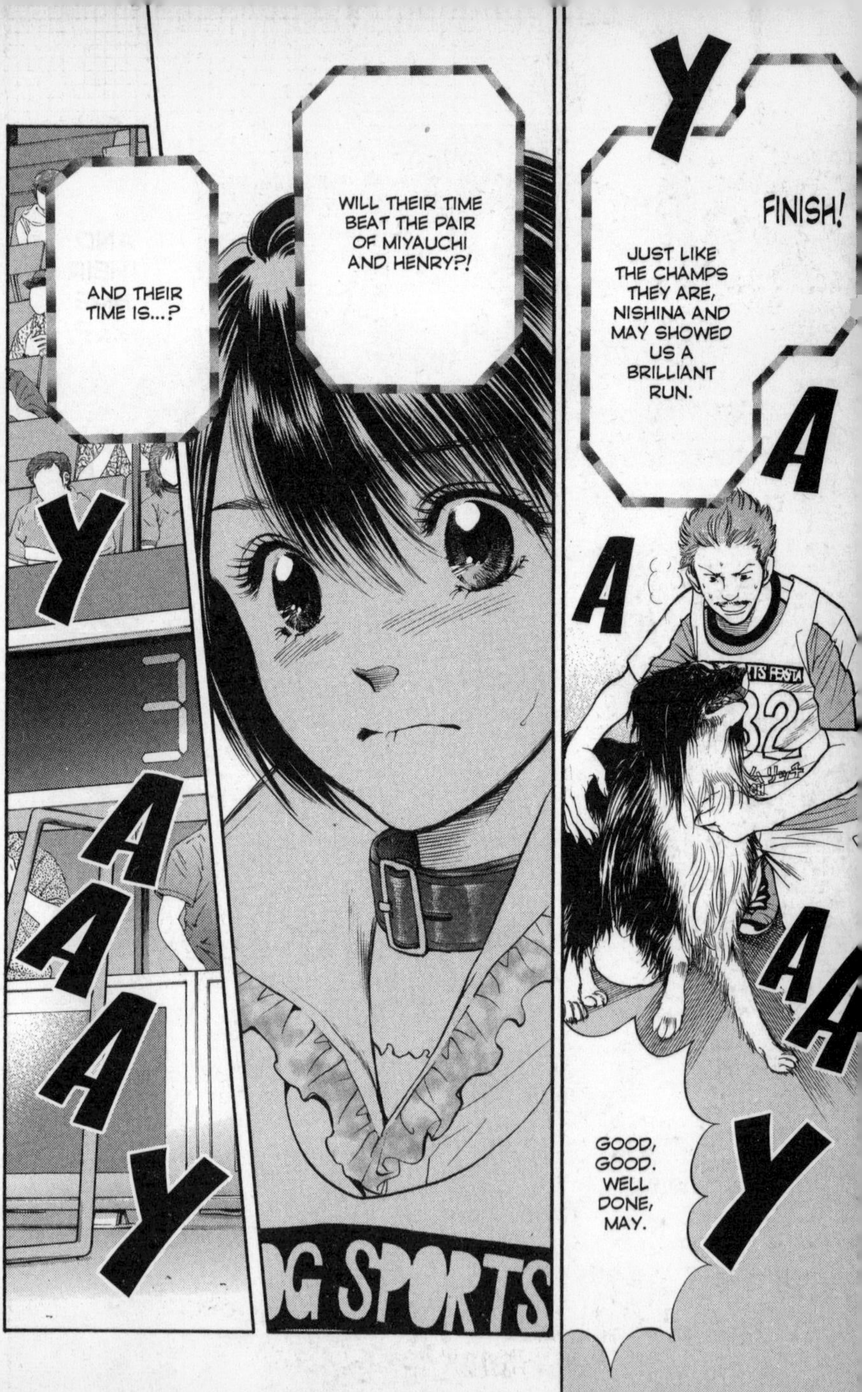
FINISH!
JUST LIKE THE CHAMPS THEY ARE, NISHINA AND MAY SHOWED US A BRILLIANT RUN.
YAAAAY
GOOD, GOOD. WELL DONE, MAY.
WILL THEIR TIME BEAT THE PAIR OF MIYAUCHI AND HENRY?!
DG SPORTS
AND THEIR TIME IS...?
YAAAY

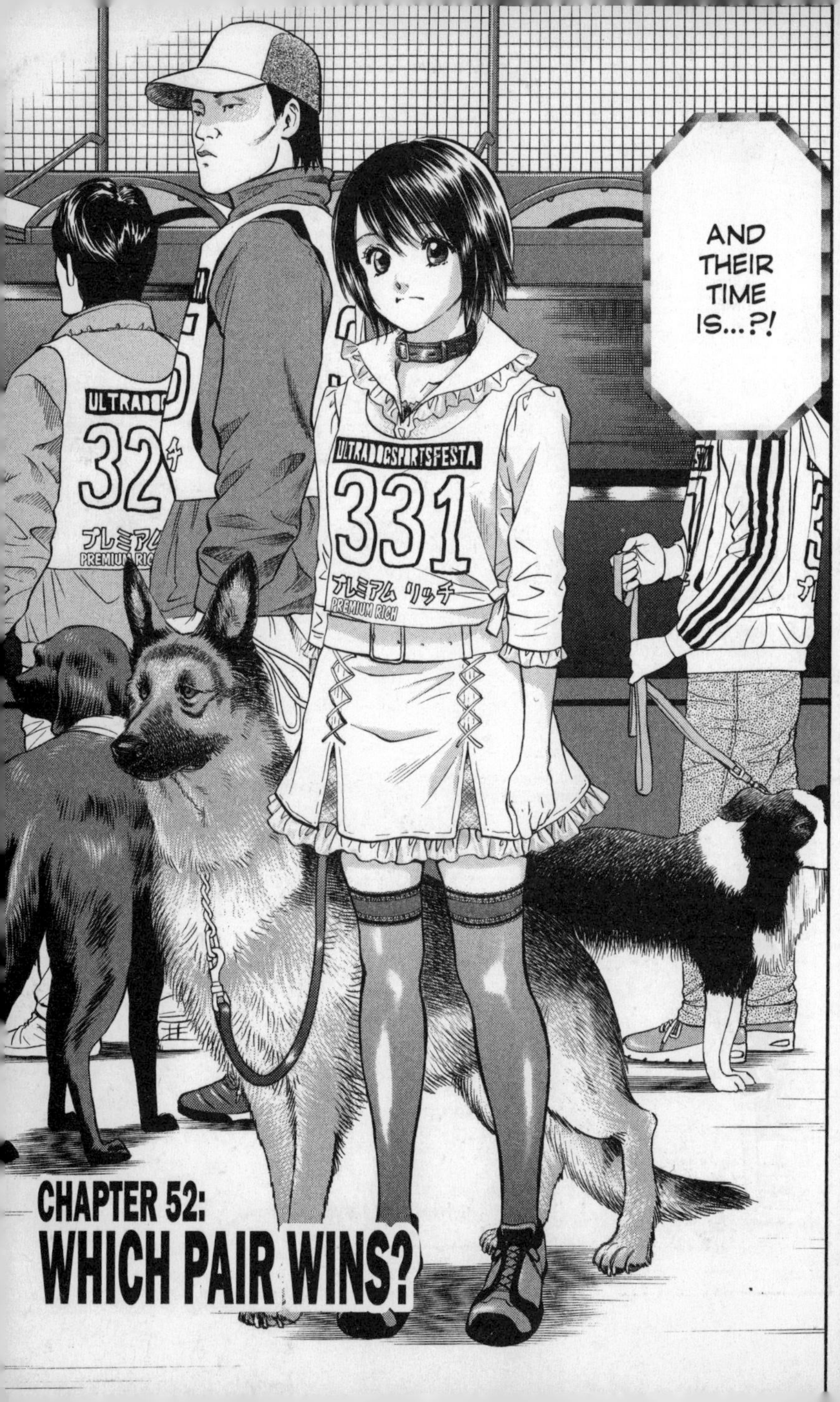
AND THEIR TIME IS...?!
ULTRADOGSPORTSFESTA
331
プレミアム リッチ
PREMIUM RICH
32
プレミアム
PREMIUM RICH

CHAPTER 52: WHICH PAIR WINS?

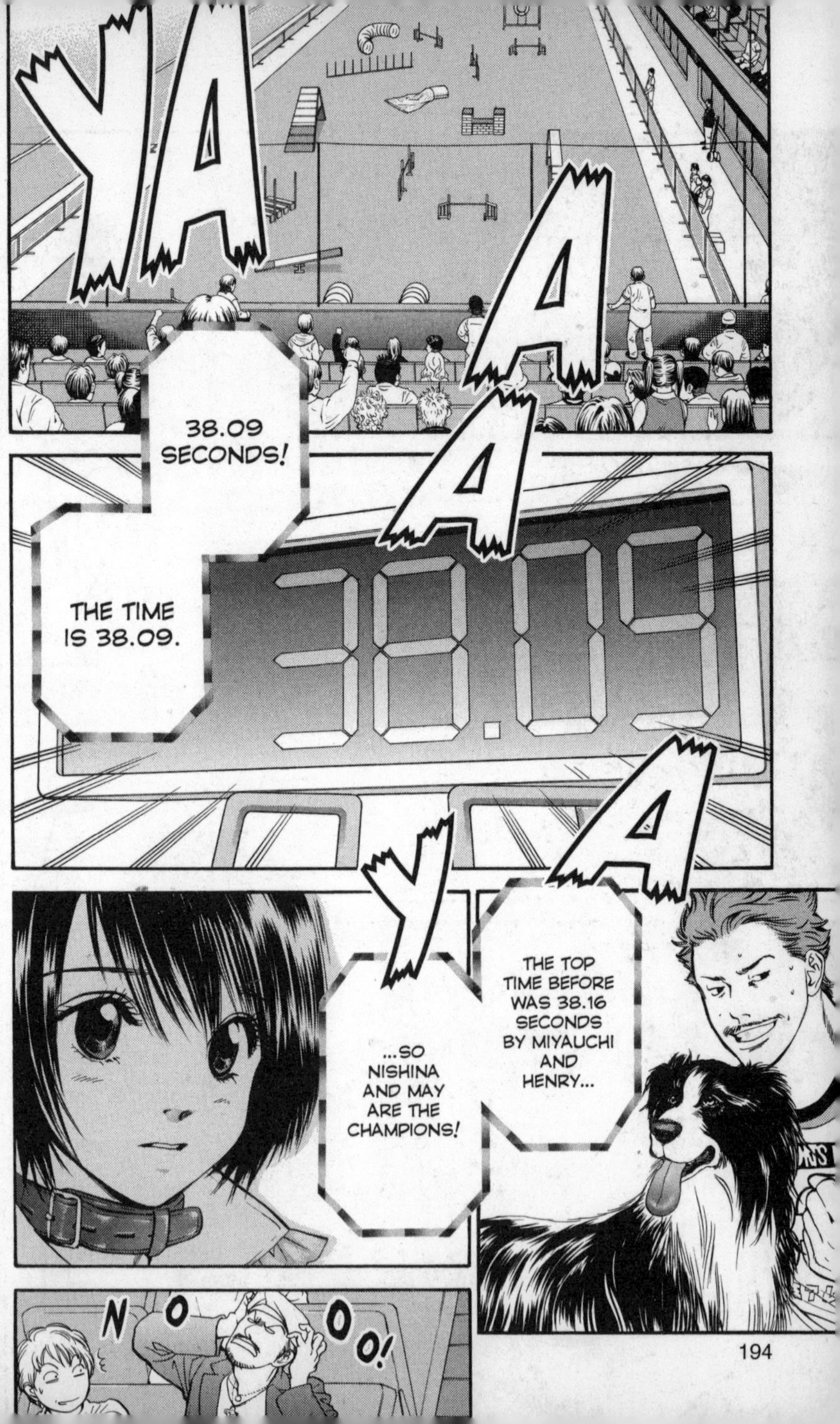

YAAAA
38.09 SECONDS!
THE TIME IS 38.09.
YA
THE TOP TIME BEFORE WAS 38.16 SECONDS BY MIYAUCHI AND HENRY...
...SO NISHINA AND MAY ARE THE CHAMPIONS!
NOOO!

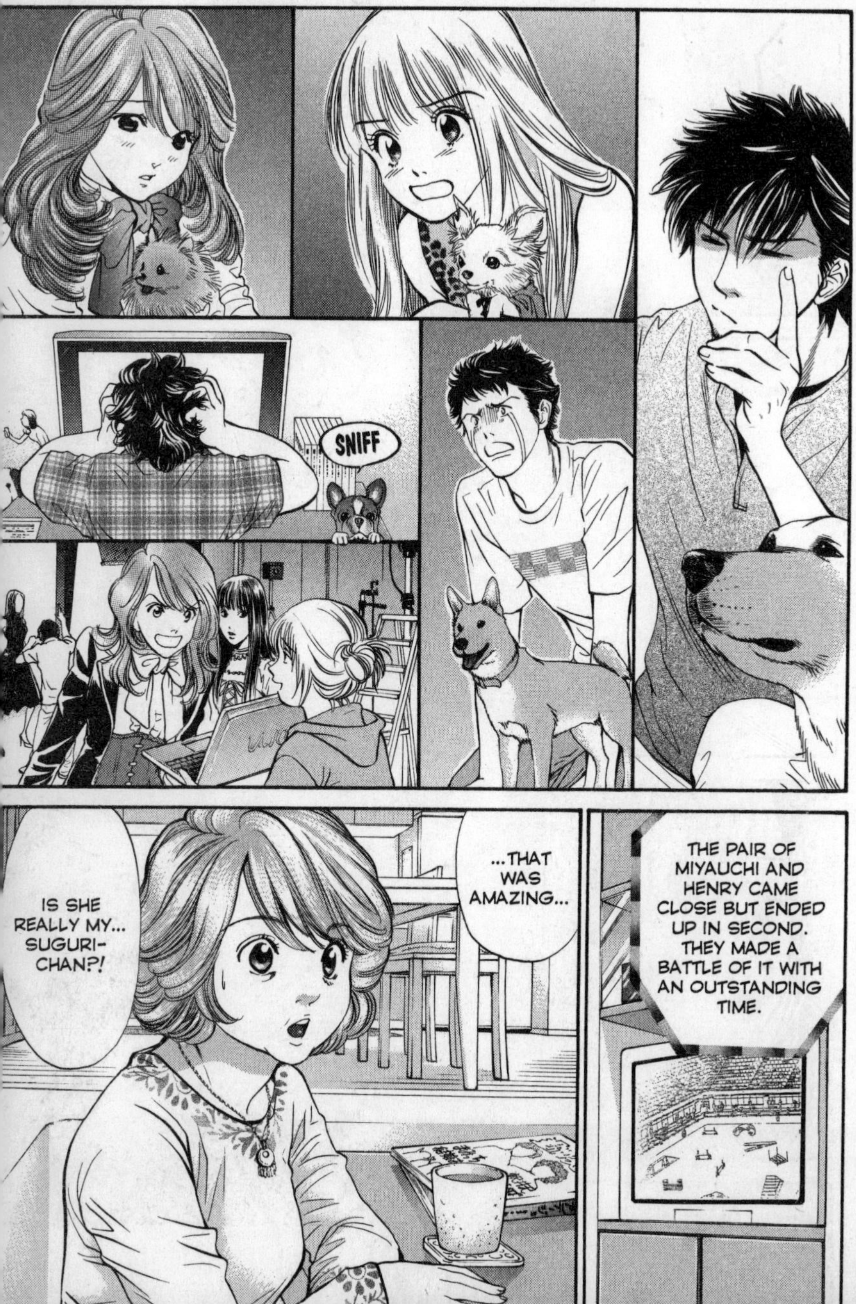
SNIFF
THE PAIR OF MIYAUCHI AND HENRY CAME CLOSE BUT ENDED UP IN SECOND. THEY MADE A BATTLE OF IT WITH AN OUTSTANDING TIME.
...THAT WAS AMAZING...
IS SHE REALLY MY... SUGURI-CHAN?!

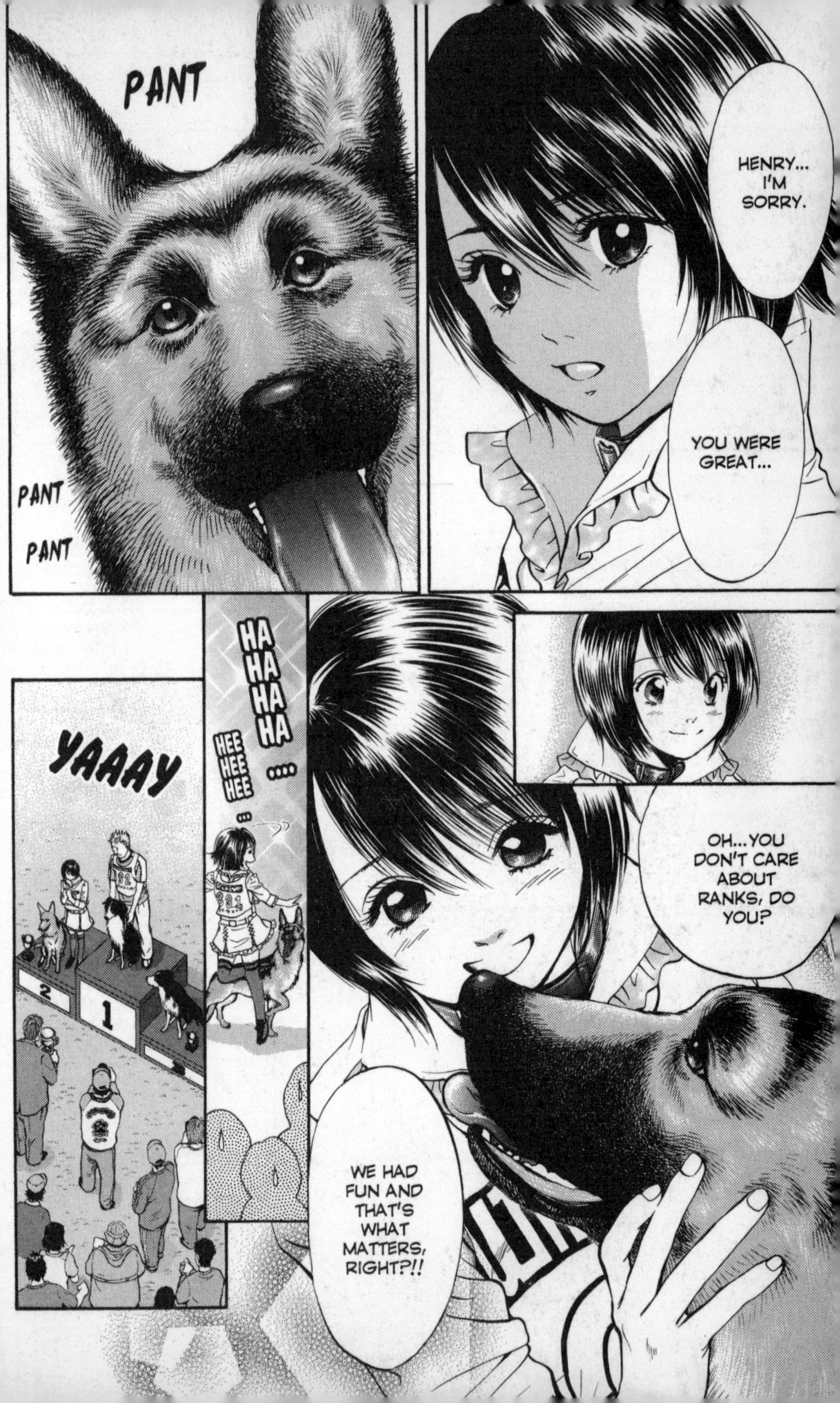
HENRY... I'M SORRY.
YOU WERE GREAT...
PANT
PANT
PANT
OH...YOU DON'T CARE ABOUT RANKS, DO YOU?
WE HAD FUN AND THAT'S WHAT MATTERS, RIGHT?!!
HA HA HA HA ....
HEE HEE HEE ...
YAAAY

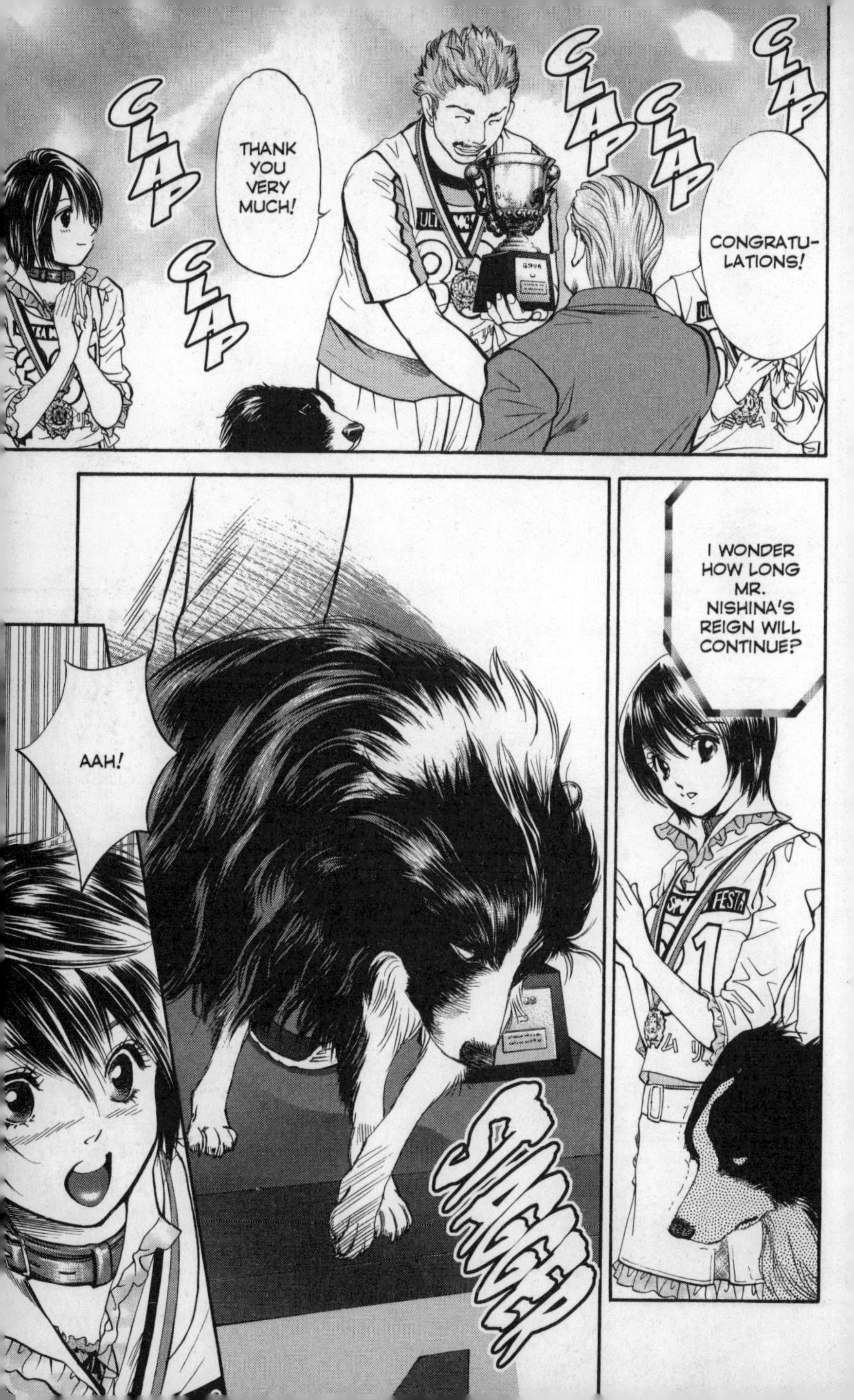
CLAP
CLAP
CLAP
CONGRATULATIONS!
THANK YOU VERY MUCH!
CLAP
CLAP
I WONDER HOW LONG MR. NISHINA'S REIGN WILL CONTINUE?
AAH!

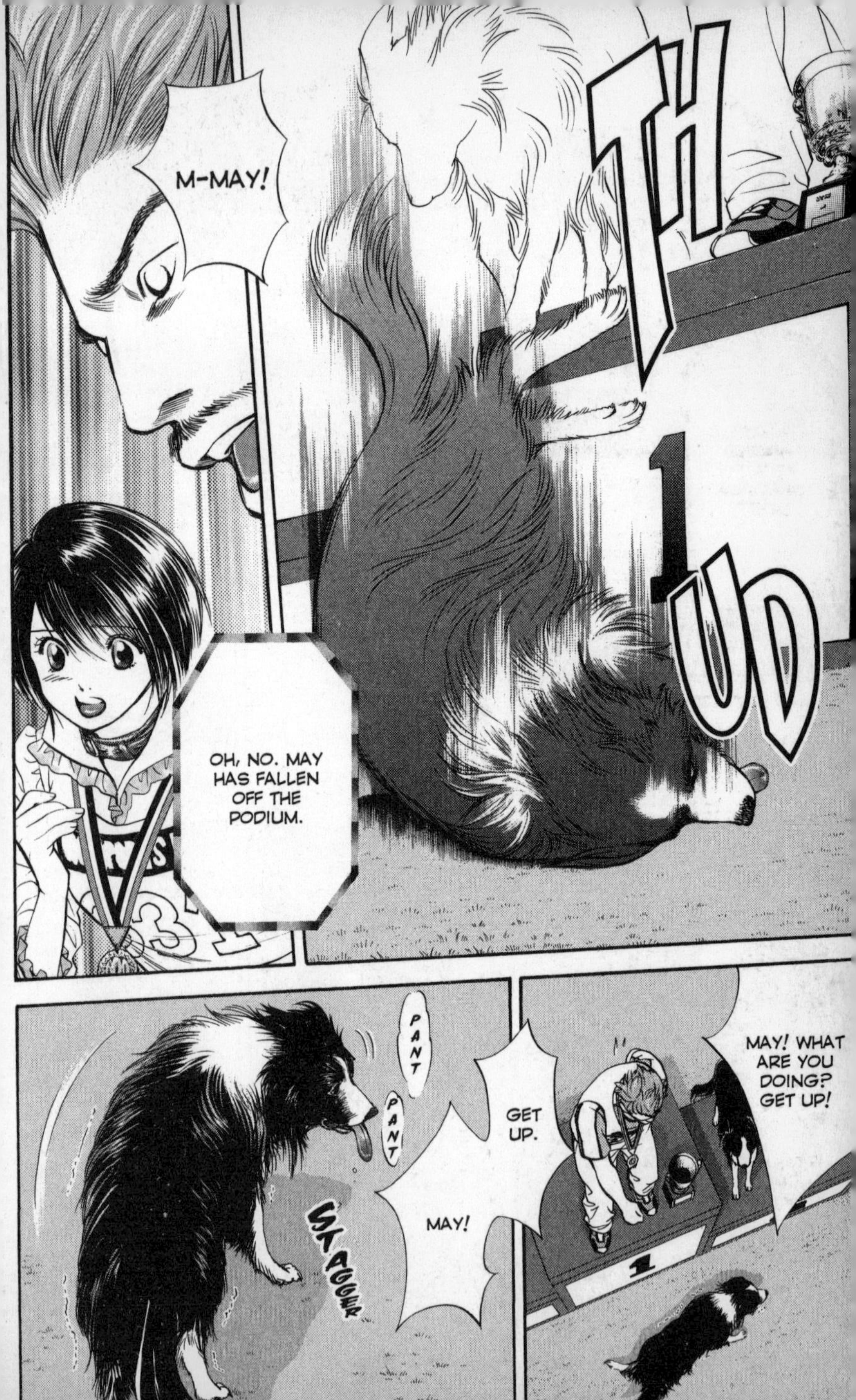
THUD
M-MAY!
OH, NO. MAY HAS FALLEN OFF THE PODIUM.
MAY! WHAT ARE YOU DOING? GET UP!
GET UP.
MAY!
PANT
PANT
STAGGER

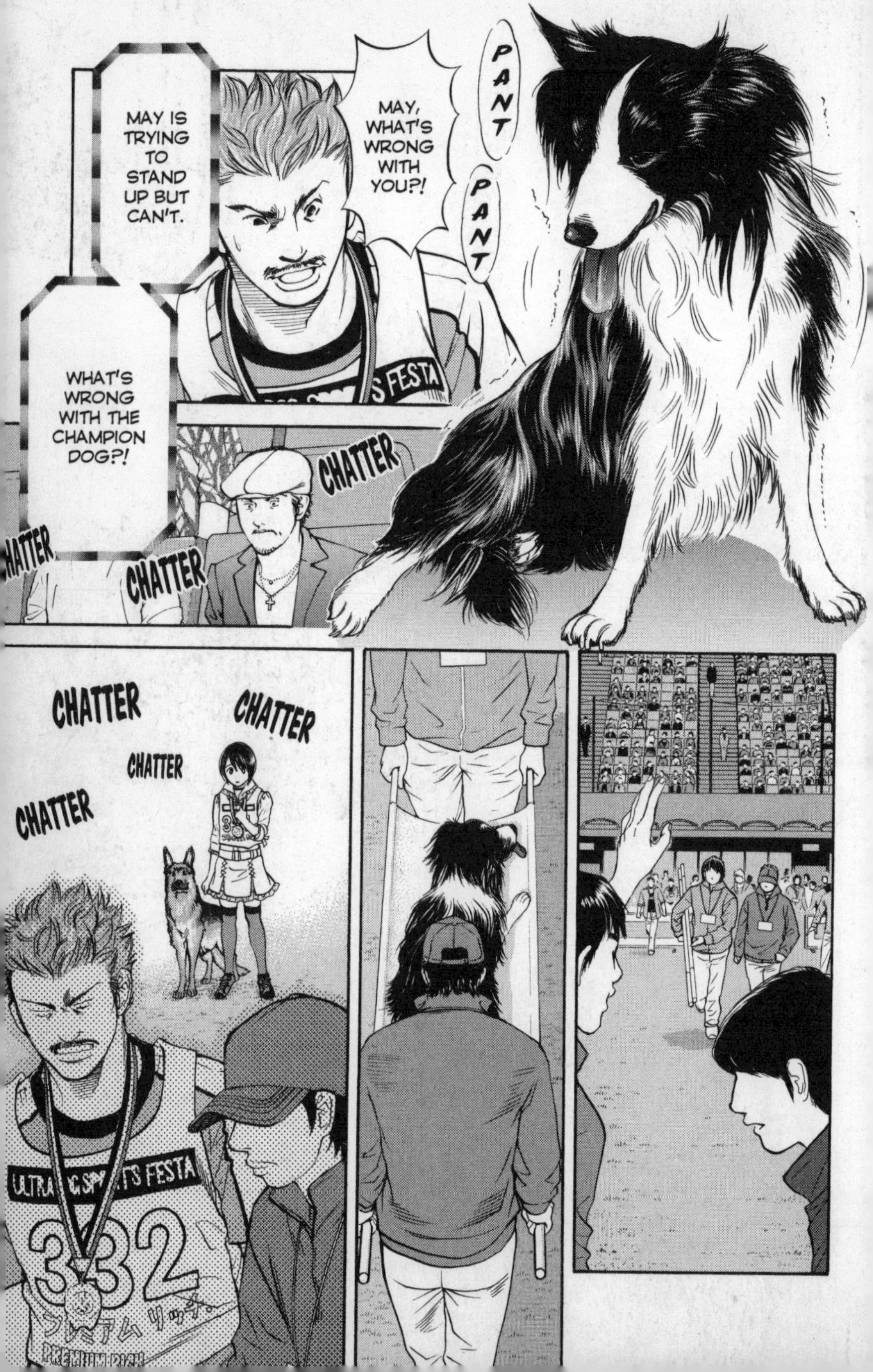
PANT
PANT
MAY, WHAT'S WRONG WITH YOU?!
MAY IS TRYING TO STAND UP BUT CAN'T.
WHAT'S WRONG WITH THE CHAMPION DOG?!
CHATTER
CHATTER
CHATTER
CHATTER
CHATTER
CHATTER
CHATTER

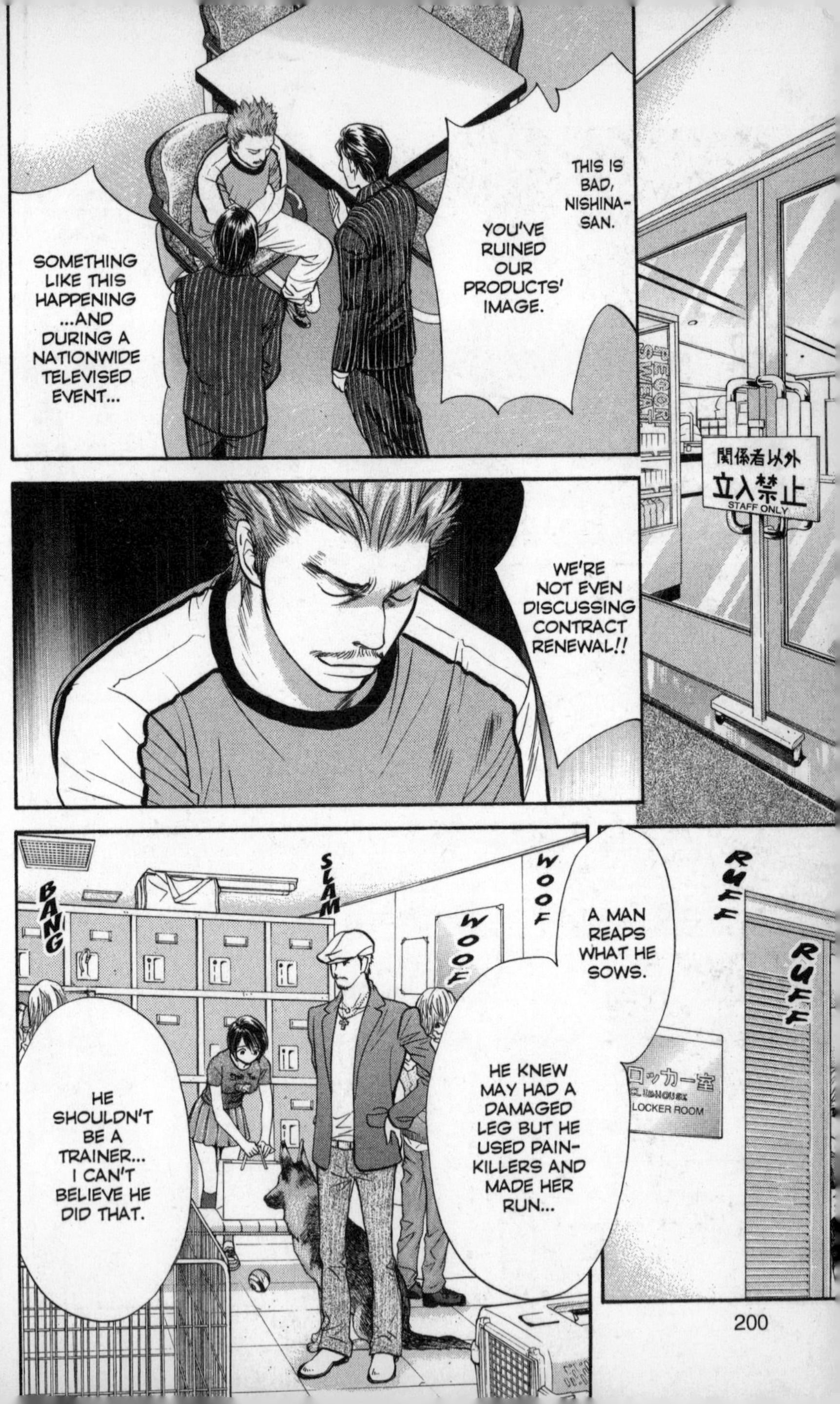
関係者以外
立入禁止
STAFF ONLY
THIS IS BAD, NISHINA-SAN.
YOU'VE RUINED OUR PRODUCTS' IMAGE.
SOMETHING LIKE THIS HAPPENING ...AND DURING A NATIONWIDE TELEVISED EVENT...
WE'RE NOT EVEN DISCUSSING CONTRACT RENEWAL!!
RUFF
RUFF
ロッカー室
CLUBHOUSE
LOCKER ROOM
WOOF
WOOF
SLAM
BANG
A MAN REAPS WHAT HE SOWS.
HE KNEW MAY HAD A DAMAGED LEG BUT HE USED PAIN-KILLERS AND MADE HER RUN...
HE SHOULDN'T BE A TRAINER... I CAN'T BELIEVE HE DID THAT.

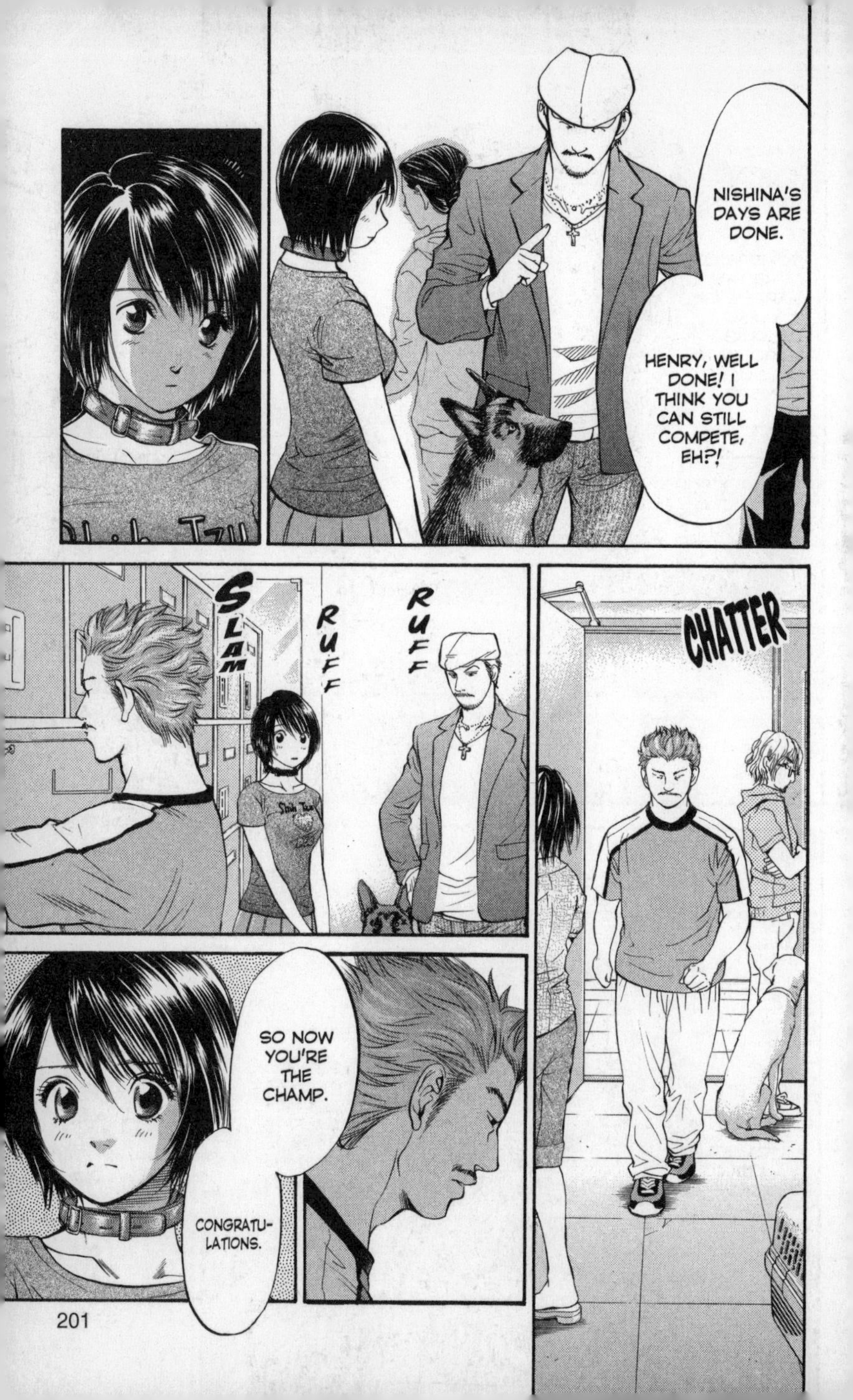
NISHINA'S DAYS ARE DONE.
HENRY, WELL DONE! I THINK YOU CAN STILL COMPETE, EH?!
CHATTER
SLAM
RUFF
RUFF
SO NOW YOU'RE THE CHAMP.
CONGRATU-LATIONS.

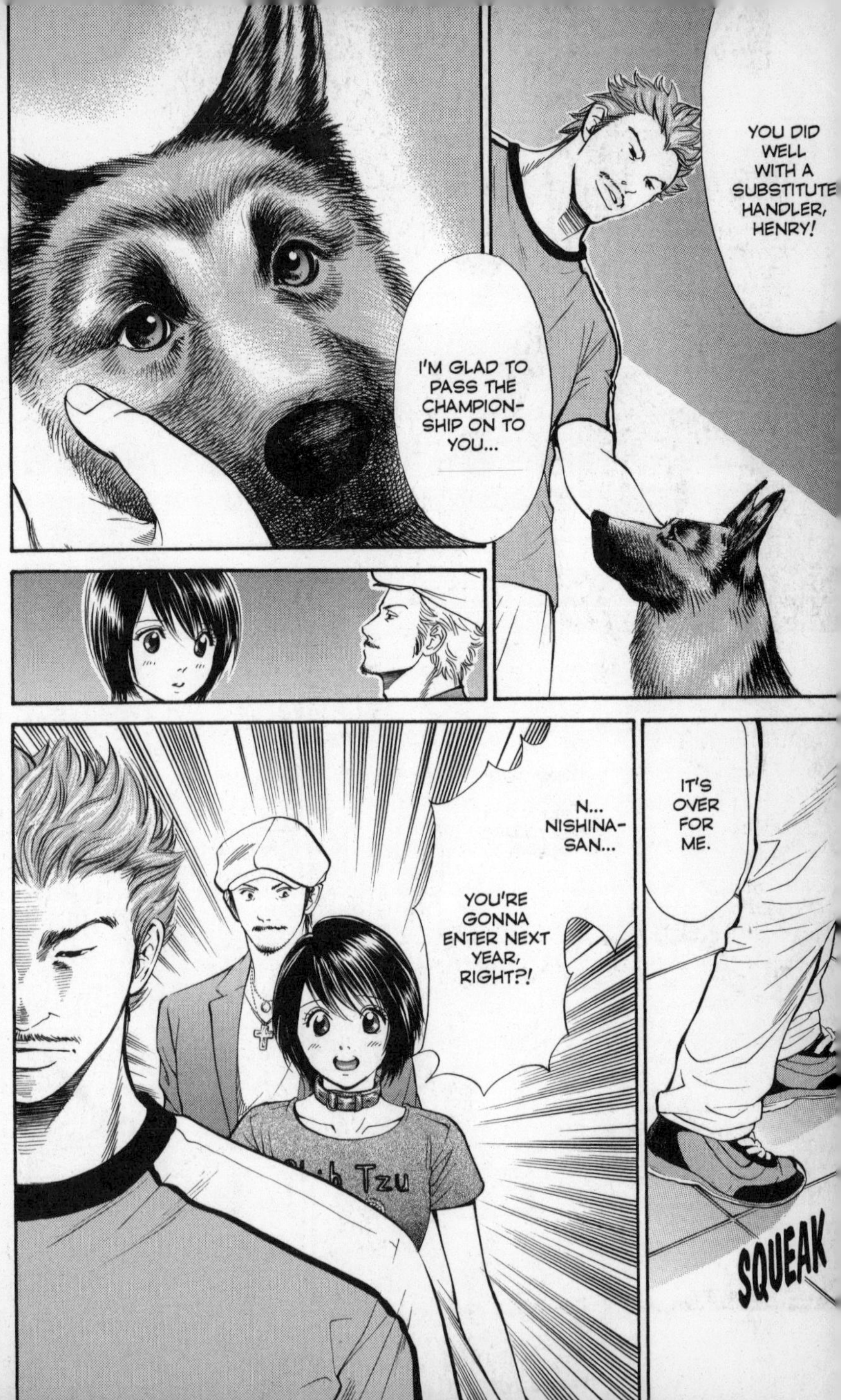
YOU DID WELL WITH A SUBSTITUTE HANDLER, HENRY!
I'M GLAD TO PASS THE CHAMPION-SHIP ON TO YOU...
IT'S OVER FOR ME.
SQUEAK
N... NISHINA-SAN...
YOU'RE GONNA ENTER NEXT YEAR, RIGHT?!

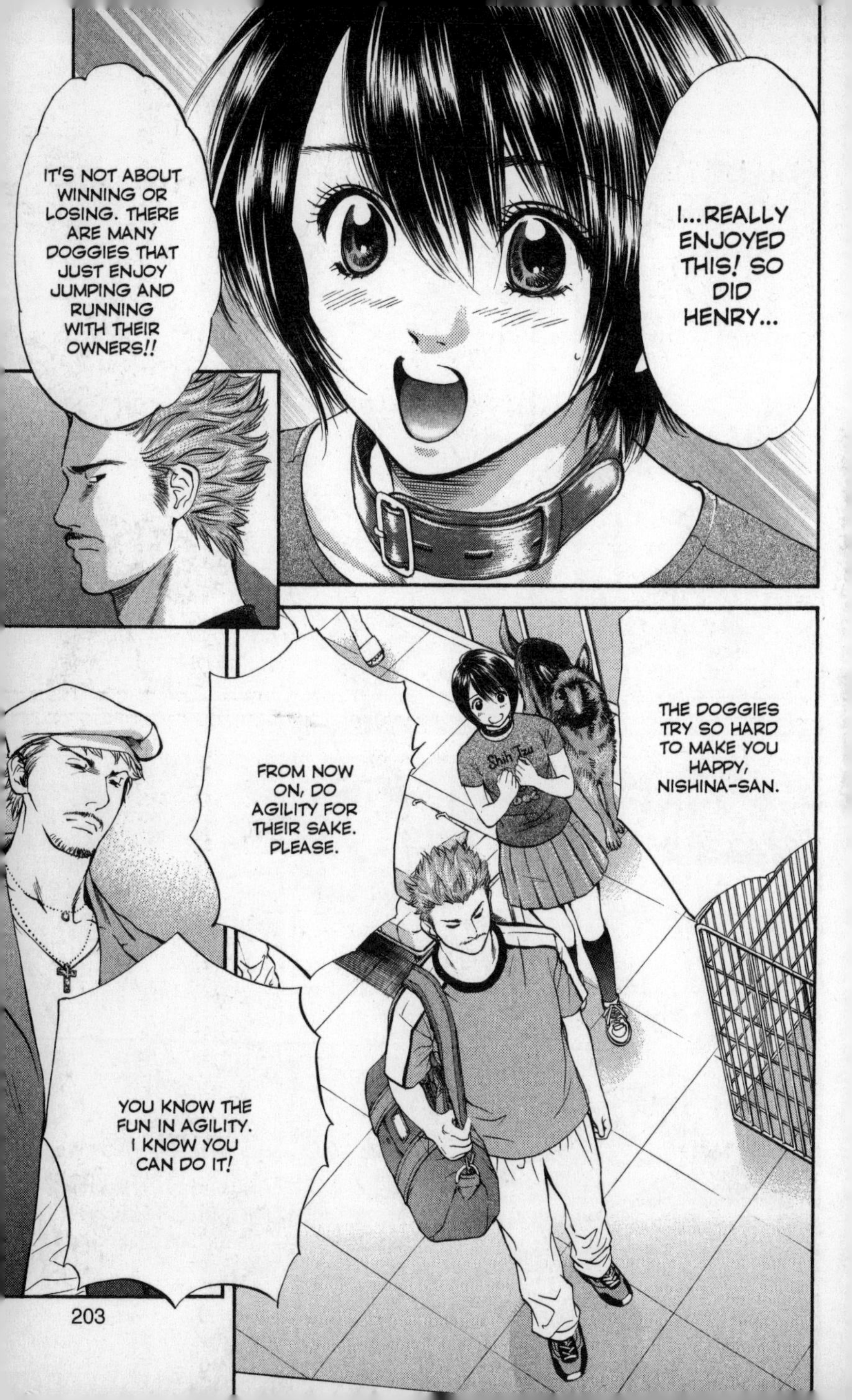
I...REALLY ENJOYED THIS! SO DID HENRY...
IT'S NOT ABOUT WINNING OR LOSING. THERE ARE MANY DOGGIES THAT JUST ENJOY JUMPING AND RUNNING WITH THEIR OWNERS!!
THE DOGGIES TRY SO HARD TO MAKE YOU HAPPY, NISHINA-SAN.
FROM NOW ON, DO AGILITY FOR THEIR SAKE. PLEASE.
YOU KNOW THE FUN IN AGILITY. I KNOW YOU CAN DO IT!
Shih Tzu

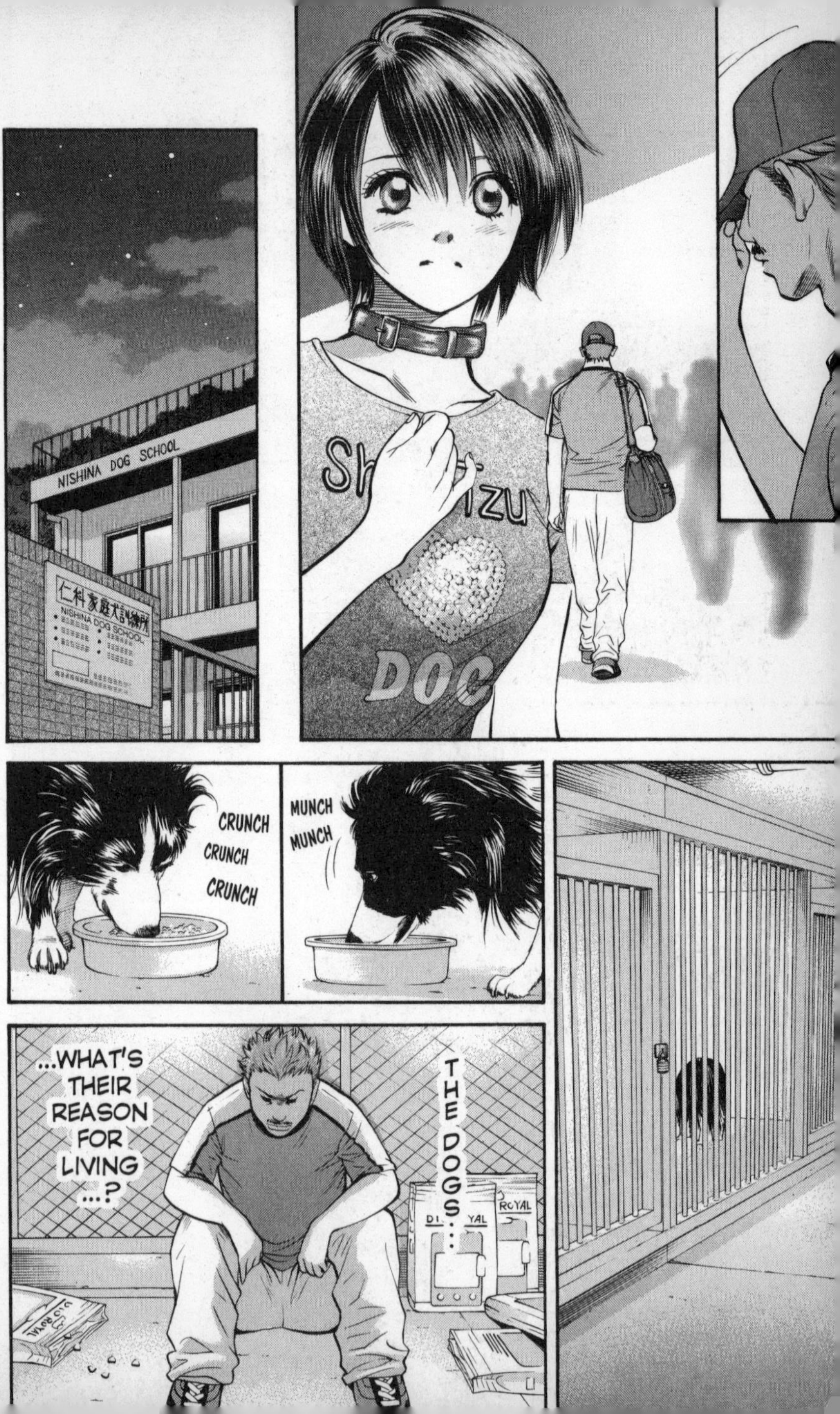
NISHINA DOG SCHOOL
NISHINA DOG SCHOOL
MUNCH MUNCH
CRUNCH CRUNCH CRUNCH
THE DOGS...
...WHAT'S THEIR REASON FOR LIVING ...?
ROYAL

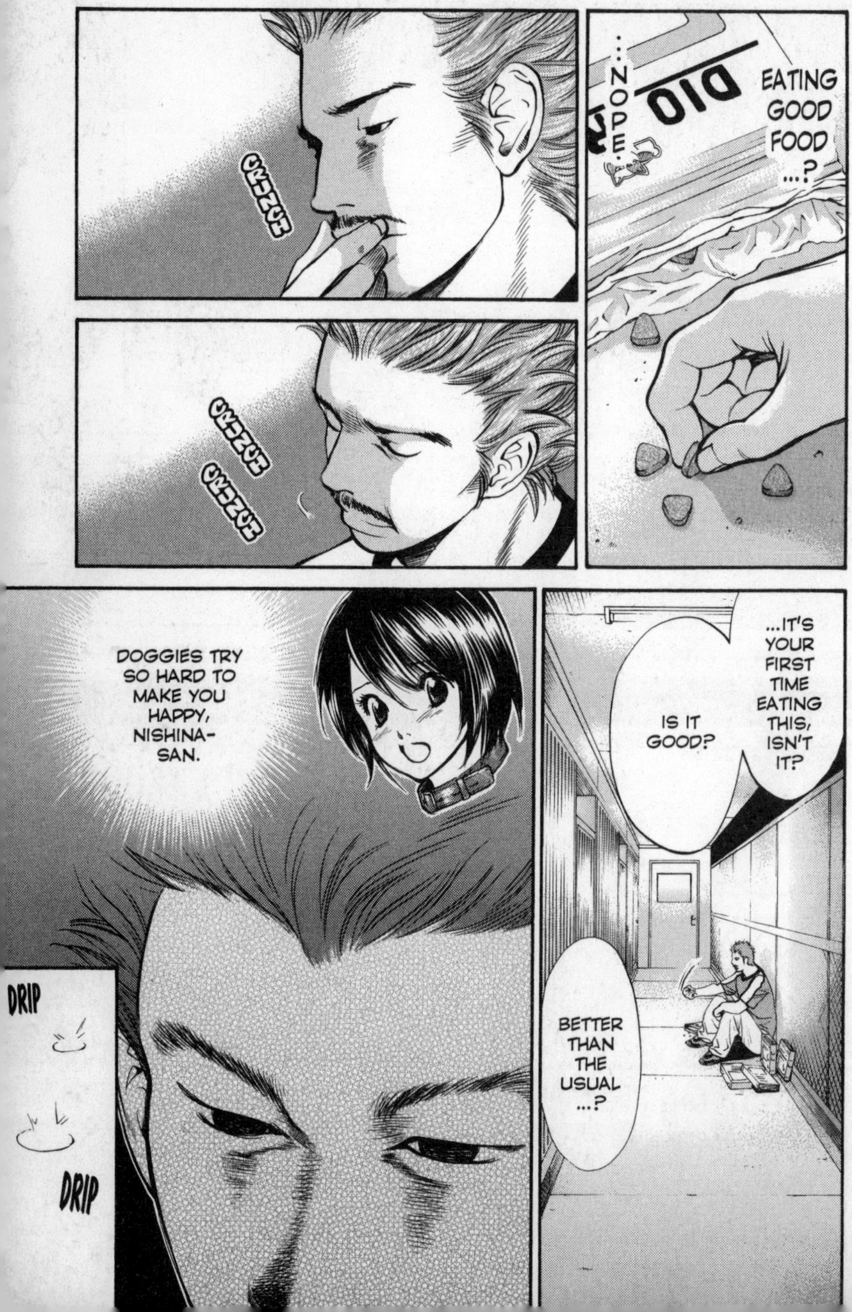
EATING GOOD FOOD ...?
...NOPE.
CRUNCH
CRUNCH
CRUNCH
...IT'S YOUR FIRST TIME EATING THIS, ISN'T IT?
IS IT GOOD?
BETTER THAN THE USUAL ...?
DOGGIES TRY SO HARD TO MAKE YOU HAPPY, NISHINA-SAN.
DRIP
DRIP

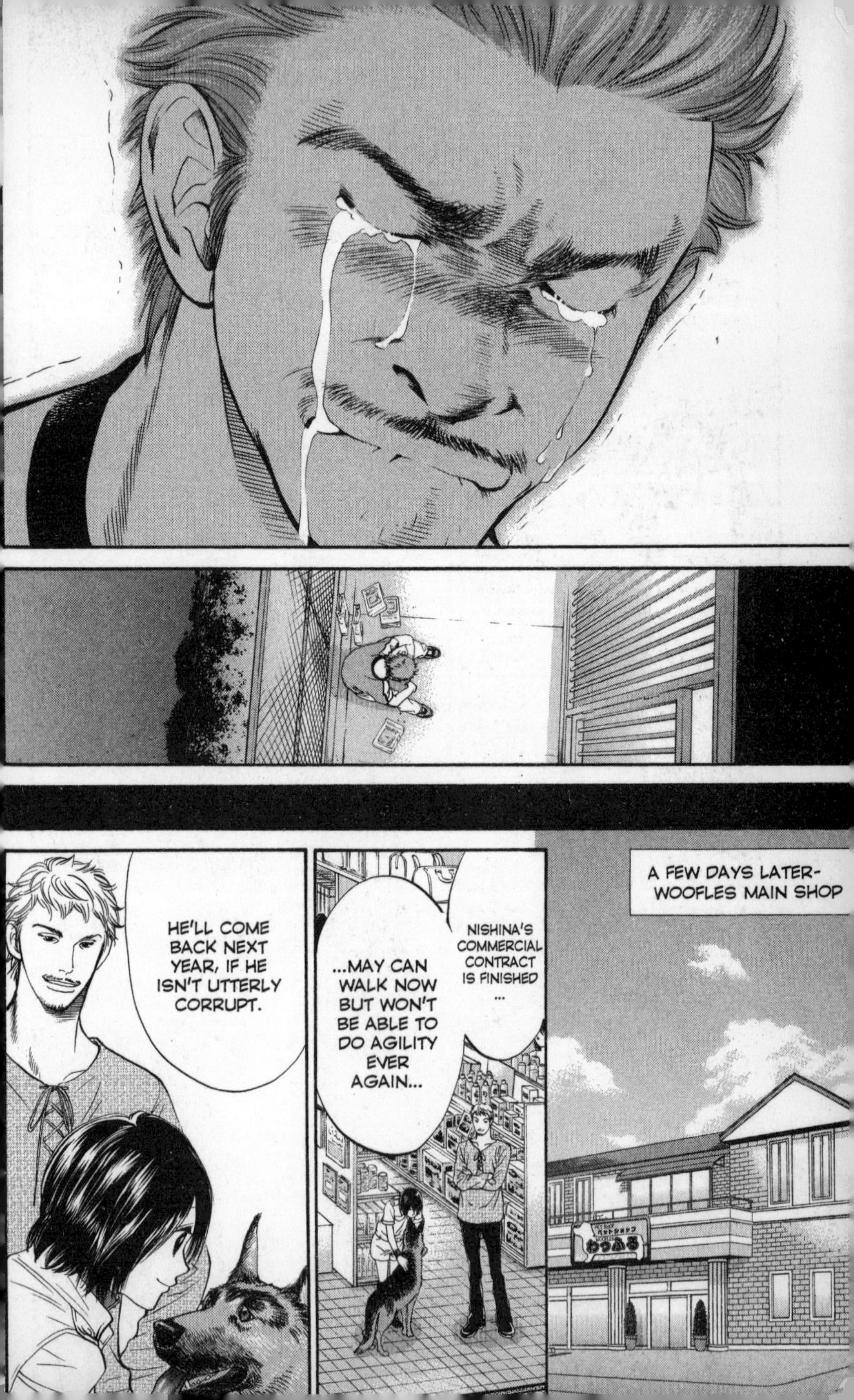
A FEW DAYS LATER-
WOOFLES MAIN SHOP
NISHINA'S COMMERCIAL CONTRACT IS FINISHED ...
...MAY CAN WALK NOW BUT WON'T BE ABLE TO DO AGILITY EVER AGAIN...
HE'LL COME BACK NEXT YEAR, IF HE ISN'T UTTERLY CORRUPT.

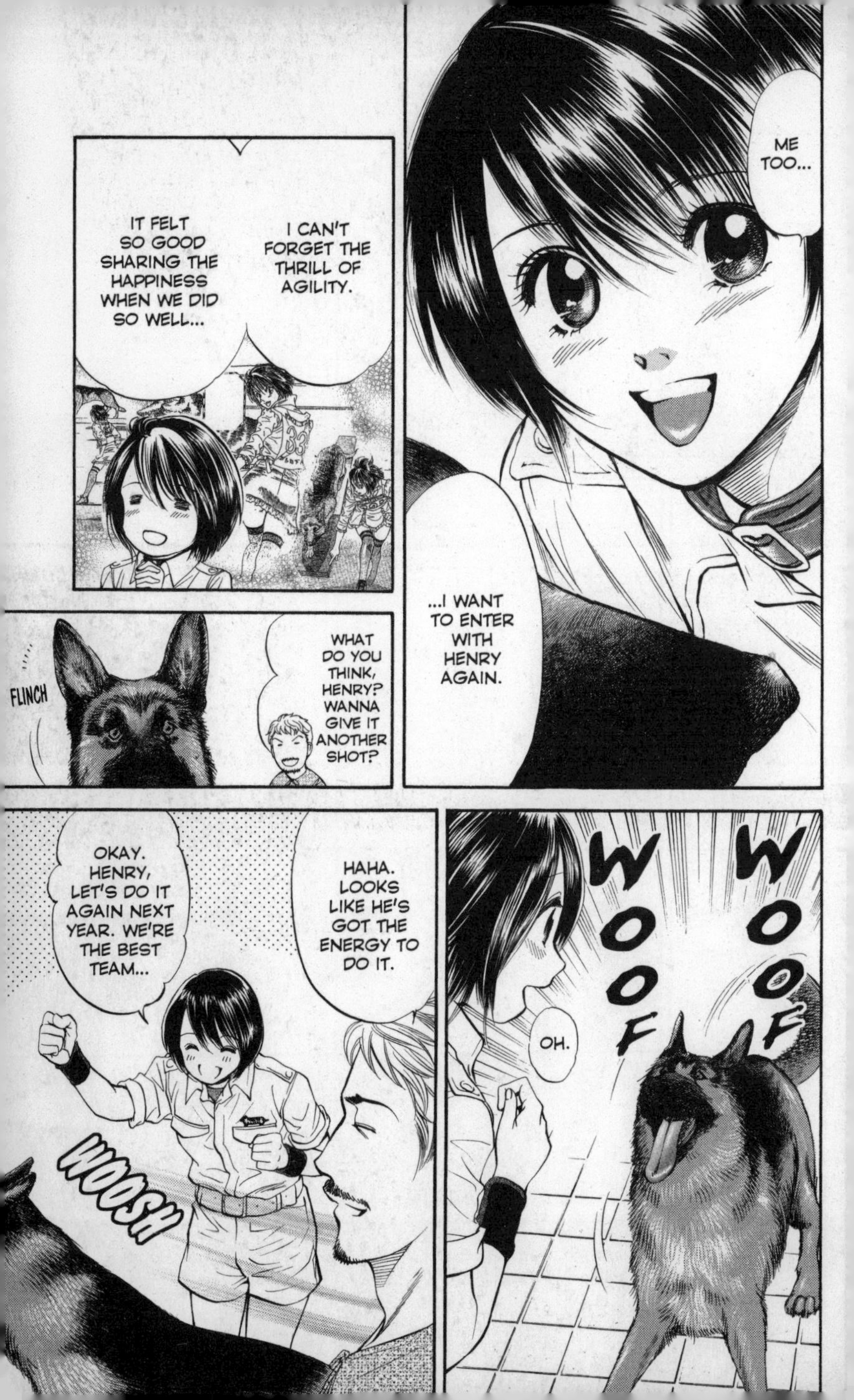
ME TOO...
...I WANT TO ENTER WITH HENRY AGAIN.
I CAN'T FORGET THE THRILL OF AGILITY.
IT FELT SO GOOD SHARING THE HAPPINESS WHEN WE DID SO WELL...
WHAT DO YOU THINK, HENRY? WANNA GIVE IT ANOTHER SHOT?
FLINCH
WOOF
WOOF
OH.
HAHA. LOOKS LIKE HE'S GOT THE ENERGY TO DO IT.
OKAY. HENRY, LET'S DO IT AGAIN NEXT YEAR. WE'RE THE BEST TEAM...
WOOSH

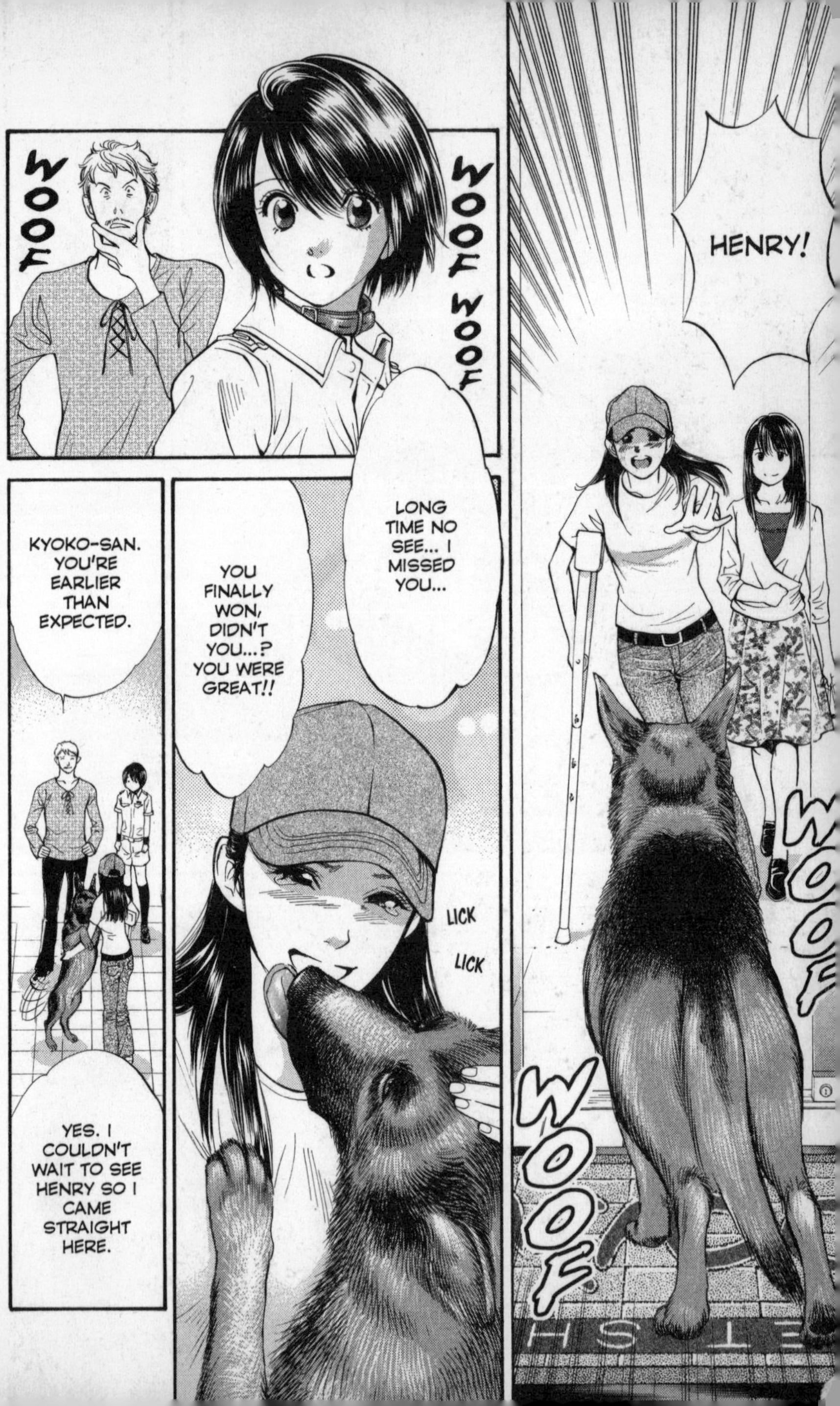
HENRY!
WOOF
WOOF
WOOF WOOF WOOF
WOOF
LONG TIME NO SEE... I MISSED YOU...
YOU FINALLY WON, DIDN'T YOU...? YOU WERE GREAT!!
LICK
LICK
KYOKO-SAN. YOU'RE EARLIER THAN EXPECTED.
YES. I COULDN'T WAIT TO SEE HENRY SO I CAME STRAIGHT HERE.

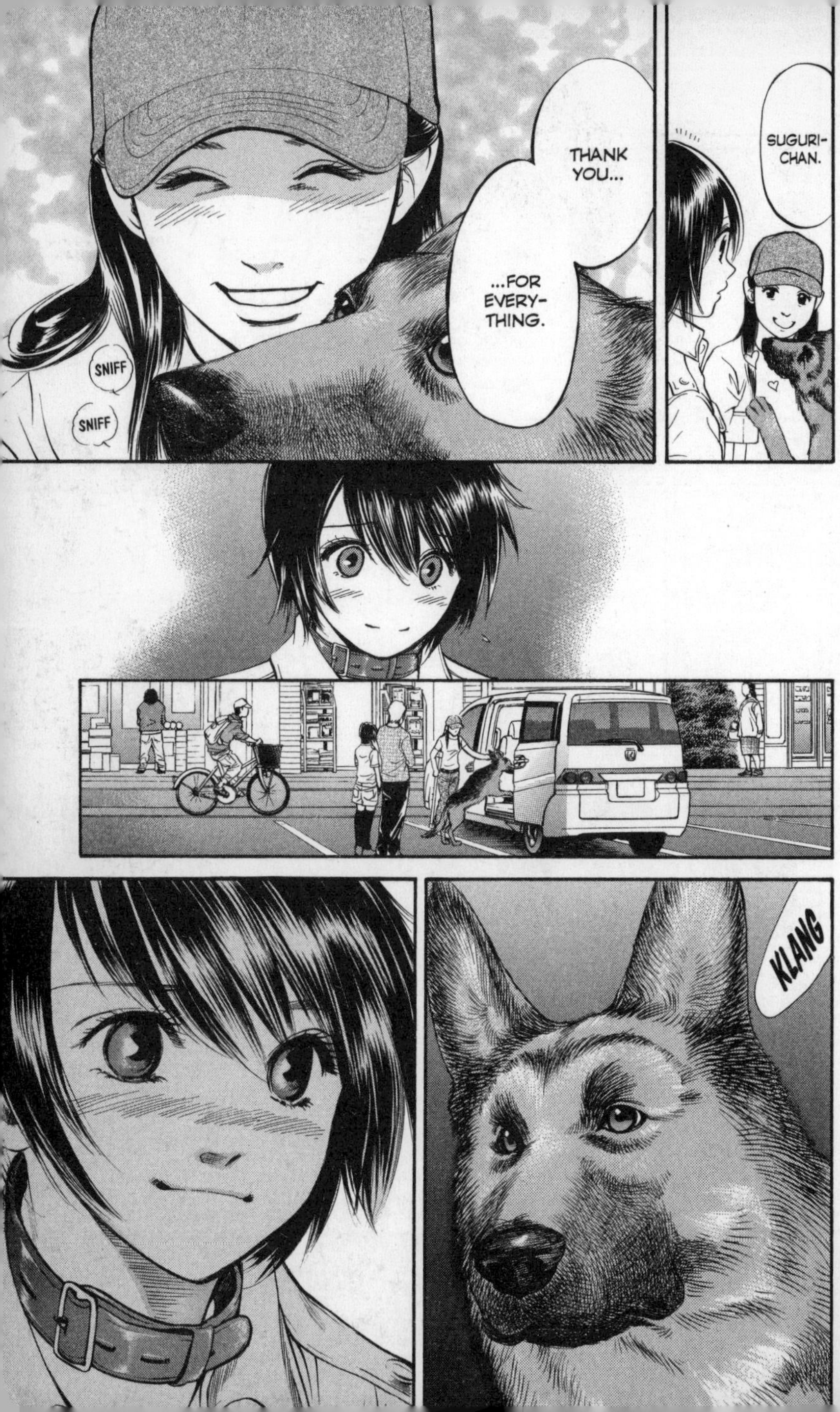
SUGURI-CHAN.
THANK YOU...
...FOR EVERY-THING.
SNIFF
SNIFF
KLANG

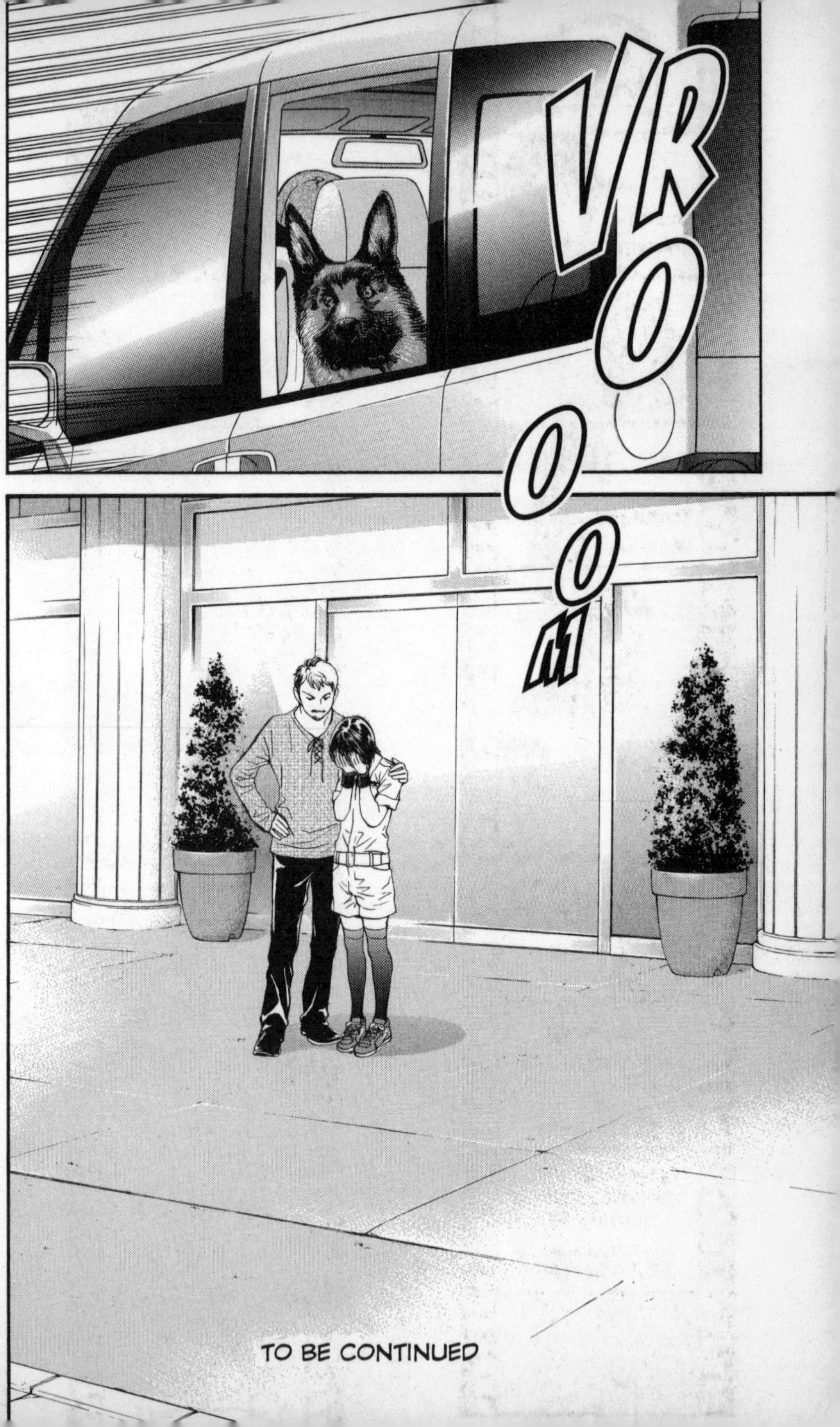
VROOOM
TO BE CONTINUED

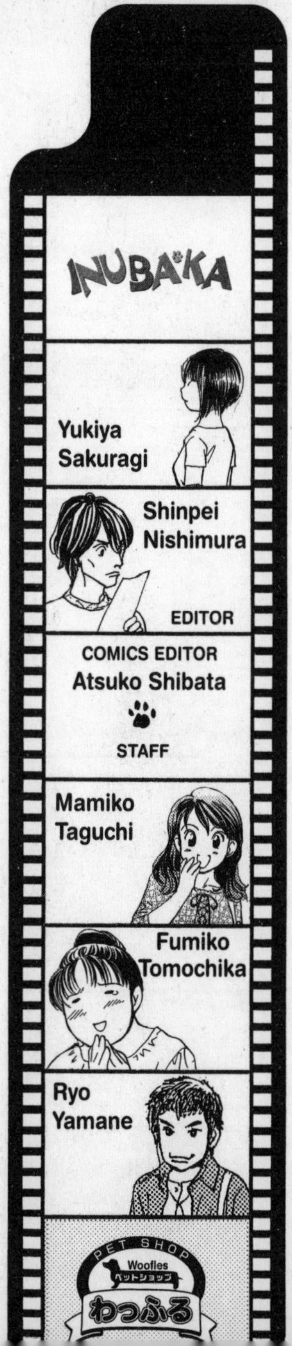

INUBAKA
Yukiya Sakuragi
Shinpei Nishimura
EDITOR
COMICS EDITOR
Atsuko Shibata
STAFF
Mamiko Taguchi
Fumiko Tomochika
Ryo Yamane
PET SHOP
Woofles
ペットショップ
わっふる

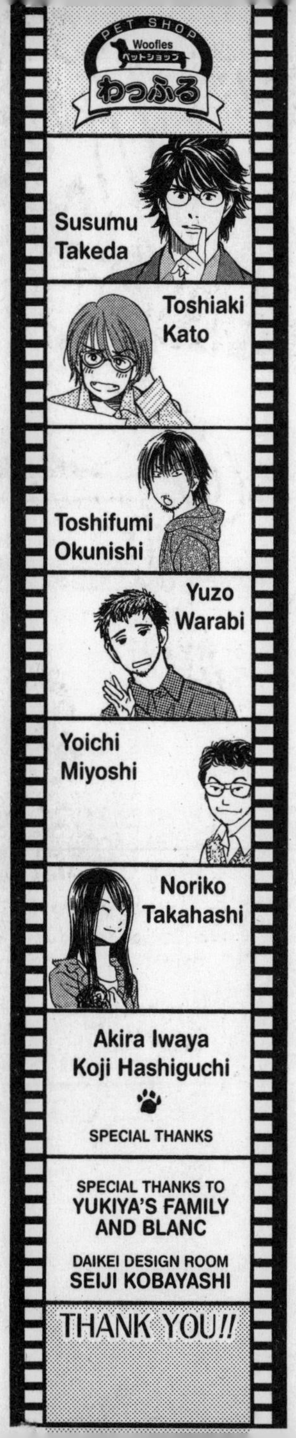

PET SHOP
Woofles
ペットショップ
わっふる
Susumu Takeda
Toshiaki Kato
Toshifumi Okunishi
Yuzo Warabi
Yoichi Miyoshi
Noriko Takahashi
Akira Iwaya
Koji Hashiguchi
SPECIAL THANKS
SPECIAL THANKS TO
YUKIYA'S FAMILY
AND BLANC
DAIKEI DESIGN ROOM
SEIJI KOBAYASHI
THANK YOU!!

INUBAKA

Everybody's Crazy for Dogs!

From Daimon-san in Tokyo

🐾 Ken-chan (mutt)

I met Ken-chan (a female) at a Seeing Eye Dog training center. Daimon-san's son thought she was a male and named her "Ken." She got so used to being called Ken. The thing beside Ken-chan is a statue of her made by her owner's friend.

Yukiya Sakuragi

Her face is very girlish. The statue of Ken-chan is excellent. It really does look like her. But Ken-chan seems to be saying that she's cuter than it (lol).

From Arino-san in Hokkaido

Shu-kun (miniature dachshund)

Shu-kun weighs 8 kg and is powerful, big and very friendly. He is four years old and childish but he burps and coughs like an old man!

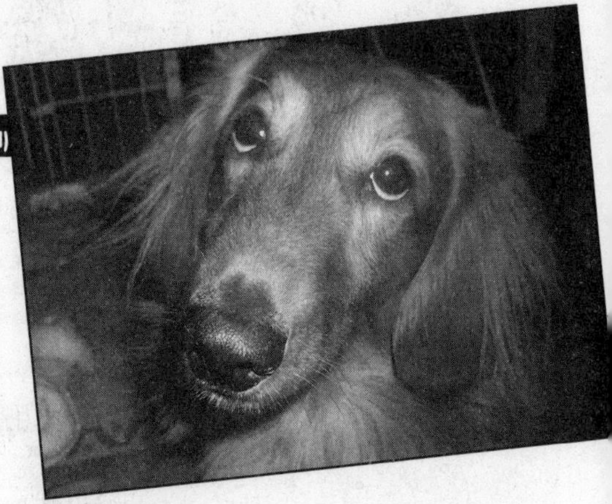

Yukiya Sakuragi

8 kg...Wonderful! (lol). I've heard some dogs are like old men but that's really funny... I laughed (Sorry!). But even those characteristics are very cute after all, aren't they?

From Sudo-san in Osaka prefecture

Koko-chan & Lavi-chan (Labrador retrievers)

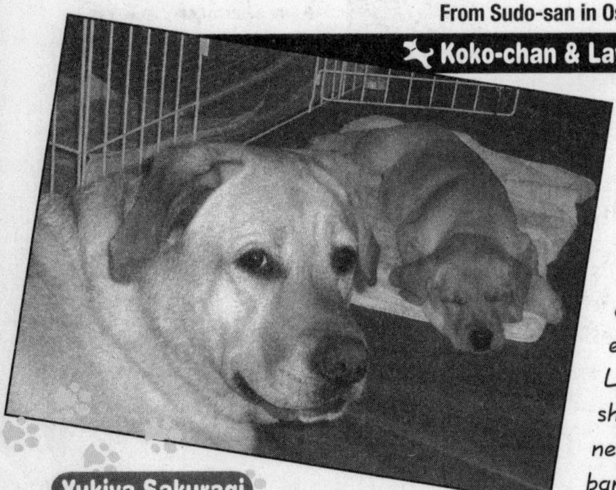

Koko-chan is six years old and Lavi-chan is a one-year-old. They aren't kin but they have a very good relationship—almost like a real parent and child! When Lavi gets scared when she's barked at by the neighbors' dogs, Koko barks back as if sticking up for Lavi!! Lavi likes the reliable Koko.

Yukiya Sakuragi

Dogs have strong bonds just like humans. I feel at peace just looking at their good relationships.

Inubaka

Crazy for Dogs
Vol. #5
VIZ Media Edition

Story and Art by
Yukiya Sakuragi

Translation/Hidemi Hachitori, HC Language Solutions, Inc.
English Adaptation/Ian Reid, HC Language Solutions, Inc.
Touch-up Art & Lettering/Kelle Han
Cover and Interior Design/Hidemi Sahara
Editor/Ian Robertson

Editor in Chief, Books/Alvin Lu
Editor in Chief, Magazines/Marc Weidenbaum
VP of Publishing Licensing/Rika Inouye
VP of Sales/Gonzalo Ferreyra
Sr. VP of Marketing/Liza Coppola
Publisher/Hyoe Narita

Printed in the U.S.A.

Published by VIZ Media, LLC
P.O. Box 77010
San Francisco, CA 94107

10 9 8 7 6 5 4 3 2 1
First printing, October 2007

VIZ MEDIA

www.viz.com
store.viz.com

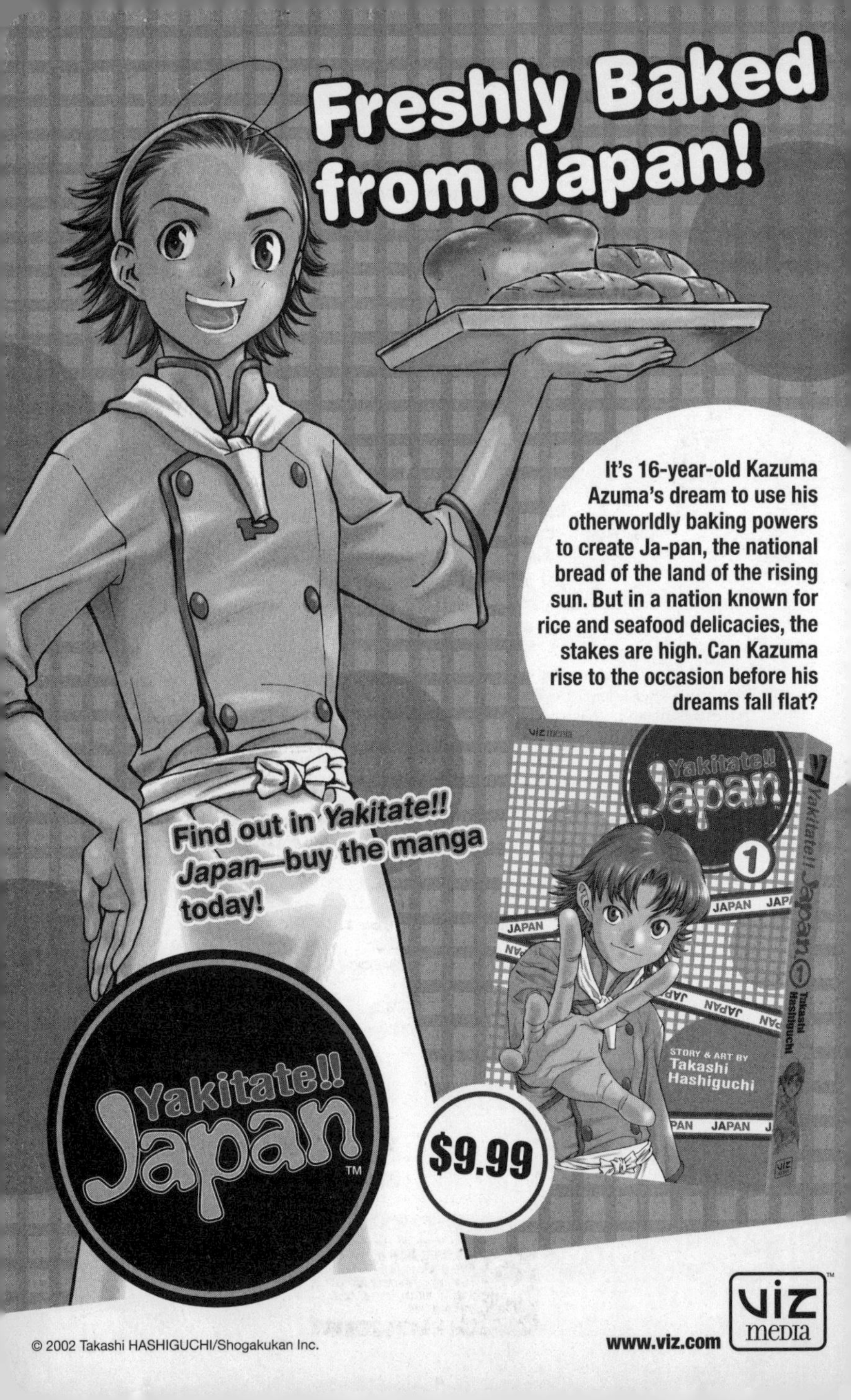
Freshly Baked from Japan!
It's 16-year-old Kazuma Azuma's dream to use his otherworldly baking powers to create Ja-pan, the national bread of the land of the rising sun. But in a nation known for rice and seafood delicacies, the stakes are high. Can Kazuma rise to the occasion before his dreams fall flat?
Find out in Yakitate!! Japan—buy the manga today!
Yakitate!! Japan™
$9.99
Yakitate!! Japan 1
STORY & ART BY Takashi Hashiguchi
© 2002 Takashi HASHIGUCHI/Shogakukan Inc.
www.viz.com
VIZ media

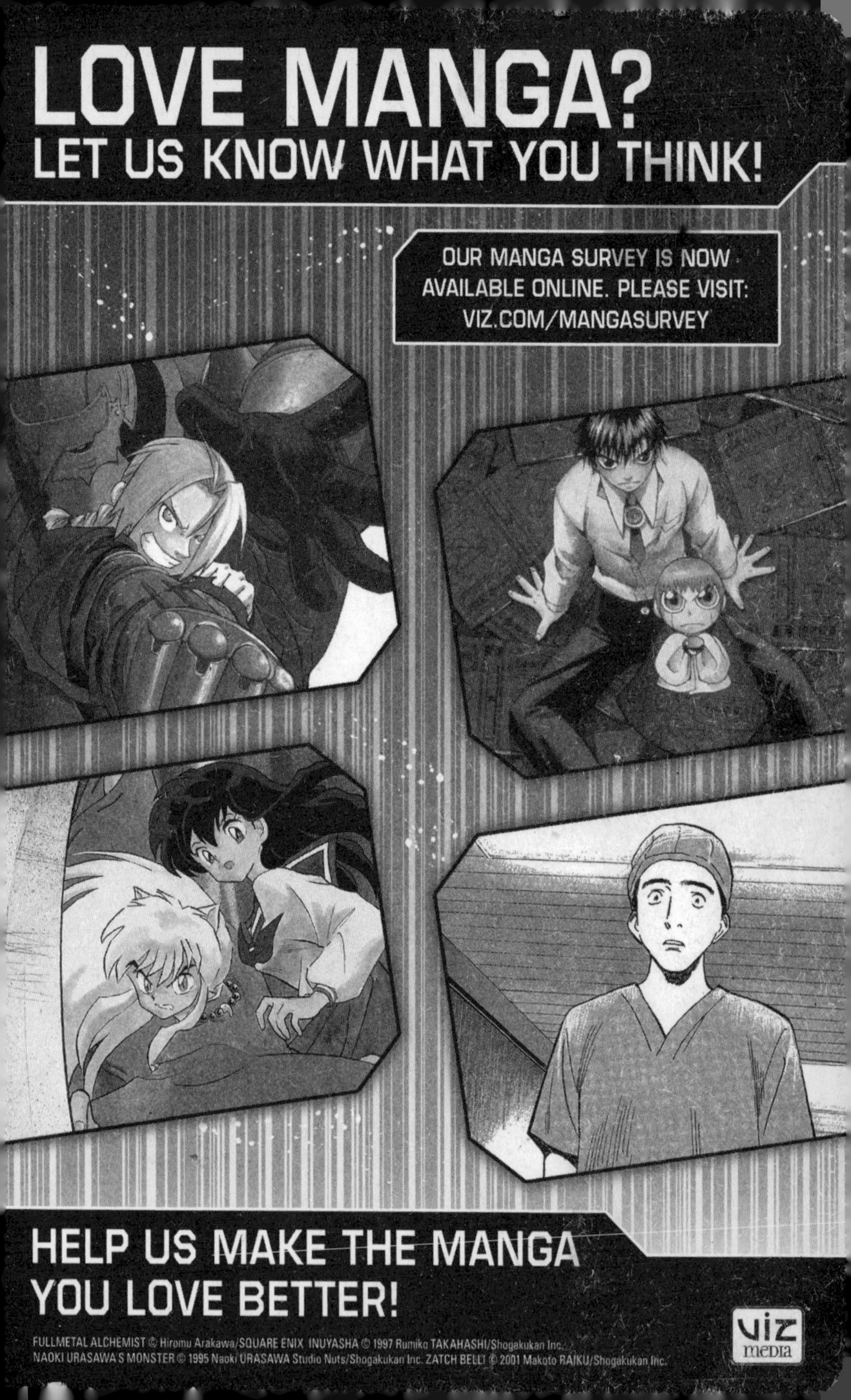